THE USES AND ABUSES OF FORECASTING

Other books by the STAFF group of SPRU

THINKING ABOUT THE FUTURE: a Critique of *Limits to Growth*
(*Eds. H. S. D. Cole, C. Freeman, M. Jahoda and K. L. R. Pavitt*)

THE ART OF ANTICIPATION: Values and Methods in Forecasting
(*Eds. S. Encel, P. R. Marstrand and W. Page*)

WORLD FUTURES: the Great Debate
(*Eds. C. Freeman and M. Jahoda*)

GLOBAL SIMULATION MODELS: a Comparative Study
(*J. Clark and H. S. D. Cole*)

THE POVERTY OF PREDICTION
(*Ian Miles*)

THE USES AND ABUSES OF FORECASTING

Science Policy Research Unit, Sussex

Edited by
Tom Whiston

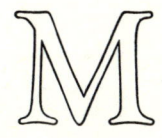

M

© Science Policy Research Unit, Sussex 1979

All rights reserved. No part of this publication may be reproduced or transmitted, in any form or by any means, without permission

First published 1979 by
THE MACMILLAN PRESS LTD
*London and Basingstoke
Associated companies in Delhi
Dublin Hong Kong Johannesburg Lagos
Melbourne New York Singapore Tokyo*

*Printed in Great Britain by
Billing and Sons Ltd
Guildford, London and Worcester*

British Library Cataloguing in Publication Data

University of Sussex *Science Policy Research Unit*
 The uses and abuses of forecasting
 1. Forecasting
 I. Title II. Whiston, Tom
 519.5′4   CB158

ISBN 0-333-26064-3

---

*This book is sold subject
to the standard conditions
of the Net Book Agreement*

Contents

Preface	vii
Acknowledgements	ix
List of Contributors	x
Introduction	1

1. The Development of Forecasting: Towards a History of the Future   *Ian Miles*   5
2. Economic Forecasting   *Frank Blackaby*   42
3. Market Forecasting   *Mark Abrams*   54
4. Transport Forecasting: Fixing the Future   *Jonathan Gershuny*   64
5. The Brighton Marina: a Case study in Arbitrariness, Uncertainty and Social Welfare in Planning Models.   *Roy Turner and Sam Cole*   93
6. Manpower Forecasters as Lobbyists: a Case Study of the Working Group on Manpower Parameters for Scientific Growth 1965–8   *Kevin McCormick*   108
7. Population Forecasting: Social and Educational Policy   *Tom Whiston*   143
8. Shadows on the Seventies: Indicative World Plan, the Protein Gap and the Green Revolution   *Pauline K. Marstrand and Howard J. Rush*   182
9. The Accuracy of Long-Term Forecasts for Non-Ferrous Metals   *William Page and Howard Rush*   201
10. Forecasting the Forces of Nature   *John Gribbin*   229
11. Telecommunications   *S. Encel*   248
12. Long-Range Forecasting and Policy-Making – Options and Limits in Choosing a Future   *Bjorn Wittrock*   267

13 The Political Limits to Forecasting	*Edward Wenk, Jr*	289
14 Interests, Hopes and Fears – Can We Change the Future?		
	Sam Cole	323
15 The Uses of Forecasting: Some Concluding Comments		
	Tom Whiston	344
Subject Index		351
Name Index		354

Preface

The members of the STAFF team (Social and Technological Forecasting for the Future) have over the course of the last few years produced a wide range of books and articles devoted to a critique of 'futures forecasting', both at the level of methodology and also in relation to planning and policy-making.

The forecasting programme of the Science Policy Research Unit (SPRU) at the University of Sussex receives its central support from the Social Science Research Council and the majority of contributors to this book are members of, or associated with, this programme. As will be seen from the list of contributors, however, there are a few additional names in the present volume. This was thought to be necessary in view of the wide range of topics (and requisite knowledge) which are considered.

There is also another reason. SPRU, and in particular the STAFF programme, has through the course of its research articles and major publications[1] derived both a flavour and a methodology of its own (isolating the dangers of 'trend forecasting' and emphasising the role that scenario-structures and 'normative' forecasting have to play). It was therefore thought that a consideration of such a topic as 'The Uses and Abuses of Forecasting', which emphasises the policy dimension, then a range of opinions by specialists in the field, would not only provide a balanced programme but would also serve to present to the reader a divergence of views, and emphasis, which is essential if he is to gain full critical insight into the relationship of forecasting and policy-making.

One man's meat is another man's poison, and in this sense the reader will no doubt find a range of approaches and points of view – some authors placing much weight upon the 'theoretical side' of their topic, whilst others prefer to consider the pragmatic turn of events. There are, however, certain common points. Probably all contributors would agree that you cannot foresee the future – there is no crystal ball. At best one can consider the implications of certain policies if continued into the future; the restrictive nature of many forecasts (either with respect to explicit or implicit assumptions); and the always present dangers of complicity in relation to the policy-making body on the one hand and the forecaster on the other. Over and above this common ground, emphasis varies according to the preferential selection of the contributors.

As to contributors, two names do not appear, but they should. Namely Chris Freeman, Director of SPRU and Marie Jahoda, Director of the STAFF programme. Theirs is the hidden hand.

December 1978 T. W.

NOTE

1 E.g. *Thinking about the Future: a Critique of* Limits to Growth (ed. H. S. D. Cole *et al,*); *The Art of Anticipation* (ed. S. Encel, P. R. Marstrand and W. Page); *World Futures: the Great Debate* (ed. C. Freeman and M. Jahoda).

Acknowledgements

The editor and publisher wish to thank the following for permission to reproduce material in this book: Pergamon Press with respect to Edward Wenk's chapter, 'The political limits of forecasting' which is based in part on his book, *Margins for Survival* (forthcoming); Rio Tinto-Zinc, who provided part of the financing of the research for the chapter, 'The accuracy of long-term forecasts for non-ferrous metals' (W. Page and H. Rush); SAGE Publications for Jay Gershuny's chapter, 'Transport forecasting: fixing the future'; and The Controller of Her Majesty's Stationery Office for the tables and diagrams in Tom Whiston's chapter.

List of Contributors

M. ABRAMS, Ph.D. Director of Research, Age Concern. He has carried out extensive work in the social/behavioural sciences with emphasis on value systems and social priorities, social indicators and change in social values. Author of *The Condition of the British People 1911–45*; *The Newspaper Reading Public of Tomorrow*; *A Short Guide to Social Survey Methods*.

F. BLACKABY, M.A. Deputy Director, National Institute of Economic and Social Research. Editor of *National Institute Economic Review* and the author of *The Medium Term: Models of the British Economy* (ed. with G. D. N. Worswick), and *An Income Policy for Britain* (ed.).

H. S. D. COLE, B.Sc., A.R.C.S., D. Phil. Senior Research Fellow, SPRU. An ex-physicist, concerned with urban planning research, and with the application of forecasting and planning methods. Also the theory of modelling and world models. Author of *Global Simulation Models* (with J. Clark) and *Thinking about the Future* (ed. with C. Freeman, M. Jahoda and K. Pavitt).

S. ENCEL, M.A., Ph.D. Professor of Sociology, University of New South Wales; visiting Professor at SPRU. A sociologist concerned with innovation, science policy, and the relations between social and technical change. Author of *Equality and Authority*.

J. I. GERSHUNY, B.Sc., M.Sc., Ph.D. A political scientist who has carried out extensive work on post-industrial society, policy analysis and technology assessment related to transport systems. Author of *After Industrial Society?* (The Emerging Self-Service Economy).

J. GRIBBIN, B.Sc., M.Sc., Ph.D. An astrophysicist, author and broadcaster, who has carried out research on climate change with SPRU. His books include *The Climatic Threat, Our Changing Climate, Climatic Change, Our Changing Universe, The Jupiter Effect*.

LIST OF CONTRIBUTORS

P. MARSTRAND, B.Sc., M.Sc., M.I.Biol. Senior Research Fellow, SPRU. A biologist, interested in environmental and health aspects of changes in technology; agricultural policy, nutrition and synthetic foodstuffs. Editor (with Encel and Page) of *The Art of Anticipation*; and (with McKnight and Sinclair) of *Environmental Pollution Control*.

K. J. McCORMICK, Ph.D. A lecturer in sociology, University of Sussex, whose research interests include manpower forecasting in science and technology, and political aspects of decision-making.

I. MILES, B.Sc. Research Fellow, SPRU. A social psychologist, working on assessment of quality of life, the interplay between society, science and technology, the psychology of the future and of futurology. Author of *Poverty of Prediction*; *Demystifying Social Statistics* (co-editor); *Progress and Problems in Social Forecasting* (co-editor with C. Freeman and M. Jahoda).

W. PAGE, B.A. Research Fellow, SPRU. A social psychologist, working on issues of technology assessment (non-modelling) forecasting techniques. He specialises in materials forecasting. Editor (with S. Encel and P. R. Marstrand) of *The Art of Anticipation*.

H. RUSH, B.A., M.A. Research Fellow, SPRU. A social psychologist whose present research interests include work on the food and agriculture section of the SPRU forecasting programme; technical change in nationalised industries and hindsight review of materials forecasting.

R. TURNER, B.Sc. Research student, SPRU, currently completing his doctoral research into the comparative structure of 'Shopping Models'.

E. WENK, Ph.D. Professor and Director of Social Management in Technology, University of Washington, USA. Previously Presidential Science Adviser, now Visiting Professor at SPRU. Author of *The Politics of the Ocean*.

T. G. WHISTON, B.Sc., M.Sc., Ph.D., C.Chem., M.R.I.C. Senior Research Fellow, SPRU. A chemist, ergonomist and psychologist, working on the interaction of educational policy and industrial and social development, technical change and skills, and industrial processes in relation to materials and energy conservation and role of government legislation.

B. WITTROCK, Ph.D. Research Associate, Department of Political Science, University of Stockholm, Sweden. Has recently specialised in studying the progress of the Swedish Secretariat for Future Studies, and the relationship of governmental structure and futures science policy.

Introduction

Concern with the future is as old as mankind; but only within the recent past has this concern developed into systematic exploration of the possibilities that lie ahead. Forecasting is today a standard procedure in government departments, in industry, in the agencies of the United Nations and in many research units all over the world. Most of these efforts have a practical purpose: to help policy-makers in their difficult decisions. The consequences of these decisions may affect not only the present generation, but our children, grandchildren and beyond. Because forecasting thus exercises some influence, however indirect, on all our lives, everyone who thinks about the future, in hope or fear, should have access to appraising for himself the nature of the influence that forecasting has. The purpose of this book is to provide such access.

Forecasting can be undertaken for short- or for long-time perspectives; it can deal with minor or with major issues; with relatively isolated or with global matters; restrict itself to the examination of the likely consequences of current policies or examine the implications of alternative policies; it can use one or more of the available forecasting techniques from simple extrapolation of current trends to the imaginative construction of scenarios; it can rely on theories or proceed on *ad hoc* empirical data; appear quantitatively precise or qualitatively vague; it can be based on conservative, reformist or radical views about social change; it can be available only to its sponsors or be made public; and finally – from the point of view of this book – it can be so bedevilled with technicalities of a high order that even full publication provides only spurious access to all but a handful of experts; or it can deliberately be directed to a wider audience.

Keeping this vast diversity in mind I have tried to collect in this text as wide a range as possible of forecasting exercises and comments on their assets and liabilities. As a result the chapter titles may at first glance appear to lack a common theme. But this is deceptive; they have more in common than the titles suggest. While each contributor no doubt expresses, to some degree, a differing focus of interest, they all comment on the uses of forecasting in relation to policy-making. For all contributors are intensely concerned with the central questions of the way in which a particular forecasting procedure compromises or attempts to control the future in relation to some particular political or ideological bias rather than presenting for consideration a range of possibilities from which a more rational or equitable selection might be made.

In so doing the various authors have attempted, where possible, to address themselves to the motivation, financing and institutional factors which controlled the forecast; to assess the relationship between forecasting and policy-maker; to assess the effects (if any) and effectiveness of the forecast; and finally to comment upon any bias which may have become apparent through critical analysis – in particular whether or not this was of an ideological, organisational, methodological or personal nature. Only through such an analysis is it then possible to comment on how such forecasts might be better performed. The extent to which these matters are applicable to the areas examined varies a great deal. But the aggregate insight gained provides, I hope, a useful critical review of the experience of forecasting in relation to policy-making in a variety of contexts.

It might be pointed out here – even though the reader of the following chapters will quickly become aware of it anyhow – that there is no uniformity in the political outlook of the various contributors. Some operate within the current system; others criticise and attack it. This is, I believe, as it ought to be if one wishes to convey an impression of the range of assumptions and attitudes current in the forecasting field.

The book begins with an historical and socio-political perspective on forecasting as an intellectual enterprise. The importance of Miles' chapter lies in his insistence that forecasts are socially embedded and that we may be too close to present-day events to throw off our somewhat time-dependent perceptual lenses, even when our vision is directed to the future. Other forecasters may not share his point of view, but it is one that needs to be taken seriously.

This chapter is followed by a series of sectoral forecasting issues. Blackaby, concerned with the problems of economic forecasting (i.e. the limitations of econometric modelling), describes current British practices in this most important field and examines their degree of success. From the macro-problems of economic forecasting the text moves to the micro-problems of satisfactorily understanding changing value-systems of individuals. This provides an interesting juxtaposition of arguments, which in essence reflects a dilemma of all forecasting: both macro-studies and insight into an individual's behaviour and the problem of individual differences are required. Forecasters have not yet learned to combine them.

The chapters which then follow deal with transport and urban development; education and manpower; resources; and socio-technological systems.

Gershuny's chapter, sub-titled 'Fixing the Future', emphasises the way in which a particular forecast may effectively foreclose any further examination and become a self-fulfilling prophecy. Gershuny makes a strong plea for a 'rational' approach to policy-making, in order to ensure adequate discussion of an appropriate range of alternatives and thereby to overcome unduly restrictive and deterministic thinking. In short to impose a 'what if' philosophy into forecasting and policy-making.

Public inquiries are intended to function as safeguards against such self-fulfilment. Turner and Cole in their chapter lay a fair degree of criticism at the door of public inquiries, both with respect to their limited terms of reference (close to Gershuny's point) and in relation to the nature of so-called 'experts' who may serve a tribunal or inquiry.

The next two chapters, McCormick's and Whiston's, are concerned with the way in which education policy may be adversely affected by comparatively narrow forecasting techniques; or at least how support and rationalisation of policy is provided by restrictive forecasting techniques. Current concerns with unemployment, with manpower forecasts and with respect to the education–industry link serve in these chapters to introduce a wider range of debate.

There then follow three chapters (Marstrand and Rush; Page and Rush; Gribbin) which deal, respectively, with food and agriculture policy, materials forecasting, and climatic forecasting. These three chapters demonstrate that forecasting in areas which have a high 'physical' component is just as dependent on assumptions as forecasting in social areas. Superficially it might be thought that systems modelling, quantification and other precise techniques are more easily undertaken in these areas. This is patently not the case.

Encel is concerned with technological innovation and, further, serves to emphasise the valuative nature and social implications of technological developments and the need for thorough analysis prior to policy formulation in these areas. What all these chapters have shown implicitly is explicitly the focus of Wittrock's, Wenk's and Cole's chapters: the assets and dangers of attaching forecasting directly to the political realm.

Wittrock deals with a successful arrangement in describing the formation and progress of a group in Sweden (the Swedish Futures Secretariat, formed as an outcome of Myrdal's *To Choose a Future* report) which is attached to the Swedish Cabinet Office. He emphasises the ability of the Secretariat to cut across government departments and immediate vested interest groups and thereby widen the policy debate.

This seemingly healthy development is, however, countered by Edward Wenk's chapter. Wenk has previously been a senior science adviser to several US Presidents; his experience has made him sceptical about the use of long-term forecasts in policy formation; the political process, being what it is, must give priority to short-term interests, even where a long-term strategy exists.

Cole in his overview of the function of global forecasting outlines the importance of individual future-entrepreneurs and the nature of their mutual recriminations. He suggests caution with respect to the value we place on global forecasts, but nevertheless recognises their 'catalytic' function.

In the last short chapter I abandon editorial neutrality, and argue the case for the possibility of influencing policy through a particular type of forecasting.

1 The Development of Forecasting: Towards a History of the Future

IAN MILES

THE USES OF HISTORY

As far as we can tell, human beings throughout history, when able to take their attention off immediate necessities, have been interested in the future. This interest takes and has taken diverse forms, but it is never merely a disinterested appraisal of an unfolding historical record. Whether it involves studying the entrails of animals or the output of computers, writing accounts of fictional voyages or arranging graphs and matrices, forecasting is part of the social construction of the future, of the making of history. It is inseparable from wider processes of social change and conflict, whether it appears to be superstition, tabulation, objective analysis or partisan programme-building.

The course of development of ideas about the future is, like an exotic culture, all the more fascinating for being unfamiliar – indeed, it is very poorly charted. And just as the confrontation of cultures may shock us into recognising that our own culture is a human construct rather than *the* natural order of things, so can a history of forecasting enable us to identify the social origins of present approaches to the future, that are rendered indistinct more by proximity than by distance. This should set the scene for the discussions of present-day futures studies in following chapters.[1]

It is common for historical overviews of an area of research to paint a picture of inexorable evolution: science advances, exorcising with its hard light the spectres of superstition and ideology. It is as if scientific knowledge, and the principles of scientific practice, exist suspended in nature, and history represents the gradual approach of humanity towards these perfect realities. The present chapter will take the contrasting approach of seeing science as a social product. Scientific practices and theories have been created and developed under particular historical circumstances, during which science has been subjected to a division of labour, specialisation and awarding of status. The production of knowledge is a human practice in a material world which includes such social factors as commitments, values and conflicts as well as the physical or social objects of immediate study.[2] This human practice is formed within particular social relations, rather than conforming to an ahistorical ideal.

It can be misleading to set out to draw firm boundaries between scientific and pre- or non-scientific forecasting. In our secularised age, the mystique of science – evoked by the use of jargon, quantitative analysis, complicated techniques, expertise – may be used to suggest that some forecasts are somehow more objective, neutral and disinterested than others. However, a basic perspective informing this chapter is that forecasting – as more orthodox fields of science – depends crucially upon commitments and assumptions that are not merely technical. This is not to say that some work is not more technically adequate than others, nor that technical adequacy is an unimportant criterion. But it is important to recognise that as well as employing the techniques (and the symbols and social relations) of contemporary science, 'scientific' forecasting draws upon a base of social practices that is shared by other ways of creating images of the future. All forecasts reflect values and interests, hopes and fears; and none are purely disinterested assessments of possible future histories. It is therefore inadequate to conceive of forecasting as a neutral practice that can be used or abused. Forecasting is part and parcel of the creation of human history.[3] This chapter sets out to throw some light on the ways in which this role of the image of the future has been developed as a constitutive element in the historical process.

PRE-INDUSTRIAL FUTURES: FROM THE GOLDEN AGE TO UTOPIA

Appeals to science and scientific rationality have not always been seen as necessary for adequate knowledge of the world; indeed, they have been influential only for a short span of human history. In traditional societies, conceptions of the future would be substantiated in terms of the cosmologies embedded in folklore and religion. In ancient civilisations the systems of astronomy, meteorology and mathematical analysis, that were developed in parallel with agriculture, maritime trade and architecture, would also have been important. Whether history was seen as an unfolding linear path, or as a series of cycles, myths of creation were intimately linked to eschatology. Analogies were drawn between human life and the natural order, and attempts to chart the course of human affairs were often modelled upon the forecasts of natural phenomena made possible by the systematic — if 'pre-scientific' — articulation of knowledge about physical and biological processes.

Forecasts of the fate of individuals, the outcomes of marriages, treaties or battles, can be traced back into our early history. They may well have always been bound up with the systems used in making decisions related to recurrent economic activities: when to plant, harvest, set sail, and so forth. Astrology, numerology and divination would be seen as exact and logical procedures, applicable to natural and human affairs alike; sharp distinctions between a natural world of facts and a social world of values were not drawn.[4] But forecasting social, as opposed to individual, change, is another matter. It seems likely that concern with defining better and worse ways of living, with the future of whole communities, and with principles of social choice, was established only when the pace of social change became such that, while important cultural continuities were retained, shifts in the established order were visible over the short run.

Utopian writing, in which a vision of an alternative mode of social organisation is outlined, is one expression of such a concern with societal change. If only as a commentary on the present, utopias are intended to play some role in guiding the actions which will shape the future. It is, however, significant that the earliest fictional utopias we know of are not set in a this-worldly future. Instead, they are set in a mythical past, or in an alternate present or other-worldly future in which supernatural agencies operate.[5]

The earliest Western utopian writings were not presented as fiction, although with hindsight we may classify them as such — if also, as in the case of Plato's *The Republic*, as a lot more besides. *The Republic* (fourth century BC) represents Plato's response to the bloody strife and the breakdown of the established social order associated with the Peloponnesian War. Rather than appealing to the natural sciences, Plato built his case for an ideal state by means of a philosophical discussion in which he outlined principles for structuring the social world. But this ideal state could only have existed in the past in his analysis: his contemporary society is portrayed as no more than its decaying residue.

Different devices were used by Iambulus in his *Islands in the Sun* (written around the turn of the first century BC, a time of slave uprisings). Iambulus set out an alternative present: a utopia displaced in space rather than time and (according to Winston, 1976) presented in a language based upon that of the travel literature which had grown up in the wake of Alexander's conquests. Like later utopian and science fiction writers, Iambulus established a sense of authenticity by the literary devices of pseudo-science, providing a wealth of concocted geographical, botanical and similar information along with his outline of a more perfect society. But the society described is one in which, as Finlay (1967, p. 8) says, 'Iambulus rather massively mixed the fabulous with the critical': social reform was not enough to ensure a good society, and he even wrote of changes in human physiology.

Leaping the centuries, the great watershed in utopian writing was of course the work that gave the genre its name – Sir Thomas More's *Utopia* of 1516. More was writing at a time of momentous social changes. The growth of commerce and population, and later industry, in medieval Europe had in many respects been achieved at the expense of large sections of the peasantry. As merchant capital took root in, and widened, the cracks in the feudal economy, poor people were rendered vulnerable to social and economic disruption: Cohn (1957) has traced out the form of the consequent revolutionary millenial movements. Throughout Europe, large sections of the poor saw their struggle against the established social order as anticipating a new reality, as helping to actualise the restoration of an earthly paradise. The utopia of these poor and dispossessed was a supernatural alternative society, but unlike Iambulus, they believed it to lie in their immediate future.

More's *Utopia* was a decisive break with the millenial revolutionary and literary utopian traditions. While Plato set his ideal society in a past forever lost, and Iambulus could only achieve consistency in his portrait of a collectivist, highly productive society by contradicting physical realities, More proposed an alternative present which depended upon changed political circumstances, rather than a changed natural order. Like Iambulus, More wrote at a time of major geographic discovery, and his ideal society was set on an island bearing much physical similarity to Britain. It was the social order that was totally transformed – More portrayed a rational society that was a human product – the result of a 'revolution from above'. It was the first, and in many ways the most ambitious, of a series of works which reflected the emergence of the absolutist monarchies of the late feudal state and may have given them some encouragement in their attempts at guiding social change – although certainly More was not optimistic about his vision being influential on the Tudor monarchy.

The flux in sixteenth-century Britain had made a new sense of the practicability of utopia possible, and this is what underlies the creation of the modern utopia. More's writing reflects the growing power of monarchical rule (and his ideal order was founded by the benevolent King Utopus) and the reduction of that of the old aristocracy as an emergent class of merchants were favoured; and the enclosures which displaced peasants from their land as much agriculture was transformed by commerce from growing food to producing wool. More reacted against the misery associated with these changes, proposing instead a planned society in which communistic social organisation made abundance serve the people's welfare. (As the role of private property grew, the prospect and potential of social ownership of the means of production became less appealing to utopian writers oriented, as most of them were, towards the groups in society whose power was largely based on private property.) The new social order, though creating misery, was one of unprecedented potential for economic production. A world without scarcity could be envisaged as technologically feasible. But it was unclear to More how far production might be expanded, and what human problems might emerge, and his utopia is a frugal one. Various, quite restrictive, forms of social engineering are proposed as means of preventing excess developing amid wellbeing.

The idea of an improved social future which could be realised by human action, without supernatural intervention, was thus established. Grasping the possibility of change, however, was not the same as forecasting the processes whereby change could be brought about. Later analysts were to identify social classes as decisive here – the industrial capitalist class, and the proletariat, most notably – with some emphasis in the twentieth century on the role of scientists and engineers. But in More's time these classes and groups were numerically insignificant or non-existent. Recognising that the merchant class would never seek spontaneously to order their operations according to human need rather than profit, More could only look, despairingly, to the monarch as a revolutionary force.

THE 'NEW SCIENCE' AND THE FUTURE

Many utopian narratives followed on More's heels: Sargent (1976), surveying English-language utopian works, reports eight in the sixteenth, thirty in the seventeenth, more than thirty in the eighteenth, and over three hundred in the nineteenth century. But until the eve of the Industrial Revolution More's successors would rarely follow him in according much significance to the sufferings of the poor or in proposing sweeping social transformations (Berneri, 1950; Finlay, 1967; Morton, 1969).

It was in the seventeenth century that decisive steps were taken in establishing a new social order – capitalism – and with it a new philosophy. As the basis of social power was shifted from the hierarchical feudal order to one determined by the ownership of capital (and later by the ownership and control of the means of production), so was social consciousness reshaped and the dominance of modern science initiated: neither process was mechanical, each being a social practice that contributed to the other (Easlea, 1973; Foucault, 1970; Sohn-Rethel, 1975). As commodity production expanded and the role of money became central, so quantification achieved a more central role in science (Young, 1978). A society increasingly regulated by market 'laws' rather than traditional political power produced a cosmology of natural law rather than one of organic harmony. And while Newton combined his interest in physics with study in alchemy and eschatology, and regarded his laws as themselves standing in need of explanation, his successors came to identify science with reductionism, and regarded the discovery of laws *as* explanation.

It took centuries for the new science to be fully applied to economic production. But future-oriented writers could already grasp some of its potential early in the seventeenth century. Bacon's influential *New Atlantis* (1627), for example, which placed great emphasis on science's role in increasing the wealth and order of society, is an elitist and in many respects conservative vision. But as part of Bacon's campaign to establish the 'new science' of the seventeenth century in Britain it eventually bore fruit which took such institutional forms as the Royal Society, a somewhat less grandiose version of the Solomon's House described in *New Atlantis*.

In addition to its elitist, patriarchical view of ideal society, *New Atlantis* had limitations as well as achievements as a forecast and programme for science-based 'modernisation'. Among these limitations may be cited Bacon's view of future scientific development being based on a specialisation of stages in the research process (with different scientists carrying out literature searches, field research, experiments, theoretical syntheses, applications of results, etc) rather than on the fragmentation of knowledge into a number of disciplines such as did take place.[6] Nor have the scientific communities which have existed since the time of Bacon ever achieved such independence from commercial interests and the state as he imagined – perhaps his king's lack of enthusiasm for Bacon's work encouraged this view.

The various successful technological predictions in *New Atlantis* – artificial flavourings, artificial metals, submarines, aircraft, and so on – are presented in passing in the text; they are not plot elements as they would be in modern science fiction. The exciting promises of the new science are outlined as symbolising the advance and consolidation of power, rather than as components of a future society, in whose creation through the substantial transformation of the present they must have inevitably played a part. Like so many of the optimistic technological forecasters of the twentieth century, Bacon was not concerned with providing an image of a world in harmony with human needs, an analysis of the prospects for liberation and an end to oppression. The focus is on the achievements, rather than the ends, of technological civilisation. An emphasis on status and supremacy remarkably similar to that of the world of advertising (only sexual titillation is missing) is evident here; this is the effective promotion of the brand-name of science and the prestige of scientists (if not their sex-appeal).

New Atlantis was a small part of a surge of activity which achieved, over a period of centuries, the establishment of a new system of production and a new conception of science as dominant in Western society. Although retrospectively this may appear to be a logical evolution from a benighted to a more rational state of affairs, the outcome of events was by no means evident to those participating in them. Some of the utopian fiction of seventeenth-century England actively opposed the changes emerging through application of the Baconian programme, and called for a return to a pre-Civil War, royalist state by depicting the harmony and stability of such a world (Morton, 1969). On the other hand, there were movements, like the Levellers and Diggers, which pressed for major changes in power and property relations, but which did not necessarily reject all that the 'new science' stood for – indeed, this science and its fruits could be part of the new world they wanted.[7] But the form of this 'new science' was itself in flux: astrology and alchemy flourished, as did remarkably different traditions of neo-Platonism, Rosicrucianism, etc (Yates, 1974). Astrology provided one way of applying analytic procedures to foretell the path of human lives, whose richness and unpredictability lay beyond the scope of other approaches – especially in a time when major social changes were opening up possibilities for new ways of life, new careers, new freedoms and constraints. Almanacs were widely distributed in the seventeenth century, providing commentaries (often in mystical, 'disguised' language) and predictions about social affairs; while millenial prophecies were declaimed by radical religious sects (Hill, 1972).

In the new conditions of capitalist society, another approach to social forecasting eventually was to achieve rather more lasting success. The new scientists, through the approach of 'political arithmetic', had attempted to apply rigorous methods of measurement and analysis to social affairs, in the process laying the basis for the development of statistical science. One of the key features of England through most decades of the seventeenth century was the confusing pattern of conflict and shifting alliances of different social groups that traced a path through civil war, restoration, and revolution. Numerical information was seen as providing a possibility of transcending opposing sectional interests and of a value-free means of making rational policies which might unit them (Likewise, a continuing theme of much utopian fiction of this period was the search for a constitutional resolution to the conflicts of elite interest groups.) At first political arithmetic was informed by a concern with analysing social change – like today's so-called policy sciences, it was associated with various forms of social forecasting. Sir William Petty, who coined the term 'political arithmetic' and pioneered quantitative explorations of human life, would take up, for example, such issues as the desirability of different alliances – thus he compared the relative strength of Britain and France in order to forecast the likely outcomes of naval war. On another occasion, discussing the advantages for trade and industry of the expansion of London, he forecast the city's future population levels – his forecast for 1800 was five million Londoners, half of the entire anticipated English population. As Strauss (1953) amply details, Petty's work teems with fascinating speculation about possible and desirable social arrangements and plans.[8]

But much of the impetus was taken out of such studies of social change and policy alternatives by the establishment of political stability and economic growth after the Glorious Revolution of 1688, and the decreasing scope of state intervention in subsequent years. Both political arithmetic and utopian fiction reflected this waning of social criticism and concern with long-term change (as is discussed by Buck, 1977 in respect of political arithmetic, and Morton, 1968, in respect of utopian writing). An image of social order as the result of recognising and conforming to natural laws was promoted, with society portrayed in terms parallel to those of the Newtonian solar system. Political arithmetic was used to justify the social order. Sometimes this took the form of demonstrating the naturalness of the *status quo* (Atkins and Jarret, 1978), sometimes it involved forecasts depicting the disastrous consequences of social reform. Armytage (1968) cites Robert Wallace as arguing in 1761 that utopian societies would collapse under the weight of their inevitable population growth; and at the end of the eighteenth century Malthus notoriously applied the 'principle of population' to demonstrate the supposed impossibility of freeing the world from hardship and inequality.

But one other application of political arithmetic to forecasting did flourish in the eighteenth century, and while its focus was also on demography, this was guided as much by financial considerations as by disinterested science. This involved the estimation of the life expectancies of individuals, a project at first of most value to those state officials charged with granting annuities as a means of raising finance. A close colleague of Petty, John Graunt, is generally attributed with establishing demographic science with his *Natural and Political Observations . . . Upon the London Bills of Mortality* (1962); it was not long before his ideas were extended, by astronomers and early probability theorists such as Hoggins, Halley, de Montmort and Bernoulli, to the preparation of life tables, which could be used to calculate the life expectancies of people of different ages. The first life assurance company to use such material in its calculations was established in 1762, and the 'Equitable's' success reinforced belief in the applicability of statistical forecasting techniques to human affairs.[9]

The prediction of an individual's chances of a short life, as a matter worthy of financial speculation, is a far cry from the imaginative construction of social alternatives. The economic growth of the eighteenth century was, however, laying the foundations for a new, and more future-oriented, stage of capitalist development: industrial capitalism. It was in the second half of this century that the first novels to be clearly set in a distant future were written. *The Reign of George VI* (1763), by an anonymous English writer was, by all accounts, a remarkably unimaginative glorification of the future of a wise monarchy (Clarke, 1973). (Armytage, 1968, cites two French novels, *L'An 2440* (1770) and *L'An Deux-Mille* (1790) as other early fictional futures.)[10] Toward the turn of the century, deeper possibilities for social change were sensed, as in Blake's contrast of green and pleasant England, the spreading dark, satanic mills, and a new Jerusalem. (Later, Mary Shelley's *Frankenstein* (1818) was to cast a different allegorical perspective on the ambiguous achievements of modern science.)

The industrial revolution, simultaneously marked by the creation of new technologies (and a new dynamic of technological change) and that of a mass, urban working class, made the reconceptualisation of utopia from a matter for speculative geography to one for futurology, an urgency. The late eighteenth century provided material for Adam Smith's vision of progress founded on the development of industry under the stimulus of self-interest, and for Malthus' influential identification of ultimate constraints on social improvement. Blake's fantastic poetry, and Spence's utopian novels, argued not for progress within the existing social order, but for a radical change of direction. A new world was in the making – but what sort of world was it to be?

THE INDUSTRIALISATION OF THE FUTURE

The late eighteenth and early nineteenth century saw England's rapid transformation into an industrial nation, with people moving to the cities at an unprecedented rate. The hardships created and exposed in this time of flux were increasingly subject to analysis by the means and language of science, especially as they provoked rebellious and revolutionary action. For example, a 'statistical movement' was established in the early nineteenth century (Cullen, 1975), rather as the turmoil of the 1960s led social scientists to proclaim a 'social indicators movement' (Miles, 1975). But the social indicators movement has been closely tied to forecasting and to such creators of images of the future as Daniel Bell (Kleinberg, 1973). In contrast, the professional gentlemen involved in the early Victorian statistical movement had little concern with depicting the improved world that would result from the social reforms they championed, such as improved and widespread education and centralised public health measures.

Despite increasing emphasis on the application of science to social problems, and a clear awareness of living through a time of major social change, very little of the early nineteenth-century literature discusses future trends in the topics addressed. Even Malthus' population projections were not 'calibrated' to predict Britain's future. They remain in the realm of social philosophy as a statement about the human lot, rather than directly taking issue with the human prospect (unlike present-day Malthusians, as even the title of Heilbroner's book, 1974, testifies). But Malthusian ideas did figure prominently in many political debates of the day, and are believed to have helped prepare the ground for, and structure, the 1834 reform of the Poor Law, for example. Political economists were being called upon to discuss social and economic policy, and the state was increasingly interested in obtaining more comprehensive data for use in policy-making. Levels of government expenditure remained fairly low throughout the nineteenth century; except for wartime expenses they rarely exceeded 10 per cent of the gross national product. In consequence, although there was an increasing formalisation of the knowledge used by the state in its economic activities, there was little incentive to determine the precise effects of policies, or the future financial consequences of present commitments in any detail.

Not only conservatives and reformists sought to apply rigorous analysis to problems of social change; radicals, more overtly interested in changing reality than in forecasting it, exposed startling new possibilities for fundamental social transformations. Marx, who with Engels wrote scathingly about utopian socialism in *The Communist Manifesto* (1848), often saw his project as being the development of a scientific socialism.

Marx is often held responsible for the atrophy of utopian thinking — a serious charge today, when it may be argued that workers in the Western industrial countries are hardly encouraged to consider a radically different future when the main alternatives to industrial capitalism appear to be indicated by professedly Marxist states. (This is one reason for radicals considering it important to develop an adequate Socialist analysis of the dynamics and shortcomings of these states — thus such journals as *Critique* and *Labour Focus on Eastern Europe*.) While it is undoubtedly correct that Marx put most of his effort to understanding the laws of motion of the capitalist system, and assessing the possible foci and agents of qualitative changes in that system, it is also apparent that throughout his work there are two types of consideration about the future. The first concerns the tendencies and counter-tendencies of development of capitalism, and portions of *Capital* and the *Grundrisse* are a working-out of the futures that may result from their unfolding — including the future prospects for revolution. The second concerns the broad shape of the higher form of society which revolutionary change could create, and Ollman (1977) has recently set out in some detail the arguments and conclusions Marx established here.

In criticising the utopian writings of other socialists, Marx was arguing against the extrapolation of limited analyses into the distant future, against the setting up of rigid 'menus for the cook-shops of the future' in place of sensitive programmes and demands for change, and against the glamourisation of disembodied scenarios which, lacking obvious links to present reality, were more a means of demonstrating intellectual prowess than a guide to action. These points are all tied to the dialectical approach which he used: since human beings and social circumstances reciprocally affect each other, engaging in the process of socialist revolution itself lays the basis for a new social consciousness. Detailed speculation about future human needs and practices based on observation of current circumstances, then, would lack a scientific basis.

Many utopian schemes and fictions were produced in the first half of the nineteenth century, despite the force of Marx's analysis, and political activists often chose fiction as a means of presenting their ideas. Morton (1968) recounts that the utopian novel, *Un Voyage en Icaria* (1840) by the French socialist Cabet inspired the foundation of Icarian colonies in Texas. Owenites on occasion presented their social platform in millenial, quasi-religious terms (see, e.g., Oliver, 1971). Sargent (1976) has listed the outstanding themes of English-language utopias of this period as: the nature of an equitable economic system, with much attention paid to socialist and cooperative organisation; the communitarian ideal and its limitations; and the 'woman question'. As at the present time, then, social ferment was calling into question distinctions drawn between the personal and the political, and challenging the social divisions structured around sex as well as those based directly on class.

As well as once more addressing matters of fundamental social change, utopian fiction changed in other ways under the impact of industrial capitalism. For much of the nineteenth century, as earlier, utopian programmes did often focus upon establishing colonies in virgin lands, and utopian fictions would be set in as yet undiscovered regions of the globe, admittedly. But as the whole world was increasingly incorporated into a single economic system, such utopias became increasingly implausible. Fictional depictions of revolutionary ideas and actions were increasingly set in terms of possible futures for one's home country and, by extension, for the whole world.[11]

The remoulding of Britain as an industrial nation was a protracted process, but two watersheds in parliamentary politics – the 1832 Reform Act and the repeal of the Corn Laws in 1846 – marked the new dominance of industrial capitalists. The Chartist movement, with its claims for popular suffrage, waned after its failures of the 1840s and a relatively stable period of economic growth was achieved. The amalgam of industrial and landed interests that was the British ruling class was now less troubled by the threatened extension of popular uprisings from home or the European continent.

One of the striking features of industrial capitalism is its tendency to produce periodic economic crises. Such crises are not planned, of course – the competitive, contradictory substance of its social relations limit any serious planning to that which can smooth the rougher edges off its development – but they are vital to economic restructuring which is itself necessitated by the accumulation of process and product changes made by individual firms. Each major crisis involves the throwing of workers out of employment, and evokes a restructuring of political and ideological forces as well as the technological changes needed to re-establish growth. Each major crisis has been associated with a new shift in dominant images of the future. Unemployment, wage cuts, and more recently cuts in social services, are part of the price paid by workers for resolution of the crisis. Having paid this price in the 1830s and 1840s, the English working class was invited to join in the new era of prosperity which they had made possible.

The new industrial era was widely seen as promising continual material progress; the austerity of necessity proposed by More in *Utopia* was now more often replaced by abundance (as in both reformist and radical critiques of capitalism) or austerity through choice (as in the utopian colonies, and, later, in William Morris' work). The mid-nineteenth-century 'futures debate' was almost free of Malthusian gloom – expansion was henceforth to be the keynote, and some social reforms actually benefited industrialist and worker alike.

One exception to this optimism is worth noting, for William Stanley Jevons was very conscious of revising Malthus in the light of the rise of the industrial system, in *The Coal Question* (1865). 'Our subsistence no longer depends upon our produce of corn. The momentous repeal of the Corn Laws throws us from coal upon corn. It marks . . . the ascendancy of the manufacturing interest, which is only another name for the development of the use of coal' (p. 173, 2nd edition, 1866). Jevons argues that increasing consumption levels are of more significance than population growth.

Jevons presented in this book an analysis with many similarities to modern energy forecasting studies. Extrapolating coal consumption rates, and assessing the probable reserves of coal and the potential for alternative energy sources, he concluded that future energy demand would outstrip supply and thus place limitations upon increasing material progress. While creating a stir – it was mentioned in Parliament by J. S. Mill, for example – Jevons' work was less in tune with its time than Malthus had been. Malthus had argued that society was always near an imbalance of food supply and demand, and that social reforms could tip the balance dangerously, at a time when the expansion of industry and empire could not but profit from these arguments. But Jevons' energy crisis lay in the distant future, and its prescriptive import was merely that social reforms should not be delayed on the assumption of continuing growth; so the response was to set up official investigations of coal reserves rather than to accept the analysis as of vital relevance.

PANDORA'S PROPHETS

Jevons' work approaches the kind of specialised forecasting of a small set of quantitative parameters that became very important in the mid-twentieth century – although typically the recent forecasts are dealing with less momentous, less long-term problems. Jevons himself helped pave the way for these developments with studies of economic fluctuations, from which he produced diagrams, which could be useful for business forecasting (Keynes, 1936). Studies of this sort proliferated in the last quarter of the nineteenth century when a major economic crisis once more drew attention to economic trends and cycles and to their social implications. But systematic business forecasting could not be developed to any extent from these analyses until economic statistics were widely available, and statistical economic forecasts are largely a product of the twentieth century (see Spengler, 1961).

The late-nineteenth-century depression provoked political turmoil in much of Europe. In Britain, whose imperial position was insulation against the deepest shocks, it nevertheless shook the idea that social progress was a matter of consensus, and that social reforms could be introduced steadily without major conflicts. The nascent 'policy sciences' were thrown into disarray: for example, the National Association for the Promotion of Social Science virtually collapsed on account of the polarisation on party lines of a reform issue. Abrams (1968) describes the annual congress of the National Association, which served as a forum in the 1860s and 1870s for technocratic researchers and reformers to discuss what reform policies might be scientifically sound. For over a quarter of a century the mixture seemed to work, and a philosophy of enlightenment (knowledge about problems and reforms will secure consensus) seemed to be validated; but in 1885 the Association split over the question of temperance. Similar storms had struck the other institutions of Victorian 'policy science', too: Abrams (1968) cites attempts to disband the 'overly political' statistics and economics section of the British Association for the Advancement of Science, and conflict in the Royal Statistical Society over a report presenting a quantified argument for nationalising the railways.

The crisis of the late nineteenth century, with its high levels of unemployment, resulted in a number of important changes in British society. Many workers organised themselves into new unions, and joined the socialist groups that eventually formed much of the base of the Labour Party (Nairn, 1964). Pressures for reform were stronger, and gained intellectual support through the poverty studies of Booth and his colleagues, and the difficulty of explaining mass unemployment in terms of workers' morale and motivation. Thus incentive was provided for an institutionalisation of reform by the British state, paving the way for an interventionist welfare state whose information needs influenced the later development of forecasting.

Reformist Fabian-style socialism was a powerful influence, too, on one of the most powerful writers of fictional futures, H. G. Wells. Aldiss (1974) recounts how many Victorian science fiction novels were suffused with the nagging awareness of a subordinated class.[12] Wells' *The Time Machine* (1895) takes this awareness into the future, charging it with pseudo-Darwinian ideas. This tale depicts class divisions rigidifying into biological ones, concluding with the ultimate pessimism of entropic decay. Wells, of course, was not content to remain a novelist: he produced essays and lectures about the future (e.g. *Anticipations of the Reaction of Mechanical and Scientific Progress Upon Human Life and Thought*, 1901), was arguing at the turn of the century for futurology, and later tried to realise his scheme for an 'Open Conspiracy' of scientists to achieve a world state. As Aldiss (1974) notes, Wells turned more and more after the First World War to creating statements rather than fictions, to argue for a world ruled by scientific rationality. His anti-Marxist commitments, however, especially as developed in the wake of *Anticipations*, left him seeking agents of reform in extra-human intervention (*In the Days of the Comet*, 1906) or catastrophe – although one of his earliest novels (*When the Sleeper Awakes*, 1899) did deal with a future workers' revolution.

In *The World Set Free* (1914), this era of reason was ushered in through a world atomic war, a device Wells was to use again in his technocratic *The Shape of Things to Come* (1933). Contemporary futurologists can sometimes be heard speculating about the necessity for a sharp shock to bring about the changes in consciousness they seek. But the wars of this century have to date played no such role – except in so far as they have provided opportunities for socialist revolutions in relatively underdeveloped parts of the world, which is hardly what Wells was looking to. What these wars have, however, achieved – in addition to immense physical devastation and destruction of human potential – are steps towards the science of the future which Wells advocated, although, again, it is doubtful that this is the neutral science that Wells envisaged. Calling for greater organisation of resources around a shared goal than ever before, these great wars are turning-points in forecasting. Their undermining of the notion of necessary human progress, and revelation of the possibilities of genocide (and even race 'suicide'), have also deeply penetrated modern thought about the future – perhaps this very depth is a reason for the refusal of most futurologists to even consider the question of the conditions for ensuring peace seriously.

The First World War necessitated the active intervention of the State in British economic affairs. But while British government expenditure rose sharply from 15 per cent to 75 per cent of the national income, no integrated national planning apparatus was constructed. Some steps towards planning had already been introduced by the welfare provisions introduced shortly before the war, but during the emergency only piecemeal enlargements were made to the planning apparatus (Ward, 1976). Even with the continued costs of social services and the evident vulnerability of the British economy after the war and during the Great Depression, there was no attempt to emulate the national planning begun in the Soviet Union in the early 1920s, although accounts of such planning found a receptive audience among both socialists and technocrats in the West. Liberals debated at length the possible conflicts between planning and individual freedom.[13] The increasing severity of capitalist economic crises and the growing political challenge of workers' movements was making an increased role for state planning – whether of a fascist or liberal variety – more and more urgent. During the interwar years different strategies were tried out in different industrial countries, but since the war state planning has been established as a major force in all of them (Warren, 1972).

Between the two world wars, interest in the future, too, took very different forms in Britain and the United States. While England fought off recognising its decline as an imperial power, the publishers Kegan Paul commissioned a series of books in which prominent intellectuals gave their views on the likely future of different areas of human activity.

Notable in this series are the opposing views of the role of science in the future given by J. B. S. Haldane, who argued in *Daedalus* (1923) that scientific progress made for social progress (and scientific socialism), and Bertrand Russell, who drew attention to the use of science for oppression and destruction in his *Icarus* (1924). British demographers caught the public eye by forecasting a likely decline of the population. (This forecast was advanced in many industrial countries during the Great Depression, and was matched by eugenicists with forecasts of a declining level of IQ due to the supposed relative size, fertility of groups differing in test performance.)

The same period saw much more emphasis on the practical aspects of short-term forecasting in the United States, both from business and academics. This interest, probably related to the US's relative size, prosperity and continuing displacement of agricultural workers, was made easier to put into practice as systematic business forecasting, by the availability of improved economic statistics. Indeed, already before the First World War a commercial service was issuing predictions of cyclical economic changes. The Harvard Index Chart used by J. H. Proxmire gave quite accurate short-term forecasts up until the First World War, but in later years its usefulness proved to be much diminished, and many other forecasting instruments were developed. Hanson (1951) recounts that in the 1920s five forecasting agencies alone served 35 000 subscribers. Their accuracy record was not particularly impressive (Cox, 1930; Fels and Hinshaw, 1968), but they may have been of use in identifying on-going booms and slumps and were certainly widely regarded as useful. But, following the Harvard Index Chart into obsolescence, these forecasting devices failed to provide reasonable predictions in the unreasonable conditions of the Great Depression, and never regained their prestige after their failure to predict and deal with the 1929 stock market crash. A similar failure of forecasting occurred in the 1970s, as we shall see later.

The boom—bust cycles of the 1920s were a source of concern not only to business, however: they created major crises in many workers' lives as unemployment levels fluctuated. Social scientists were employed by successive US governments in a number of major research projects on social and economic trends, and began to apply techniques of trend extrapolation and systematic qualitative analysis to social and technological forecasting. Along with the New Deal and increased state planning in the United States, came such reports as *Technological Trends and National Policy*. Carried out under the direction of sociologist William F. Ogburn, this study included assessments of the track record of technological forecasts, attempts to predict technological trends, and assessments of possible social implications: the emphasis on technology is in keeping with the belief that social problems stem from difficulties faced by human nature and culture in keeping pace with social change.[14] These studies supported a new emphasis on social and economic planning as a system of balancing the growth process, while studiously avoiding raising doubts about the existing structure of business and its systems of technological change.

In the uncertainty and growing gloom of the interwar period, then, we find the first large-scale attempts to develop a systematic set of scientific methods for forecasting social and economic changes.[15] In the United States, such social analyses were in keeping with the shift from an optimistic and relatively *laissez-faire* economic situation (with a proliferation of short-term economic forecasts) to the need to shore up the existing structure of power relationships through increased State intervention and the New Deal (and reports for the President on the directions of social, economic and technological trends – see Bernstein, 1968). It is interesting to note that this was the period in which the technocracy movement, with its plans to place the American future in the hands of a scientific elite, flowered (Elsner, 1967); and that the 1930s were the 'golden age' of science fiction, when pulp magazines depicting the vast powers of future scientific civilisations (remarkably similar in all but their technology to suburban America and its nightmare images of the 'yellow peril') also flourished (Ashby, 1974).

In different countries the problems of the interwar years met with different political resolutions: the New Deal was benign in comparison with fascism and nazism. While their form depended upon the balance of political forces in each country, these widely varying outcomes were in common sought to defend the national capital and capitalist system against internal and external threats. Thus they ultimately insulated the very relations that were the source of crisis from being overturned by that crisis. The differing and partial national solutions finally resulted in the conflagration of the Second World War, which was to mark the take-off of futures studies (as of rocketry; two Wellsian dreams). Henceforth the debate was less to be concerned with the desirability of planning, and more with its techniques.

LIVING IN THE FUTURE

We now live in a world dreamed of, anticipated and predicted – with varying degrees of accuracy – by forecasters of the past. The applications of science and technology have transformed vast areas of the physical and social worlds. Advanced industrial societies are crucially dependent on science and technology for their daily activity and future expansion. Shambling out of Solomon's house. Frankenstein's monster bears both artificial flavours to please the senses, and medical instruments to prolong and enhance life.

The power of modern technology was effectively demonstrated in the Second World War, where new means of destruction wreaked unparalleled havoc, and immense strides were taken in speeding up technological development. National States learned, as in the previous war, from their experiences of economic management and organising of crash programmes (for example, for the development of nuclear weapons). They also learned the utility of applying scientific methods to military problems, thus developing the fundamentals of operations research (as the later US space programme was to stimulate the development of systems analysis).

The demand for forecasts boomed after the war, with military forecasting continuing to play an important role. The US Army began its series of long-range technological forecasts in the late 1940s, while the first of many 'think tanks', RAND, was established for the US military in this period. Maintaining high levels of military expenditure was an important means of State economic management (Horowitz, 1969). The Cold War conditions that this facilitated and sustained provided incentives to study emerging technologies of destruction and the possible circumstances of future wars. Organisations like RAND became high-status centres of multidisciplinary research, where academics could share the authorship of projects with representatives of both sides of the military-industrial complex.

The threat of nuclear war was the subject of many studies in this period, including Herman Kahn's first two books; and the disastrous potential of open, full-scale warfare also led to a search for new strategies for containing conflict. With the increasing importance of Third World countries as resource and investment sites for US interests, counter-insurgency strategy was a boom area of research here: the notorious Project Camelot brought attention to some of these studies in a spectacular way (Horowitz, 1967).[16] Camelot, designed so to forecast the risks of revolutions in Latin America so as to enhance the ability of the US state to determine the futures of these countries, was only aborted when a European futurologist whose cooperation had been sought leaked details to Chilean politicians.

Forecasting for military purposes is nothing new of course: kriegspiel has a long tradition (for example Wilson, 1970). What is new is the massive scale of resources poured into such efforts, and of the importation and development of social science here, which has had significant effects on the practice of forecasting for non-military purposes. Even kriegspiel has been reconstructed by contemporary science, in the form of game theory. And game theory, apparently a highly formalised, mathematical body of analytic procedures, is not neutral when applied to forecasting: Horowitz and Katz (1975), for example, argue that as well as being a convenient weapon in power struggles between different branches of the military, game theory both incarnated and inspired a rigid foreign policy. Other techniques that are commonplace in forecasting research were developed in the think tanks – delphi technique, scenario analysis and the like.

Military forecasting has played an important role in setting the pace of futures studies, indeed it is something of a skeleton in the cupboard for many contemporary forecasters – just as war is a plausible future which is dismissed with immense complacency in most forecasting works. The space race – itself stimulated in no small way by military interests – has also played a notable role in providing techniques of analysis for goal-directed futures research. But economic forecasting of various kinds also boomed in the long period of relatively crisis-free economic expansion in the 1950s and 1960s in the West. (Not that crises were ever all that far away. For example, the influential Paley Report on Raw Materials (1952) was set up after the alarm about raw materials shortages associated with the Korean War.) This interest in economic forecasting coincided with a new emphasis on planning, both on the part of large companies and national States.

Large industrial firms grew in the wake of the war into transnational corporations; these offered increasing scope for, and required increasing attention to, coordinated activities (as argued by Galbraith, 1967). The accelerated rate of technological innovation, and the increasing scale of industrial projects (meaning more expense and longer lead times) made for greater risks in failure and delay, and thus an increased need for corporate planning (Mandel, 1975; Rosenhead and Thunhurst, 1978). Private and nationalised industry thus took up and elaborated many of the techniques of long-term technology and economic forecasting; occasionally they would commission full-scale futurological studies (like Unilever's *Britain 1984*, Brech, 1963) to sound out their medium- and long-term social environments.[17]

Economic forecasting was also expanded and developed under the impetus of growing State expenditure in the postwar period (see for example Gough, 1977). Not only high levels of military expenditure were used to promote economic stability; other forms of demand management, and later more extensive economic planning, were deployed to limit unemployment and secure the profitability of private industry (O'Connor, 1973; Warren, 1972). These tendencies were particularly marked in Western Europe; in France in particular they led to wide-ranging intellectual developments in which the concepts of prospective planning, and forecasting were closely linked.[18] Economic forecasting has been the main focus of development, however, and has largely been institutionalised: McMahon (1965) found that the six OECD countries he studied all used short-term forecasting in budgetary and monetary policy-making, with some states also using it in wage regulation and indicative planning.

Since 'mixed economies' cannot engage in comprehensive planning, given the continued private goal-setting and business rationality of major industrial sectors, these economic forecasts may play a number of roles. As well as attempting to estimate the consequences of interacting private and state decisions, for example, they may be used to create a common image of the future which can partially substitute for a deliberate coordination of sectional interests – a ghostly kind of planning! What they do not do, of course, is indicate possible future directions of change which challenge the existing economic order. By not admitting radical alternatives into the analysis – they are 'politically unfeasible' – the forecasts may be used to reinforce the acquiescence of subordinated groups to the demands of this social order – persuading people that wage rises or welfare service expansion are out of the question, for example.

Official forecasts are not alone in simultaneously performing both technical and ideological functions. It is common to find private agencies producing national economic forecasts, in addition to those prepared by state statistical and economic officials. Several factors make this a lucrative business, among them the recurrent suspicion that official forecasts are intended more to produce a desired response than to provide a dispassionate account of tendencies of development and the outcomes of current policy. The forecasting procedures of the OECD, for example, came under heavy outside criticism as well as provoking conflict among OECD staff, in 1975–6 (Anon, 1976a); since revising its procedures, OECD forecasts have often diverged from those of its member governments. In principle, it is to be welcomed that alternative sources of technically competent forecasts are available. But while corporate planners have been well aware of the need to scrutinise official forecasts carefully, and to enlist expert analysis where necessary, there is little evidence of workers' organisations developing such capabilities: the plurality of economic forecasts that are available continues largely to reflect a one-sided set of interests rather than pluralism.

The long economic boom that followed the Second World War had confounded the forecasts of many economists, who had expected a relapse into stagnation; instead short-run forecasts had to be revised upwards, as a historically unprecedented period of rapid growth was achieved. But in recent years, the factors which sustained the boom – a world division of labour and monetary system based on US hegemony, profitable technological change, and economic management through State expenditure – have increasingly become sources of new problems – inflation, monetary instability, conflicts over trading arrangements, unemployment (Gamble and Walton, 1976; Mandel, 1975; for a more orthodox view, see McCracken, 1977). Even before the economic crises of the 1970s unfolded, the late 1960s were a time of social upheaval – the events associated with Czechoslovakia and France in 1968, student and ghetto uprisings, Northern Ireland, the 'counter culture'. Harbingers of qualitative change, or merely cues for ushering in new techniques of conflict resolution – whatever their significance, these events were largely unforeseen in the forecasting literature of the preceding years, which had been heralding the 'end of ideology' (Kleinberg, 1973; Miles, 1978).

There is not much to wonder at, in this failure to forecast the eruptions of the 1960s. The main approaches used in forecasting relied upon extrapolation – either of quantitative trends (or cycles) as in economic forecasting, or of qualitative trends as in the case of many social forecasts both explicit and implicit. By projecting past patterns of change without any sensitivity to the possible future transformation of quantitative factors into qualitative changes, or the creation of countertrends by the self-same forces that set trends in motion, forecasters confine themselves to envisaging the perpetuation of the *status quo*.

The assumption that the future will be pretty much like the present, with perhaps a little more 'modernisation' flowing from economic growth and technological progress, has in some historical periods proved the most accurate forecasting instrument. Probably it has helped make the present pretty much like the past, although it is only one of many systems contributing to social reproduction; it can hardly be singled out for special blame here, or even be cited as a particularly manipulative force (as in conspiracy theories of forecasting). But our social system, in continually undermining its own foundations, creates both periodic crises and the conditions for consciously oppositional forces to develop. As in the decade of the 1970s, these circumstances imply a search for alternatives to deterministic methods of forecasting, and for new images of the future.

THE UNFORESEEABLE FUTURE

As in the 1920s, economic forecasts have again been discomfited recently by a series of events which rendered many established procedures obviously invalid. Thus in 1973–4 national economic forecasts were widely inaccurate, under-estimating the rapid growth of recession and the onset of recession (Anon, 1974; Zucker, 1975). Unlike the interwar forecasting scene, however, the recent economic crisis has led to an intensification of research work rather than a widespread loss of faith; like the earlier period, we are witnessing an increased interest in forecasting social and technological changes, in order to address issues clearly missing in the orthodox economic approach. Indeed, there has been much hope pinned on 'the systems approach' as providing integrated – and therefore, hopefully, more accurate – images of the future.

The scale of contemporary industrial activity is such that much information is both vital and cheap to acquire relative to other investments. Thus attempts are being made both to deepen and broaden the scope of economic forecasting – for example, with private consultants setting up extensive data banks and computer simulation models to predict the future of countries and groups of nations. Likewise there is more interest in combining economic forecasts with forecasts of other social changes (which are often held to account for economic anomalies).

Various factors had already stimulated the growth of social forecasting before the economic crisis broke in the 1970s. For example, a demand for forecasts was produced by the growing involvement of the state in social affairs – for purposes of macro-economic management, to cheapen the costs to industry of health, education and other social infrastructures, to contain or defuse opposition to existing tendencies of development, and to cope with the disorganisation that these tendencies have left in their wake. Demographic predictions were, for example, sought by a wide range of agencies, who would also be interested in studies of the problems for which they were held responsible. Urban and transport forecasting became almost as lucrative as redevelopment and property speculation. Especially in the United States, techniques of systems analysis and computer simulation, developed in the space programme, were employed first to these areas of forecasting and then to a wide range of state activities – with often farcical results (Hoos, 1972). Especially after the eruption of social conflict in mid-sixties America, applications of such approaches to social forecasting were common, as policy-makers sought a pleasing pattern and cheap 'Great Society' programme which would, they hoped, paper over the cracks.

The mid-sixties saw a rapid expansion of futurology. A steady stream of conferences, research groups and journals flowed forth, and hopes were raised that different forecasting studies and methods could be synthesised into a general science of the future (Cornish, 1977). Technocratic policy scientists, progressive corporate planners, and intellectuals aware of the persistence of poverty and ignorance amidst continuing economic growth, were drawn into the attempt to develop viable images of the future.[19]

Much of this new surge of futures research has actually relied on the most primitive methods of extrapolation and naive speculation simply applied to a wider range of issues. A number of more complicated approaches have, however, also been developed – scenario analysis techniques, delphi, computer simulation. Just as a theoretically informed, critical use of extrapolation can be valuable as an assessment of tendencies of development, if not as a deterministic prediction of the future, these more sophisticated approaches may have a contribution to make to understanding the present and creating the future. But, given the ways in which the production of knowledge is structured in contemporary society, these newer approaches are more often used to remain faithful to the *status quo*. Their technical complexity makes them difficult for many people to understand, and may reinforce the idea that the future is so complicated that it should be left in expert hands. Yet underlying even the most sophisticated quantitative analysis is a core of assumptions that are political, not solely technical. Often the complexity simply serves to play a set of canonical variations upon ideological 'common-sense' themes or conservative extrapolations (Miles and Irvine, 1978). Rather than advancing social understanding, they more often play a mystificatory role – however useful they may be for, or however removed they are from, the technical needs of planners. Forecasting is not being abused here (except in so far as there is fudging of technical issues), because it is never neutral to begin with.

It is not to claim that all forecasts share precisely the same content;

rather, to argue that the dominant features of forecasting are structured by a set of dominant – but not monolithic – interests. Futurology has produced its optimists and pessimists, although the possibilities of violent conflict are not often addressed (except by counter-insurgency 'experts' and military strategists), nor are means of checking the militarisation of the world discussed (exceptions here include the World Order Models Project and the work of peace research groups). The possibilities for transcending capitalist social relations, furthermore, are very seldom raised in the futures literature – and when they are, the image of 'socialism' portrayed is horrendous indeed!

Images of the future of the West, portrayed in the futures literature, have overwhelmingly been fairly complacent visions of post-industrial society. (See Marien, 1977; Kleinberg, 1973.) It is only recently that concerns about mass unemployment have resurfaced in the futures literature. In-depth studies of the future of industrial societies have tended to be limited to compilations of sectoral studies with little overarching analysis or general theoretical perspective – this is true even of the six volumes of *Plan Europe 2000* devoted to education! Nevertheless, a shopping-list of forecasts seems to be in demand, now that there is so much uncertainty about future directions of social change: thus in addition to the familiar business forecasting agencies, there have recently been established a number of private agencies (Boucher and Willson describe more than twenty at work in the United States) which provide data on a wide variety of social trends, and/or collate forecasts made in specialist journals.

Where studies concern the future of the whole world, rather than simply that of industrial countries, the gloomy Malthusian debate, rather than the sanitised perspectives of post-industrial society predominates (see Freeman and Jahoda, 1978). Here, forecasts range from threats of imminent ecological doom unless drastic action is taken, to prophecies of superabundance on condition that nobody upsets the boat. In locating questions about world futures firmly as technical debates concerning resource availability and technological change, the literature has by and large diverted its gaze from the socio-political underpinnings of world inequality. The oppression of Third World peoples is seen, not as a historical product of a particular pattern of social development, but as a natural consequence of 'underdevelopment' or 'overpopulation'.[20]

Contemporary forecasting differs vastly from the concern with the future expressed in earlier periods – a consequence of the rapid rate of technological change and the growing concentration of power in large corporations and state bureaucracies, and changes in educational levels and social organisation. The variety of forecasting methods available has mushroomed, there have been created new specialisms within futures studies (including the specialism of the 'expert generalist'), and glossy works of futurology are now often directed at a mass audience rather than at limited elites. But while all these changes are strikingly apparent, there are striking continuities in the study of the future.

Forecasting studies are usually commissioned and formulated according to the interests of dominant social groups. The images of the future which dominate these studies, which in turn contribute to the general formulation of ideas about the future, correspond to these interests. The diversity of forecasting techniques conceals the reliance of many upon extrapolation, on the projection, forward in time, of relationships characterising the present (Miles and Irvine, 1978; Miles 1978; Miles 1975). Forecasting studies overwhelmingly take the present order of social relationships as universal rather than as something that was created and may be transformed through human action. The very system of social relationships which creates a demand for more and more study of the future, places severe limits on our conceptions of future relationships.

But it is too simplistic to view the history of the future as solely a succession of adaptations to avert threatened change in the social organisation of power. Certainly the main thrust of scientific forecasting has been to contain challenges to the existing system: thus the political arithmeticians responded to the radicalism of the Puritan revolution, Malthusians and the Victorian statistical movements to the working-class upsurges of the Industrial Revolution, and the interwar trend to the discontent of the Depression era. But alternative images of the future have also repeatedly been developed, in the social analyses of Winstanley, Marx and many later revolutionaries, for example, and in the form of fictional utopias.[21]

Contemporary policy science and future studies may not only reflect responses to some of the challenges experienced by the dominant social order but also reproduce some of its contradictions and allow these challenges to bear fruit. In some cases, radical social critics have been able to mobilise enough resources to produce futures studies which can compare with the most advanced work in terms of technical sophistication — for example, the Bariloche world model (Herrera, 1977). Third World social scientists have, as this example indicates, achieved some success in gaining support for their challenges to Western views of the future, perhaps because of their common (if ambiguous) appeal to anti-colonialist, nationalist and socialist mass and elite movements alike. But, in general, the forecasting literature shows little sign of penetration by radical currents in the industrial countries. The revolutionary rhetoric of some Soviet studies is no exception: only the ecological movement has evoked much response among futurologists. While recent years have been the occasion for a marshalling of scientific expertise for oppositional social movements, and alternative plans are being prepared by community action groups and workers' organisations (e.g. the Lucas Aerospace workers' alternative corporate plan, see Elliot 1977), the images of an alternative future that result typically address only a localised range of questions and are often, in that respect, liable to be given a purely utopian interpretation. Nevertheless, alternative futures, and possible ways of realising them, are depicted in many serious works of radical analysis.[22]

The concern with alternative futures for world society expressed in such literature, whose theoretical apparatus is actively orientated towards fundamental social change, means that it is something that future researchers ignore at their own peril. While such perspectives remain the object of considerable controversy in academic circles, the crises of the social sciences in the last decade restimulated interest in them. Meanwhile 'systems' approaches and the idea that a focus on the future can achieve a synthesis of disciplines, have often been advanced as providing a holistic view of social change; one that is less in conflict with the mainstream traditions of social science. The current world crisis seems likely to produce, at an intellectual level, the confrontation of these perspectives, and with this, an increasing confrontation of opposing images of the future.

There are opportunities for interventions to be made by social critics in forecasting – when the advantages of reaching its audience does not mean the vitiation of aims and analysis with an inadequate language and methodology. At present forecasting is effectively monopolised by the perspectives under whose aegis its dimensions and form have been largely staked out.

Far from being neutral, it exists largely to secure an alienated and alienating social order. It remains to be demonstrated how far the elaboration of alternative perspectives upon its terrain is dependent upon the reconstruction of that social order itself. Likewise it remains to be established how far this reconstruction can be facilitated through our striving to create alternative forms of forecasting and richer images of the future.

NOTES

1. The wide historical scope necessitates rather drastic compression of substance and, no doubt, a degree of over-generalisation: I hope that the extensive bibliography can go some way towards helping readers offset these problems. The discussion is also tied almost exclusively to Western images of the future, and, within these, to English-language sources stemming mainly from the United Kingdom and United States. No doubt the greater length and labour required for a more comprehensive study would be well repaid; on the other hand, at least the focus here should clarify aspects of what has been the historically dominant tradition.
2. This is a perspective that may be easier to illustrate with reference to a 'fringe' science, such as forecasting is now often seen to be. For studies in other areas of natural and social science which contribute to this analysis, see Blackburn (1972), Easlea (1973), Evans, Irvine and Miles (1978), Rose and Rose (1976), Young (1971, 1973), Mendelsohn, Weingart and Whitley (1977).
3. Miles and Irvine (1978) elaborate this argument with especial reference to the development of forecasting technique. Miles (1978) focuses on ideological dimensions of contemporary futures research. Sandberg (1976) presents detailed analysis of forecasting and planning based largely on Scandinavian examples. Rosenhead and Thunhurst (1978) address operations research in these terms.
4. The fate of astrology in modern times is interesting: in England, at any rate, it has emerged as a popular social philosophy (although one appealing to different groups) at times of crisis such as the mid-seventeenth century, the late nineteenth century, and the last third of the twentieth century (Howe, 1967; Russell, 1974).
5. The after-life of religious cosmologies, like such rewards for the blessed as Valhallah, Paradise or the Isles of the Blessed, like the folksy never-never lands of Cockaigne, Faery and even the Big Rock Candy Mountain, lies in the individual, rather than the societal, future. But apocalyptic and messianic religious visions, in contrast, as sometimes developed by groups suffering long-lasting oppression, did propose the ideas of a final day of judgement or reckoning, when historic wrongs would be righted and a divine 'social' order established.
6. It might be argued that Bacon was simply well ahead of his time, and that the division of scientific labour by the stage, rather than the subject matter, of research is currently proceeding apace. McLean (1978), for example, argues that computerisation facilitates this tendency in social research.
7. Probably the newest approximation to a utopia stemming from such sources is the work of Gerrard Winstanley: see *The Law of Freedom* (1652). Bacon himself could simultaneously favour 'the effecting of all things possible' and science for 'the relief of man's estate'. It is with William Blake and Mary Shelley that the possible contradictions here are first unfolded.
8. Jonathan Swift's brilliant essay, *A Modest Proposal*, occasioned by his distrust of the uses of political arithmetic, is a brilliant and still-relevant satire on the claimed neutrality of quantitative policy analysis. His

demonstration, in deadpan prose, that the raising of Irish children for cannibalisation would immeasurably benefit the United Kingdom, is echoed only shallowly in verve and wit by recent parodies of technocratic rationality like *Report from Iron Mountain* (Lewin, 1967).

9. The life-table is the paradigm of a common modern approach to forecasting the fate of individuals – for example, versions of it are employed in applied social research for social work and social control, e.g. in predicting crime, the success of managers, etc.
10. The latter anticipates Kahn and Wiener's futorological opus (1967) by almost two centuries. But these authors are not alone in drawing their titles from the past: *The Art of Conjecture*, used by de Jouvenel for his influential book (1967) was originally used by Bernoulli (1713).
11. It is no innovation of modern science fiction to situate fictional alternative societies in outer space – Lucian of Samosata described other-worldly societies in the second century AD – but it is only in recent years that space travel has been sufficiently realistic for its fictional deployment to transcend satire or adventure yarns.
12. Aldiss also outlines the genre's defining feature as its concern with the future achievements and consequences of scientific development of science, giving these a far more central place than did, as noted earlier, Bacon in *New Atlantis*. He sees Mary Shelley's *Frankenstein* (1818) as the paradigmatic science fiction novel, a striking allegory of the problems of scientific progress directed by individual ambition. With Wells, scientific marvels and horrors flow thicker and faster than the victims of Frankenstein's monster in a Hollywood movie.
13. See Boucher (1977) for a survey and bibliography of forecasting research in the Soviet Union. On the evolution of the liberal debate, see Sandberg (1976).
14. On Ogburn, his work and times see Duncan (1964), Gilfillan (1968), Miles (1975), Miles and Irvine (1978).
15. Demographic forecasting predates this to some extent, but even here the method of components projection was not widely applied until the 1920s. It was also in this period that forecasting of election results was developed on any scale.
16. On scholarly inputs to US involvement in Indochina, see Chomsky (1969, 1973).
17. Although forming the subject of countless conferences, bibliographies, and even of an annual directory, corporate planning is not yet established in all the largest companies. In surveying large industry in the UK, Higgins and Finn (1977) found that while almost all of the 'Times Thousand' firms engage in long-range financial planning, some one in five do not practise corporate planning. The journal *Long Range Planning* carries useful, if sanguine, reports of developments in this field.
18. The *Prospective* group of Gaston Berger, active through the 1950s, influenced the process of French planning. In 1970 the Commissariat Général du Plan issued an impressive series of futures studies concerned with urbanism, ways of life, telecommunications, and so on, while as early as 1963 a study of France up until 1985 was undertaken. During the 1960s Bertrand de Jouvenel established the *Futuribles* project, which has helped to

impart a European flavour to futures studies, and under whose auspices a series of seminal futurological conferences were organised in the early 1960s (with Ford Foundation support).

19. Klein (1977) notes American science fiction as undergoing significant changes in the mid-sixties, too; it veered from a focus on optimistic tales of distant futures to pessimistic portraits of the near future. He relates this to the changing circumstances of the genre's audience – technical white-collar workers whose rising status and autonomy at work were being checked for the first time. We have not been able to discuss here Orwell's *1984* or Huxley's science fiction novels (such as *Brave New World* and *Island*), which have played a significant role in crystallising popular images of the future.

20. Malthusian forecasts also play a significant ideological role in debates over the future of the industrial countries. However idealistically ecological issues may be pursued by activists, the occlusion of the social relations underlying economic, pollution and resource crises in Malthusian forecasts means that they may play various roles supportive of these social relations. For example, 'limits to growth' ideas have been cited as, among other roles: providing a rationale for the restructuring of world production under the dictates of transnational corporations; providing a plausible argument for their control of world resources; and supporting social Darwinism and reductions in living standards. See Atkinson and Kusch (1977), Balibar (1978), Enzensberger (1976), Golub and Townsend (1977), among others.

21. In a series of assessments of utopian literature, Darko Suvin has argued that 'science fiction is historically part and parcel of a submerged or popular "lower literature" expressing the yearnings of repressed social groups' (Suvin, 1974, p. 256), and that 'sudden whirlpools in history which both further and permit its emergence in literature – the times of Iambulus, More, Fourier, Morris, or indeed our own – have therefore the makings of great ages of science fiction' (Suvin, 1976, p. 242). Indeed, new utopias are currently being created within science fiction, notably Le Guin's *The Dispossessed* (1974) and Callenbach's *Ecotopia* (1978). (It is instructive to contrast Le Guin's libertarian socialist vision with the 'scientific' socialism of Haldane's *The Man With Two Memories* (1976)).

22. Thus Mandel (1969) concludes his outline of *Marxist Economic Theory* with discussions of future social possibilities. The East German writer, Bahro (1978) has produced an analysis of radical possibilities in the 'state socialist' countries. In a recent conference of futurists on desirable future worlds, Markovic (1978) attempted to outline a model for a 'humanistic socialist' society, based on his experience of the Yugoslavian experiment; while this paper, focusing exclusively on an image of a desirable future as it does, may be the exception that proves the rule, it is strictly in line of descent from Markovic's previous studies grounded firmly in the present. Amin (1974) and Frank (1976) have also written on the more ominous development of what they term the '1984' scenario, starting from a focus on the world system of international capital. Listing the whole range of relevant studies and sources here would be impossible; for more bibliographic information see Boyle and Harper (1976), Griffiths, Irvine and Miles (1978), Livingstone (1975), Pateman (1972), BSSRS (1977), Tallahassee Science for the People (1977), Miles (1978).

BIBLIOGRAPHY

Abrams, Philip (1968), *The Origins of British Sociology*, Chicago and London: University of Chicago Press.
Aldiss, Brian W. (1974), *Billion Year Spree*, New York: Shocken.
Amin, Sumir (1974), Towards A New Structural Crisis of the Capitalist System? *Conference on Multinational Corporations in Africa*, Dakar: UNALEDP.
Anon. (1974), 'Theory deserts the forecasters', *Business Week*, 2337 (24 June) pp. 50–4.
Anon. (1976a), 'Independence at the OECD', *Business Week*, no. 2429 (26 April), p. 92.
Anon. (1976b), 'The trouble with forecasting world economies', *Business Week*, No. 2429 (20 April) pp. 88–92.
Armytage, W. H. G. (1968), *Yesterday's Tomorrows*, London: Routledge and Kegan Paul.
Ashby, Michael (ed.) (1974), *The History of the Science Fiction Magazine, Part One, 1926–1935*, London: New English Library.
Atkins, Liz and Jarret, David (1978), 'The significance of significance tests', in J. Evans, J. Irvine and I. Miles (eds.), *Demystifying Social Statistics*, London: Pluto Press.
Atkinson, Pat and Kusch, Johan (1977), 'Limits to growth or limits to capitalism?', *Science for People* no. 33, 12–14.
Bahro, Rudolf (1978), *The Alternative in Eastern Europe*, London: New Left Books.
Balibar, Etienne (1978), 'Irrationalism and Marxism', *New Left Review*, No. 107, pp. 3–18.
Berneri, Marie Louise (1950), *Journey Through Utopia* (1971 ed.), New York: Shocken.
Bernstein, Barton J. (1968), 'The New Deal: the conservative achievements of liberal reform', in B. J. Bernstein (ed.) *Towards A New Past*, New York: Random House.
Blackburn, Robin (1972), *Ideology in Social Science*, London: Fontana.
Boucher, Wayne I. (1977), 'Forecasting when the future is known: the case of the Soviet Union', in W. I. Boucher (ed.) *The Study of the Future: An Agenda for Research*, Washington: National Science Foundation.
Boucher, Wayne I. and Willson, Katherine (1977), 'Monitoring the future', in W. I. Boucher (ed.) *The Study of the Future: an Agenda for Research*.

Boyle, C. and Harper, P. (1976), *Radical Technology*, London: Wildwood House.
Brech, Ronald (1963), *Britain 1984*, London: Darton, Longman and Todd.
BSSRS (1977), *Ecology: A Critical Reading Guide*, London: BSSRS/SCANUS.
Buck, Peter (1977), 'Seventeenth-century political arithmetic: Civil strife and vital statistics', *Isis 68* (241) pp. 67–86.
Callenbach, Ernest (1978), *Ecotopia*, London: Pluto Press.
Chomsky, Noam (1969), *American Power and the New Mandarins*, New York: Pantheon; Harmondsworth: Penguin Books.
Chomsky, Noam (1973), *The Backroom Boys*, London: Fontana/Collins.
Clark, Sir G. N. (1948), *Science and Social Welfare in the Age of Newton*, London: Oxford University Press, partly reprinted in Anthony Oberschall (ed.) (1972), *op. cit.*
Clarke, I. F. (1973), 'The discovery of the future 1750–1850', *Futures, 5*, pp. 494–5.
Cohn, Norman (1957), *The Pursuit of the Millenium*, London: Secker and Warburg (1970, Paladin).
Cornish, Edmund (1977), *The Study of the Future*, Washington: World Future Society.
Cox, Garfield V. (1930), *An Appraisal of American Business Forecasts*, Chicago: University of Chicago Press.
Cullen, M. G. (1975), *The Statistical Movement in Early Victorian Britain*, Hassocks, Sussex: Harvester Press.
de Jouvenel, Bertrand (1967), *The Art of Conjecture*, New York: Basic Books (originally published in France, 1964).
Deutscher, I. (1964), *The Age of Permanent Revolution: a Trotsky Anthology*, New York: Dell.
Dobb, Maurice (1963 rev. of 1946), *Studies in the Development of Capitalism*, London: Routledge and Kegan Paul.
Duncan, Otis Dudley (ed.) (1964), *William F. Ogburn: On Forecasting and Social Change*, Chicago: University of Chicago Press.
Easlea, Brian (1973), *Liberation and the Aims of Science*, London: Chatto and Windus (for Sussex U.P.).
Elliot, Dave (1977), *The Lucas Aerospace Workers' Campaign*, London: Young Fabian pamphlet no. 46, Fabian Society.
Elliot, Dave and Elliot Ruth, (1976), *The Control of Technology*, London: Wykeham Press.
Elsner Jr, Henry (1967), *The Technocrats*, Syracuse, New York:

Syracuse University Press.
Enzensberger, Hans Magnus (1976), 'A critique of political ecology', in *Raids and Reconstructions*, London: Pluto Press.
Fels, Rending and Hinshaw, C. Elton (1968), *Forecasting and Recognising Business Activity Turning Points*, New York: National Bureau of Economic Research and Columbia University Press.
Finley, M. I. (1967), 'Utopianism ancient and modern' in K. H. Woolf and B. Moore (eds.) *The Critical Spirit*, Boston: Beacon Press.
Foucault, Michel (1970), *The Order of Things*, London: Tavistock.
Frank, Andrew G. (1976), 'Economic crisis. Third world and 1984', *World Development 4*, pp. 853–61.
Freeman, Chris and Jahoda, Marie (eds.) (1978), *World Futures: The Great Debate*, London: Martin Robertson.
Galbraith, J. K. (1967) *The New Industrial State*, London: Hamish Hamilton.
Gamble, Andrew and Walton, Paul (1976), *Capitalism in Crisis*, London: Macmillan.
Gilfillan, S. Colum (1968), 'A Sociologist Looks at Technical Prediction', in James R. Bright (ed.), *Technological Forecasting for Industry and Government 1968*, Englewood Cliffs, N. J.: Prentice-Hall.
Golub, Bob and Townsend, Joe (1977), Malthus, 'Multinationals and the Club of Rome', *Social Studies of Science*, 7, pp. 201–22.
Gough, Ian (1975), 'State expenditure in advanced capitalism', *New Left Review*, No. 92, pp. 53–92.
Griffiths, Dot, Irvine, John and Miles, Ian (1978), 'Social Statistics: Political Perspectives', in J. Evans, J. Irvine and I Miles (eds.) *Demystifying Social Statistics*, London: Pluto Press.
Haldane, J. B. S. (1976), *The Man with Two Memories*, London: Merlin.
Hansen, Alvin H. (1951), *Business Cycles and National Income*, New York: W. W. Norton.
Heilbroner, R. L. (1974), *An Inquiry into the Human Prospect*, New York: Norton.
Herrera, Amilcar (ed.) (1977), *Catastrophe or New Society?* Canada: IDRC.
Higgins, J. C. and Finn, R. (1977), 'The organization and practice of corporate planning in the U.K.,' *Long Range Planning*, 10 (4), pp. 88–92.
Hill, Christopher (1972), *The World Turned Upside Down*, London: Maurice Temple Smith (Penguin, 1975).
Hoos, Ida R. (1972), *Systems Analysis and Public Policy: A Critique*, Berkeley: University of California Press.

Horowitz, David (ed.) (1969), *Corporations and the Cold War*, New York: Monthly Review Press.

Horowitz, Irving Louis (1967), *The Rise and Fall of Project Camelot*, Cambridge, Mass.: MIT Press.

Horowitz, I. L. and Katz, J. E. (1975), *Social Science and Public Policy in the United States*, New York: Praeger.

Howe, Ellis (1967), *Urania's Children*, London: William Kimber.

Irvine, J., Miles, I. and Evans, J. (eds) (1978), *Demystifying Social Statistics*, London: Pluto Press.

Keynes, J. M. (1936), 'William Stanley Jevons 1835–1862', *Journal of the Royal Statistical Society 94*, pp. 516–48.

Klein, Gerard (1977), 'Discontent in American science fiction', *Science Fiction Studies*, *4*, pp. 3–13.

Kleinberg, Benjamin S. (1973), *American Society in the Post-industrial Age*, Columbus, Ohio: Charles E. Merril Pub. Co.

Le Guin, Ursula (1974), *The Dispossessed*, New York: Harper and Row.

Lenin, V. I. (1917), *The State and Revolution*, English edition 1965, Peking: Foreign Languages Press.

Lewin, Leonard C. (ed.) (1967), *Report from Iron Mountain*, Harmondsworth: Penguin.

Livingstone, Dennis (1975), *A Bibliography of Positive Alternative Futures*, Troy, New York: Rensselaer Polytechnic Institute (mimeo).

Mandel, Ernest (1969), *Marxist Economic Theory*, London: Merlin Books.

Marien, Michael (1977), 'The two visions of post-industrial society', *Futures*, 9.

Markovic, Mihailo (1978), 'Humanist socialist vision of future', paper presented at conference on *Alternative Visions of Desirable Societies*, Centro de Estudios Economicos y Sociales del Tercer Mondo, Mexico City, April 1978.

Marx, Karl, and Engels, Frederick (1848), *The Communist Manifesto*, (reprinted in Marx-Engels: *Selected Works*, 1968, London: Lawrence and Wishart).

McCracken, Paul, et al. (1977), *Towards Full Employment and Price Stability*, Paris, OECD.

McLean, Mick, (1978), 'The computerization of social research', in J. Evans, J. Irvine and I. Miles (eds.), *Demystifying Social Statistics*, London: Pluto Press.

McMahon, C. W. (1965), 'A general survey of the procedures and problems of official short-term economic forecasting', in OECD, *Techniques of Economic Forecasting*, Paris, OECD.

Mendelsohn, E., Weingart, P. and Whitley, R. (eds.) (1977), *The Social Production of Scientific Knowledge*, Dodrecht, Netherlands: D. Reidel.

Miles, Ian (1975), *The Poverty of Prediction*, Farnborough: Saxon House.

Miles, Ian (1978), 'Dangers of futures research', in Jib Fowles (ed.) *Handbook of Futures Research*, Dorsey, Illinois: Greenwood Press.

Miles, Ian and Irvine, John (1978), 'Social forecasting: Predicting the future or making history?' in J. Evans, J. Irvine and I. Miles (eds.), *Demystifying Social Statistics*, London: Pluto Press.

Morton, A. L. (1969), *The English Utopia*, London: Lawrence and Wishart.

Nairn, Tom (1964), 'Anatomy of the Labour Party', *New Left Review*, 27, 28, reprinted in Robin Blackburn, 1977 (ed.), *Revolution and Class Struggle*, London: Fontana/Collins.

National Resources Committee, (1937), (Report of the Sub-committee on Technology) *Technological Trends and National Policy including the social implications of New Inventions*, Washington DC: US Government Printing Office.

Nordhauser, Norman, (1973), 'Origins of federal oil regulation in the 1920s', *Business History Review*, 47, pp. 53–71.

O'Connor, James (1973), *The Fiscal Crisis of the State*, London: St James.

Oliver, W. H., (1971), 'Owen in 1817: The millenialist moment', in Sidney Pollard and John Salt (eds.), *Robert Owen: Prophet of the Poor*, London: Macmillan.

Ollman, Bertell (1977), 'Marx's vision of Communism: a reconstruction,' *Critique*, 8, pp. 4–41.

Pateman, Trevor (1972), *Counter Course*, Harmondsworth, Penguin.

Report of the President's Research Committee on Social Trends (1933), *Recent Social Trends in the United States*, New York: McGraw-Hill.

Rose, Hilary and Rose, Steven (eds.) (1976), *The Political Economy of Science* and *The Radicalization of Science*, London: Macmillan (jointly titled *Ideology of/in the natural sciences*).

Rosenhead, Jonathan, and Thunhurst, Colin (1978), 'Operations research and cost-benefit analysis: Whose science?' in J. Evans, J. Irvine and I. Miles (eds.), *Demystifying Social Statistics*, London: Pluto Press.

Russell, Eric (1974), *History of Astrology and Prediction*, London: New English Library.

Sandberg, Ake (1976), *The Limits to Democratic Planning*, Stockholm: Liber Förlag.
Sargent, Lyman Tower (1976), 'Themes in Utopian fiction in English before Wells', *Science Fiction Studies*, *3* (3), pp. 275–82.
Shaw, Martin and Miles, Ian (1978), 'Social roots of statistical knowledge', in J. Evans, J. Irvine and I. Miles (eds.) *Demystifying Social Statistics*, London: Pluto Press.
Sohn-Retehel, Alfred (1975), 'Science as alienated consciousness', *Radical Science Journal* no. 2/3, pp. 65–101.
Spengler, Joseph J. (1961), 'Quantification in economics: Its history', in Daniel S. Lerner (ed.), *Quantity and Quality*, Glencoe: Free Press.
Strauss, E. (1954), *Sir William Petty's Portrait of a Genius*, London: The Bodley Head.
Suvin, Darko (1974), 'Radical rhapsody and Romantic recoil in the age of anticipation', *Science Fiction Studies*, *1*, pp. 255–69.
Suvin, Darko (1976), 'The alternate islands: a chapter in the history of science fiction', *Science Fiction Studies*, *3*, pp. 239–48.
Swift, Jonathan (1729), 'A Modest Proposal for Preventing the Children of poor people in Ireland, from being a Burden to their Parents or Country; and for making them beneficial to the Publick', in *Swift: Gulliver's Travels and Other Writings*, ed. Miriam Kosh Starkman, (1962), New York: Bantam Books.
Tallahassee Science for the People (1977), *Reading Lists in the Making: Periodicals that Progressive Scientists Should Know About*, Tallahassee, Florida: Progressive Technology Co PO Box 20049.
Ward, Benjamin (1976), 'National economic planning and policies in twentieth-century Europe', in C. M. Cipolla (ed.), *The Fontana Economic History of Europe* (Vol. 5, *The Twentieth Century*, Part 2), London: Fontana/Collins.
Warren, Bill (1972) 'Capitalist planning and the State', *New Left Review*, No. 72, pp. 3–29.
Wilson, Andrew (1970), *War Gaming*, Harmondsworth: Penguin.
Winstanley, Gerrard, *The Law of Freedom and Other Writings* (ed. Christopher Hill), Harmondsworth: Penguin.
Winston, David (1976), 'Iambulus' Islands of the Sun and Hellenistic literary Utopias', *Science Fiction Studies*, *3*, pp. 219–27.
Yates, Frances A. (1975), *The Rosicrucian-Renaissance*, London: Paladin.
Young, Robert M. (1971), 'Evolutionary biology and ideology – then and now, *Science Fiction Studies*, *1*, pp. 77–206.
Young, Robert M. (1973), 'The evolutionary and ideological contexts of

the nineteenth-century debate on man's place in Nature', in Mikolas Teich and Robert M. Young (eds.), *Changing Perspectives in the History of Science*, London: Heinemann.

Young, Bob (1978), 'Why are figures so significant? in J. Evans, J. Irvine and I. Miles (eds.), *Demystifying Social Statistics*, London: Pluto Press.

Zucker, Seymour (1975), 'How good are the CEA's forecasts?' *Business Week*, No. 2368 (Feb 17) p. 24.

2 Economic Forecasting

FRANK BLACKABY

THE EVOLUTION OF SHORT-TERM ECONOMIC FORECASTING

The boundaries of economic forecasting are not easy to draw. The economist may be inclined to say that virtually any forecast of the future state of the world has an appreciable economic content – or, if it does not, so much the worse for the forecast. There are not many forecasts which do not need, somewhere, some economic concepts – such as the problem of the allocation of a given volume of resources between different ends – or some form of economic analysis, such as the reaction of producers and consumers to relative price changes. This chapter limits itself to one part of this large field – to the evolution of the forecasting of the movements of the economy as a whole, and the influence which these forecasts have had on policy.

So far as economic policy was concerned, the need for short-term economic forecasting was the consequence of the Keynesian revolution. So long as it was believed that there was nothing much that the Government could do to influence the general course of the economy, there was little point in setting up any body within the Government to try to forecast the course which the economy was going to take. Governments, however, emerged from the Second World War with a new doctrine – that it was their responsibility to attempt to maintain the full employment which the war had brought, and that it could be done by the manipulation of demand. In the words of Sir Robert Hall, economic adviser to the British Government in the early postwar period, the broad rule was 'to stimulate demand when it is deficient and to restrain it when excessive'.[1] A policy of this kind of course requires an assessment of whether demand is going to be deficient or excessive; and since there is a time-lag before policy measures become effective, the policy clearly requires an economic forecast. Short-term economic forecasting therefore began after the war within the Government service as an attempt to forecast the future movements of total demand in the economy, as a background to a Budget decision on whether to stimulate or to restrain it.

The initial forecasting in the United Kingdom was conducted in a body known as the National Income Forecast Working Party: and the title indicates the form which the forecast took. It was essentially based on the forecast of the components of national expenditure – and indeed, in a much more elaborate form that is still the basis of official short-term economic forecasting thirty years later. The forecasting in the early years was not based on an econometric model; the economic advice of various departments was brought together for a view on the likely course of exports and imports, of private fixed investment and so on; and the figures were presented as a forecast of the expenditure table, at constant prices, in the national accounts. This forecast of demand was compared with the course of potential output, and this was the basis for a recommendation to the Chancellor of the Exchequer about the need for tax increases or tax decreases.

Since those early days, short-term economic forecasting has evolved both inside and outside the Government. Within the Government, the basic principle of forecasting has remained the same – that of forecasting the movements of expenditure components of the national income; but the process has become more and more elaborate. A formal computerised model began to be used in the later half of the sixties, and the Treasury has now the largest macro-economic model in use in the United Kingdom.[2] Before 1969, there were only partial indications of the forecasts which the model gave in the Chancellor's Budget speech. From 1969 onwards, the forecasts have been published in abbreviated form in the Financial Statement which accompanies the Budget. However, this published forecast sets out only some of the numbers; the more sensitive parts of the forecast, such as the forecast of earnings, prices, or the balance of payments, are not presented in this way. The Treasury's forecasting model is available for use by outsiders, and indeed there are groups which make regular use of it for constructing their own forecasts. Some of the problems of doing this are discussed below.

Meanwhile, the practice of making short-term economic forecasts began to spread outside the Government service as well. In one case, the Government deliberately encouraged the setting up of a separate forecasting unit in the National Institute of Economic and Social

Research, so that there could be some kind of independent check on the numbers put forward by the forecasters within the Government; the National Institute began publishing quarterly economic forecasts in 1959. Since then other forecasting units have been established at the London Business School and at the Department of Applied Economics at Cambridge; and a number of stockbroking firms also publish forecasts. Large firms have begun increasingly to recognise that their sales prospects are closely linked to general economic development; they therefore also provide a market for forecasts of the movement both of the UK economy and of world developments as well.

TECHNIQUES OF SHORT-TERM ECONOMIC FORECASTING

There are three different ways of making short-term economic forecasts. One is to conduct a survey of business intentions; a second is to use leading economic indicators; a third is to construct an econometric model of the working of the economy.

The use of business surveys as a way of forecasting short-term economic developments has been widely practised by conjunctural institutes on the Continent; and in the United Kingdom both the *Financial Times* and the Confederation of British Industries also put regular questions to samples of businessmen. In order not to load the surveys with an indigestible proliferation of numbers, and in order to make it possible for the businessmen (who are usually managing directors) to answer without the need to set up a large statistical apparatus, the questions are usually in the 'up/same/down' mode. For example, businessmen are asked whether their general optimism about the state of the economy is greater, the same, or less than it was in the previous survey. The presentation of the results then charts the movement of the excess of ups over downs. Various attempts have been made to match the movement of these 'net answers' with economic series; one of the difficulties is that business opinion tends to be rather volatile, with fairly substantial swings between optimism and pessimism at four-month intervals. Perhaps the most useful of these survey questions are the questions about the investment intentions. More generally, it has not proved easy to convert the answers to these questionnaires into good numerical forecasts of the main economic magnitudes.

The practice of using leading economic indicators sprang from work done on the analysis of business cycles in the United States. It was suggested that there were some series which regularly moved in advance of the economic cycle; and by the observation of these leading indicators, governments and industry could be warned in advance of the coming of a recession or a boom. The basic analysis consists of plotting the movement of past cycles of economic activity, and then attempting to establish which series appeared to move in advance of the general movement of national product. The apparatus of leading economic indicators is most fully developed in the United States; there has been a recent examination of cyclical indicators for the postwar British economy[3] and the Central Statistical Office now publish regular series in *Economic Trends*. The main criticism of leading economic indicators is that they tend to give too many false signals; the comment has been made in the United States that they signalled seven of the last three recessions.

In short-term economic forecasting, the growth industry has been in the construction of econometric models. The argument for these is that they embody some theory about how particular economies work: they have relationships of imports to national product, with some influence of relative prices, and the relationship of consumers' expenditure to consumers' incomes, and so on.

The original constructors of econometric models for the United States and the United Kingdom economies envisaged that as time went on their econometric structures would become more and more secure, and they would be able to forecast with increased confidence and increased accuracy, and in great detail, so that eventually they would be able to provide firm forecasts for the evolution of the demand for products of individual industries. That is not in fact how matters have developed. The underlying patterns of behaviour in these economies have not been as stable as the original model builders hoped. It is not simply that the coefficients on the variables in the various equations have changed substantially; it is rather that there have been increasing doubts about the proper specification of those equations. Further, economies have moved into uncharted territory: in particular, the Western industrial economies have in recent years experienced rates of inflation for which they had no precedent in the previous twenty-five years. This inevitably means that patterns of behaviour become unpredictable; for example, there has been virtually universal surprise at the way in which, in a period of accelerating inflation, the proportion of personal income which is saved appears to have risen rather than to have fallen. In general, there is much less agreement now than there was ten years ago about the proper specification to represent the working either of the United States or the United Kingdom economy.

Thus, for example, different models of the working of the British economy embody significantly different pictures of the way in which the rise in money earnings is determined. In one view, the demand for labour (as measured by unemployment) is still important, in spite of the coincidental rise in the level of unemployment and the rate of inflation over the last seven years. A price expectations term is included in the relationship, so that the rise in earnings is represented as a function of the level of unemployment and price expectations. A second view about the determinants of the rise in money earnings gives no place to the demand for labour, but presents a relationship which models the wage bargaining process; the rise in earnings depends on the movement of past prices, and on the past movement of real post-tax earnings. There is a third view, that the rise in money earnings is largely indeterminate, depending amongst other things on the extent to which the trade union movement is or is not willing to cooperate in general with Government policy, and that therefore in forecasting no equation should be used. These three different views obviously imply different conclusions for policy. Partly because of different explanations for the rise in money earnings, different models of the UK economy do not produce the same answers about the effects of an exchange rate change; in some, the effect is substantially eroded in a relatively short time, and in others the erosion is significantly less substantial, and takes longer.

However, even if there were an agreed model of the working of the UK economy, there would still be substantial problems in producing agreed forecasts. A great deal of the actual process of making a forecast, using an econometric model, consists of fixing the future pattern of 'residuals'. For each equation, it is possible to compare for the past the series of numbers which the use of the equation produces with the actual series of recorded numbers; they rarely coincide precisely, and there is usually a 'residual'. It often happens that for the most recent set of observations there may be a fairly sizeable, and sometimes a fairly constant residual. The problem then arises of what to do about inserting residuals into the forecasts. One can assume that they represent some chance factor which will not recur: and in that case one puts in a zero residual for the future. Alternatively, one can assume that they represent some factor not in the specification of the equation which has shifted the relationship in some permanent way; in that case, one would probably continue the residual at some average of its past figure in recent observations. Finally, there is the possibility that the residual has been growing and that the actual observations have been diverging increasingly from the forecast observations; in that case, if one has a residual which appears to have been increasing over time, one might decide to allow it to continue to increase. The pattern of a forecast is substantially influenced by the decisions which in fact are taken about these residuals, so that different groups using the same econometric model may nonetheless come up with completely different forecasts.[4]

THE ACCURACY OF SHORT-TERM ECONOMIC FORECASTS

There is obviously no single simple answer to the question: 'Have short-term economic forecasts been accurate?' Indeed there are appreciable technical difficulties in assessing the accuracy of any individual forecast. First of all, it is possible – indeed probable – that during the period which the forecaster covered, some economic policy actions were taken which the forecaster did not assume in his forecast numbers. (Some forecasts are explicitly made 'on unchanged policies' – though it is often quite difficult to say what unchanged policies are: other forecasters indicate what kind of policy measures they think will be taken during the period of the forecast.) The question therefore arises whether the forecast should be corrected for the unanticipated policy measures; any correction which is made assumes precise knowledge of the effect of the policy measures, and there may be considerable uncertainty here. Secondly, problems arise from the revision of the basic data on which the forecasts are made and this can produce complications. For example, let us suppose that a forecaster, using past figures for consumers' expenditure up to and including the year 1977, makes a forecast of consumers' expenditure in 1978; he will present both the actual figures expected in 1978, and the percentage change from 1977. Subsequently the first estimate of consumers' expenditure in 1977 is revised upwards. When the forecast for 1978 is eventually compared with the first estimate of the actual figure, it appears that the *level* of consumers' expenditure was correctly forecast, but the forecast of the year-on-year percentage change from 1977 to 1978 was too low. Is this forecast to be considered correct or incorrect?

Perhaps the summary conclusion to be drawn from the various studies of the accuracy of short-term economic forecasting[5] is that in the sixties and early seventies the general direction of the movement of the economy was usually predicted correctly; the forecasters tended to be right about the years of relatively rapid output growth and the years of relatively slow growth. They can legitimately claim they did better than chance, or better than naive forecasting procedures. However, there was a fairly massive forecasting failure for the years 1974 and 1975; none of the main forecasting bodies appeared to have foreseen the size of the depression of those two years – and that conclusion also applies to forecasts made immediately after the rise in oil prices. In general, it does not appear that the accuracy of short-term forecasting has improved over time – and this is again a conclusion which applies both to the United Kingdom and to the United States. It is an open question, therefore, whether the increased sophistication and elaboration of the econometric models used for forecasting has or has not produced a more accurate picture of the workings of the economy.

THE INFLUENCE ON POLICY

It is without question that short-term economic forecasts have influenced economic policy. Once some concept of demand management had been accepted, governments were virtually forced to take some view of future economic developments when coming to economic policy decisions which were likely to affect the short-term movements in their economies. Certainly the amount of attention paid to forecasts has varied from administration to administration, and from politician to politician. For example, in the United Kingdom between 1970 and 1972 the Conservative administration appeared not to be particularly concerned with demand management, and appeared not to have paid a great deal of attention to forecasts in designing its fiscal policy; it was more concerned with long-term reforms. However, it was forced sharply back into the business of demand management by the increase in unemployment between 1970 and 1972, and at the beginning of 1972 it was once more engaged in calculating the size of fiscal stimulus which would be needed to bring the figure of unemployment down substantially by the end of 1973.

Forecasts do not, of course, influence economic policy in any automatic or mechanical way. In the United Kingdom a forecast, once prepared, is passed up through the hierarchy of senior civil servants in the Treasury, who may express their scepticism about one or other aspect of the forecast structure. When they look at the forecast produced by the Treasury model, they will compare it with forecasts made by reputable forecasting institutions outside the Treasury – for instance, the forecasts published in the National Institute Economic Review or those published by the London Business School; and the politicians in turn may also take advice from outside sources. Further, in the United Kingdom, economic policy in general, and Budget policy in particular, has ceased to be the exclusive province of the Chancellor of the Exchequer and the Prime Minister; the main line of economic strategy has become a matter for Cabinet discussion, and here again it is open to other Cabinet ministers to take outside economic advice, or to take the advice of their specialist advisers, if they so desire.

One of the great difficulties of forecasters is to impress on the users of the forecasts the wide margin of errors in the figures. There is no great point in presenting decision-makers with a large array of alternative possibilities; in the end, some kind of central view has to be taken. But, although margins of error can be stated, there is no effective substitute for the actual experience of basing policy on a particular forecast which then goes significantly wrong. Mr Macmillan, in his experience at the UK Treasury, learnt what little weight should be put on balance of payments forecasts; for example, in his autobiography he comments, in relation to a balance of payments forecast: 'My confidence in the accuracy of figures of this sort is just about as much as I have in Old Moore. The fact is that nobody can make these calculations accurately . . . when we complain, we are just told that it is too bad.'[6] Indeed politicians in general tend to be rather hard on the forecasters: they get little praise when they are right, but extensive blame if they are wrong. Thus a number of Conservative ministers complained bitterly that the Treasury forecasters had been wrong about the rise in unemployment through 1972, and indeed seemed on that occasion to be trying to shift the blame onto the forecasting team. The relationship between politicians and the forecasters is therefore something of a love/hate relationship; the politicians cannot do without forecasts for any length of time, but when they do take notice of a new forecast they do consider it to be the duty of the forecasters to be right.

In general politicians, much as they grumble about forecasts, nonetheless use them. There have been two significant academic schools of thought which have criticised the process of basing short-term economic policy on forecasts; as yet, however, their influence on actual policy has been limited. One such strand of criticism of forecasting and demand management is monetarist. Here the proposition is that the Government should limit its policy to setting a particular target for the rise in money supply; and once that target has been set, it should simply intervene, by influencing interest rates or controlling the supply of credit, to keep the rise in the money supply in line with the target figure.

The argument is that with such a rule the economy would be self-righting; if the rise in the money supply showed signs of being excessive, the measures the Government would take to bring the figure down would deflate the economy as necessary; likewise the Government would take action mainly by reducing interest rates if the rise in the money supply appeared insufficient. However, in general governments which have adopted monetary targets have tended to use them rather as one additional item of economic policy, and not to rest the whole of the economy exclusively on the management of the money supply; the proposition that the use of monetary targets makes short-term economic forecasting unnecessary has not in general been accepted.

The second proposal for a short-term strategy of economic policy which did not require an economic forecast was put forward by certain Cambridge economists.[7] This proposition was: 'Tax rates should be set, not by reference to a short-term forecast, but in such a way that the full employment yield of taxes falls short of public expenditure by an amount equal to 1 or 2 per cent of GNP.'[8] This proposition rested on a certain observed constancy of the net acquisition of financial assets by the private sector. However, not long after this suggested simple rule had been propounded, the observed constancy broke down; the net acquisition of financial assets of the private sector increased to 6 or 7 per cent of GNP; and consequently the simple rule was clearly no longer applicable. It had a brief influence on policy in the early months of the Labour Government in 1974, but it is no longer particularly significant for policy-making. This attack on the process of basing demand management policy on short-term economic forecasts must also be considered to be unsuccessful.

MEDIUM-TERM AND LONG-TERM MACRO-ECONOMIC FORECASTS

There is no doubt that short-term economic forecasts influence economic policy. It is much more open to question whether at the present time medium-term macro-economic forecasts have much influence. Certainly it is true that for some sectors of the economy – notably the energy sector – there are medium-term and long-term projections of energy demand which influence the pattern of investment decisions. But these projections tend not to be closely linked to any detailed medium-term macro-economic forecast; indeed in most Western industrial countries at the moment there is simply a large question-mark over any medium-term or long-term projection of the future growth of real national product.

The medium-term macro-economic figures which Western governments have elaborated and presented in the past have always tended to be more in the nature of targets than forecasts. They have tended to indicate the way in which the government hopes the economy might develop in the medium term, rather than the way in which it was expected to develop. The medium-term figures, in short, have been more in the nature of plans than forecasts. Recent years have seen a decline in the practice of macro-economic medium-term planning in Western industrial countries. One of the few countries in the West with a continuous history of medium-term economic plans is France; the latest French plan is relatively short of numbers, and is more in the nature of a description of the desirable direction of evolution of the French economy and indeed of French society. In the United Kingdom, official medium-term planning has virtually ceased to exist. The shock of the total failure of the National Plan dealt the procedure a blow from which it has not recovered. Thus there is no official indication of the expected, or planned, growth-rate during the period in which North Sea oil comes on stream; and unofficial medium-term forecasts show widely divergent views about the underlying productive capacity of the British economy. Thus the Cambridge Economic Policy Group takes the view that a 5 per cent growth in real national product is needed between 1976 and 1985 in order to bring unemployment down to 800 000 by the end of the period. The underlying growth-rate in the London Business School projection into the medium-term is about half that of the Cambridge Group; and the National Institute medium-term projection comes about half-way between.

This high degree of medium-term uncertainty is largely a consequence of the extended recession which the Western industrial world has experienced since 1973. As a consequence, international organisations such as OECD now no longer make the confident projections which they have made in the past 15 years. Thus in 1960, the OECD boldly projected a 4·1 per cent growth-rate for the aggregate real national product of member countries for the next decade. By the mid-sixties, it was clear that this trend growth-rate was being exceeded, and in 1965 the figure was revised upwards to 4·6 per cent. When the time came to make a new ten-year projection in 1970, it was for an aggregate growth-rate of 5·1 per cent; and up to 1973 the actual course of aggregate national product for OECD countries as a whole did not diverge much from this trend line. So for a period of thirteen years it appeared safe to say that the Western industrial nations in total were growing at a trend rate of 4–5 per cent a year, and were likely to continue to do so.

This trend has been radically broken since 1973. It is not simply that the aggregate real national product of OECD countries taken together failed to rise in 1974, and fell in 1975; since 1975, in spite of the loss of two years' normal growth, there has been no recovery to the rates of growth experienced in the 1960s. The OECD in a recent report[9] considered it possible, as from 1975, that OECD countries taken together could reasonably aim for a 5·5 per cent annual growth-rate of real national product. However, this was no longer labelled a projection, but a scenario; and the rate of growth between 1975 and 1978 has fallen far short of this figure.

It is therefore an open question whether for some reason there may have been some kind of mutation in the potential growth-rate of the Western industrial world; and it cannot be claimed that economists can provide a definitive answer to the question whether this is so or not. The present contribution of medium-term macro-economic forecasting to policy is relatively small.

NOTES

1. Hall, R. L. in the preface to J. C. R. Dow (1963), *The Management of the British Economy 1945–60*.
2. The Treasury publishes a technical manual describing its macro-economic model, available from HM Treasury, Parliament Street, London SW1.
3. O'Dea, D. J. (1975), *Cyclical indicators for the post-war British economy*, Cambridge University Press.
4. For a discussion of some of the problems of differences in models, see Laury, Lewis and Ormerod, 'Properties of macroeconomic models of the UK economy: A comparative study', *National Institute Economic Review*, No. 83, February 1978; Christ, C. F., 'Judging the performance of econometric models of the US economy', *International Economic Review*, Vol. 16, No. 1, 1975; and *Demand Management*, edited by M. Posner, Heinemann Educational Books, forthcoming.
5. Ash, J. C. K. and Smyth, D. J. (1973), *Forecasting the UK Economy*, Glasgow: Saxon House, Kennedy, M. C. (1969), 'How well does the National Institute forecast?' *National Institute Economic Review*, No. 50, November 1969; McNees. S. K. (1975), 'An evaluation of economic forecasts', *New England Economic Review*, November/December 1975; McNees, S. K. (1976), 'The forecasting performance in the early 1970s', *New England Economic Review*, July/August 1976, pp. 29–40; Osborn, D. R., 'National Institute gross output forecasts: A comparison with US performance', *National Institute Discussion Papers No. 1*.
6. Macmillan, Harold, (1972), *Pointing the Way*, London: Macmillan, p. 222.

7. For a discussion of this particular approach, see F. Cripps, M. Fetherston and W. Godley, 'What is left of New Cambridge?', *Economic Policy Review*, March 1976, No. 2.
8. Lock, Kit, *op.cit.*, p. 47.
9. *Towards Full Employment and Price Stability*, OECD, June 1977.

3 Market Forecasting

MARK ABRAMS

In both the public and private sectors of the economy the manager frequently has to cope with social and economic changes brought about by forces beyond his control: changes in population size and composition, the redistribution of income between age-groups and social classes, technological and business innovations introduced by other managements, changes in society's values, geographical shifts in population, a fall in the birth-rate, an expansion in the propensity of married women to go out to work, the increasing fragmentation of the population into one-person and two-person households, and so on. Management may, of course, wait until such changes directly affect demand for its goods and services and then react as best it can. Increasingly, however, management tries to anticipate these broad changes and their consequences and to adjust its own policies and behaviour appropriately beforehand.

In addition to these external pressures encouraging the manager to forecast future developments that are likely to affect his operations, there are internal ones generated by his own wishes to bring about change by, for example, adopting a new advertising policy, using a different chain of distribution, breaking into new markets, modifying his product, etc.

In both these situations – the 'external threat' and the 'internal initiative' – forecasts are of most help in management's decision-making when they are both quantitative and time-spaced – e.g. that the contemplated new Sunday newspaper will reach a circulation of 500 000 in the first year of publication, 1 000 000 after two years, and then stabilise at 1 500 000 from the third year on; or that the number of cars per person in Great Britain will be 0·292 in the year 1980, 0·353 in 1990, and 0·382 by the end of the century. In real life such time/quantity precision is rarely attainable, and the wise forecaster (learning from the history of the population projections made by Registrars-General) will aim to produce variant forecasts (i.e. a range based on different assumptions); and the sensibly cautious manager will seek a policy that will enable him to cope with all the variants offered him.

Whatever techniques of analysis he employs, the market forecaster, for the most part, draws his data from two main sources: published governmental and other administrative statistics, and the findings of surveys carried out among samples of the relevant population. (To these he not infrequently adds a third ingredient – his own personality structure; this may well affect the range of initial assumptions he makes – and therefore the range of forecasts he makes; his personality may also colour the implications he discovers in his forecasts.) But whatever data and statistical techniques he employs the market forecaster, faced with a particular problem, will find himself working within particular constraints. They are:

1. In different markets, management is able to bring to bear on the future different levels of manipulation to support its decisions about the future. In some, management is able substantially to reinforce its decisions for change by the use of advertising, publicity, sales promotions, etc; in others these devices for engineering the future are of very limited value.

An example of the former situation is provided by the history of the early postwar J. Arthur Rank Organisation's film *Hamlet*. When in 1947 a start was made with filming, the Organisation sought a forecast of how many adults in this country, if left to themselves, would pay to see the film during both its West End and general release. The forecaster set about his task by carrying out interview surveys of the cinema-going behaviour and film tastes of the total population aged sixteen and over. Obviously, the probable audience would be less than the total 36 million people in this age-band, and the first step in designing the questionnaire for the surveys was to include a series of questions that filtered out the probable patrons from the total. These filter questions were in terms of the respondent's age, sex, educational background, social class, frequency of cinema-going, proximity to one of the cinemas in the J. Arthur Rank circuit, taste in films (as manifested in past attendances), views about Shakespearean drama, etc.

The final outcome of these filters was a forecast that, 'if left to themselves' no more than one-half of all those aged sixteen to forty-four and one-sixth of those aged forty-five or more would go to see the film. But the surveys also showed that approximately 20 per cent of the non-probables could be turned into patrons if they: (a) learned more about the stars appearing in the film, Laurence Olivier and Jean Simmons; (b) were not exposed to the 'threatening' information that Shakespeare was the author of the original play; (c) could be given a one-sentence account of 'the plot' in the vocabulary and emotions that were normally deployed by the sub-editors of the Sunday and daily newspapers most widely read by these 'possibles'.

The higher audience forecast was vindicated ('proved correct') because publicity for the film concentrated heavily on the 'stars' and crystallised Shakespeare's play into a single sentence that promised narrative, action, violence and sex: 'This is the story of a man who, because he could not make up his mind, destroyed those he had most loved'.

Clearly, these means of attaining sales forecasts by acting almost directly on demand are less likely to be used, and when used less likely to be effective, in the markets for capital goods; few buyers of electricity generating stations are likely to change their behaviour because they are shown photographs of the engineers who will be involved in their construction. In capital goods markets forecasts of demand that yield an unattractive future usually have to be accepted.

2. In different industries there are differences in the flexibility of the end-uses to which an industry can apply its plant, manpower, and raw materials. Normally, the greater this flexibility the less pressing is the need for investment in forecasting: the same factories, workers, machines, retail outlets can be used for the production of maxi-skirts when fashion decrees that mini-skirts are passé; the same plant can turn cocoa beans into either milk chocolate or plain chocolate; and superfluous cinemas can be turned into profitable bingo halls within a few weeks with only the slightest of structural changes. By contrast, in industries where the uses to which resources can be put are almost unique (and where these resources are costly), forecasting is a major management need. Electricity generating plants cannot do anything else except generate electricity, and once built are likely to last thirty or even forty years. Similarly, giant oil-tankers are of very little use other than for transporting oil long distances, and they too usually have long lives. In both instances the cost of inaccurate forecasting can be formidable.

There is not much flexibility in the end-uses to which a theatre can be put, and accordingly some would-be theatre builders are prepared to go to considerable lengths to find out something about future theatre audiences before proceeding to reach a decision. An example of this is the forecasting study carried out in the middle 1960s for one of the outer

London boroughs with a total population at the time of approximately 250 000. There was already a small theatre (seating capacity just under 400) within the borough's boundaries, but its lease would run out in the early 1970s; as a first step in deciding what to do those responsible needed to have forecasts of the probable long-term future audiences for a theatre either on the site of the present one or one located elsewhere in the borough.

The researchers started by examining the past records of the existing theatre. These showed that over a period of several years the average weekly attendance, in spite of a steadily increasing population in the borough, had remained fairly constant at around 45 per cent of capacity; even this low average level, however, was only achieved because of audiences approaching 100 per cent of capacity on Saturday nights and during the Christmas pantomime season. The size of audiences had also varied considerably between different plays: a Chekhov play resulted in a weekly average audience of 33 per cent of capacity, while a Ben Travers farce raised attendance to 70 per cent of capacity.

From the past the researchers turned to the present. Over a period of two months in the middle of the year audiences visiting the existing theatre were asked to complete a questionnaire designed to reveal some of the main characteristics of the theatre's patrons. The replies showed that (over that period) in the average audience: women outnumbered men by more than five to four; people aged sixteen to thirtyfour accounted for half the total; well over one-third of the patrons were members of households where the head was in a professional or managerial job; nearly two-thirds had come to the theatre by car; most had come with one or two other persons; the average audience consisted of two very different types of patron – a majority who had attended the theatre only once or twice over a period of three months, and a tail of addicts who came two or three times a month; sometimes they visited a West End theatre but then it was part of a special occasion that included a meal in a restaurant; half the average audience lived within the borough's boundaries, and almost all the remaining half came from adjacent boroughs; one important finding related to patrons' tastes – the 'regulars' put as their favourites modern serious plays (*The Caretaker*, *A Severed Head*), and classical plays (*The Cherry Orchard*, *She Stoops to Conquer*), but what brought in the all-important marginals (those who, when they came, doubled the size of the audience) tended to be the comedies and thrillers (*Rookery Nook*, *Dial M for Murder*, *Tons of Money*, etc).

On the basis of findings such as these the researchers might well have gone ahead with their forecasts and recommendations; however, given the inflexibility of the end-uses of a new theatre, they studied in much the same way the theatre audiences in two other outer London areas. The results for all three were so similar that they felt confident that their original findings held true for any semi-suburban theatre and its audience.

Satisfied on this point they then related their findings about composition of the audience to the present and expected class and age composition of each ward in the theatre's catchment area; from this they concluded that with a different site (more central for the sort of people likely to visit a local theatre) and with a balance of plays slightly tilted in favour of comedies, musicals and thrillers, a new theatre with a maximum seating capacity of 500 and plenty of nearby parking spaces for the Saturday night 'bulge' audience could be operated successfully. So far the forecast has proved to be broadly accurate.

3. Markets also differ in the ease with which management can assemble from its own administrative records the information needed for a dependable forecast. In the two exercises described above some of the relevant information was already available in this form. But where management is contemplating a substantial change (for example by breaking into relatively new markets) this advantage is lacking, and the forecaster has to start by generating new data – at least new to his client. An example of forecasting under these conditions is to be found in the postwar history of the *Manchester Guardian*.

By the beginning of 1950 the newspaper's management was certain of three facts: that the paper's then circulation of 140 000 had increased substantially over the 1939 figure; that the rate of expansion was slowing down; and that the rate of expansion had been greatest in the Greater London area. Apart from this last geographical fact they did not know who were these new readers; nor did they know how many more people with the same characteristics were non-readers of the *Manchester Guardian*, where they were located, and what prevented them from becoming readers.

To obtain this information interview-surveys were first carried out among separate samples of regular *Manchester Guardian* readers in Greater Manchester, in a group of Northern provincial cities, and in Greater London. An analysis of the results indicated the traits of *Manchester Guardian* readers in the expanding Greater London area – that 78 per cent of these readers had in common at least six out of ten characteristics:

1. They were in professional (e.g. teachers, social workers, civil servants) or managerial jobs.
2. They were centre or left of centre in politics.
3. They had received full-time education beyond the minimum school-leaving age.
4. They were readers of either the *Observer* or the *Sunday Times*.
5. Went either regularly or occasionally to church, chapel or synagogue.
6. Said that they were 'very interested' in international politics.
7. Said that they were 'very interested' in economic and social problems.
8. Said that they were 'very interested' in party politics in Britain.
9. Said that they were 'very interested' in American affairs.
10. Said that they were 'very interested' in literature and books.

But only 35 per cent of *Manchester Guardian* readers in Greater Manchester exhibited six or more of these characteristics: they were more likely to have had no formal education beyond elementary school, were much less inclined to be left of centre in their politics, much less interested in international politics, American affairs, social problems, etc; and they either read no Sunday newspaper at all or else limited themselves to the *Sunday Chronicle* or the *Sunday Express*.

As a next stage in the data collection, interviews were carried out in the three areas with samples of non-*Manchester Guardian* readers; in each area the sample matched the *Manchester Guardian* readers in terms of age, sex, income and occupation. The findings showed that in the Greater Manchester area only 15 per cent of these non-readers exhibited six or more of the ten constellations of traits that marked the typical new *Manchester Guardian* reader, i.e. it looked as if circulation here had almost reached saturation point. But in the Greater London sample as many as 45 per cent of non-readers of the *Manchester Guardian* registered six or more of the traits. They were currently mainly readers of the *Daily Telegraph, The Times* and the *News Chronicle*, and were, according to their own reports, readers of these papers almost as much as the result of habit rather than because of any particular attributes of the paper that they particularly liked or admired.

However, this 45 per cent of Greater London non-*Manchester Guardian* readers who recorded six or more *Manchester Guardian* traits divided into two groups: the 12 per cent who said that if they could not get their usual paper they would switch to the *Manchester Guardian*, and the remaining 88 per cent who named some other national daily. (This question was asked before any mention of the *Manchester Guardian* had been made by the interviewer.) Clearly, it was in the newspaper interests, knowledge, attitudes, etc, of this latter group that the greatest uncertainty about the future of the *Manchester Guardian* lay. Their later answers showed that while most of them had heard of the paper, a majority had never read a copy, that even on the basis of hearsay they could not suggest anything either good or bad about the paper, and the most frequent description they offered was that it was a parochial Northern, provincial paper, and as such was the sort of paper they might well read if they lived in the North; this was particularly true of readers of the *News Chronicle* and *The Times*, who thought it was a paper probably read by Northerners who were educated, cultured, intelligent, and thoughtful (i.e. very much as they saw themselves).

From these and similar data the forecasters concluded that under certain circumstances (e.g. availability before breakfast in those Greater London boroughs with double the national proportion of people with a terminal education age of 18 or more; changing the contents of the front page from local classified advertisements to national and international political and social news, putting more emphasis on feature articles), within a year any circulation it lost in Greater Manchester would be made good by new readers in Greater London and the Home Counties, and that within two years its circulation would have increased by between 40 per cent and 60 per cent (which end of this range it achieved would depend upon the quantity and quality of the publicity and advertising that accompanied the changes).

Here again then we have an example of a forecast arrived at through a series of filter questions put to samples of the relevant population, but here the filters go well beyond the usual socio-demographic ones of sex, age, social class, etc, to take in the much more imprecise factors of values, taste and product images.

One more example is given here to illustrate the need to take account in market forecasting of product-loyalty and intensity-of-product use. During the 1950s most Western countries were operating transatlantic liners and some were beginning to consider seriously a policy of retiring some of their older ships and replacing them with new liners. In Britain this turned on the question of building a third 'Queen', and accordingly it was decided to carry out a survey into the transatlantic travel habits of existing patrons of the 'Queens' and their attitudes towards sea and air transport in order 'to throw some light on the different hypotheses underlying purely statistical forecasts of future traffic.' Accordingly, at the end of 1959 a survey was carried out among people in the

United States and in Britain who had travelled on the 'Queens' at any time during the preceding twelve months.

Since it was known that Americans were consistently and substantially the major contributors to the passenger lists, little need be said about the British consumers: well over half the latter travelled first class, a large majority were men, most of these men were middle-aged or elderly, and nearly three-quarters of these British first-class travellers had made the trip for business purposes. Clearly, the future demand from British travellers (at the high-cost, luxury end of the market) depended upon the extent to which the management of British industry remained in the hands of elderly men prepared to spend two weeks on the trip to New York and back again. The forecasters, perhaps pessimistically, decided that the future for such British entrepreneurs was safe, but all the same they concentrated their attention on the then American patrons of the 'Queens'.

Barely half of these travelled first class; only 7 per cent of the Americans had made their last trip for business purposes – two-thirds had made the crossing in order to have a vacation in Europe, and almost all the remainder were visiting relatives in Europe; these latter overall proportions were even higher for those who travelled cabin class or tourist class. When they were questioned on product-loyalty barely 30 per cent of the Americans expressed a clear preference for transatlantic travel by the 'Queens' (as compared with nearly 50 per cent of British patrons), and indeed of those who had crossed the Atlantic in the previous twelve months less than one-third had in all their transatlantic travels during the previous fifteen years always travelled by 'Queens' both ways. Moreover – and this brings us to the question of intensity of product-use – these 'Queens' addicts turned out to be comparatively infrequent transatlantic travellers; the younger Americans were less addicted to exclusively 'Queens' patronage, and at the same time made many more crossings. Indeed, no more than half the younger, first-class American respondents said that their next transatlantic crossing would be by sea and, even then, not necessarily by 'Queens'. Nearly half of all the Americans said that if the 'Queens' were no longer operating they would not miss them. Indeed, of all those Americans who said they planned their next trip by 'Queens', only 13 per cent said that if the 'Queens' were not available they would travel by a ship similar to the 'Queens'; the rest were prepared to settle for any kind of liner or, indeed, for air transport.

Thus, the socio-demographic filter questions (age, class, etc) suggested a possible decline in future transatlantic travel by Americans on

'Queens'-type vessels, and the product-loyalty and intensity-of-product-use filters strengthened this pessimistic forecast. The final conclusion was that by the time a new 'Queen' had been built and launched on the transatlantic route it could count on the support of no more than 57 per cent of the then type of younger American patron of sea travel, and that 79 per cent of the then type of British patron of the leisurely, luxury, and sea-based means of pursuing business would still be in the market.

The examples presented here point to four predictive elements that can be sought for in any market. By the use of sample surveys it is usually possible to divide the total population into relevant sub-groups defined in terms of age, sex, social class, income, educational background, life-cycle stage, occupation, etc, and then calculate the contribution of each sub-group to the total market.[1] Then for each sub-group it is possible to construct four indices: an Index of Penetration, an Index of Fidelity, an Index of Intensity, and an Index of Growth; their respective measures would be attained by finding out:

Penetration: What proportion of the sub-group are present consumers of the product?
Fidelity: in each sub-group what is the proportion of present consumers to the number of those who have ever used the product?
Intensity: what is the weight of consumption of present users in each sub-group?
Growth: in each sub-group what is the ratio of new consumers (e.g. obtained in the past six months) to all present consumers?

In the ideal world the forecaster would have at his disposal the findings of several surveys spread over time, and each would yield measures of all four indices.

Even more importantly, the survey would discover the attitudinal determinants of each index figure, and also how far each section of the population will retain its attitudes and behaviour over time, and also how far those who replace it over time in a particular stage of the life-cycle will adopt the attitudes of those who have been replaced. (There is strong evidence from the annual reports of the National Food Survey over the past forty years that many of the food preferences of young prewar housewives stayed with them as they moved into middle age and then into old age. And examples of the replacement phenomenon can probably be found in the annual reports of the National Readership

Survey where the findings suggest that today's readers of the *Sun* and the *Daily Mirror* are the sons and daughters, and even grandchildren, of those who read the war-time *Daily Mirror*, where strip-cartoon Jane managed to lose her clothes almost every day and where, under the slogan of 'Publish and be damned', the editorial content — either in the news or the features — could be relied upon to produce an ephemeral sensation at least once a week.)

And this, of course, is the central difficulty of market forecasting — the problem of measuring present consumption attitudes, of discovering what past circumstances have generated them, and then of ascertaining to what extent present attitudes will persist and what new attitudes are likely to emerge in the future. In many situations the present and the past may well be the prologue to the future, but in market forecasting we have scripts which are subject to revision by the author, the director and, above all, by the audience.

NOTE

1. *In developing this analysis of a market the author is indebted to 'Rationalising Sports Policies', Council of Europe, Committee on Sport, Strasbourg, 1977, and particularly to the paper by Prof. Brian Rodgers of Manchester University, 'An International Perspective on Sport'.*

4 Transport Forecasting: Fixing the Future

JONATHAN GERSHUNY

There is no one single future to be forecast. The future is, to a greater or lesser extent, determined by our own actions; to the extent that we have discretion in our activities we must think, not of *the future* but of *alternative possible futures*. This is particularly important in the case of transport, which has been seen over the last century to be a major causal variable in the pattern of social change; in choosing a future transport system we are also choosing the much wider system of social relations that will be dependent on the particular transport provisions. The choice of transport system is thus an especially important part of public policy-making, and forecasting must play a significant role in choice. This paper will look at two particular examples – motor vehicle forecasting, and airport demand and capacity forecasting – in order to throw some light on the nature of this role.

CONDITIONAL AND UNCONDITIONAL FORECASTS

The concept of rational policy-making is helpful in formulating a view of the appropriate form of forecasting. Rationality is an attribute, not of some particular policy, but of a particular process of choosing a policy. A rational policy-making process is one in which all the available options for action are considered, and as a result of that consideration the option with the most preferable consequences is chosen.[1] This suggests a role for forecasters: a forecast that is to be useful to a rational policy-maker must take as its starting-point the alternative available courses of action and correctly identify the various consequences of their adoption. Forecasts help policy-makers to make the connection between means and ends by showing what happens *if* particular actions are taken. A policy-relevant forecast cannot therefore consist of a single unconditional prediction – such a prediction contains no implications for action.

Without taking the argument too far at this early stage, it is necessary to establish this distinction between conditional and unconditional forecasts. It is certainly true that some unconditional forecasts are necessary inputs to the policy-making process – predictions of the weather, for example. There is, within broad limits, a single future pattern weather, but while the average policy-maker cannot do anything to affect that pattern, he must nevertheless take action to cope with its effects. In deciding on which course of action to adopt, the policy-maker himself formulates a set of conditional forecasts in response to the unconditional prediction: 'It is going to rain tomorrow' (unconditional prediction). '*If* I harvest my crop today *then* . . . , *if* on the other hand . . .' (conditional forecasts responding to the prediction).[2] Clearly there are two different sorts of views of the future involved here. In one case the prediction refers to events which are outside the control of the decision-maker, which must be dealt with simply as circumstances; in the other the predictions take the circumstances as given, and examine the results of alternative responses to them. In this paper I shall be dealing with the second category, conditional forecasts concerning the effects of discretionary actions.

The confusion between these two categories of prediction is at the nub of the argument in the following sections. Forecasters who are in reality in the second category – or so I shall argue – often contend that they are in the first. In the examples considered below I will argue that forecasts which are presented as unconditional predictions are in fact single 'if . . . then' statements which have been abstracted from a full set of alternative conditional forecasts. The effect of such misrepresentations is to make the policy-making process less rational. They disguise as inevitable future events which in fact require the cooperation of policy-makers – this illusion of inevitability confirms policy-makers in courses of action which themselves bring about those events. Forecasters predict future levels of demand, policy-makers adjust the supply to meet this demand, and that adjustment generates the predicted level of demand. Where such interconnections between supply and demand exist, forecasting may have the effect of fixing the future – of preventing that process of consideration of feasible options which is the essence of rationality.

Two different sorts of factors underlie the role of forecasters in the fixing of the future. The first is the frequent complication of methods used in forecasting. Social systems are themselves extremely complex, and there is a tendency for the models which represent them also to be complex. Some of the difficulty of the forecasting methods may be necessary, given the nature of social processes. Alternatively, however, the complexity of models may be unnecessary, and stem from the forecaster's intention to hide, disguise or mystify his methods and assumptions. In any case, whether intentional or not, the complexity of forecasting methods does have a tendency to make the assumptions which underlie particular predictions invisible to those not directly involved in developing those methods. This opaqueness may have the effect of making conditional forecasts look like unconditional predictions – if the assumptions are not visible, it is easy to forget that they are there.

The second factor leading to the 'fixing of the future' is the exclusion of particular policy options and other contextuating circumstances from consideration. Once a set of policy alternatives has been excluded, the policy or policies which are left are converted from variables to constants. If, to get ahead of the argument, all alternatives to a road-building programme are excluded in traffic forecasts, the predictions are converted from being relatively conditional to being apparently unconditional – the road-building policy is reinforced, and the future has been fixed. The effect, as will become clear, is of a vicious triangle.

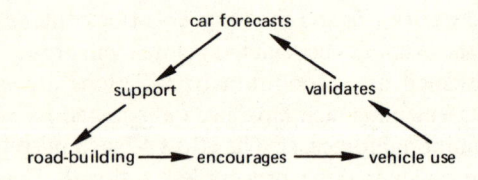

```
                    car forecasts
               ↙                 ↖
          support               validates
         ↙                           ↖
road-building ——→ encourages ——→ vehicle use
```

The nature of bureaucratic systems of administration is to exclude alternatives. This exclusion enables the application of the specialised expertise necessary for efficient and rational detailed policy-making. But nevertheless it does lead to a fixing of the future – and hence to a paradoxical non-rationality.[3] We will return to this discussion of the proper contribution of forecasting to a rational policy-making process, but before doing so, we shall consider the case studies in some detail.

THE TRRL FORECASTS OF MOTOR VEHICLE NUMBERS

The transport forecasting methods used by the Transport and Road Research Laboratory have a long history[4] but the discussion here will concentrate on the two most recent examples published in 1974 and 1977 respectively. These forecasts are of particular importance; they are, as we shall see, actively used in the formulation of public policy, and indeed they form part of what has been referred to as 'The National Traffic Forecasts'.[5]

The 1974 forecasts[6]
The basic TRRL approach is to predict future numbers of cars as a function of three variables, national income, motoring costs, and time. A summary of the 1974 forecast (LR650) is shown in Figure 4.1.[7]

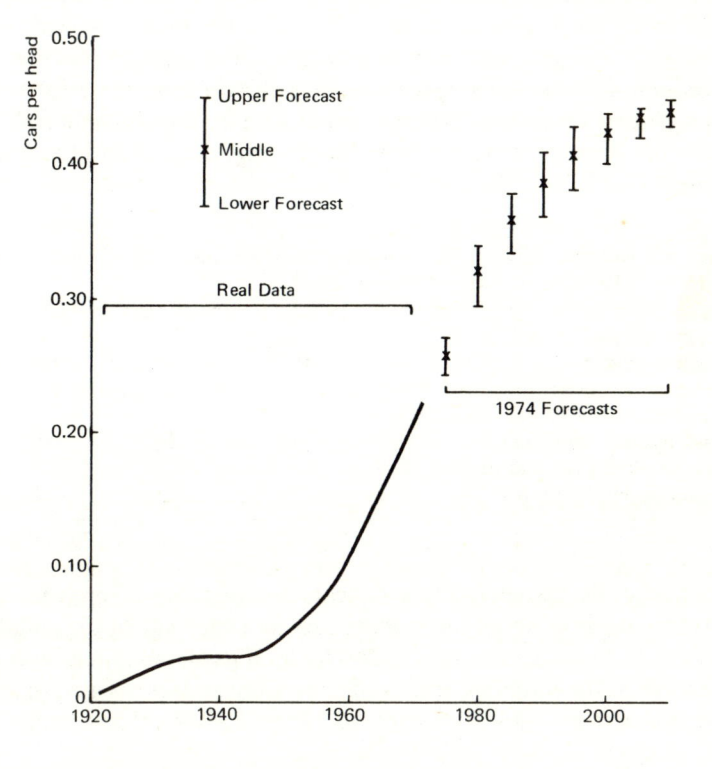

FIGURE 4.1. 1974 TRRL forecast

The basic form of the motor car growth model is the logistic curve, and the mathematical function which is used is (somewhat simplified):[8]

$$Y = \frac{s}{1 + (\text{motoring costs})^{-as} x (\text{national income})^{-bs} x c^{-cs(\text{time})}}$$

whether Y = car numbers
and a, b, c and s are constants.

For any values of motoring costs and national income at any point in time, this function will yield a prediction of numbers of motor cars.

The first question to ask about this sort of model is: how sensitive is it to alteration of its variables? The answer seems to be that it is not particularly responsive to changes. The upper and lower limits to the forecasts depicted in Figure 4.1 are derived by permutating costs and income assumptions; the upper limit is based on the highest assumed rate of income growth and the lowest cost growth, the middle estimate is based on middle income and cost assumptions, and the lowest estimate is derived from the lowest income growth and the highest cost growth assumptions. Particularly past the end of the century, the results of making either of the two extreme sets of assumptions become rather similar. By contrast, consider the effect of varying one of the constants (Table 4.1).

TABLE 4.1 Relative effects of varying cost, income and saturation rates on LR650 predictions of cars in 2000[9]

Assumed saturation level(s) *(cars per head)*	0·35	0·45	0·55
Upper extreme cost and income assumptions (millions)	19	25	31
Lower extreme cost and income assumptions (millions)	17	23	29

The effect of the extreme costs and income assumptions taken together leads to a range of about one million cars on either side of the middle forecast. The effect of varying s makes for a range of six million cars on either side of the actual forecast – a 25 per cent variation as against a 4 per cent variation. And as we shall see, all three of the values of s are in fact possible.

Clearly, the choice of a value for this parameter s is of crucial importance. Once it has been chosen, the forecast follows almost irrespective of the values chosen for the cost and income variables. Why is s so important? The parameter s is the limiting value to which the function tends – the other constants and variables determine merely how long it takes to get to this limit. In real terms, s is the state of market 'saturation', at which everyone who is likely to want a motor car has one already. It appears that the modelling process depends principally on the choice of a value for saturation.

How then is a value of s decided upon? The logistic nature of the model suggests a solution. Figure 4.2 shows the relationship between the rate of growth of car numbers and the absolute number of cars; assuming that the car growth pattern is logistic (see note 8), there should be a linear relationship between the percentage growth-rate and the absolute number. The most direct approach to forecasting the saturation level is simply to find some real combinations of car numbers and growth-rates, plot them on to a graph and fit a straight line through them – the saturation level is where the growth-rate declines to zero. The TRRL procedure makes three estimates, using this procedure on three

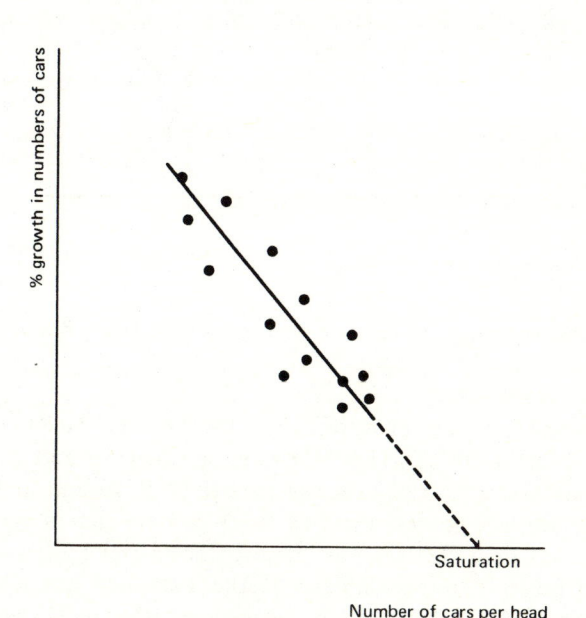

FIGURE 4.2. Determination of saturation point – an idealised version

different sorts of data.[10] The first category of evidence is time-series data for the UK. By looking at yearly growth-rates and ownership levels, the TRRL arrive at a saturation level of 0·34 (Figure 4.3a). They cast doubt on this low estimate, however, by comparing it with estimates on the same basis for the USA which arrive at a forecast of saturation at 1·23 cars per head – which they consider 'clearly unrealistic'. Their explanation for this result is that economic factors disturb the forecast, and accordingly they recalculate the saturation level, taking account of 'economic factors which change from year to year', as something between 0·36 and 0·41.

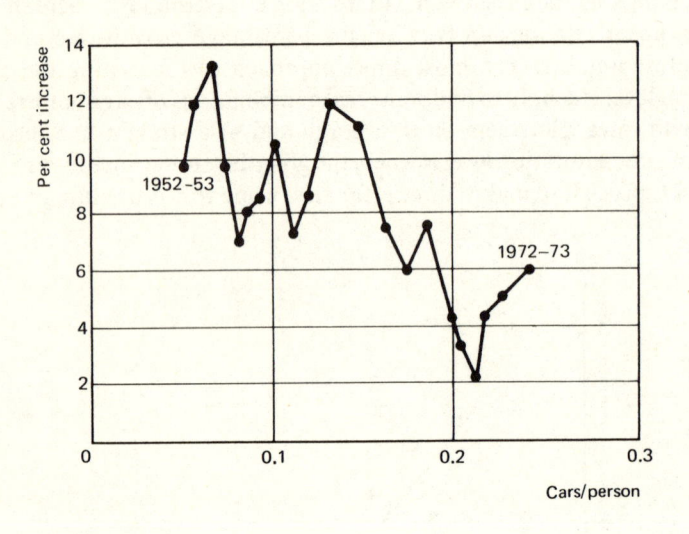

FIGURE 4.3a. Percentage increases of cars per person, Great Britain 1952–73

The second category of information used by the TRRL is cross-sectional data for the UK. They take rates of ownership and increase in the various UK countries over the period 1965–70 and arrive at a saturation estimate of 0·66 (Figure 4.3b). When the exercise is repeated for the period 1970–72, however, they get the answer 1·72, which they choose to discount; instead they exclude the Scots counties and arrive at an estimate of 0·51, which they consider to be rather more reasonable. The final category of evidence they cite is again cross-sectional, but this time comparing countries (Figure 4.3c). The results of this third exercise

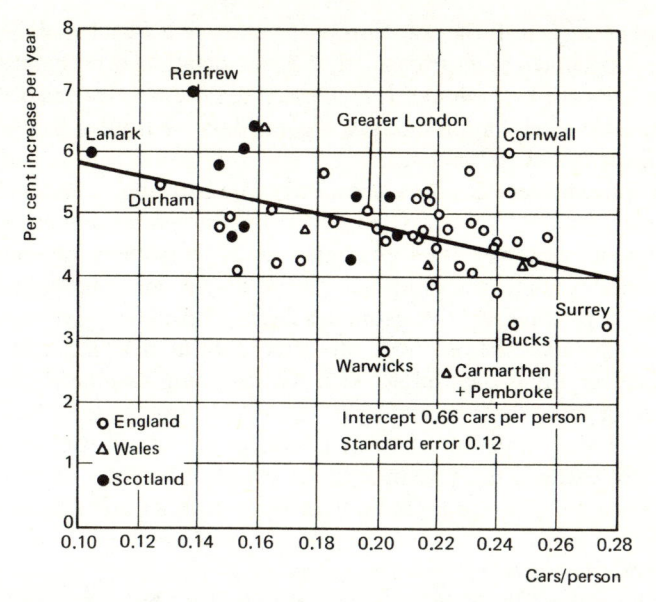

FIGURE 4.3b. Growth-rates of cars per person, Great Britain 1965–70

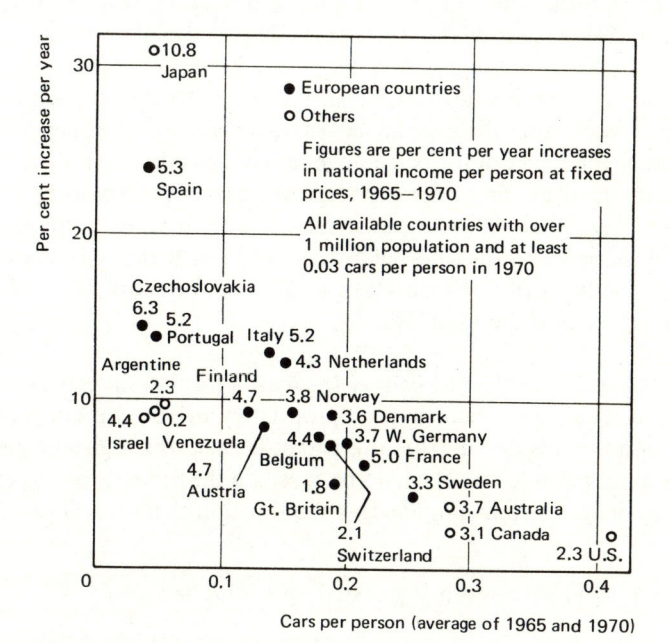

FIGURE 4.3c. Growth of car ownership in selected countries from 1965–70 in relations to ownership level and economic growth

are rather unclear. If the non-European countries are excluded then the answer appears to be approximately 0·3, but including other countries – particularly the US – would seem to increase the estimate considerably. (There is another way of interpreting this data – but we will return to this in the following section.)

We will consider this procedure rather more critically later, but for the moment we should draw two things from this discussion. The first is that the model, although it is presented as a fearsomely complicated mathematical function, is in fact a very simple one. The only really important parameter is the saturation level s, and all the other variables and parameters make very little difference to the model. Once s has been chosen everything else follows. The second thing to note is that the process of choosing s according to the TRRL procedure is itself very simple – merely a matter of fitting a straight line to a scatter of points and then extrapolating it. In fact the whole apparently complicated process comes down to no more than a job for ruler and graph paper.

The 1977 forecasts

The philosophy of this later set of forecasts (LR799) is very similar to that of the earlier publication; the precise model, however, is slightly different. The author of the forecast explains:

> ... some of the data are not consistent with a strictly logistic growth curve. The basic observation is that over a long time period the relationship between the percentage rate of growth of car ownership and the level of car ownership y is not linear, as it would be if the logistic model applied ... but is curved. The curvature implies that the S-shaped growth cruve reaches half of the saturation level over a shorter time period than it takes to achieve the second half of the growth to saturation (LR799: 3).

If we look at Figure 4.3c we can see the reason for the concern – clearly this data would be much more appropriately fitted by a curve. The implication that is drawn from this is that instead of a logistic curve, a rather more suitable model would be based on the power growth curve. This (again somewhat simplified) is the function that is used:[11]

$$Y = \frac{s}{1 + [\text{Time} \; x \, (\text{motoring costs})^a \, x \, (\text{national income})^b]^{-n}}$$

where s, a, b and n are constants

And again we find that the choice of saturation level is much more important than assumptions about the variables.

TABLE 4.2 Relative effects of varying cost, income and saturation rates in LR799 predictions of car ownership in 2000[12]

Assumed saturation level(s) (car per head)	0·40	0·50	0·60
Upper extreme cost and income assumptions (millions)	22·0	25·5	27·8
Lower extreme cost and income assumptions (millions)	20·9	23·1	24·3

The difference in the scale of the two classes of effect is not quite as marked as in LR650 but nevertheless it is still clearly the saturation level that determines the forecast.[13] The effects of the new form of the forecasts can be seen from Figure 4.4.

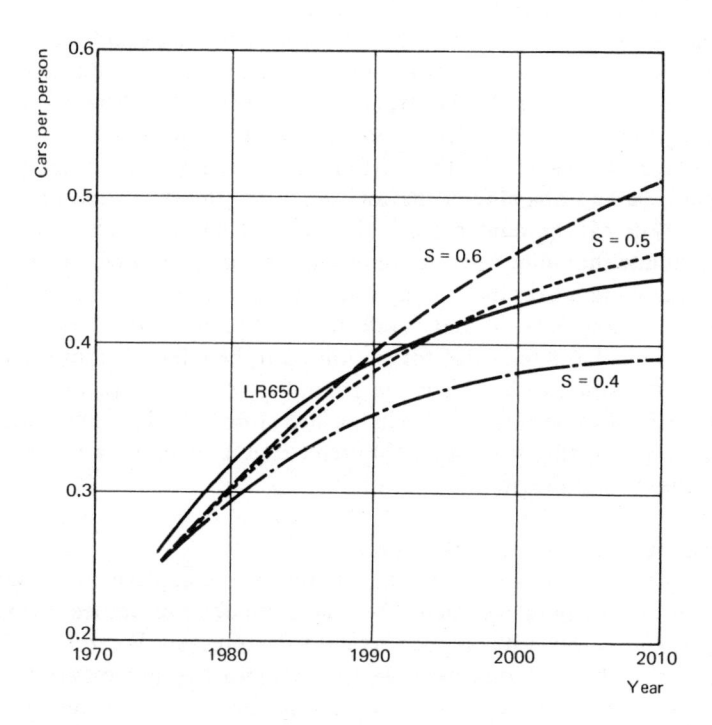

FIGURE 4.4. Comparison LR799 of middle forecasts with those in LR650

The new forecast growth curves initially lie somewhat below the 1974 predictions, but as time passes the new forecasts maintain a higher rate of growth than the old ones. Slower initial growth is compensated for by faster growth at the end of the century so that by the first decade of the next century the forecasts from the two different sorts of model would be more or less the same. The LR650 forecast in Figure 4.4 has an s value of 0·45 – if the later forecasts had contained an estimate for $s = 0·45$, the estimates from 2000 onwards would have been very similar. In the event, however, 0·5 is given as the most likely value in the 1977 forecast, which leads to eventual forecasts of vehicle numbers rather higher than those of 1974.

This is a rather odd situation. The only solid information available is that the rate of growth of car numbers is rather slower than previously forecast – the actual number of cars in 1975 (13·7 million) was some 400 000 fewer than that forecast in 1974. The 1977 publication, as in the quotation above, clearly suggests that this shortfall must mean that the *form* of the model is incorrect. This certainly does not follow logically – it is equally possible that the model was correct in 1974 but that a lower value of s should have been chosen. In sum, the shortfall from the previous forecast leads to two connected changes. First, the logistic relationship is replaced by the power growth function which has a slower initial growth-rate, but a faster subsequent rate of growth, so that the longer-term forecasts from the two functions are substantially identical. Second, having abandoned the logistic curve, the data presented in Figure 4.3c can be reinterpreted. The logistic model required that a straight line should be fitted to these data; the power growth model on the other hand makes the assumption that the relationship between the size of the car population and its rate of growth is curvilinear (see Figure 4.4). On this basis the value for saturation to be inferred from Figure 4.3c may be increased – this is the grounds given for the increase of s from its 1974 value of 0·45 to 0·5 in the latest forecasts. The result of the short-term shortfall from the 1974 predictions is therefore a *raising* of the long-term forecast!

Criticisms of the forecasting procedure
Even accepting for a moment the validity of the approach (the next section will dispute it), there are still a number of rather serious objections to the way it is applied in the TRRL forecasts. We will start by considering the least important. First, this forecasting process is clearly extremely arbitrary. There is no way that historical or other trend data can be used as *evidence* for any future trend. If, indeed, it is assumed that

growth will inevitably be according to some particular function, then data do to some extent lead to a prediction – but a prediction which is conditional on that assumption. The previous discussion suggests that the grounds for making the assumptions necessary in this case are extremely flimsy. Take the crucial choice of a value for saturation: the available evidence (as we see from Figures 4.3a, 4.3b and 4.3c) is contradictory, so the forecaster is free to choose at his whim. In LR650 the choice of saturation level is justified thus:

> None of the methods described above gives by itself a convincing estimate of saturation level and the estimates vary somewhat . . . 0·3 . . . 0·4 . . . 0·5. . . . In previous forecasts a saturation level of 0·45 has been used . . . the previous figure will be retained (LR650: 57).

And the later forecasts show a similar willingness to pick and choose among alternative conflicting possibilities.

> The long-term trends in Britain have been shown to have an element of consistency but this was not sufficiently strong to provide a basis of extrapolating them to the long-term future. On the one hand, linear extrapolations of growth-rates since 1953 suggested a value of s of about 0·35, but on the other, study of a longer period showed evidence that the underlying trend was not in fact linear, so that 0·35 provide only a lower bound . . . saturation seems unlikely below around 0·5 cars per person (LR799: 10).

In neither case is there unambiguous concrete evidence to suggest any particular value for s; the choice in the final event is determined entirely by the private and non-technical motives and intuitions of the forecaster.

Furthermore, we may get some clue as to the nature of these motives by considering the change in the form of the forecasting function in LR799. The available evidence was that car ownership was growing more slowly than had previously been forecast. Lowering the saturation level would have made the forecasts based on a logistic curve assumption consistent with the latest data – and would also have considerably reduced the size of the more distant forecasts. This option was, however, neglected in favour of the switch to the power growth curve – which had the effect of actually increasing the forecast. We might, somewhat unkindly, suspect that it is the author's own prejudice that the eventual levels of car ownership will be high that lead him to choose those technical options which lead to high forecasts. He certainly has no unexceptionable evidence on which he could base that choice.

Secondly, even with these arbitrary assumptions there are still serious methodological problems. It is not logically correct to argue from a cross-sectional observation towards a longitudinal forecast. Cross-sectional curves may shift over time; when they do, a generalisation from a cross-section will lead to a misleading forecast. Thus it is simply not correct to suggest that because the USA is richer than the UK and has more cars, when we are as rich as the USA is now, we will have as many cars as the USA has now. Nor is it logically correct to say that because at one point in time there is a trend observable in the ownership and growth-rates between the poorest and richest regions in the UK, that the trend will continue over time. Indeed there is internal evidence in LR799 which neatly demonstrates this point (see Figure 4.5).[14]

The trend for each successive five-year period would suggest a continually rising saturation level. Thus, 1953–8 would suggest a saturation level of less than 0·3, 1958–63 of around 0·5, 1963–8 of

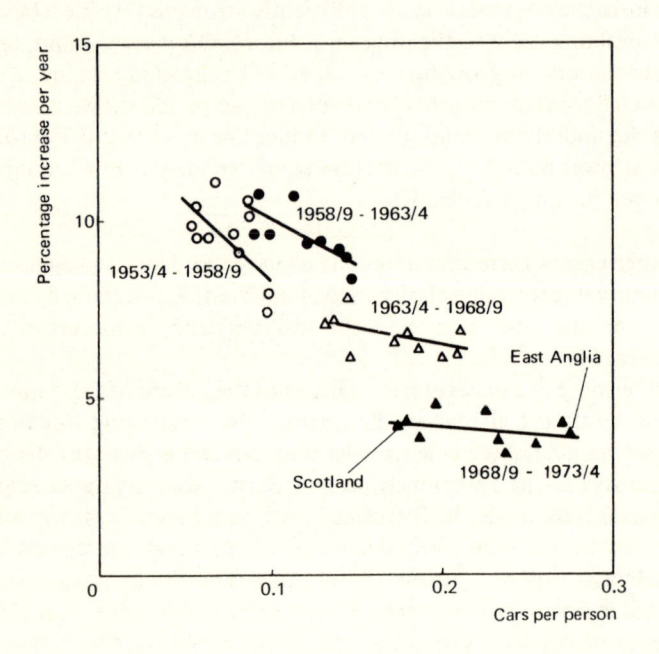

FIGURE 4.5. Growth of car ownership in regions of Great Britain, 1953–74

around 1 and 1968–73 of considerably more than 1. Nevertheless the trend over time appears to be quite independent of these cross-sectional ones; taking, for the purposes of rough estimation, the UK averages as the centre of gravity of the scatter of points for each period, the trend of these averages is apparently such as to forecast a saturation level of hardly more than 0·3. So in this case the cross-sectional picture would give a misleading forecast of the pattern of change.[15]

These first two objections are, however, minor in comparison with the third – that the forecasters suppress all those contextual circumstances which might lead to variations in the forecast. The most important of these is the choice of public policy but, before we come to policy, let us consider some of the others. We have already mentioned that motoring costs and economic growth, though included as variables in the model, seem to contribute little to the actual forecasts. Now this *may* mean that they are in fact irrelevant, that car numbers will rise irrespective of what happens to people's incomes and the cost of motoring. This is possible, but on the face of it hardly likely; much more likely explanations are either that the assumed likely values of these variables used in the forecasts are insufficiently extreme to give an adequate picture of the possible variability, or that the model tends to under-estimate the importance of these variables. There is evidence to suggest that both of these things are happening.

The values used in the forecasts are apparently chosen with a view to facilitating high predictions. The national income forecasts are rather biased upwards.

> Between 1951 and 1975, real Gross Domestic Product rose by an average of 2·5 per cent per year. . . . Although growth has been less in the more recent years there is no reason to think this downward trend will continue . . . alternative forecasts have been made assuming 2, 3 and 4 per cent annual growth of GDP from 1977 onwards (LR799: 14).

Four per cent as an upper estimate is perhaps not over-optimistic, but the assertion of 2 per cent as the lower limit is definitely insufficiently pessimistic. And similarly the cost alternative estimates appear unduly biased downwards: the three alternatives for the price of petrol are 0, 2, and 4 per cent growth-rates – so that the fastest rate of economic growth would leave petrol costs on the high extreme price rise assumption in the same relationship to incomes as in the present – we can easily imagine much more extreme assumptions.

The effect that these variables have on the forecast is determined by assumptions about the cost and income elasticities of demand for cars. The effect of varying the elasticities is shown in LR799, but only in the context of the medium values of the variables, with the result that the effect appears to be small. When the forecasts are made the extreme assumptions for the values of the variables are in fact made together with the medium elasticity assumptions. In LR799 there is no forecast which combines extreme values with extreme elasticity assumptions; however in the appendix to LR650 there is just such a forecast, which is reproduced here as Figure 4.6.

The middle forecast here is of course the same as that shown in Figure

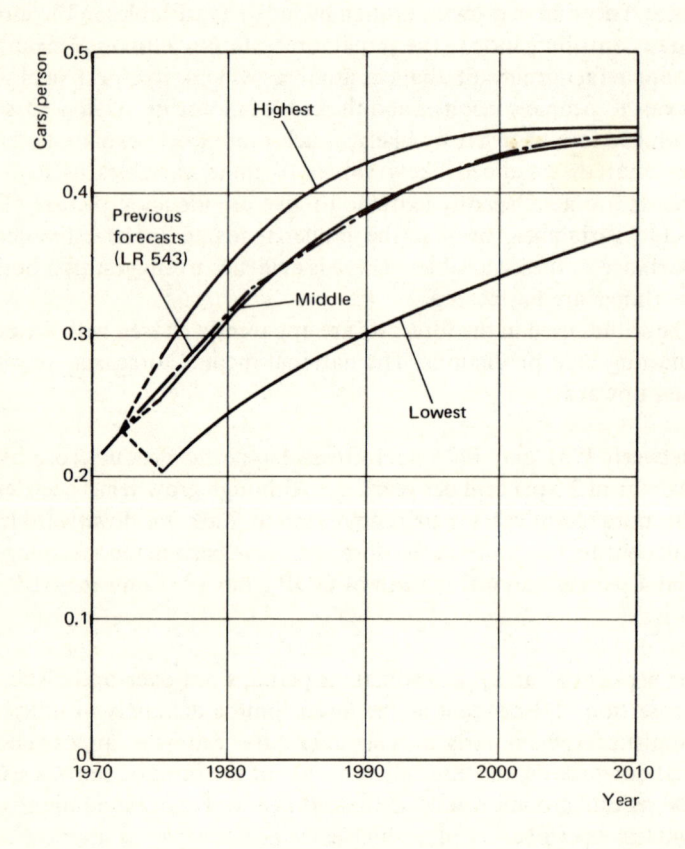

FIGURE 4.6. Comparison of forecasts of cars per person with middle and extreme assumptions

TABLE 4.3 LR650 – Upper and Lower Forecasts with Medium and Extreme Elasticity Assumptions[16]

		1980	1990	2000	2010
Lower Forecasts	Medium elasticities	·29	·36	·40	·43
	Extreme elasticities	·25	·30	·35	·38
Upper Forecasts	Medium elasticities	·34	·42	·45	·45
	Extreme elasticities	·36	·43	·45	·45

4.1 above – but the variation is very much greater. Table 4.3 compares the variations with the medium and the extreme elasticity assumptions. In other words, using the extreme elasticity assumption, together with the lower (and yet still much too high) growth and price assumptions, the lower bound is reduced by about 3 million cars. Perhaps prudently, information is not provided to enable a similar calculation for the later forecasts.

And there are of course other variables. Technical change must have some importance – after all the growth of the motor car is itself to some extent a process of substitution for a previous pattern of bus and rail transport. In the same way, in the long term, other technologies might succeed the motor car for some functions. Or, more radically, communications might substitute for transport, or urban design reduce the need for it. In point of fact none of these things seems particularly likely to come about *of its own accord* – but they certainly could be promoted as a matter of deliberate public policy.

It is this issue of public policy which is the main contributor to the indeterminacy of the transport future – and yet it is one which the TRRL forecasts most steadfastly refuse to contemplate. The justifications claimed for this exclusion are twofold. The first is that including policy variables is difficult: 'It is therefore desirable . . . to show the effects of alternative policies. In this report *it has not been possible* to go far towards policy dependent forecasts . . .' (LR650: my emphasis). The second sort of justification is used in LR799 and slightly contradicts the earlier position; here the justification for the entirely extrapolative approach to forecasting is that 'there are strong underlying social and economic forces at work that make the future course of car ownership largely inevitable, or at least hard to restrain deliberately'. In other words, policy, it is claimed, does not have a very significant influence. We should note here that the forecast is not in fact independent of policy – an extrapolative forecast relies on a continuation of current lines of policy. This is recognised in LR799: the forecast

... does not explicitly recognise the influence of other factors such as policies adopted towards road provision, traffic restraint and public transport support; continuation of current policy trends on such matters is implicitly assumed (LR650: 8).

In effect, the TRRL forecasts *predict policy as part of their forecast* – it is the effect of this implicit prediction which is the basis for the most serious criticism of the TRRL procedure.

The assertion that their activities have the effect of fixing the future is of course strenuously denied by the TRRL forecasters. They base their defence on two legs. Firstly, they claim that they have very little impact on road-building policy. Secondly, they argue that roads do not generate new traffic, and hence that any influence they may have on policy formulation does not result in any increase in vehicle numbers.[17] These arguments are both rather doubtful. There is extensive evidence in the scientific press as to the use of the forecasts in motorway planning enquiries, both as general justifications for road-building and as a part of the cost-benefit assessment procedure.[18] The Leitch Report on Trunk Road Assessment finds that the cost benefit assessment is very sensitive to the vehicle forecasts.[19] We can only conclude that the vehicle forecasts do influence policy.

The second point is more difficult to answer. We cannot prove in general that road-building does generate traffic, since we have no way of conducting adequate experiments. We can, however, look for natural experiments; one such is provided by the Severn Bridge. In ten of the eleven years for which statistics are available, the average yearly growth in use of the bridge was 3·7 per cent. In the remaining year (1972) the growth was 24·0 per cent.[20] 1972 was the first year of operation of the new London to Bristol motorway. Reference to a road map reveals that, with or without a motorway, all traffic from London to South Wales must pass over the bridge, so the diversion of existing traffic from other routes is not a credible explanation for the phenomenon. The clear inference to be drawn is that the completed motorway caused the extra traffic. We might sensibly, therefore, stand the TRRL's position on its head. We have in fact no reason to suppose that anyone at all would use motor cars if no facilities were provided for their use. We have no general evidence in either direction but, given the choice of assumptions, it would seem sensible to hold that people's consumption *is* largely determined by facilities available to them, rather than assuming that it is *not* so determined, as the TRRL argument suggests.

This then is the evidence for the vicious triangle argument. The forecasts are arbitrary, being dependent on numbers chosen at the discretion of the forecasters. They influence the formulation and implementation of road-building policy. And it seems probable that the road-building programme generates traffic so as to lead to a vindication of the forecasts.

FORECASTS OF DEMAND AND CAPACITY IN LONDON'S AIRPORTS

The most serious flaw in the case against the TRRL forecasting procedure is that there is no available evidence of the effect of *varying* public policy. We cannot tell what the effect of an overall reversal of the transport policy from emphasis on private to public transport would be, simply because it has not happened. We can however suggest an analogy which may illustrate the effect of a reversal of public policy on the forecasters' fix. This analogy is the controversy over the proposed Third London Airport.

The issue as a whole has been very extensively reviewed, so I do not propose to rehearse the events again here.[21] Instead I wish to focus attention narrowly on the forecasting process. Forecasting airport capacity involves making predictions of a number of variables (Figure 4.7).

The most important of these variables is the number of passengers who wish to use the airport; it has effect in two ways. The first is a direct

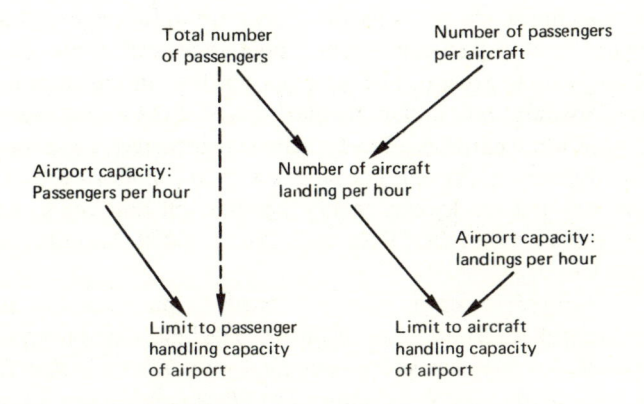

FIGURE 4.7. Forecasting airport demand and capacity

effect – airport terminal buildings are of finite size and have a maximum capacity of passengers. Passenger handling constraints have not been the issue, however, in the debate over the third London airport; none of the four major forecasts of capacity have seen passenger handling as leading to the necessity for a new airport. The second, indirect, effect has been the major concern, and we will concentrate on this; it is the effect of the number of passengers on the number of aircraft landing at the airports. The aircraft handling capacities of the airports has given rise to considerable worry and a predicted shortfall of take-off and landing facilities has been the basis for the arguments for a new airport.

We should notice that all of these variables have a discretionary element to them, which relates both to public policy and to technical change. The number of passengers per aircraft can be affected by technical change – the building of larger aircraft – or by economic measures to encourage airlines either to use larger aircraft types, or to fill the aircraft with more passengers. The total number of passengers wishing to use an airport may be affected by varying the alternative transport available – in this case, by building a channel tunnel, for example – or by varying the desire for travel, by increasing or decreasing the promotion of tourism, or by diverting traffic to other areas, which might involve promoting regional airports. Airport capacity may be varied by increasing the technical efficiency of the ground control of aircraft movement, or by varying the pattern of use of airport runways. Passenger handling capacities may be varied by modifying arrival and departure facilities or by building new terminals.

Any single forecast of some airport's future demand and capacity must therefore make a lot of assumptions. It must assume a particular pattern of technical change, a particular pattern of future investment in the airport, and a particular public policy towards travel and the transport system in general. The forecasts which we discuss here made a set of such assumptions, and, particularly because the assumptions they made about future patterns of investment were incorrect, these forecasts have actually been disproved. The point I wish to emphasise is that these forecasts were potentially elements in the same self-fulfilling process as previously described in the TRRL case. We should at this point turn to the forecasts.

The first three forecasts were appended to public policy papers arguing the need for a new London airport. The first is to be found in the *Report of the Interdepartmental Committee on the Third London Airport* (1962), the second in the White Paper *The Third London Airport* (1967), and the third in the *Report of the Commission on the Third London*

Airport (the 'Roskill Report' of 1971). Each of these reports contained an, in essence, unconditional prediction that the London airports would very soon run out of capacity and that therefore a new one should be built. The fourth forecast is contained in *Maplin: Review of Airport Project* (1974); it argues that airport capacity will be ample for at least the next twenty years and hence that no new airport is needed.[22]

These forecasts are all made in slightly different ways and over differing timespans. Yet by careful examination of the reports it is possible to compare them. What follows is pieced together from fragmentary evidence in the published material.

The first stage in each of the forecasts is the estimation of future numbers of passengers (Figure 4.8).

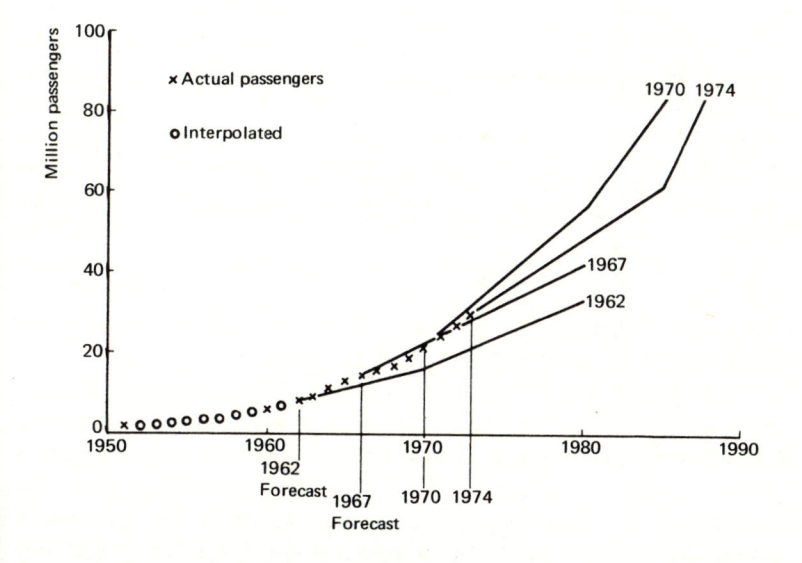

FIGURE 4.8. London Airports passenger forecasts

The most important fact about the growth of the number of air passengers during the 1960s is that the *rate* of growth of passenger numbers was itself growing (that is, the growth-rate was doubly exponential). The result of this was that the three estimates of traffic based on 1960s data were each upward revisions of previous forecasts. After 1970, however, the rate of increase slackened, so the 1974 forecast was a downward revision of the Roskill version. (We might note in passing that this is not a *necessary* conclusion – the 1974 review committee could certainly have assumed that the slackening of growth was simply a temporary phenomenon; they chose not to do so, however.)

To move from here to estimates of the number of aircraft landings it is necessary to make assumptions about the number of passengers per aircraft (the load factor). All of the forecasts assumed that the load factor would increase over time; the earlier forecasts seem however to have under-estimated the rate of increase (Figure 4.9).

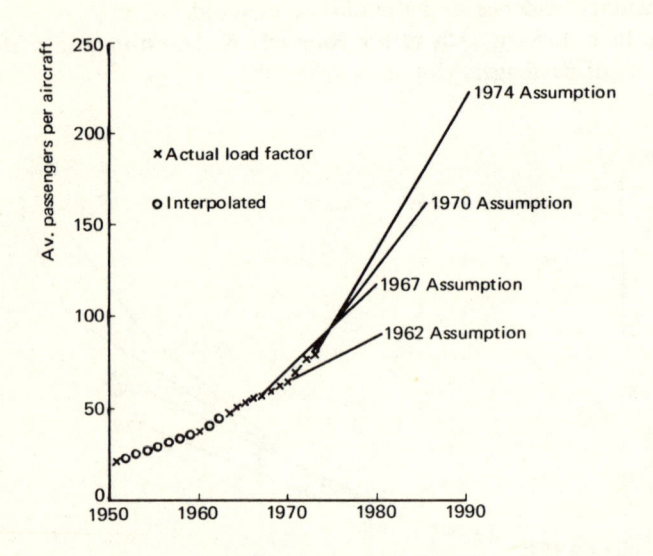

FIGURE 4.9. Load factor assumptions

As a result, the rate of growth in the number of aircraft landings is considerably lower than that of passengers (Figure 4.10), and the forecast rate of increase generally decreases over time.

Finally, we turn to estimates of airport saturation levels (Figure 4.11). In no case does the passenger handling impose a constraint, though in the 1974 forecast passenger saturation, while still beyond the time horizon, does occur before landing capacity saturation. We see again that the estimates have been revised upwards twice over the period – in 1970 and in 1974.

When we plot the various forecasts of traffic on to these various ceilings we see the different forecasts of saturation. The 1962 and 1967 forecasts were of saturation in around 1970, the 1970 forecast was of

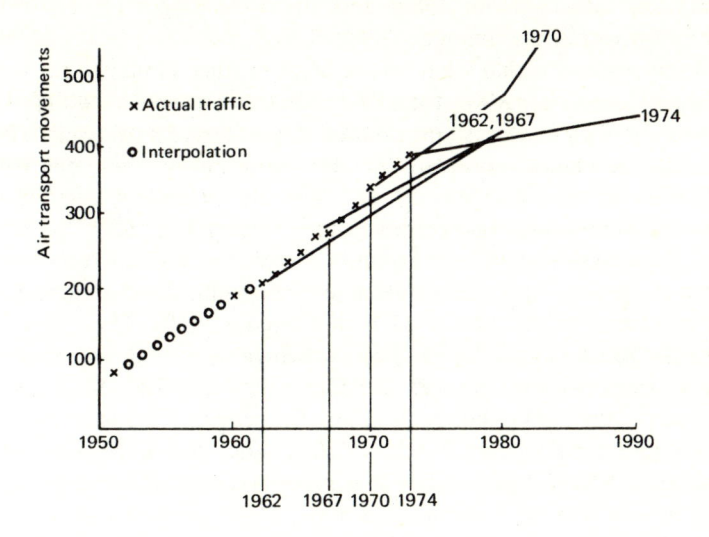

FIGURE 4.10. London Airports air traffic forecasts

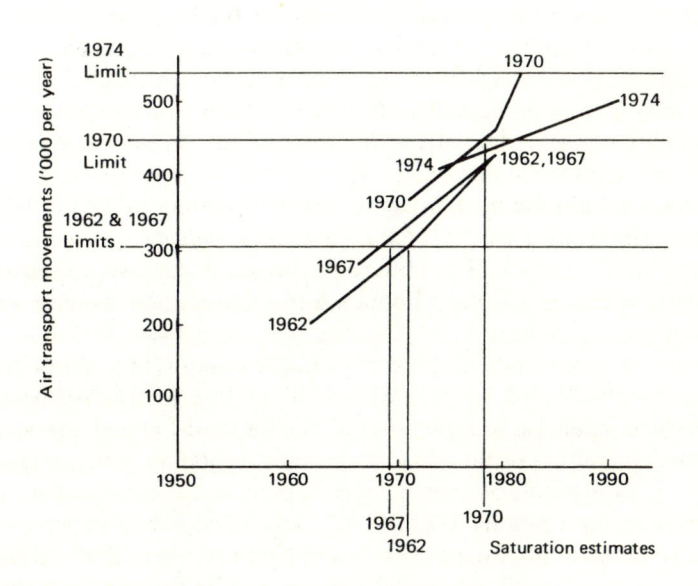

FIGURE 4.11. Estimated traffic and saturation levels

saturation rather before 1980, and the 1974 forecast was of no saturation within the timespan of the forecast.

My hypothesis is that what we see here is rather similar to the road transport forecasts made by the TRRL – but with one crucial difference. As with the TRRL forecast, the London airport forecasts were made in a way that excluded consideration of variation in the contextual variables – in this case airport and aircraft technology – and in a manner which excluded the consideration of alternative policy options – here, the investment in new ground-control systems and runways at existing airports. And this is not merely hindsight, these options were available and indeed canvassed in the middle 1960s. The improved ground-control option, for example, was suggested by the aeronautics expert Alan Stratford who gave evidence on behalf of the Stansted residents at the 1965 public enquiry into the proposed Stansted airport. He pointed out that the Chicago (O'Hare) and New York (Kennedy) airports both handled around twice as many takeoffs and landings as did Heathrow at that time. Similarly, in 1967, *The Economist*, commenting on the White Paper, pointed out both the discrepancies between the UK and US estimates of airport capacity and that the forecast did not take adequate account of the likely influence of big jets on aircraft load factors. (It also went on to suggest a number of other alternative policies to airport capacity extension, including the further development of vertical take-off aircraft for short-haul purposes, and the building of the channel tunnel.) So clearly there was contemporary argument about the possibility of radical alternative transport futures. But in spite of the availability of these alternatives, the forecasting exercises were essentially unconditional – they gave high and low alternatives reflecting uncertainty, but gave no alternative forecasts relating to the available policy options. Just as the TRRL case, they *embodied* assumptions about future policies. The difference between the two examples, however, is that in the third London airport case, these assumptions were not to be vindicated.

They were not vindicated because of public opposition to the policy, which eventually led to its reversal. The 1962 Interdepartmental Committee report led to a proposal to build a third London airport at Stansted; public opposition delayed the implementation of this, and led first to a (non-statutory) public enquiry, then to a government policy review and the resulting 1967 White Paper. The White Paper itself caused extensive public opposition, which led to another delay and then to the appointment of the Roskill Commission. The Roskill Report was the subject of extensive public debate, which delayed the building of the

Foulness airport project to such an extent that when the project was finally abandoned as a result of the 1974 reassessment, the site had hardly been cleared preparatory to construction.

It may well be that had the Stansted airport been built as a result of the 1962 Report, Heathrow would have reached a saturation level by the late 1960s – simply because the public authorities would not have made the investments necessary to extend its capacities. And similarly, had the new airports proposed by the 1967 and 1971 policy statements been constructed, the saturation levels they predicted would by now have been vindicated. Certainly there were errors in the forecasting procedures; the increases in load factors were systematically underestimated. But correcting these technical errors does not substantially change the picture – after all, even taking the comparatively low 1974 estimate of air traffic growth, in combination with the 1970 assumption of the airports' capacities, we still get an estimate of saturation soon after 1980. The central factor which produces the prediction is the assumption about investment policy in the existing airports. The first three reports embody the assumption of low levels of investment and hence predict the need for a new airport. The new airport was blocked by public opposition, and hence investment in the existing airports was forced on the Government, and so the forecasts of impending saturation were repeatedly falsified. The crucial change in the 1974 report was an assumption of 'load spreading' from peak periods to other parts of the year. Would this load spreading have occurred if construction of new runways had been undertaken in the late 1960s? It is certainly questionable. We might add that since 1974, although the number of passengers has continued to increase, the number of air transport movements at Heathrow and Gatwick has stayed roughly constant. In short, and by contrast to the TRRL case, the policies taken for granted within the forecasts were not implemented, other policies were as a result forced on the authorities . . . and the existing airports now operate at a level 25 per cent higher than that originally suggested as being their saturation level without any impending need for new construction.

CONCLUSION

We must start this conclusion with a question: why does unconditional forecasting, this process of fixing the future, take place, given that forecasters might be supposed to be contributing to a rational decision-making procedure? At the beginning of this chapter, two different sorts of partial answers were suggested. The first had to do with the complexity of the forecasting process – in some cases doubtless necessary – but in others used to remove arguments from a political to a technical plane. The second related to the nature of bureaucracies, and their operation by a process of subdivision of tasks. The TRRL was originally established as an institution for carrying out technical investigations into traffic safety and transport engineering. It has a specialised division ('Access and Mobility') responsible for transport forecasting and a *separate* division (the Special Research Branch) responsible for dealing with policy issues. It is not surprising, therefore, that the forecasting procedure has a technical, apolitical character; its character is determined by the organisational structure of the TRRL.

The third London airport controversy has a similar explanation. An inspection of the membership list of the Interdepartmental Committee called to consider the need for a new airport in 1962 reveals thirteen out of fifteen, including the chairman, to be members of the 'aviation community'.[23] The issue was captured from the start: all subsequent discussion took for granted that a new airport would sometime be built. Consider the terms of reference of the Public Enquiry at Stansted (which led to the 1967 White Paper): 'To hear and report on local objections relating to the suitability of the choice of Stansted for an airport . . . but not to question the need to provide a new third London Airport'.

Any forecasting process needs to exclude *some* alternatives. But, as in the examples we have discussed, exclusion results in a reduction of the rationality of the policy-making process. Is there anything we can do to avoid this sort of irrationality? There are two possible approaches.

The first is rather idealistic. It would involve the development of an independent 'staff' forecasting capacity within government, possibly directly responsible to Cabinet Ministers after the fashion of the CPRS. It would cut through limited departmental responsibilities and instead be responsible for taking a 'broad view'. But there are still problems. How is this forecasting unit to avoid co-option by particular interests in Government, given that it would not possess any political resources of its own? Or conversely, if it were not so co-opted, how, without resources, could its critiques be effectively brought to bear on decision-makers? And finally, and most important, since this unit would unavoidably develop its own partisan 'view' on policy issues, how could we be certain that this view would ultimately be less myoptically exclusive than that of the 'line' departments?

The second possibility is rather more pragmatic. It would involve finding — and presumably paying — informed groups outside government to oppose official forecasts in an authoritative manner. They may have no position, and no resources of their own, but they would at least be free to join with or even mobilise opposition in a manner not available to a governmental body. And the existence of a plurality of such groups would at least provide a set of *alternative views* for open public discussion and comparison.

It was in effect just such outside opposition which overthrew the London airport's forecast. If one may venture a forecast at the conclusion of a critique of forecasts — the same may well happen to the TRRL forecasts. It may well be that such opposition, utilising informed expert opinion in public debate, may be the best available answer to the transport — and other — forecasters' fix on the future. The Department of Transport's apparent acceptance of the Leitch Report's proposal of open access to an improved forecasting procedure may herald a substantial change in public policy.

NOTES

1. See H. E. Simon (1957), *Administrative Behaviour*, New York: Macmillan, (2nd edition) and 1947 (1st edition):

    The task of rational decision is to select that one of the strategies which is followed by the preferred set of consequences. . . . The task of decision involves three steps: (1) the listing of all the alternative strategies; (2) the determination of all the consequences that follow upon each of these strategies; (3) the comparative evaluation of these sets of consequences.

2. It should be stressed that for the sake of simplicity of exposition, conditional and unconditional here are used to refer only to the possibilities for action that are or are not envisaged within the forecast. Thus, an unconditional forecast may still be a probabilistic one — 'there is a 20 per cent probability that it will rain tomorrow' — whereas a conditional forecast will always make a prediction that is dependent on some prior *action* — 'if . . . then. . . .'

3. This 'Paradox of specialisation' was formulated by R. A. Dahl and C. E. Lindblom (1953), *Politics, Economics and Welfare*, New York: Harper

    When one specializes he focuses on certain categories of repetitive events . . . men can become specialists only by *ignoring some of the variables*. Hence a calculation that is rational in the short run or with respect to certain limited goals may prove to be irrational in the long run or with respect to different goals.

4. The first in this line of forecasts was J. C. Tanner, 'Forecasts of future

numbers of vehicles in Great Britain', *Roads and Road Construction*, 40, 1962. This was followed by J. C. Tanner, 'Forecasts of vehicle ownership in Great Britain', *Roads and Road Construction*, 1965; A. H. Tulpule, 'Forecasts of vehicles and traffic in Great Britain: 1969' (Road Research Laboratory, LR 288, 1969); and A. H. Tulpule, 'Forecasts of vehicles and traffic in Great Britain: 1972' (Transport and Road Research Laboratory, LR 543, 1973); the two forecasts we shall be discussing here, whose methodology descends directly from these earlier efforts, are to be found in J. C. Tanner, 'Forecasts of vehicles and traffic in Great Britain: 1974 revision' (Transport and Road Research Laboratory, LR 650, 1974) and J. C. Tanner, 'Car ownership trends and forecasts' (Transport and Road Research Laboratory LR 799, 1977).
5. UK Department of the Environment, *Consultative Document on Transport Policy*, London: HMSO, 1976.
6. The discussion here concerns Tanner (1974), *op. cit.*
7. Source: Tanner (1974), *op. cit.*, Table 10.
8. We should introduce here two subtly different mathematical functions employed in the TRRL forecasting exercise, the 'logistic curve' and the 'power growth curve'. These are both S-shaped curves, describing bodies that grow at rates inversely proportional to their sizes – the bigger they get, the slower they grow. In the case of the logistic curve, the relationship between the size and the rate of growth expressed as a proportion of size is linear. In the case of the power growth curve this relationship is curvilinear, so that, while at first the decline of the growth-rate is rapid, as the bodies get bigger this decline gets slower. The logistic curve is symmetrical about its point of inflection; the power growth curve, because of its faster initial decline of growth-rate, is lopsided, showing a faster rate of growth relative to the logistic in the later stages of its development. Both curves (in the general case) tend towards a maximum value.

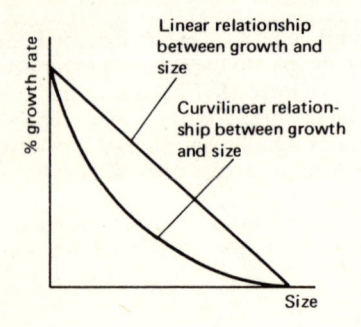

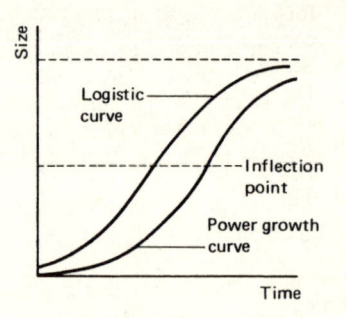

The actual relationship used in the 1974 forecast is:

$$y = \frac{s}{1 + ki^{-bs}p^{cs}e^{-ast}}$$

where y = cars per person
i = GDP per person, fixed prices
p = cost of motoring
t = year
k, s, a, b, c are constants

9. Source: Tanner (1974), *op. cit.*: 14.
10. Source: Tanner (1974), *op. cit.*, Tables A1.2, A1.5, A1.9.
11. The actual relationship is:

$$y = \frac{s}{1 + [a(t-T) + b \log i + c \log p]^{-n}}$$

where s, a, b, c, T and n are constants to be determined.

12. Source: Tanner (1977), *op. cit.*, Table 8.
13. For further evidence of this, see Tanner (1977), *op. cit.*, Tables 3 and 4.
14. Source: Tanner (1977), *op. cit.*, Figure 16.
15. J. Adams, 'Saturation Planning', *Town and Country Planning*, December 1974, claims that Tanner makes the technical error of switching the dependent and independent variables in making the linear regression estimate of the relationship between the number of cars and the rate of growth of car numbers. Adams suggests that the number of cars should in fact be the dependent variable and rate of growth the independent variable; recalculating on this basis gives a much lower estimate of saturation from cross-sectional data. I suspect, however, that both variables should, in Tanner's model, be considered as dependent, and the errors should be distributed between both variables.
16. Sources: data from Tanner (1974), *op. cit.*, figures 1 and A2.6.
17. The flavour of this defence is to be found in Vol. 2, Paper 5 of the 1976 *Consultative Document on Transport Policy*. These arguments were also put forward by one of the TRRL experts responsible for the forecasts, in conversation with the present author.
18. See, for example, *New Scientist*, 11 December 1975; 6 March 1975, 565; 11 December 1975, 648–49; 18 November 1976, 393 ('Traffic forecasts used to Justify M3'); 3 November 1977, 269. (The 'Leitch Report').
19. *Report of the Advisory Committee on Trunk Road Assessment*, London: HMSO, October 1977, 65–6.
20. The yearly statistics are as follows:

Annual Traffic Flows over the Severn Bridge

Year	Two-way vehicle flows	% growth on previous year
1966*	1 565 958	—
1967	5 832 527	—

* The bridge was opened in September 1966.
Source: *Financial Times*, 8 December 1977.

Annual Traffic Flows over the Severn Bridge

Year	Two-way vehicle flows	% growth on previous year
1968	6 458 404	+ 10·7
1969	6 815 819	+ 5·5
1970	7 301 523	+ 7·1
1971	7 823 998	+ 7·2
1972	9 702 396	+24·0
1973	10 293 121	+ 6·1
1974	10 122 167	− 1·7
1975	10 199 712	+ 0·8
1976	10 579 224	+ 3·7
TOTAL:	86 694 849	+ 576

21. See, for example, O. Cook (1967), *The Stansted Affair: A Case for the People*, London: Pan Books; P. Bromhead (1973), *The Great White Elephant of Maplin Sands*, London: Elek; and D. McKie (1973), *A Sadly Mismanaged Affair*, London: Croom Helm.
22. Other forecasts of demands on London airports not reviewed here are contained in 'UK Report of the London Airport Development Committee,' CAP 145, London; House of Commons 1957; 'Fifth Report from the Estimates Committee of London's Airports', Report, Session 1960–66, HCP 331, London: HMSO, 1964; UK Department of Trade, 'Report of the Working Party on Traffic and Capacity at Heathrow', CAP 349, London: HMSO, 1971; UK British Airports Authority, 'Forecasting Paper 72/7', 1973, unpublished; UK Department of Trade, 'Forecasts of Air Traffic and Capacity at Airports in the London Area', London: HMSO, 1973.
23. Membership of the Interdepartmental Committee

BEA, BOAC, BIA	3
Ministry of Aviation	7 (including the chairman)
Air Ministry	1
National Air Traffic Control	2
Ministry of Housing and Local Government	1
Ministry of Transport	1
	15

5 The Brighton Marina: A Case Study in Arbitrariness, Uncertainty and Social Welfare in Planning Models

ROY TURNER AND SAM COLE*

INTRODUCTION

Mathematical models are used extensively in urban planning; for example to estimate traffic flows, housing demand and the likely impact of new shopping amenities. However, there is considerable controversy surrounding the use of models in town planning. The displacement of old shops by new shopping centres and supermarkets has both social and economic disadvantages as well as advantages, as with other aspects of urban planning.

New developments inevitably generate conflicts of interest between different groups – not just between shoppers, but also between new shopkeepers and old shopkeepers and between local authorities. There may be fundamental doubts concerning the need and consequence of new planning development – and in an inquiry the role of an 'expert' may be critical. But the 'expert' may use models which serve to mystify as much as to inform. The models used may, in their morass of technicalities, conceal much controvertible thinking, and at a time when there is an increasing awareness for the need for public participation in planning decisions, the usage of such techniques that may serve to mystify and alienate the layman is of particular concern and requires careful and critical analysis.

This chapter examines some of these problems in relation to a recent public inquiry, but the comments made have wider implications for other kinds of urban and regional planning inquiries and the use of models.

THE BRIGHTON MARINA INQUIRY

History and scale of the Marina proposals

The Brighton Marina Inquiry was held in Brighton Town Hall for nine weeks at the end of 1974 (22 October – 20 December). The decision to hold an inquiry was made by the then Secretary of State for the Environment, Geoffrey Rippon, after a number of groups and individuals had aired their disapproval of the Brighton Marina Company's latest planning proposals to East Sussex County Council.[1] The scheme under investigation at the Inquiry dates from the outline application of January 1974 and contained a shopping and exhibition centre with multi-storey car-parking facilities, an entertainments complex, a hotel and 1450 residential units. The 'Marina' itself consisted of an inner non-tidal 'locked' basin and an outer tidal basin separated by a spine one kilometre long – all set within two harbour walls. This scheme was the latest in a long string of planning proposals. The first outline planning application for a marina at the present Black Rock site goes back to 1966. An Act of Parliament (the Brighton Marina Act) was passed in April 1968 authorising, within certain restrictions, the construction of the harbour and supporting development. At the end of 1970 revised plans were submitted for planning approval. Permission was granted early in 1971 and construction work started in March the same year. By the time the Inquiry had started the western breakwater was completed, as well as half of the eastern breakwater and some of the spine, so Brighton was committed to having some sort of marina by then.

The Brighton Marina Company (BMC) employed the services of several leading planning consultants as consultant and expert witnesses. The local planning authorities submitted their own evidence. To counter the evidence given by the BMC, to air various points of view and to offer alternative plans, the Marina Action Campaign (MAC) was set up as an 'umbrella' for a number of groups. This combined activity by so many diverse interest groups made the Inquiry unusual in terms of the level of financial, legal and technical opposition that the Campaign could muster. The Campaign could afford to employ a barrister for the period of the Inquiry (no mean issue) and make use of experts from the local university and other departments.

The Brighton Marina Project is a very large financial undertaking. A local community newspaper sums it up rather well:

> The Marina Company is big – its Marina may well cost £100 million (1974 prices) by the time it is finished, and this figure is twice the value of the assets owned by Tesco Supermarkets, bigger than the whole of Unigate and nearly as big as the whole of the Boots chain.[2]

In the outline proposals the BMC had earmarked 17 500 gross square metres for shopping and exhibition space. According to the consultants for the BMC: '... the amount of space allocated to general retail and exhibition usage respectively were not identified in the application....'[3] However, in the Inquiry the consultants for the BMC broke down this figure as follows: 9000 square metres for marine exhibition; 4000 for chandlery ('marine shopping'); 3000 for general shopping; and 1500 ancillary to the entertainments complex. The 3000 square metres shopping centre was to consist of a large supermarket of 2000 square metres and twelve smaller units. The 1750 car spaces would not compete for the needs of the Marina residents/berth holders, or the hotel guests who were provided in the proposals with 2600 and 300 car spaces respectively. By way of comparison Brighton town centre's Churchill Square has a multi-storey car-park with provision for about 1500 cars.

What is this Marina centre likely to bring in? The BMC consultants state: '... my analysis suggests that (in 1981) the proposed centre will attract turnover in the order of £2 410 274 (at 1971 prices)....'[4] What is immediately striking about this figure is the confidence with which this forecast is made (for a shopping centre not yet built), right down to the last pound. Fascinating though this apparent ability to predict *so* accurately is, we shall not dwell on it here. Instead let us consider the relative scale of the turnover figure for the Marina in comparison to that of Brighton town centre. For convenience shopping (which is the day-to-day purchases of goods, such as food, which make up the bulk of the expected Marina centre turnover), the 1971 census of distribution gives a figure of about £8 million turnover for the town centre. Brighton can boast of another large well-established centre that appears in the census – London Road, which is a 'high street' type centre with many of the usual large multiples – the turnover for which in 1971 was about £5 million for convenience goods.

A brief note on shopping models
At this stage it is necessary to give some idea of the nature of shopping models. All but one of the experts in the Inquiry employed a mathematical model (rather than simply adding up customers, turnover etc). We indicate the contrasting details of different models (see the first endnote) but broadly speaking they have similar characteristics. They assume, for example, that different kinds of shopping centres – town centres, local centres, corner shops, etc – have a different 'attractiveness' to customers and that this attractiveness is traded off against the effort different kinds of users have to make to use the amenities. In the 'gravity' model used by the consultants to the Marina Development Company attractiveness was assumed to depend only on the type of centre. The likelihood that people would visit a given centre was assumed to depend on the inverse of the road-distance (to some power) from the centre of the 'residential zone' to the centre in question. The total purchasing power of consumers was estimated from consumer expenditure surveys on the assumption that real incomes would not rise substantially over the next ten years.

Clearly there are many points in the modelling process where different assumptions can be made. For example, different proxy variables can be used as a surrogate for 'attractiveness' – floor-space and sales volume are commonly used.[5] Likewise, different measures of 'distance' may be used – e.g. crowflight distance, road distance, travel time, travel cost – that are not necessarily correlated with one another. Different functional relationship between these two sets of variables produce different models. Other sorts of assumptions and decisions will be discussed later. Obviously alternative assumptions will modify the resulting predictions.

The case of the Brighton Marina Company
The position of the Company with respect to the shopping (and also housing) proposals was presented by Nathaniel Lichfield and Associates (NLA), consultants hired to do the job. Of the terms of reference of the Inquiry only those for shopping need concern us here, i.e. 'the need and justification for the shopping space to be provided by the proposed development and its likely effect on existing and proposed shops in the area'.[6] The consultants' documents reiterate these objectives.[7] Notice they were paid to do two things: (1) to show that the amount asked for in the development was necessary; (2) to do an impact study to show that the proposals would not adversely affect local shops.

In addition to attempting to fulfil the above terms of reference their proof of evidence states that 'throughout the analysis when faced with a number of possible alternative assumptions we have consistently adopted the one which maximises the impact of the Marina on other centres'. To some extent this laudable aim conflicts with the terms of reference. Apart from problems with some of the assumptions there are some reasons to doubt whether this objective was actually pursued.

(a) *The justification for the centre* The demand for foodstuffs is assumed to come from three sources: owners of the associated residential development and of yachts moored in the Marina; a certain amount of 'leakage' from existing centres; *plus* purchases by day visitors to the Marina. The first is relatively fixed and based on consumer expenditure surveys, the second is small and estimated from the model and the last is based on a survey of expenditure by day trippers to a neighbouring resort. This last expenditure – largely ice-creams and similar purchases which, multiplied by the large number of expected visitors, *constituted half the expected turnover of foodstuffs* – was used to justify the need for a large supermarket. That is, the justifications for the shopping proposals *crucially* hinge on the questionable assumption of the importance attached to the 'ice-cream purchases' of day trippers.

(b) *The impact study* The relatively small impact on local centres predicted by the consultants rested on a similarly questionable assumption – that the size of the proposed centre made no difference to the expected 'leakage' from other centres. That is: *it makes no difference to their assessment whether the proposed centre has a floor-space of one square metre or ten thousand square metres.* The Marina is treated as a 'local' centre for the purposes of its impact on neighbouring local centres. Given the size of the centre and its amenities this is somewhat modest. It does, however, enable the desired prediction to be made. Their study claimed to demonstrate the need for the proposed shops and their negligible impact on other nearby centres. The estimated impact of the Marina centre is shown in Table 5.1. Despite this it was suggested in the Company's proof of evidence that the Marina might help to relieve Brighton's already over-crowded town centre. The estimated impact of the Marina centre is shown in Table 5.1(a).

The Marina Action Campaign's case
The objections to NLA's evidence – the justification of the large scale of the development by virtue of 'ice-cream sales', and its small impact on local centres by treating the Marina centre as a 'local' centre – were

raised in the MAC's proof of evidence.[8] This evidence also raised a number of other issues particularly relevant to the use of models. In the NLA model it was assumed that the Marina centre and other local centres all had the same 'attractiveness' to shoppers. In fact the Marina centre was to be much larger than the existing local centres. Table 5.1(b) shows the results of MAC's calculations using the NLA model but adjusting it to take account of an alternative assumption that the

TABLE 5.1 Estimated impact of the Brighton Marina Centre for the 1981 forecast (sales figures are in terms of 1971 prices and in units of £'000)

(a) *Forecasts using the Nathaniel Lichfield and Associates' model as used by NLA*

Centre	Computed sales (I) — No Marina	Computed sales (II) — with Marina	Impact (% change II/I)
1	549	510	93
2	415	384	93
3	655	592	90
4	615	582	95
5	729	767	93
6	985	900	91
Average Impact:			92

(The percentage impact figures in this and other tables are given to the nearest 1 per cent).

(b) *Forecasts using the NLA model as used by MAC*
The NLA model did not take account of the different size of the centres in its impact study of local centres and assumed that all the centres were equally attractive. Hence MAC slightly adapted the model in two ways. Firstly MAC assumed that by virtue of its much larger floor-space the attractiveness ('A') of the Marina would be larger than the local centres; the model was run for A = 2 (i.e. Marina doubly as attractive as local centres with 'Attractiveness' = 1) and A = 3. Secondly, MAC assumed that with its large supermarket and car-parking facilities, the Marina centre would attract car-borne shoppers whilst the local centres would attract people who would walk. 'Distances' to the Marina were reduced to account for this assumption, and the model was run again.

Centre	Computed sales (III) Marina with A = 2	Impact (% change III/I)	Computed sales (IV) Marina with A = 3	Impact (% change IV/I)	Computed sales (V) Marina with A = 2, adjusted distances	Impact (% change V/I)
1	471	86	439	80	378	69
2	346	83	318	77	269	65
3	533	81	487	74	404	62
4	491	80	430	70	378	61
5	604	83	549	75	491	67
6	815	82	744	76	619	63
Average Impact:		83		75		64

(c) *Forecasts using the MAC model*
MAC used a conventional gravity model – i.e. one in which 'attractiveness' of centres is measured in terms of floor-space.

Centre	Computed sales (VI) – No Marina	Computed sales (VII) – With Marina	Impact (% change VII/VI)	Computed sales (VIII) Marina with $A = 2$, adjusted distances	Impact (% change) VIII/VI
1	364	328	90	277	76
2	335	299	89	251	75
3	747	645	86	517	69
4	572	420	73	284	50
5	771	647	84	510	66
6	1164	1015	87	821	71
Average Impact:			85		67

Marina centre was twice or three times as attractive as the local centres. However, it is more usual to assume that attractiveness is proportional to the total floor-space of shops at the centre. MAC showed (Table 5.1(c)) that if this more common assumption was used then the likely impact of the proposed centre was twice that estimated by NLA.

Another question raised in the MAC proof of evidence was the differential impact of the Marina centre on different groups of shoppers. Very often when a new centre is built (especially one with good car-parking facilities and more remote from residential areas) it has the effect of attracting car-borne shoppers away from local shops. Since these people tend to be the more affluent, the turnover at local shops, and hence the service, is reduced more than *pro rata* to the loss of customers. If this custom is taken away, less affluent and less mobile shoppers may suffer. (Table 5.1(b), computed sales V) In fact a progressive decline – the loss of trade reducing the attractiveness of a centre in turn reducing trade and so on – leads to the closing of shops and blight. In the UK only about 50 per cent of families own cars; the less mobile often include old people and young families with children. Two residential areas in the proximity of the Marina seemed especially vulnerable.

The MAC made some estimates of what this progressive decline might look like. These are shown in Table 5.2. Whether the numbers mean anything is open to question – but if one is adopting the assumption 'which maximises the impact of the Marina on other centres', some such estimates are necessary.

In return Lichfield Associates criticised the MAC for not taking

TABLE 5.2 Progressive decline of centres

Here the attractiveness of the centres, taken here to be floor-space, is adjusted to take account of the impact in the previous time period. The initial impact is the % change as estimated using the MAC model (i.e. $100 \times VII/VI$ from Table 5.1c). To calculate the progressive decline the original floor-space was reduced by the level of the initial impact to give the impacts of the 'first iteration'. These impacts are then used to adjust the floor-space again to give the impacts of the 'second iteration'.

Centre	Initial impact	Impact: First iteration	Impact: Second iteration
1	90	91	92
2	89	89	90
3	86	85	86
4	72	59	51
5	84	81	81
6	87	87	89

sufficient account of 'topping up' versus 'main shopping'. The argument goes: for purposes of 'topping up' shopping the Marina centre is to be considered as a local centre – *equally* as attractive as other local centres; for 'main' shopping the Marina would compete with the town centre. This main/topping up dichotomy was not mentioned in the consultants' proof of evidence yet they brought it up in their critique of MAC despite the fact that they themselves showed no hesitation in adding ice-creams and bulk grocery purchases. In any case they argued that 'convenience shops which become vacant will be taken up for durable sales'. They asserted that there would be some durable 'overflow' from the Marina, some of which would go to local shops.

The Marina Company's 'last minute expert'
At this point – the last day of the inquiry – the Marina Company introduced another witness, Harvey Cole, again a leading expert on shopping. No notice of this witness was given so the MAC lawyer (who was preparing his final speech) could not cross-examine him. Harvey Cole again criticised the MAC for not distinguishing between main and topping-up purchases, and the use of floor-space as an attractiveness index. He completely ignored the previous discussion on the use of shopping models and talked only in 'common-sense' terms. By implication Harvey Cole suggests that since previous evidence based on

models was contradictory, models were unreliable and should be ignored. This was reflected in the Inspector's report.[9] On the basis of a visit to the centres in question Harvey Cole concluded that it was unlikely that local centres would lose further trade, car-borne shoppers from these areas having already switched to other larger centres in Brighton. This assertion was quite untested. In fact no empirical survey was undertaken at any time during the Inquiry except one by the MAC on the origins of car-borne shoppers arriving at the one supermarket in Brighton's town centre which has substantial purpose-built on-site parking facilities. Given the obvious rapid changes in turnover at shopping centres in the vicinity the idea that some kind of equilibrium had been reached was obviously open to question.

The results of the Inquiry
In the event, to quote the local paper – the *Evening Argus* – 'the company got just what it asked for – 3000 square metres in the main public shopping centre'.[10] National policies may have played a role in this decision. The Marina Company is eagerly advertising the Marina in national newspapers as 'Europe's largest Marina'. Clearly, the Marina is to be an international showpiece. The *Evening Argus* reports the Inspector as saying that the Marina ' . . . will keep Brighton in the forefront of Britain's holiday resorts and make a notable contribution to its *status* as a leisure, conference and residential town'.

The prestige of the final witness may also have played its part; the Inspector's report referred at some length to Harvey Cole's evidence. Only cursory mention was made of the evidence submitted by NLA and MAC. It would not be surprising if the technical debate surrounding the models and their application was beyond both the Inspector and the legal representatives of all parties involved, not to mention the public. When the Inspector's report was returned from the Minister some significant additional restrictions were stipulated. Permission was granted but Marina figures for its sales of floor-space were rigidly fixed. As a result of the Inquiry, 2000 square metres of floor-space were approved for a supermarket out of a possible 13000 square metres sales space, as approved by the Council before the Inquiry.

We shall discuss later the implications of this case study for the conduct of public inquiries. Now, we consider the apparent wide differences in forecasts made by shopping models when alternative (yet plausible) assumptions are made.

Several alternative assumptions and 'decision points' may modify the results of models. After the Inquiry a more systematic study[11] of this phenomenon was made – looking at the effects of variations in the 'gravity' and a range of other shopping models, with different levels of detail and data requirements in order to evaluate not only their different forecasting ability but also whether this was improved through additional detail. To this purpose several models, described in our fuller report, were applied to four towns in the UK – Coventry, Derby, Telford and Watford. All but one of the models have been employed in numerous studies.

There are other important factors to be considered. Models are not used to forecast the effects of immediate changes. A complex, such as the Brighton Marina, may take a decade to construct but its effects will be felt long afterwards. Thus, the data that must be fed into the shopping models – the number of people living in the area, their income, the level of car ownership, public transport, patterns of expenditure and so on – are all based on other forecasting exercises, all of which are subject to similar problems. It may be that the 'data' from these exercises are the major uncertainty in the results of a shopping model. For the Marina inquiry Lichfield Associates assumed that expenditure on foodstuffs would remain constant – a cautious assumption based on national expectations. Obviously there is room for many alternative assumptions.

CONCLUSIONS

Several related issues have been brought together in this paper. Firstly, the public inquiry system and whether it inevitably favours particular interests, secondly, whether models foster this, and finally, given that some decision ultimately has to be taken, how can this be done as fairly as possible with an awareness of what might potentially go wrong. Public inquiries are called for when the Government Minister concerned feels that there is sufficient opposition to proposed schemes to merit open public discussion. Such schemes can be, and indeed are, quite varied: for example, the Windscale nuclear processing plant; the Archway road development; and the Brighton Marina project. Public inquiries, particularly those into proposed large-scale developments such as the Brighton Marina, may be costly affairs, but then set beside the *financial costs* of these schemes themselves, the costs of such exercises may be negligible.[12] Moreover, it is often the *social costs* that form the crux of the debate in public inquiries. In some sense decisions arising from public inquiries must be compromises. Models sometimes play a role in this process of evaluation, but other assessment techniques may also come to the fore. We believe that shopping models are not developed enough to be useful, *on their own*, in public inquiries. Nevertheless public inquiries have a useful function because any proposed project allows for some manoeuvrability. There is flexibility in the planning system and, given adequate preparation, modifications and corrections can be made. 'Experimental' approaches to planning and careful monitoring of projects constitute learning by doing.

The framework in which the affairs of a public inquiry are conducted is legalistic. The inspector is a planning QC and, in the Marina inquiry, so was the lawyer representing the interests of the Marina Company. The exchange between the various bodies is through lawyers and the inspector presides over court-like proceedings. Having a lawyer to present a case is a costly affair – especially for *ad hoc* groups from the public. If vested interests are at stake (as in the case for the Marina Company) the cost of lawyers and experts becomes worthwhile. In relation to the total cost or expected returns on a proposal this expenditure may be marginal. These observations are more appropriate to public inquiries into large-scale developments. In these circumstances, where the matters in hand become weightier, more lawyers and their entourages abound, more expert witnesses are liable to appear, the procedural formalism becomes tighter, and the atmosphere is potentially more intimidating for individuals questioned or giving verbal evidence to the inquiry.

This raises the question of public participation in planning inquiries. An organisation like the Marina Action Campaign is only possible in a town where there is an articulate public with sufficient resources and willingness to make a 'case' free of charge. A university town provides this. University workers having flexible working hours, they can prepare and present evidence at the inquiry during what for most people are normal working hours. Also, they have a secretarial/stationery/xeroxing back-up. This is beyond the means of most people. There is at present in the UK no framework in financial or legal terms, that enables 'the public' to muster its own experts. It has to depend on committed individuals or the formation of *ad hoc* groups (such as the Marina Action Campaign).

It is worth considering how certain constraints in the planning system affect the formation of 'final' plans. It should be noted that local authorities are obliged to consider every planning application on its merits, unless it explicitly conflicts with approved structure plans.

At the time of the Marina Inquiry there was no *approved* East Sussex

Structure Plan – however the existing unapproved Brighton Urban Structures Plan did argue against the development of edge-of-town shopping complexes. Suppose a planning application were accepted by a local authority, and that a subsequent public outcry resulted in setting up a planning inquiry. The public inquiry would be supplied with specific 'terms of reference' by the relevant Government Minister. Debate in the inquiry would be addressed to its terms of reference. It is likely that any evidence not conforming to this procedure would be ignored despite its relevance to the eventual decision. For example in the Marina Inquiry the terms of reference are not concerned with whether the whole project is desirable or whether any alternative is to be considered. If proposals are rejected it would be *on the basis of the inquiry's terms of reference* and the developer would have to go away and rethink. In fact, in the Marina Inquiry one group did draw up an alternative Marina project – based on more local needs.

In addition, public inquiries are forums of technical debate only; they deal with planning law and planning objections. Political questions are beyond their terms of reference although technical evidence necessarily touches on them. The inquiry inspector is obliged to act as a 'technician', filtering out the relevant information to write his report. The report is 'handed-up' to the Minister (who called for the inquiry); the political decisions are made there. Thus, we have a three-tier structure: terms of reference supplied by the Minister; a basically 'technical' inquiry; and a political decision by the Minister. This is an example of a 'hierarchical' decision-making procedure in which the political and technical merits of a scheme (let alone any alternatives) are assessed *separately* and *sequentially*. There will be a tendency in such a system to pre-empt the eventual decision.[13] A 'better' structure would assess the 'political' and 'technical' merits of alternative schemes together so that issues arising out of the assessment procedure could be taken into account.

Hence, for the reasons stated – the legal and financial 'straight-jackets' that are imposed, the need to present formal technical evidence and the alienating decision-making structure – public participation in the present public inquiry set-up is inhibited. Unlike the proponents of a project, objectors often cannot attend inquiries. Other forms of evidence may be treated with less respect. The Marina Inquiry was no exception:

> On the volume of petitions and letters he received Mr Widdicombe said: I have taken these letters and petitions into account, but in my view the representations of persons who do not attend the Inquiry and

are therefore comparatively uninformed about the facts and arguments of the matter carry little weight.[14]

However, this is not to suggest that the public inquiry system should be scrapped. The Marina Inquiry and the more systematic study show how alternative assumptions in models can affect the results obtained. Underlying assumptions and different theoretical model structure amount to an ideology in the broadest sense of the word. Conflict over technical systems is healthy since it may reveal ideological commitments underlying them. A clash over technical issues may in fact politicise the debate. Public inquiries, such as the Marina Inquiry, reveal the vested interests of developers if their experts are *challenged*. In the Marina Inquiry there were many costly experts hired to *fight* the case.

Here, then, lies the advantage of the public inquiry: an open forum in which 'ideologies' may come to the fore. Such a politicised debate should be actively encouraged – for example, by affording particular objectors, who will probably have limited resources, access to legal advice, and making financial provisions for at least the preparation of evidence.

The issues dealt with in public inquiries may be complex, the basic principles may be 'common sense'; there is a need for careful analysis. In some respects, therefore, a satisfactory investigation of a planning proposal is bound to be technical. Models often serve to mystify – to contradict common-sense arguments. In the past this has often been the case. When the debate is one-sided scientific method can be used as evidence to support even the most controversial proposal. In the Marina Inquiry there was more effective opposition, a phenomenon that is becoming more widespread although it is still exceptional. There, the net effect of using another model to bring opposition to bear on the evidence of the planning consultants was that the two models neutralised each other. By bringing in a new expert witness using his 'judgement' rather than a 'model' the inspector was let off the hook of having to face up to the genuine uncertainty inherent in such forecasting exercises.

Unfortunately few, if any, checks are made on the forecasts by planning consultants. Their 'track record' is not known. It is not known whether predictions by judgemental forecasters such as the Marina Development Company's 'last minute witness' are on balance better than those of the planning models. Apart from the present study there have been relatively few studies which even attempt to compare the predictive performance of competing models.[15] If the experience of macro-economic forecasters is any guide, then models may help to produce marginally better forecasts but essentially what is employed is a judicious mixture of analysis and intuition. However, this in itself is not enough. In addition, forecasts need to be subjected to criticism if a realistic estimate of the combined uncertainty in a planning decision is to be obtained.

The discussion of different models has raised a number of questions – does the use of disaggregated models improve performance? Does the need for data make such models impractical except as an aid to the development of theory and understanding? We suspect this is the case. In general there will not be enough data to account adequately for the interests of minority groups. The models are probably useful (given the caveats above) to produce guides to expected gross turnover at different centres and estimates of the traffic flows, etc. To evaluate the interests of minority groups requires separate and more detailed study and adequate representation in the inquiry itself.

It is possible that in an ideal world all parties with a legitimate interest in a planning proposal would have equal access to expert advice and legal representation. It may also be argued that such 'balanced' argument might effectively neutralise the system. The present system only operates because it favours large interests at the expense of the small. The public inquiry usually has unnecessarily restricted terms of reference. In the end the decision rests on the judgement and bias of the officials involved. This at least should be recognised.

ACKNOWLEDGEMENTS

We are grateful to N. Dombey (and others) for comments.

NOTES

* A fuller version of this chapter is obtainable from the authors.
1. See *The Times*, 2 March 1974.
2. *Brighton Voice*, 1974, No. 18, p. 10.
3. Chris Turner (of Nathaniel Lichfield and Associates, consultants for BMC) Local Inquiry under section 35 of the Town and Country Planning Act, 1971, proof of evidence, section III.
4. Ibid; Section 156.
5. See for example, the review of NEDO (1970), 'Urban Models in Shopping Studies', HMSO, pp. 34–59.
6. These terms of reference were stated in the Secretary of State's 'Rule 6 Statement' that initiated the inquiry.
7. C. Turner, POE, sections 7 and 8.

8. H. S. D. Cole, Local Inquiry Under Section 35 of the Town and Country Planning Act, 1971, Proof of Evidence.
9. See Dorothy Nelkin (1975), 'The political impact of technical expertise' *Social Studies of Science*, Vol. 5, No. 1, p. 54 for comments on 'conflict among experts reduces the political impact'.
10. *Evening Argus*, 3 June 1975.
11. This is part of a forthcoming Ph.D. thesis by one of the authors: R. Turner, 'The use of Mathematical Models in Urban Planning; the case of Shopping Models'.
12. The 1977 Windscale Inquiry – a milestone in public inquiries in terms of the long duration of the inquiry, the volume of evidence submitted, the importance of the issues involved. The cost to the taxpayer has been estimated at about £2 million. Estimates of the cost of building the scheme vary, but £600–700 million is of the order often quoted.
13. See Jay Gershuny (1978), *After Industrial Society?* (London: Macmillan).
14. *Evening Argus*, 3 June 1975, p. 10.
15. A notable exception in this respect is an article by Stan Openshaw: 'An empirical study of some spatial interaction models', *Environment and Behaviour*, 1976, Vol. 8, pp. 23–41.

6 Manpower Forecasters as Lobbyists: A Case Study of the Working Group on Manpower Parameters for Scientific Growth 1965–8

KEVIN McCORMICK

INTRODUCTION

For the past thirty years public discussion and official policy for scientific and technological manpower in Britain has been punctuated by announcements of brave hopes and bleak disenchantment about the possibilities of using forecasting techniques to guide educational policy. The machinery of advice developed in the postwar reconstruction was largely discredited and even disowned by some of its members by the beginning of the 1960s. Yet a vigorous burst of officially-appointed forecasting activity was undertaken in the mid-1960s. By the end of the decade these official platforms had been dismantled and many of the forecasters confessed disappointment over their efforts. Another flare-up of forecasting activity appeared likely in the mid-1970s when the Minister of State for Higher Education poked among the embers and announced the necessity for manpower forecasting to guide education. On this occasion, however, no official bodies were established and the smouldering desire to use the educational system to promote economic reform awaits a new champion. Meanwhile the cycle of official resolve and retraction requires some explanation. At the present time, there is widespread disenchantment with the conceptual tools of manpower forecasting, disenchantment about the possibility of translating forecasts into effective policy recommendations, and disenchantment with the educational system as a promoter of social change. In this essay I shall attempt to unravel some of these strands of enthusiasm and subsequent disenchantment by a case study of one manpower forecasting body in the mid-1960s – the Working Group on Manpower Parameters for Scientific Growth.[1]

The Report of this Working Group under the Chairmanship of Professor (now Sir) Michael Swann received an early post-mortem in 1969 which judged the assertions about a 'shortage' of scientists and engineers to be inadequate scientific analysis and better understood as the special pleading of a partisan lobby of scientific and engineering interests.[2] The economist critics, Gannicot and Blaug, included their adverse comments in a polemical review of the interrelated body of forecasting work carried out under the umbrella of the Committee on Manpower Resources for Science and Technology (1965–8). Since the central concern of Gannicot and Blaug was to rebut the analysis of the forecasters and to advocate an alternative, more economics-informed view of manpower problems, their review did not examine closely the processes by which the forecasters reached their conclusions. Whereas Gannicot and Blaug concentrated on the processes by which the forecasters *ought* to have made their forecasts, this chapter concentrates on the processes by which they *did* make their decisions as a prelude to an evaluation of their forecasting studies.

Usually any group of forecasters have available a corpus of previous forecasts on which to draw as points of reference. In the next section it is argued that the controversies provoked by earlier forecasts had an important conditioning effect on the approach of the Swann Working Group, prompting them to seek a new methodology. Just as there was an attempt to develop a new methodology of forecasting on the part of the forecasters, there was an attempt on the part of Government to develop new institutions to relate science to technology and economic ends. The impact of this institution-building on the forecasting activity is examined in Section 3, where the influences are traced on the conception of the problem, the data collected and the nature of the forecasts. The Swann Working Group's analysis of the manpower problem is scrutinised in Section 4. Here it is argued that the forecasters were confident in their analysis of the problems, despite some confessed areas of ignorance, largely because the existing evidence was thought consistent with their model of education-industry relations. The broader set of values which sustained this model became most explicit when the forecasters put the concept of 'need' at the centre of their forecast of future employment requirements and moved on to the policy recommendations outlined in Section 5. Curiously, however, some of the central recommendations for the reform of the educational system were similar to those of the critics, Gannicot and Blaug. If we wish to examine the question of whether the forecasters were right for the wrong reasons, then it is particularly important to re-examine the processes of reasoning which the Swann Working Group used.

IMMEDIATE BACKGROUND

To Gannicot and Blaug it was surprising that manpower forecasting was re-established in the 1960s. At the beginning of the 1960s the Robbins Committee appeared to have demolished the intellectual credibility of manpower forecasting and set the stage for educational expansion despite the advice of manpower forecasters. Two factors helped in the rehabilitation of manpower forecasters; firstly, there was general interest in and sympathy for planning in economic life which accompanied the return of the Labour Government in 1964, and secondly, the Robbins Committee did not completely close the door on manpower considerations. Indeed the Robbins Report listed the development of qualified manpower as a central aim of universities. The major thrust of the Robbins critique of manpower forecasting was directed largely to blunt any arguments contrary to expansion based on manpower criteria, when a strong case for expansion was being developed on the grounds of anticipated social demand for higher education. Moreover the Robbins Committee believed that there was unlikely to be any *real* conflict between 'social demand' and 'manpower needs'. The overthrow of manpower forecasting was more apparent than real. The main significance of the controversy lay in the extent to which the techniques used, should include economic considerations.

The controversy centred on the 1961 Long-Term Demand for Scientific Manpower prepared by the Statistics Committee for the Committee on Scientific Manpower of the Advisory Council on Scientific Policy (ACSP).[3] The conclusion of the report, 'that the overall supply and demand for qualified manpower will not be very much out of balance at the end of the first five years of the decade 1960–1970', was disturbing even within the ACSP, some of whose members saw science as a political and economic resource and pressed for expansionist policies. In order to soothe their anger and that of outside critics, the ACSP claimed that the Report had been misunderstood, and that it was not complacent, for there were references to specific shortages. By putting great stress on the assumptions underlying the forecast the ACSP encouraged scepticism and undermined the Report. Thirdly they urged rejoicing that the growth of non-vocational employment meant that the day of the scientist in the general culture had arrived.[4] This emphasis on the importance of 'science-mindedness' in the general population became one of the points of bridge-building between the ACSP and the Robbins Committee. To the Robbins Committee, which was committed to expansion of the higher education system beyond that covered in the 1961 Report on the grounds of anticipated student demand, manpower forecasting became a target for attack.

The attack was well marshalled by Lord Robbins, in the body of the Robbins Report, and well supported by Robbins Committee statisticians.[5] Moreover the Robbins Committee found an ally in Sir Solly Zuckerman, who withdrew his support from manpower forecasting when giving his evidence to the Robbins Committee.[6] Later Zuckerman came back to the Robbins Committee with some support for expansion based on employer estimates of employment in 1965 made to the later 1962 Triennial Manpower Survey and the new information of scientists who had diffused into non-science occupations available from the 1961 Census of Population. The evidence was welcomed by the Robbins Committee which accepted the forecasts as minimal guides for student numbers without implication for setting upper limits.[7]

One important legacy from this episode of controversy lay in the extremely delicate position of the civil service secretariat and statisticians. Their position has always been delicate because they serviced a Committee on which their department had members as representatives and then both members and secretariat had to respond to the Reports as members of departments. In the next round of forecasting this problem was reduced by the separation of departments from membership, but the problems remained for the secretariat. In this case the problems for the future secretariat were compounded because they had a considerable share in a report which had received much criticism and which the Chairman had rejected. This controversy gave added impetus to a search for new conceptual approaches in the next round of forecasting.

The Statistics Committee had taken the view that 'demand' was more problematic than 'supply' since the target supply was already in the educational system and could be estimated given various assumptions about qualified applicants, filled places, wastage rates, and the lengths of courses. The previous 1956 attempt to forecast long-run demand using an incremental labour/output ratio appeared inadequate.[8] Therefore the 1961 forecast built up estimates of future employment industry by industry in the light of likely developments in the economy through informal discussions between departments, industrialists, and economic advisers. It was these discussions which included estimates of the costs of employment and the likely ability of industry to afford the estimated employment, which led to downward revision of earlier estimates of growth of employment.

Having seen the criticisms of their attempts to estimate demand (a measure of the employers' willingness and ability to pay) the statisticians and secretariat were ready to accommodate the next manpower committee's emphasis on estimates of need to guide educational policy.

A NEW START ON MANPOWER FORECASTING IN 1965

Between 1963–5 the institutional apparatus of Government for the prosecution of civil science and technology underwent considerable change. This upheaval had significant implications for the kind of manpower forecasting activity which was subsequently undertaken. The central Government departments (the Department of Education and Science, the Ministry of Technology and the Ministry of Labour) are outlined in Figure 6.1. The main advisory forecasting body (the Committee on Manpower Resources for Science and Technology and its Working Groups, including the Swann Committee), advised the Department of Education and Science and the Ministry of Technology. This pattern of inclusion linked the forecasting activity to the 'science budget' and linked the forecasters to the lobbies which attempted to influence the allocation of the budget. The exclusion of the Ministry of Labour, however, meant that another set of interests were not directly involved in the forecasting of the 1960s, although it has asserted its central interests in manpower policy with the demise of the forecasting bodies since 1968.

A start on the institutional changes was made by the Conservative Government in 1963 in its responses to the Robbins Report recommendations on the organisation of higher education and in response to the Trend Committee recommendations on civil science organisation.[9] For education a Federal Ministry was created to cover the spectrum from schools to universities. For civil science it was proposed to replace the Department of Scientific and Industrial Research (DSIR) by three new research councils and to replace the Advisory Council for Scientific Policy (ACSP) with a new Council for Scientific Policy composed of independent members. The proposals were undertaken by the election

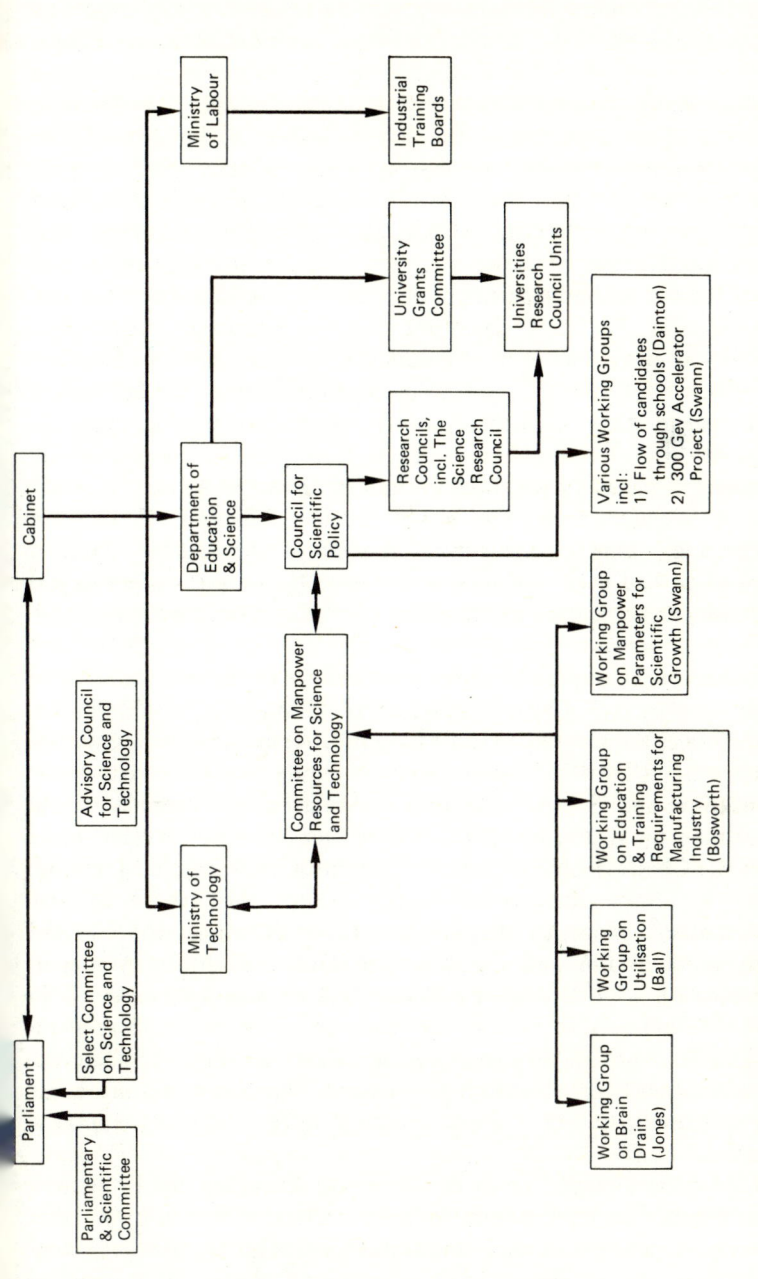

FIGURE 6.1. The structure of forecasting advice and decisionmaking in scientific and technological manpower policy 1965–68

and the new Labour Government placed the research councils under the financial control of the Secretary of State for Education and Science. Therefore the Council for Scientific Policy (CSP) had a narrower brief but stronger powers than the ACSP through its advice to the Secretary of State on the allocation of the 'science budget'.[10] For the DES the changes meant that effective systems of communication had to be developed between the various units drawn from the different traditions of the mainstream Ministry of Education officials who had regulated schools and further education and the newcomers from the office of the Lord President, the Department of Scientific and Industrial Research (DSIR) and the UGC. To stoke the 'white-heat of technological revolution' proved an even more difficult administrative problem and the Ministry of Technology was developed piecemeal through 1964–6 with the addition of further powers and responsibilities. From the original brief to stimulate four 'high-technology' industries, the Ministry acquired a wider brief for industry at large. Advice on its role was anticipated from the newly created Advisory Council on Technology. One of the central themes of the Labour Party in opposition had been that it would harness the nation's scientific and technological resources to the promotion of economic progress.

Planning was a key phrase but it implied coordination of effort too, and this was attempted by cross-memberships of the various advisory bodies and by providing a focus for coordination in the new Manpower Committee, the Committee on Manpower Resources for Science and Technology (CMRST), which reported jointly to the Department of Education and Science and to the Ministry of Technology. The Chairman, Sir Willis Jackson (later Lord Jackson of Burnley) had taken over the Chairmanship of the old Committee on Scientific Manpower from Sir Solly Zuckerman shortly before the demise of that Committee.[11] Together with three other members of the CMRST (Professors Swann and Dainton, and Dr F. E. Jones, Managing Director of Mullard Ltd), Sir Willis Jackson was a member of the Council for Scientific Policy. The remaining thirteen members of the CMRST comprised university vice-chancellors, university professors of natural science or engineering, university professors in the social sciences, industrialists in science-based industry and a representative from the TUC.

Under the direction of its very energetic chairman the Committee established a large programme of work to be undertaken by working parties at a prodigious rate.[12] Inevitably the CMRST carried over some tasks from its predecessor, the Committee on Scientific Manpower (for example, the Triennial Manpower Survey). The inclusion of 'Technology' and 'Resources' in the title was intended to indicate new directions in the broader conception of the task and the importance of economic ends, however.[13] The utilisation of manpower was to be examined by two working parties, the Working Group on Engineering Training and the Requirements of Industry under the chairmanship of G. S. Bosworth, and the Working Group on the Utilisation in Employment of Scientists and Technologists under the chairmanship of Professor J. G. Ball.[14] The flow into employment was to be examined by the Working Group in Manpower Parameters for Scientific Growth under the chairmanship of Professor Michael Swann and the flow of qualified scientists and engineers out of the economy (the 'brain drain') was to be examined by a working group under the chairmanship of Dr F. E. Jones. Through the provisions of cross-memberships, common secretariats and discussions in the CMRST the Working Groups could be coordinated, and similar provisions maintained the links with related working parties established directly by the CSP, in particular the Committee chaired by Professor Dainton which examined the flow of scientists and engineers through the school system.[15] Such was the cross-membership that the eight-man Swann Working Group included five 'chairmen'.

Although enthusiasm was in abundant evidence in the way that men holding full-time senior posts elsewhere threw themselves into multiple committees, fear was another motive. The enthusiasm for planning shown by the Council for Scientific Policy and the new Labour Government stood in marked contrast to the *laissez-faire* philosophy propounded by Lord Hailsham as Minister of Science.[16] But Lord Hailsham had been preoccupied by a model of pure science as a prototypical model society during a period of economic growth, whereas the new Labour Government was preoccupied by technology and an immediate economic crisis. Therefore when Lord Bowden warned that the current rate of growth of Government support for the Research Councils (about 13 per cent per annum in real terms or a doubling every six years) could not continue, the largely academically composed CSP was agreeable to forward planning as the alternative to arbitrary cuts.[17] The terms of reference emerged from complaints, widespread among industrialists and articulated within the CSP by Dr F. E. Jones, that university expansion was denuding industry of talent in the short run and diverting QSEs into activities which were unlikely to be of foreseeable benefit to industry. Similar fears had been voiced by Lord Todd, the Chairman of the former ACSP, who had opposed the

Robbins expansion and urged that further expansion should concentrate on technical staff to support QSEs.[18] Now the CSP invited the CRMST to investigate:

> What rates of growth of science are permissible in the Universities and Research Councils without creating serious problems for the intake of highly-qualified manpower into industry and for the long-term quality of science teaching in the schools.[19]

By the final report, however, the reference to 'parameters' had been dropped, a reflection of the shift in the preoccupations of the Committee and an abandonment of the attempt to provide quantitative forecasts.[20] The shift came after the publication of the Interim Report in 1966 and was greatly stimulated by the two 'newcomers' to the Committee.

By January 1966 the Working Group had been composed, with six members drawn from the Parent Committee (Professors Swann, Ball, Jackson, Hutton, Dainton and Dr Jones) and two members drawn from outside (Professor Pippard and Dr Davies). Professor Pippard was sought as an original thinker on the development of physics and physics education for a problem which was anticipated to disturb many physicists. Although it was likely that an additional chemist and an industrialist would be sought in ICI, a major employer of university-trained scientists and engineers, Dr Davies was invited to contribute his original thinking on science education. Yet there was little scope for originality in the first task of the Working Group. By the third meeting in July 1966 the members were discussing the first draft of the Interim Report in order to advise the CMRST on the interpretation of the 1965 Triennial Manpower Survey and to give advice to the CSP for the Secretary of State on the allocation of the Research Council budget for 1967/8. At this early stage the Committee saw their future task as long-term quantitative forecasting.

> We believe that manpower needs can and should find quantitative expression, perhaps in the form of desirable patterns of flow to be varied between subjects and with the state of university or industrial expansion; and we recommend that there should be further examinations of the feasibility of doing this.[21]

However, by 1968 the Working Party recorded that:

> It is important to complement the (Triennial) Surveys with attempts

to assess these longer-term changes even if – as we have found – the conclusions must be qualitative rather than quantitative.[22]

Within the Swann Working Group the criticisms of the short-term Triennial Surveys were given added weight by the industrialists Davies and Jones, who argued that these 'snapshots' were too much influenced by the timing of the enquiry in the optimism and pessimism of the trade cycle and that the inquiries were unlikely to be answered by those responsible for investment plans and therefore doubly unreliable as guides to future behaviour. In any event the Triennial Surveys anticipated events only three years ahead and were inadequate for the ten-year view sought for educational planning. All the past methods of long-term forecasting had been discredited, the CMRST lent its weight to criticisms of the stock-demand balancing exercise of the 1961 forecast with the complaint that a stock was an assembly of many generations not necessarily available for current employment without retraining.[23] While the CMRST could hope for guidance on long-range forecasting from computable models of the educational system by Professor Stone and information on quantitative relationships between economic performance and manpower utilisation from Professor Moser and his colleagues, in the short term they had only their beliefs.[24] Ultimately need rather than demand became the central concept in the analysis. Therefore when the Ministry of Technology statisticians appeared committed to the fine honing of statistical precision, Dr Davies urged his colleagues to select a policy issue and use logic and imagination to attack it. This was the beginning of the redirection of the Working Group's work towards curriculum reform and away from quantitative forecasting. Given that the weakest point of forecasting lay with demand, Davies argued that the solution was not the refinement of forecasting but the removal of the problem by avoiding the early specialisation in studies which created the rigidities in planning. Professor Pippard was a willing ally in tackling the problems of university curriculum reform and the Committee and secretariat saw the task as 'qualitative' forecasting, judging the balance between specialist and generalist studies.

Thus the attempt to develop a fresh approach to long-term forecasting had to wait until the Working Group could escape its immediate advisory responsibilities and negotiate a wider brief with the CMRST and the CSP. The newcomers to the Working Group ably facilitated this change of focus. However, the web of past commitments continued to influence the Working Group, particularly in the division of labour between institutions and Working Groups. The Secretariat, drawn from the newly-created Science branch of DES located in Richmond Terrace, had to be sensitive to the concerns of their new colleagues in the Curzon Street headquarters of DES and to alert members to the problems of polarising goodwill when they addressed themselves to issues of school curriculum reform and salary differentials for science teachers. If the problems of coordination were difficult within a new Ministry, then they were still relatively simple compared to the problems of securing cooperation and coordination for the Working Group across several Ministries. Cooperation and coordination within and between the CMRST and its working groups was not a problem, but the consequences of decisions about the allocation of the study programme became a problem. Although 'utilisation' was a topic for examination by another working group, it was extremely difficult to discuss demand and need without reference to utilisation, and the decision not to discuss some of the evidence on utilisation but to refer to the other Working Groups became an Achilles heel of the Final Report. Having made little headway on the extremely difficult conceptual problems of utilisation, the Ball Committee on Utilisation was pre-empted from completing its work by the intervention of the Department of Employment (formerly the Ministry of Labour) into manpower policy through its responsibilities for the Industrial Training Board and its creation of its own unit for highly qualified manpower research.

SYMPTOMS AND DIAGNOSIS IN THE MANPOWER MALAISE

The Interim Report broadly confirmed the conventional wisdom of science-based industry and some academics, who felt that industry was being denied manpower by the expansion of the universities. As a zoologist Professor Swann was not too perturbed by the small sample sizes in some of the Interim Report analysis. However, much of the subsequent data collection was directed to a strengthening of the argument which was re-stated in the main report:

> The statistics of our Interim Report were criticised on the grounds that they were by no means complete and relied in some cases on relatively small samples. It is now possible to supplement our earlier analysis with statistics over a wider field. We have, we believe, arrived at a reasonably comprehensive picture of the flow of graduate

scientists and technologists, and our new data without doubt reinforce the conclusions that we drew earlier.[25]

Throughout the analysis there was the strain of impatience from practical men who were committed to produce an analysis of the manpower situation *and* feasible policy recommendations. Therefore at a number of points a confession of ignorance or a caveat about the data or analysis was followed immediately by a 'but' or a 'nevertheless'.

> Our evidence is less complete than we would have wished. ... Nevertheless the evidence that was available confirmed to us our earlier findings – particularly the outstanding needs of the schools and industry for a greater share of the more able scientists and (to a lesser extent) of technologists – and revealed a potentially dangerous imbalance whose redress should not wait upon more refined studies.[26]

The Working Group was unlikely to be surprised by fresh evidence because of the prior definition of the problem; the main innovations lay in the concepts used to present the data, and the search for evidence was constrained by the search for variables out of which practicable policies would be fashioned.

The most striking innovation in the presentation of the manpower statistics was in the conception of a 'flow' of manpower through the schools, through higher education, through first employment and in subsequent job mobility. This attempt to model the relations between education and employment as a dynamic living system was particularly congenial to Professor Swann, as a zoologist. Although it had severe deficiencies in data, especially for technology students, where half the new supply came outside the well-documented university sector, the estimates of flows highlighted the problem of lead times, in this case ten years, before changes in the educational system could become effective in employment. This consideration gave the rationale for concentrating attention on the postgraduate level for dramatic solutions.[27]

The projections of supply anticipated university output to 1971–2, five years on from the last statistics of 1966–7. In effect this was building on the Dainton Committee view of the school population to estimate the university contribution of 70 per cent of the newly qualified scientists and engineers (the universities were responsible for 90 per cent of the new supply of scientists and approximately 50 per cent of the new supply of technologists). For the undergraduate population in science and technology faculties two projections were offered, based on different assumptions about the properties of sixth-form scientists who would proceed to university study: a 'pessimistic' assumption (63 per cent) led to a projected decline in the undergraduate population whereas an 'optimistic' assumption (a proportion increasing from the 63 per cent in 1966–7 to 75 per cent in 1971–2) led to an increase to 82 000 at the end of 1971–2.[28] The 'optimistic' growth pattern was taken to be the more realistic assumption in calculating the projected postgraduate population. With the assumption that the 1966–7 ratio proceeding to postgraduate studies would remain constant (postgraduate 43:100 undergraduate), the Working Group anticipated a postgraduate population in science and technology of 20 500 in 1971–2.[29]

Once again, *faute de mieux*, the statistics had to be seized upon to advance policy recommendations despite caveats about the heroic nature of the assumptions about the transition coefficients. For example, in a discussion of the extent to which the SRC award policy might influence the numbers proceeding to postgraduate study, the Working Group admitted:

> It would clearly be unwise to draw firm conclusions until more information is available. But this evidence points to the need for a fuller understanding of the interaction of the sources of support and of the factors shaping the demand for postgraduate work, to assist postgraduate awards policy in seeking to match the output from education more closely to requirements of employment.[30]

The familiar pattern of the caution negatived by a 'nevertheless' was used to reach the policy implications,

> It must be emphasised that these projections have been made solely to display some implications for policy: in no sense are they intended to be a prediction of what will happen . . . . We reiterate these projections explore what might happen; they do not predict what will happen . . . changes in these and other policies could invalidate our projections; nevertheless some important conclusions emerge.[31]

The projections would become predictions unless policy were changed. The *main* possible sources of change were in those factors which the Working Group was seeking to influence – the UGC, the SRC, the employers in recruitment policy and the students in applications. The Working Group was disturbed by the slowing down of the rate of growth of the output of scientists and technologists (5 per cent per annum in 1968–72 compared to 10 per cent per annum previously), even on the optimistic assumption. Thus the UGC was urged to accommodate all able applicants for undergraduate science and technology. Moreover the contrast between the projections and the UGC planning figures (82 000 versus 80 000 at the undergraduate level and 20 500 versus 17 800 at the postgraduate level in 1971–2) was highlighted to argue the case for priorities for undergraduates rather than postgraduates and advanced course work rather than research training. Otherwise the 'internal university pressures' would frustrate the particular UGC planning figures and the pattern of priorities which the manpower committees were advancing on the basis of estimates of long-term requirements.

The discussion of requirements had to be based on articles of faith once the Triennial Surveys were admitted as suspect. Yet the Triennial Surveys remained a linch-pin of the diagnosis. This paradox can be best explained by noting the use of the Triennial Surveys to build up a picture of the universities as insufficiently responsive to the demands of industry and schools, a use borrowed from the parent CMRST.

> Neither the schools since 1956 nor industry since 1959 have been able to achieve employment corresponding to stated demand. By contrast the increase of employment in higher educational establishments and in the public sector has on occasion reached or even exceeded the stated demands.[32]

The CMRST and the Swann Working Group believed that employer demands (in the sense of anticipated requirement), understated need (in the sense of what the manpower forecasters felt was good for them and the economy), so that the case about absolute numbers was linked to the fair shares issue too.

> We do not know how many scientists and technologists are at present required by employers or will be in the future. The picture is particularly uncertain in respect of industry. A full account must await the results of the current (1968) Triennial Survey, though there are signs of shortage. We are, however, in no doubt that two sectors in particular – industry and the schools – need, for their own welfare and that of the economy, a much greater injection of scientists and technologists; and that for most of the 1960s the pattern of

employment of graduates in this field, particularly of the most able, has been at variance with this need.[33]

The possibility that the numerical shortfalls were indicators of overestimate rather than that shortage was not discussed; although the manner in which employers apparently coped with the shortfalls raised the question of substitution. The employment of arts and social studies graduates in production departments, the appearance of QSEs in technician roles, and the proportions of professional institution members who reported posts in management and administration further undermined the usefulness of a forecasting technique which attempted simple translations from educational discipline to occupational category in fixed coefficients in the manner of the Triennial Survey.[34] Despite their expressed dissatisfaction with this inflexible form of forecast the Working Group found it difficult to escape the logic of fixed coefficients, even in the imaginative piece of research commissioned for the long-term forecasting.

Jobs in research and development were regarded as having close links with educational preparation, whereas for many other jobs a specialised scientific or technological preparation was not thought necessary, although a general background in these subjects was thought desirable. It was evident to the Working Group that although jobs in industrial R and D had risen in absolute numbers, these jobs accounted for a declining proportion of scientists and technologists employed in industry.[35] Therefore the Working Group set out to gauge the growth of these occupational developments and assess the implications for the future balance of specialist and generalist education through the secondment of Mr McCarthy from ICI to the DES.

The terms 'specialist' and 'generalist' could be defined either by educational or by employment characteristics.[36] In educational terms, the specialist has concentrated on one subject of study to the exclusion of others whereas the generalist has studied a variety of subjects. In employment terms, the specialist has studied to the equivalent of graduate level in a narrow range of specified disciplines or undergone lengthy training whereas the generalist occupation could be undertaken after relatively short specialist training by someone of appropriate intellectual powers and personal qualities. McCarthy then attempted to quantify the extent of both types of educational provision and employment opportunities in Britain and America, and concluded that less than 20 per cent of graduates in Britain emerged from generalist studies in the early 1960s compared to the 65–75 per cent of American students who received generalist education. The reliance on published data from the Robbins Report meant that there was some over-simplification of curriculum content and that there were some important omissions, notably the ex. CATS, the 'new' English universities and the Scottish universities.[37] The significance of these omissions lay in the extent to which the study produced an outdated caricature. Some educationalists, however, objected to the very gross nature of comparisons, for example, doubting whether the British first degree should be compared with the American first degree without the inclusion of the HNC level qualification. In considering employment opportunities, it has been hoped to comb company records using indices of 'generalism' and 'specialism' but this was abandoned in favour of a more broadbrush assumption that science-based specialists were employed mainly for R and D.[38] In neither country did the proportion of qualified scientists and engineers in R and D in manufacturing industry exceed 40 per cent. Therefore, a mismatch between the proportions in specialist education and specialist job opportunities was detected in British education, which produced educational specialists far in excess of occupational specialists.

The logic was somewhat incongruous. Although the Working Group was anxious to break the presumed automatic link between 'good degree' results in science-based specialists courses and academic or government research employment, specialism in education was linked to specialism in employment (and similarly for generalism) in the characteristic fixed input-output coefficients of manpower forecasting. There was the added colour that 'generalist studies must relate to society' and by a procedure of presumption and definition (e.g. the use of terms such as 'technological society') the McCarthy and Swann Reports considered only science-based generalism. The term 'generalist education' was at best ambiguous, covering an enormous variety of educational courses from the attempted interdisciplinary courses, to 'cafeteria courses' and even the mixes of main courses and 'tool subjects', and at worst a deception on liberal education.[39]

The concentration on patterns of education stemmed from the Working Group's conviction that 'motivation' was the crucial issue in the flow of manpower and the belief that motivation was shaped within the educational system. Although employers were urged to recruit vigorously, the central issue was held to lie in the preferences of students shaped by school and university.

The vital issue is however the motivation of the individual. It is of great importance to change a widespread belief that academic research is the only respectable outcome of a scientific education.[40]

Two kinds of evidence were marshalled to support this account. Firstly, the statistical information on first and substantive employment of first degree and higher degree graduates collected from the UGC and the University Appointments Board was interpreted as if the employment reflected a set of preferences. By a highly dubious inference it was assumed that the pattern for 'good degree' students indicated, in some pure unconstrained sense, the 'real' motives of less academically able students.[41] The inferences were linked to two social surveys initiated by the University Appointments Boards; the first was a national survey of 1960 graduates undertaken by Professor Kelsall and the second a survey of careers of graduates beginning postgraduate study in 1957–8, undertaken by Dr Rudd. These studies added broad confirmation to the patterns of flow observed in the main statistical series and the questions on the timing of occupational choices revealed substantial proportions who had not decided on careers until during their undergraduate courses, particularly in physics.

Marked differences in the propensity to enter industry between physics and chemistry/technology higher degree students had been noted in the Interim Report and now it was held that the pattern of tastes was the result of tastes acquired in the educational system.[42] At the undergraduate stage a higher proportion of chemistry graduates (41·8 per cent) compared to physics graduates went into research or further academic study (36·2 per cent) and conversely a lower proportion went into industrial employment (see Table 6.1). But at the postgraduate stage a lower proportion of chemistry higher degree graduates (16 per cent) compared to physics (26·8 per cent) entered university employment and a higher proportion (17·8 per cent versus 10·4 per cent) went into industry. Therefore the main report supported the image of a self-feeding academic system, particularly in physics research manpower, which had been the starting-point of CSP concern.

The image of a self-feeding system carried important moral overtones of blame and serious political implications for the science budget. The responsibility for the patterns of flow into employment was put squarely on academics when the Working Group asked the rhetorical question, 'Are they (students) to be blamed for preferring the academic world here or abroad (even without a permanent post) to industry or school teaching in this country?'[43] The political implications were pointed up in the informal responses to the physics lobby when they were pointedly

TABLE 6.1 First employment of first degree graduates, by discipline: 1966 (in %)

	Higher education and research			Schools, colleges and teacher training				Indus-try	Govern-ment	Other Train-ing	Other Home Employ-ment	Other Employ-ment Over-seas	Others	Total	Total
	Research & Further Academic Study	Univers-ities	Total	Teacher Train-ing	Schools	Further Edu-cation	Total								
Chemistry	41·8	1·0	42·8	11·0	2·1	0·4	13·6	31·5	2·8	0·7	0·6	2·4	5·8	9·4	100·0 (1957)
Physics	36·2	0·8	36·9	9·1	2·2	0·4	11·8	34·0	5·1	0·5	0·8	3·1	7·6	12·1	100·0 (1651)
All science	31·2	2·0	33·1	14·1	3·6	0·8	18·6	26·3	4·8	4·7	0·7	3·5	8·3	17·2	100·0 (9859)
All technology	15·6	0·2	15·9	1·2	0·3	0·3	1·8	61·5	5·3	0·2	0·0	5·0	9·5	15·4	100·0 (5613)

Source: Extracted from Table 23, *The Flow into Employment of Graduate Scientists, Engineers and Technologists*

TABLE 6.2 First employment of higher degree graduates, by discipline: 1966 (in %)

	Higher education and research			Schools, colleges and teacher training				Indus-try	Govern-ment	Other Train-ing	Other Home Employ-ment	Other Employ-ment Over-seas	Others	Total	Total
	Research & Further Academic Study	Univer-sities	Total	Teacher Train-ing	Schools	Further Edu-cation	Total								
Chemistry	14·0	16·0	30·0	0·1	2·3	4·2	6·7	17·8	2·9	—	0·1	28·2	14·3	42·6	100·0 (826)
Physics	10·1	26·8	37·0	0·2	2·1	2·5	4·9	10·4	8·9	0·2	0·4	18·2	20·1	38·9	100·0 (473)
Total science	11·8	23·0	34·8	0·3	2·1	3·6	6·0	12·1	6·9	0·3	0·6	21·2	18·2	40·3	100·0 (2334)
Total technology	14·4	8·3	22·7	—	0·1	3·6	3·7	33·7	4·0	0·1	0·1	13·5	23·5	37·2	100·0 (991)

Source: Table 26 *The Flow into Employment of Scientists, Engineers and Technologists*

told that the support for their expensive researchers came directly from industry, and that they ought to make a more effective contribution. The proposal for the 300 GEV accelerator was an issue which bulked large in the discussions of the CSP.[44] As Chairman of the CSP Working Group on the 300 GEV accelerator project, Professor Swann was in a strong position to draw parallels between manpower and financial flows.[45]

The physics lobby could muster a number of rejoinders, for example that the descriptions of physics and industry had been overdrawn, and that the roots of any problem lay in industry and its inadequate utilisation of physics manpower. The physicists countered that only accidents of history had separated physics and engineering departments whereas this split had not occurred in chemistry, therefore the proper comparisons of employment should be physics and engineering versus chemistry and the policy solution should be greater possibilities for student transfers between departments.[46] Again objecting to the goodies versus baddies contrast with the chemists, the physicists objected that the success of the chemists had been to push a larger proportion of first degree graduates into higher degree studies so that university expansion had drawn from a relatively larger pool of able candidates and not starved industry in the short run. The relatively happy relationship between the chemical industry and university chemists was alleged to result from the more enlightened nature of the chemical industry. For example, the adverse comments on Ph.D. training made by some industrialists to the Working Group were contested by representatives from the chemical industry in their discussions.[47] Why the chemical industry should be different was not discussed although there is a suggestive clue in the papers on technological innovation where it appears that much chemical innovation is planned through large research programmes whereas much innovation in physics occurs through major discontinuities which industry rarely has the capacity in skilled manpower to exploit.[48] If the innovations stem from planned programmes then it is more likely that the utilisation of manpower is planned.

Despite the influence of Professor Swann and the use of flow concepts, the Working Group was accused of using machine metaphors rather than organic metaphors in their analysis of the labour market. More pointedly, Blaug and Gannicot asserted that this defective perspective was linked to the forecasters' operation as a lobby pleading a special interest.[49]

At one level it could be argued that the manpower forecasters were simply ignorant of the social sciences. This charge would be difficult to sustain however for social scientists were included on the parent body

(Professors Stone and Moser on the CMRST) and several members of the Working Group had been involved in collaborative social science enterprises.[50] Although aware of the social sciences, it could be argued that the social sciences were not useful for their analysis. There is some truth in this comment. The Moser-Stone contributions were hopes for the future. Yet the Working Group sought data from Professor Kelsall, Dr Rudd and Mr Hutchings. In this sense social scientists were useful but the concepts and theories in schemes of interpretation were not taken up. The Working Group's belief that 'the day is past when universities were for the elite only' contrasts sharply with Professor Kelsall's report title, *Graduates: the Sociology of an Elite*.[51] The data available in the Hutchings survey on the different social backgrounds of students in different faculties did not receive comment.[52] Sex and social class did not appear to cross the minds of the Working Group. Yet politicians and social scientists were sensitive to these variables as part of a scheme of explanation of 'shortage'.[53]

However, sex and social class were not variables which could give scope for dramatic policy intervention, nor did they yield clear clues to long-term policy for a body trying to work through the SRC and UGC. The other major variable ignored was salary. The Working Group did not attempt to examine detailed evidence on salary movements.[54] Subsequent salary data collection did not support the claim of a shortage of scientists or engineers.[55] The avoidance of salary data could rest on two assumptions, the first was that salary was unimportant in motivation on the supply side and the second was that salary was unimportant as a factor on the demand side. At some point the Working Group appeared to advance the first view, preferring to concentrate attention on tastes for jobs rather than financial reward in a discussion of job mobility.[56] However the main premise was the acceptance of industrialists' complaints that any attempts to compete with other sectors were negated by the principles of fair comparison used in the civil service and in universities.[57] As members of professional institutions, individual members of the Working Group were aware of salary surveys which indicated relatively low salaries for engineers, but there was little point in studying the matter if the Working Group believed that industrialists could be only exhorted to recruit vigorously (which did not imply salary increases) and the main policy recommendations were to Government on pay policy.[58]

This view of industry's inability to compete was not accepted in some of the evidence presented to the Working Group, but this selective use of data reflects the use of the social survey data without reference to the schemes of interpretation which underlay their collection.[59] To adopt these alternative schemes of interpretation would have led the Working Group outside its terms of reference, outside its definition of the problem, outside its agreed division of labour with other Working Groups, and outside the policy levers on which it hoped to exercise influence.[60]

FROM DIAGNOSIS TO CURE

> The diagnosis, let alone the cure, of the malaise that affects the British economy is clearly far beyond our terms of reference. The Report of the Working Group on Migration has recently displayed some symptoms of this malaise, and other Groups are examining particular aspects of it. We have therefore confined our attention largely, though not entirely, to the task of bringing about improvements through the education system, and particularly through higher education. Our recommendations . . . attack only one corner of a vastly complicated situation. The measures we propose for education, or indeed any others, will not in themselves suffice; they depend for their success on complementary developments in employment. Only through joint action by education and employers, especially in industry, can progress be made in solving present manpower problems.
>
> *Nevertheless* we propose that education take the initiative in dealing with these problems.[61]

The final report of the Working Group had diagnosed the existence of vicious circles in the manpower flows in the sense of a self-feeding system in academic research, especially physics, and a less than desirable flow into industry which had a poor substance and reputation largely because of the inadequate flow of able scientific and technological manpower. The problem for policy was to break into these circles. As stated in the first paragraph quoted above, the diagnosis and policy recommendations were even-handed on both universities and industries. The ubiquitous 'nevertheless' sold the pass on that point however. This sermon on salvation through science was preached mostly to the universities since it was believed that the educational system could be more readily controlled and changed, in contrast to industry. Control for universities and coaxing for industry left an asymmetry in the final report.

The Working Group received a good deal of evidence that the poor state of industry was a deterrent to potential entrants, and said so.[62] The evidence came from industrialist members, from witnesses in oral and written evidence, and from the Jones Working Group. But the Swann Working Group wished to avoid repetition of the Jones Working Group and wished to avoid the self-fulfilling prophecy of suggesting that graduates are unlikely to enter industry because of its poor state. Therefore little of this material was discussed in the Report: even the discussion of the Training Boards was extremely brief and the recommendation did not visualise the control of industry through Government agencies, only the opportunity for industry to use the 1964 Industrial Training Act to control education and training provision.[63]

Just as the language of economic crisis is explicit in the Final Report, the language of war, generalship and campaign is implicit in the recommendations which divided into the short-term measures (or tactics) and measures for the longer term (or strategy).

Many of the short-term recommendations to the educational system were re-statements of measures already put into effect by the UGC and the SRC, but repeated with vivid invocations to 'drastic action' and bold experimentation. In its recommendations on the scale and proportions for the student population and the 'pump-priming' support for more vocationally oriented courses, the UGC was following the Swann Working Group lines of thought.[64] Although viewed with distaste, the Working Group accepted that the UGC should bow to the pressure of applicants in making provision for faster growth in arts and social science undergraduate places relative to science and technology.[65] Encouragement was given to several SRC initiatives such as those in pure science associated with industrial interests (Cooperative Awards for Pure Science) and the revision of support for advanced courses with sixty courses of industrial relevance given a priority classification.[66] Although the SRC might chafe at the language of the Working Group deliberations, with its relative harshness for universities and indulgence for industry, it was faithful to the spirit and purpose of reform. The participation of assessors from the UGC and SRC in all the Working Group discussions meant that there was a ready translation of thinking into policy before the recommendations were even finalised.

While tactical dramatic intervention was sought through the changes in the scale and type of postgraduate study, the longer-term strategic reforms were addressed to undergraduate curriculum reform. While the short-term changes were the more controversial, the proposals for broader courses stimulated by the McCarthy Report were received with general approval. Again the Working Group picked its way carefully towards the politically acceptable solution. Professor Pippard proposed restructuring university education towards a generalist degree awarded after two years with the possibility of specialist study to a Master's degree standard after a further two years, or a Diploma after one year. The appeal of the proposal lay in its call to adapt institutions and courses towards a system on the verge of mass higher education for two years at least, *and* the insistence on strict selection for the specialist courses. Although egalitarians and selectivists might rejoice, the Swann Working Group distanced themselves from the proposals as 'interesting', 'provocative', but 'hardly practical'.[67] The basic objection was that the proposals were unlikely to be politically acceptable – 'requiring too much of an upheaval in our accustomed habits to be readily acceptable'.[68] It was taken as evidence of a lack of interest in practical politics that the proposal retained the term 'centres of excellence', which had caused offence in many universities and had been replaced in official language by the term 'focal centres of specialisation'. The Working Group preferred to emphasise the term generalist and to cite examples of known developments. This strategy rested on the assumption that curricula were better developed by university teachers than by central committees. In this sense the ambiguity of the generalist concept was a strength since it left open many possibilities for local interpretation. It is likely that the success of an advisory body will depend on the alliances which it can build with outside interest groups and for the longer term the Working Group were sensitive to the autonomy of their peers in the universities.

One senior civil servant described the CSP and its associated committees as 'in-service training for Fellows of the Royal Society'. The nub of truth in this remark can be seen in the extent to which the Working Group became responsible for carrying out many of their own recommendations. When the Working Group recommended that the Committee of Vice-Chancellors and Principals carry out curriculum studies, the Working Group contained two vice-chancellors.[69] When the Working Group recommended the development of generalist curricula, they could look to their own institutions.[70] When the Working Group made recommendations to the UGC they included an assessor and a future chairman of the UGC and similarly when they made recommendations to the SRC they had included an assessor and future members.[71] When the Working Group made recommendations to Government, they included a future chief scientist to the Department of Industry.[72] And when discussions on industry – education relations were raised in professional bodies, the Working Group could carry its message into the Council of Engineering Institutions, the Royal Society, the Institution of Mechanical Engineers, the Institution of Electrical Engineers, the Institute of Physics, the Royal Institute of Chemistry and the Institution of Metallurgists.

In retrospect the recommendations to experiment still appear sensible because the Report highlighted the enormous gaps in our knowledge about how the educational system functions. There was ignorance about the curriculum, and therefore about the utility of 'specialist' and 'generalist' categories, hence the need for a recommendation on curriculum investigations. Some contemporary research by Hutchings suggested that the extent of specialisation in physics courses had been overstated.[73] There was ignorance about the influence of course structures on student career preferences and several studies suggest a much more limited influence on students by faculty than is supposed in the Swann Working Group.[74] Finally there was even ignorance about the extent to which the education system could be controlled as distinct from administered, for it was not clear how far SRC award policy or UGC grants influenced the growth of university research staff.

AN EPITAPH FOR SCIENTIFIC AND TECHNOLOGICAL MANPOWER FORECASTING

In 1976 the House of Commons Select Committee on Science and Technology, a Committee of Members of Parliament which advises Parliament on scientific and technological affairs (see Figure 6.1), urged the Government to resume forecasting and the Triennial Surveys and to give science and technology special treatment in higher education.[75] The Government rejected the advice on the Triennial Surveys and the resumption of forecasting on the grounds that: (a) the very success of the efforts to build up the stock of qualified scientists and engineers raised very serious problems of survey inaccuracies as the numbers grew; (b) the magnitude of the survey posed additional administrative burdens on companies when satisfactory alternative sources of information were available on employment in the Population Censuses; and (c) there were several problems in the interpretation of the surveys.[76] This recent exchange of views underlines two points in this chapter. There is the perennial desire of politicians to gear the educational system to industrial requirements and there is the change of view of

Government about the possibilities of achieving such a relationship through forecasting.

It is clear that the problems of interpretation were known to Government and to the forecasters at the beginning of the 1960s. Yet despite the published caveats and the diffidence about their meaning, the Triennial Surveys were used to build a case against an educational system failing to meet the requirements of industry and schools. At the end of the 1960s that argument was badly undermined by two developments. Firstly the Gannicot and Blaug critique challenged the intellectual credibility of short-term forecasting based on employer opinions and long-run forecasting based on needs identified by a group with a clear vested interest. This cautionary message to Government to be wary of partisan accounts appears to have been absorbed. Since 1969 Government has tended to rely on intramural inquiries on broad national issues, for example, from the Department of Employment, or to the extramural agencies on more specific manpower issues, for example, National Economic Development Office inquiries on the manufacturing industry or the Committee of Inquiry into the Engineering Profession.[77] In all these inquiries salary has been more prominent as an area for data collection and as an indicator of the state of the labour market and the discussion has been more informed by economic analysis.[78] Perhaps the more damaging attack on short-run forecasting and the 'shortage' conclusion came with the second development, the cut-back of industrial recruitment programmes in the early 1970s.[79] Newspaper headlines proclaimed 'Engineers fight for jobs'.[80] And with the change from a Labour to a Conservative Government in 1970, Mr Heath became the first postwar British Prime Minister to caution against the over-production of graduates.[81] From Morrison and Attlee through Churchill and Eden to Wilson, for a quarter century, British Prime Ministers had emphasised the importance of the educational system to industrial vitality against a background of 'shortage'. Although the present (at time of writing) Labour Government has expressed concern about the quality and quantity of engineering education, there is a possibility that the manpower problems of British industry will be tackled directly through the examination of utilisation. This was the line of inquiry which the Swann Working Group closed off a decade ago.

The longer-term recommendations for broader-based generalist science courses met with agreement from supporters and critics alike. Shortening the lead time for planning through shifting the start of specialisation on to postgraduate study or training was attractive to those concerned with manpower issues, but a criticism of premature specialisation had been an important feature of the Robbins Report on educational grounds. Yet it is clear that the specific science-based generation concept rested on inadequate information about university curricula and dubious models of the ways in which education relates to jobs and employment. Again it is not clear how need was expected to be translated into demand by employers other than by their need to recruit from among the able who would inevitably go to university.[82] It is not clear that employers have been able to go beyond fairly bland statements of their requirements of the educational system, which usually emphasise character and motivation, and it is not clear that they are prepared to commit resources to training to the kinds of levels hoped for by the Swann Working Group.[83]

One defence offered sometimes for planning is that a plan unlocks resources, providing a stimulus to decision-making and action. Without the plan, it is argued, there will be no criteria for decision-making. Given that governments find it difficult to avoid decisions, it is attractive to governments to have a plan. In the case of the Swann Working Group it could be argued that the Working Group protected the morale of the scientific community by producing an agreed report which provided a rationale for implementing the slowing down of the rate of growth of Research Council spending. In this way the scientific community was protected against arbitrary cuts. Moreover the Interim Report had paved the way for the major battle on the science budget, the 300 GEV accelerator project, by drawing attention to the relative flows of physicists into industrial employment compared to academic and government employment. In 1967 the CSP was asked to comment on the proposal that Britain should contribute to the proposed 300 GEV machine for research into nuclear physics at an estimated cost of £180 m. After approving comments from the SRC and CSP, the Government declined to participate, noting that the project would take a large proportion of the SRC budget and make little contribution to the economy through technology or trained manpower. The CSP report was a shrewd document in recommending participation on scientific grounds, subject to safeguards on costs and the SRC budget for other disciplines, for the listed advantages and disadvantages included the economic and manpower cases. It was widely recognised within the CSP that the safeguards could not be given but the unpleasant decision was left to Government and cross-disciplinary squabbles were contained.[84] To defend forecasts and plans as aids to decision-making is a weak defence if the decisions themselves are judged undesirable by their outcomes. Although the UGC accepted the relatively faster rate of growth of arts and social science rather than science and technology undergraduate places, to the chagrin of some Swann Working Group members who favoured the direction of applicants, the UGC continued to adopt the old two-thirds science and technology versus one-third arts and social science ratio on the capital programme. This policy owed much to the shortage and national need accounts which had emerged from the forecasting bodies. It was not stopped until the UGC was investigated by the Committee on Public Accounts.[85]

The Swann Report was a highly political document. It was political by definition, for the Committee's terms of reference were to advise on policy, but it was political in the more popular sense too, in that the Report was an astute contrivance, drafted with an acute ear to soundings on the politically acceptable.

By the time that the Swann Committee was concluding its business it had become embroiled with another strident interest group within the educational system: the radical students. This group posed a challenge to the scientific community whether its views were expressed as critiques of the perversion of science for industrial-military purposes or as romantic rejections of economic growth.[86] Dismay about the radical students was acute among some members of the Swann Committee because the challenge came from within the universities and because a critique of economic growth undermined the basis of the Committee's work. Once the goal of economic growth and the application of science and technology to socially approved purposes was accepted, then the Swann Committee's task could be seen as the identification of technological imperatives. The technological imperatives model of social development is a very apolitical process because the element of choice is de-emphasised and the political task becomes a largely administrative affair.

In the Swann Working Group model of science – higher education – industry relations, industry was becoming increasingly dependent upon scientific knowledge and expertise. Industry was viewed as the source of wealth and determinant of the standard of living in industrial society, ('the most immediately productive sector').[87] Because it was dependent upon scientific and technological expertise, industry would be forced to recruit from the major suppliers of expertise in the higher education system.[88] Industry would be forced because, although this pattern was evident only in the science-based sectors in the 1960s, it was anticipated that traditional industries would either disappear or would become transformed by the diffusion of scientific and technological applications.

Recruitment from higher education would be forced because the 'more able' would continue into higher education. These developments were seen as part of an unfolding logic of social development, what the working Group termed 'the inexorable march of science and technology'.[89] From this model of technological society the task for forecasters is that of the identification of the 'imperatives' or preconditions for economic and technological growth. One of the central imperatives is the recognition of an interventionist role for the state, for example, in underwriting the demand for science and technology and in underwriting the supply of highly qualified manpower. Although outside their terms of reference, the Swann Working Group urged Government to favour industrial R and D through fiscal and procurement policies.[90] On the educational front, it seemed quite natural that Government should seek to match the educational system to the requirements of industry.

Similar models of technological imperatives had their intellectual champions in the early 1960s.[91] They had their critics too. The critics emphasised the variety of social arrangements compatible with advanced industrialism.[92] In Britain some political commentators emphasised the similarities in structure and functioning of the two major political parties, whereas other commentators emphasised the importance of ideological differences in shaping conduct.[93] In 1970 the new Conservative Government challenged the necessity for the kind of economic planning developed in the 1960s. Having been closely associated with the 'white heat of technological revolution', the forecasting bodies lost favour as that vision faded. That vision had faded before the electoral demise of the Labour Government. The forecasters had lost faith in forecasting and the administrative departments had grown lukewarm in their support. Technology had been oversold in the general view and education had been oversold in the Swann Report. The change of Government set the seal on the final disbanding of the forecasting bodies.

A decade later, interviews with the former members of the Swann Working Group revealed a sense of disillusionment with various aspects of forecasting. Some members of the Working Group rejected the possibilities for forecasting in the light of the large number of unknowns in both supply and demand factors.[94] Other members of the Working Group were disappointed by the failures of the various bodies – industry, the universities and Government – to translate recommendations into effective policy. The universities were thought to have been slow to respond to the initiatives of the UGC and the SRC. Industry disappointed by recruitment cutbacks, the slow development of training and post-experience provision, and continuing reports of wide-spread malutilisation of professional manpower. However, former members of the Secretariat were much less disappointed with the Reports and activities of the Working Group, which may indicate a more sanguine view of the power of advisory bodies to influence events.

It remains to be seen whether the intramural planning and consultation documents which have tended to replace advisory bodies will be any less prey to partisan interests or more effective in stimulating public awareness of planning issues. Although it became the medium of a partial view the Swann Working Group had attempted to stimulate discussion of manpower problems and policies through conferences and the scientific press.[95]

The Swann Report was very much a document of its time, sharing with many other reports the belief that the educational system could be a ready instrument of social policy.[96] An awareness of our limited understanding of the past, a greater humility on the part of educationists, and a more modest expectation of the educational system's ability to shape our future might be the more important legacies of these exercises in forecasting. Such an epitaph has been provided by Sir Michael Swann:

I know that I myself have contributed handsomely to the notion that education is the best or even the only way to put the world outside to rights. In a report on scientific manpower, which dissected the ills of science and technology, the Committee of which I was Chairman came down unhesitatingly and with my encouragement and firm approval, in favour of university education as the only practicable way of curing the woes of British industry. Academics did not like the idea, but not so far as I can make out, because they doubted the power and influence of education. They simply didn't like the implicit criticism of universities. It is right, of course, that educationalists should believe in what they do, and forgivable if they somewhat oversell their wares. But it is a dangerous situation when they acquiesce in an illusion. For it must soon become all too clear that a society where education is doubled and quadrupled does not suddenly become different and better. There are a few signs of such a realisation already.[97]

NOTES

1. I have many debts for generous help and encouragement. Professor Chris Freeman and Tom Whiston invited a manpower contribution and provided a stimulus to follow a longstanding interest in manpower policy development. Members of the Working Group – Sir Michael Swann, Professor Sir Frederick Dainton, Professor Sir Brian Pippard, Dr F. E. Jones, Professors Hutton and Ball – gave time from their busy lives for interview. Dr Davies responded directly to my questions. The Institute of Manpower Studies Joint Research Support Fund provided financial assistance for my travels. Timothy John McCormick, born 20th October 1977 added urgency to my study and reminded a distracted father that the future is as worthy of contemplation as the past.
2. K. Gannicot and M. Blaug 'Manpower Forecasting since Robbins: a science lobby in action', *Higher Education Review*, Vol. 2, No. 1, September 1969.
3. Advisory Council for Scientific Policy (1961), *The Long-Term Demand for Scientific Manpower*, Cmnd 1490, London: HMSO.
4. Advisory Council for Scientific Policy (1962), *Annual Report 1960–61*, Cmnd 1592, London: HMSO.
5. See, for example, Committee on Higher Education, *Higher Education: Report*, Cmnd 2154, HMSO, London (especially Chapter 6). See also C. A. Moser and P. R. G. Layard, 'Planning the scale of higher education in Britain: some statistical problems', *Journal of the Royal Statistical Society*, December 1964.
6. *Higher Education: Evidence*, Part 1, Vol. B. pp. 431–3.
7. *Higher Education*, para. 189–94.
8. The 1956 forecast had assumed 1:1 labour output rates and a 4 per cent per annum rate of economic growth, whereas over the period 1956–9 the growth of qualified scientist and engineer employment had been 8·5 per cent with a rate of economic growth of only 2·1 per cent.
9. For a discussion of the controversies over Government policy for civil science and technology in this period, see Norman Vig (1966), *Science and Technology in British Politics*, Oxford: Pergamon Press.
10. P. Gummett and R. Williams, 'Assessing the Council for Scientific Policy', *Nature*, Vol. 240, 8 December 1972.
11. Professor (now Sir) Michael Swann joined the Committee on Scientific Manpower in 1963.
12. The programme was set out in an interim report, *A Review of the Scope and Problems of Scientific and Technological Manpower*, Cmnd 2800, London: HMSO, 1965.
13. The 1965 Triennial Survey broke new ground by the inclusion of technicians but the provisions for this development had been made by the Committee on Scientific Manpower, *Report of the 1965 Triennial Manpower Survey of Engineers, Technologists, Scientists and Technical Supporting Staff*, Cmnd 3103, London: HMSO, 1966.
14. The Bosworth Working Group reported in *Education and Training Requirements for the Electrical and Mechanical Manufacturing Industries*, London: HMSO, 1966, but the Ball Working Group submitted only an

internal report before the disbanding of the Standing Committee, the Committee on Manpower Resources for Science and Technology in 1969.
15. *Report of the Enquiry into the Flow of Candidates in Science and Technology into Higher Education*, Cmnd 3541, London: HMSO, 1967.
16. Lord Hailsham, *Science and Government*, Eighth Fawley Lecture, University of Southampton, 9 November 1961.
17. Council for Scientific Policy, *Report on Science Policy*, Cmnd 3007, London: HMSO, 1966, paras. 9–12.
18. Advisory Council for Science Policy, *Annual Report 1963–4*, Cmnd 2538, London: HMSO, 1964.
19. *Report on Science Policy*, p. 13.
20. Parameters was dropped between the Interim Report (Cmnd 3102) and the Main Report (Cmnd 3760). An additional reason for the omission was that parameter was too esoteric a term for a report intended for a wide readership and political impact.
21. *Interim Report*, Cmnd 3102, p. 27.
22. *The Flow into Employment of Scientists, Engineers and Technologists*, Cmnd 3760.
23. *Report of the 1965 Triennial Manpower Survey of Engineers, Technologists, Scientists and Technical Supporting Staff*, Cmnd 3103, para. 41.
24. *Ibid.*, paras. 50–2, 79–80.
25. *The Flow into Employment of Scientists, Engineers and Technologists*, Cmnd 3760, para. 4.
26. *Ibid.*, para. 66.
27. *Ibid.*, Figures 1 and 2, and para. 18.
28. *Ibid.*, paras. 23–31, and Annexe G.
29. *Ibid.*, paras. 28–9 for a discussion of two further projections which worked backwards from the UGC planning figure to examine different distributions between coursework and research.
30. *Ibid.*, para 37.
31. *Ibid.*, paras. 23–32.
32. *Interim Report*, Cmnd 3102, para. 21.
33. *The Flow into Employment of Scientists, Engineers and Technologists*, Cmnd 3760, p. viii, paras 88–90.
34. *Ibid.*, paras. 93–9.
35. Ministry of Labour, *Occupational Changes 1951–61: Manpower Studies No. 6*. London: HMSO, 1968 and *Electronics: Manpower Studies No. 5*, London: HMSO, 1967.
36. A summary of the study was attached as Annexe F to the Main Report, Cmnd 3760, and a full account was published as *The Employment of Highly Specialised Graduates: a comparative study in the U.K. and the U.S.A*, Science Policy Studies No. 3, Department of Education and Science, London: HMSO, 1968.
37. McCarthy assumed that the omissions would cancel each other out, for example, that the ex.CATS as *specialist* institutions would have *specialist* courses which outweighed the multidisciplinary emphasis of new universities and the common core of Scottish universities; *ibid.*, p. 8.
38. For example, generalist jobs required 3 months' training or less whereas specialist jobs required 1–2 years' training.

39. For an example of the attempted identification of 'liberal' with 'vocational', see B. Holloway, 'Higher Education and Employment: a view from the interface' in F. R. Jevons and B. Turner (eds.) (1972), *What Kinds of Graduate Do We Need?* London: Oxford University Press.
40. *Interim Report*, Cmnd 3102, p. 26.
41. *Ibid.*, para. 33.
42. *The Flow into Employment of Scientists, Engineers and Technologists*, Cmnd 3760, para. 192.
43. *Ibid.*, para. 158.
44. Council for Scientific Policy, *Second Report on Science Policy*, Cmnd 3420, London: HMSO, 1967, para. 54.
45. *The Flow into Employment of Scientists, Engineers and Technologists*, p. 3.
46. *Ibid.*, para. 61–2.
47. *Ibid.*, para. 113.
48. Compare the accounts of innovation in physics-based industry (Professor Pippard) and innovation in chemistry-based industry (Dr Neuth), *ibid.*, Annexe D.
49. K. Gannicot and M. Blaug, *op. cit.*
50. Professor Hutton had collaborated with a sociologist in a study of engineers (J. Gerstl and S. P. Hutton (1966), *Engineers: the Anatomy of a Profession*, London: Tavistock) and Duncan Davies had interpreted economics for technologists: D. Davies and M. C. McCarthy (1967), *Technological Economics*, London: Wiley.
51. R. K. Kelsall et al. (1970), *Graduates: the Sociology of an Elite*, London: Methuen.
52. Hutchings had noted that a higher proportion of applied scientists compared to pure scientists come from the top income groups and from independent schools.
53. Among the politicians, Mrs Williams and other Ministers launched a campaign to secure more female entrants to engineering studies and among social scientists, Celia Davies noted the pool of ability among girls not proceeding to further study: *Changes in Subject Choice at School and University*, London: Weidenfeld and Nicholson, 1967.
54. *The Flow into Employment of Scientists, Engineers and Technologists*, Cmnd 3760, para. 181.
55. G. C. Wilkinson and J. D. Mace (1973), 'Shortage or surplus of engineers: a review of recent U.K. evidence', *British Journal of Industrial Relations*, vol. 2, no. 1.
56. *The Flow into Employment of Scientists, Engineers and Technologists*, Cmnd 3760, paras. 192–5.
57. *Ibid.*, para. 182.
58. *Ibid.*, para. 183, yet the interim report urged employers to 'bid'; *Interim Report*, para. 41.
59. E. Rudd, 'The rate of economic growth, technology and the Phd', *Minerva*, vol. VI, no. 3, Spring 1968, especially pp. 381–2.
60. The Working Group was not entirely averse to stepping outside its terms of reference, however; see the Main Report, *Cmnd 3760*, p. vii.
61. *Ibid.*, p. 3 (my emphasis).
62. *Ibid.*, para. 6.

63. *Ibid.*, para. 187.
64. *Ibid.*, para. 119.
65. *Ibid.*, p. vii.
66. *Ibid.*, paras. 120–2.
67. However the Working Group reproduced the proposals in Annexe E in order to stimulate discussion; *ibid.*, pp. 106–10.
68. *Ibid.*, para. 168.
69. These were Swann (Edinburgh) and Dainton (Nottingham). In addition the Standing Committee, the Committee on Manpower Resources for Science and Technology, included Venables (Aston in Birmingham) and Bragg (later at Brunel).
70. In addition Duncan Davies and his colleagues could point to the development of industrial science at Stirling University.
71. Professor Dainton became Chairman of the UGC in 1973 and Dr Davies was a member of the SRC in 1969–73.
72. Dr Davies became Chief Scientist in the Department of Industry in 1977.
73. D. Hutchings (1971), 'First degree courses in physics', *The Physics Bulletin*, vol. 22.
74. Hutchings found the correlation between course structure and student employment destinations; *ibid.*
75. House of Commons Select Committee on Science and Technology, *Third Report – University–Industry Relations*, HCP 680, London: HMSO, 1976.
76. *University–Industry Relations*, The Government's Reply to the Third Report of the Select Committee on Science and Technology, session 1975–6, Cmnd 6928, London: HMSO, 1977.
77. See, for example, (a) Department of Employment, *Employment Prospects for the Highly Qualified*, Manpower Paper No. 8, London: HMSO, 1974, (b) NEDO, *Shortages of Qualified Engineers*, London, 1975.
78. *Ibid.*, see also the British Association for the Advancement of Science, *Education Engineers and Manufacturing Industry; A Report to the British Association Coordinating Group*, University of Aston, Birmingham, August 1977.
79. See NEDO, *op. cit.*
80. *Guardian*, 5 July 1971.
81. *House of Commons Debates, Official Report*, 1972, vol. 836, pp. 193–5.
82. *The Flow into Employment of Scientists, Engineers and Technologists*, p. 3.
83. In a paper which voiced its scepticism of attempts to provide numerical forecasts, the CBI reported the main concern of employers in terms such as 'poor personal ambition and little professional commitment; a lack of flexibility, breadth of vision and creativity in problem solving; need of close supervision; and deficiencies in inter-personal and communicative skills'; 'Qualified scientists and engineers – industry's requirements from the higher education system', *Supplement to CBI Education and Training Bulletin*, May 1976. The 1975 CEI Survey of Professional Engineers, however, noted relatively greater dissatisfaction among members with initial industrial training than with formal education, CEI, *The 1975 Survey of Professional Engineers*, London: CEI, 1975.
84. Council for Scientific Policy (1968), *The Proposed 300 GEV Accelerator Project*, Cmnd 3503, London: HMSO.

85. Committee of Public Accounts, *Third Report*, 1969–70, London: HMSO, paras. 114–63.
86. See, for example, the paper by Professor Swann and the subsequent discussion at the Liberal Science Conference, Liberal Science and Technology Panel, *The Sources and Uses of Scientific Manpower*, Orpington: Laser, 1969.
87. *Interim Report*, Cmnd 3102, para. 7.
88. See note 8.
89. *The Flow into Employment of Scientists, Engineers and Technologists*, p. 32.
90. *Ibid.*, para. 180.
91. See, for example, C. Kerr et al. (1960), *Industrialism and Industrial Man*, Cambridge, Mass.: Harvard University Press, and J. K. Galbraith (1967), *The New Industrial State*, London: Hamish Hamilton.
92. See, for example, the discussion of sociological perspectives in P. Halmos (ed.) (1964), *The Development of Industrial Societies: Sociological Review Monograph*, No. 8.
93. Compare, for example, R. T. McKenzie (1955), *British Political Parties*, London: Heinemann', and S. Beer (1965), *Modern British Politics*, London, Faber.
94. Professor Sir Frederick Dainton, 'The siren song of manpower planning', *New Scientist*, 7 April 1977, and for some wry comments D. Davies, 'The short and the long term', in F. R. Jevons and H. D. Turner (eds.), *op. cit.*
95. See, for example, the letter from the Chairman of the Working Group asking for responses to the Interim Report, *Nature* 5065, 26 November 1966.
96. At the other end of the educational system, this was the era which saw an attempt to tackle social and economic inequality through 'compensatory education'.
97. Professor Swann, *New Scientist*, 22 October 1970.

7 Population Forecasting: Social and Educational Policy

TOM WHISTON

INTRODUCTION

Planning without prior knowledge or reasonable expectations is a risky business. In an attempt to minimise the risk element in planning, then, limited cognisance of future estimates is often relied upon. However reliance upon 'future estimates' is itself a risky business. We merely, therefore, replace one form of risk-taking for another. The extent to which such associative risk can be minimised is dependent upon several major resources: time, effort, expertise, comprehension, theory development and methodological sophistication – as applied to population forecasting. A critical failure in any one of these resources may ensure a gross error or distortion in any attempt at 'future prediction'. And always one is faced with the dilemma that modelling of dynamic processes centred on past or present events may be of only very limited application to the future. People's attitudes (and actions) change. This being so, then the 'honest forecaster' – viewed here as one who openly 'qualifies' his estimates according to the limitations of his own assumptions – is more desirable than the forecaster who distorts by selection without explicit presentation.

Now in many areas planning horizons are usually comparatively short-term. The temporal scale over which we feel we can sensibly control, modify or influence, is of the order of a few months or at most five or seven years. Continual monitoring, review and problem redefinition is the order of the day – for instance with respect to 'economic control'. However certain plans, once initiated, may take decades or even centuries to implement (the development of economic and industrial empires; the building of a cathedral) and implicit in the plans is the overriding assumption that there will be people around in the future with similar values or tastes.

Similarly we must recognise that planning is *necessarily selective* – and commitment often concedes irreversible consequences (e.g. population policies which are enshrined in sterilisation campaigns form a particularly significant example of a potentially sad use of erroneous forecasting); on the other hand, the starvation or malnutrition of a significant proportion of a nation's populace, through the non-implementation of an appropriate food/agricultural policy may reflect not only an abuse of authority, but also an abuse of forecasting – in the sense of unjustified ignorance. Between over-use and under-use lies a precipitous path. Error may lie in the formulation of the forecast itself (for a forecast, like a policy, is formulated) or with the selective interaction of policy and forecast. Abuse may reside in use or non-use.

This chapter seeks to explore some population forecasting attempts and their subsequent interaction with 'policy'.

It was suggested above that much policy-making relates to comparatively short time-scales – no more than a few years; in this sense demography (of 'already born populations') is on fairly safe ground, where mere head-counts suffice (though these are difficult enough to achieve – see Appendix I to this chapter) and assumptions relate primarily to the life expectancy of particular age-groups and certain net migratory influences. Thus the head-count of 0–5 year-olds of the UK population tends to define the school population which will 'move through' the 5–10 year-old portion of the education system for the next 5 years (and for corresponding later periods); the 0–10 year-olds reveal the pattern for the next 10 and so on.

Similarly the distribution profile for the age group 0–16 tells us much about new entries into the future 'work-force population' (for constant male and female participation rates) over the next 16 years and the age-group 50–65 tells us quite a bit about the scale of pensions over the next period (15 years) and to a more limited degree the load-factor on the NHS, the number of hospital beds which may be required, etc. To a much more limited degree, the distribution in the present 0–15 age-group informs us of social service requirements 50–65 years from now – but we do not make our plans now! Equally, and of considerable importance from the standpoint of long-range planning, a complete monitoring of a country's population now, tells us in some ways more about the distant future than it does about tomorrow. Embodied in this irony is the argument that whilst mortality and migratory rates (wars and epidemics notwithstanding) may remain fairly constant, fertility-rates may show significant fluctuations and shifts. We are thus in the position of possibly being able to forecast some population characteristics in the long-term future with more confidence than we are able to adequately account for the near. Demographic considerations are therefore a combination of projection/forecasting based on assumptions relating to longevity and procreativity of present populations; the finer the mapping of the present and the better we understand the socio-cultural determinants of procreativity the greater the potential for planning and 'rational policy'.

Forecasting comes more into its own when the lead times for policy enactment are greater than the age-cohort which we can describe, and this implies estimating the 'unborn'. The assumptions in regard to fertility-rate should then be carefully considered, together with the cyclic nature of number of births due to the uneven distribution of previous generations.

On the 'applied side' the potential use for demographic forecasts might seem to be immense – e.g. social services, education, housing, market profiles, employment, etc, – not to mention with respect to population policy itself. However there are wider and more subtle socio-political uses, where the estimation of future population may be seen as a political tool (see Meadows and Meadows, 1972 and subsequent critiques (Cole et al, 1973 and Freeman and Jahoda, 1978) for example). This is not to say that political objectives are acceptable or unacceptable – but it does suggest that there must be much care taken in analysing the forecasting procedure and assumptions, and the subsequent relationship to policy-making. Dissemination factors may be critical here since 'in-house' criticism may not reach the 'lay' policy-makers. Population forecasts and demographic analysis occur at many levels ranging from local (sub-national) resource-spending issues to global considerations and, whilst in the former case there are often detailed demographic data available, in the latter it is only in very aggregate form. We will examine three 'levels' of forecast here in order to assess the effect on policy. But before considering them in any detail, it is perhaps worth making a few general points which relate to most demographic predictions.

Firstly as to methodology, the forecasting of future population size and structure depends on four main factors: (i) accurate mapping of the present population distribution; (ii) assumptions concerning fertility rates (and family completion cycles); (iii) assumptions regarding mortality rate; (iv) corrections due to net migratory effects – at local or national levels: migration also carries implications, to a lesser degree, at the global level, if one recognises a socio-cultural modification of fertility rates. A failure of any one of these factors may 'upset' a forecast (or may even help it), and the longer the time-scale considered, the greater the room for 'multiplier effects' to operate in relation to the forecast.

Similarly, the greater the degree of aggregation – e.g. across countries or ethnic groups, with differing fertility rates, then the greater the room for error.

Secondly, as to policy formulation: population estimates, whether of the single 'best fit' types, or of the 'variant' form, do not *imply* policy, but they should merely provide background for policy. Factors and difficulties which apply now may not operate in the future; for example in relation to localised food shortages and global population growth, many policy-makers (and the public who support them in office) view 'the problem' in one of two ways: either policy geared to population reduction, and/or increased food supply through an agricultural policy. However there is much evidence to support arguments about a malfunctioning distribution and allocation dimension to the problem. Modification of this problem implies, in part, a change in situation ethics.

Similarly, in debates concerning ethnic relations relative to population growth; to *assume* a constant fertility-rate is to provide the means of a biased forecast and unjustified policy.

Policy can never be 'neutral' but it can aim to be equitable and rational. The extent to which a particular policy is fed by a one-sided forecast is a measure of its social arbitrariness. The ultimate test perhaps is the degree of impartiality of the forecasting techniques and the mode of selection for policy.

Thirdly, as to detail: trends and mere numbers are not sufficient. We are influenced by changing attitudes and the past. With respect to attitudes, family size is changing and despite reduction in absolute numbers there is an increase in the number of households occurring – of great importance to housing policy; with respect to the past, previous 'birth bulges' (despite present falling fertility-rates) will almost certainly ensure future mini-bulges which are of particular importance to the social services and to educational policy. Without 'detail' in such forecasting areas imprecision in planning occurs, which might have high social costs.

It cannot be argued too strongly that if justifiable policy decisions are to be made based on demographic considerations then there is an essential requirement for detailed and thorough demographic analysis. Demographic forecasting or projection is in itself a very hazardous profession — and one which belies the smooth curve observed in so many over-confident predictions. It is perhaps ironical that as we move from narrow to wider organisational levels, from sub-national issues to global considerations, then we find an inverse relationship between the demographic data available on the one hand, and the importance of the issues requiring clarification on the other.

For as Figure 7.1 indicates, as we move from sub-national policy issues through national issues on to international regional issues and finally to global issues, though the panorama for decision-making becomes increasingly important (often tragically so), the strength of the data base diminishes.

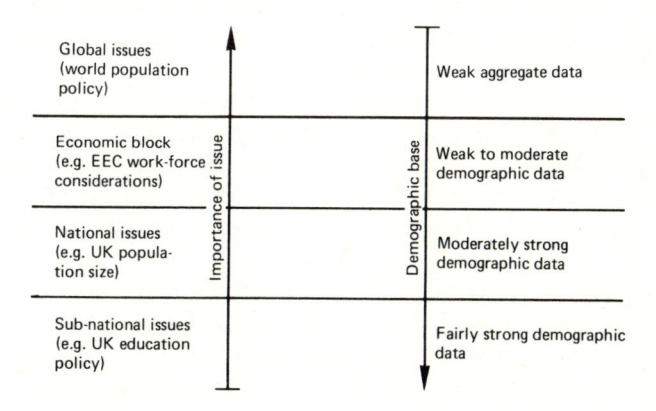

Importance of issue	Demographic base
Global issues (world population policy)	Weak aggregate data
Economic block (e.g. EEC work-force considerations)	Weak to moderate demographic data
National issues (e.g. UK population size)	Moderately strong demographic data
Sub-national issues (e.g. UK education policy)	Fairly strong demographic data

FIGURE 7.1. Decreasing demographic base as policy problems increase in severity

There is perhaps a lesson to be learnt from this which centres upon a consideration of 'system boundaries'. As the boundaries become looser, as we move from sub-national to global issues, then a demographic description becomes necessarily (?) weaker. At the same time we must also recognise that the policy-making/control dimension which parallels the expansion of system boundaries also becomes weaker. Perhaps there is a symbiotic or structural/functional relationship to be identified here. On the one hand global issues are poorly defined in demographic terms. Equally there is a poorly defined power structure (e.g. the UN) to implement policy. At national levels the reverse is true; some national governments have more powers of jurisdiction, more autonomy and hence in some senses more power of control. At the same time they often possess a surer demographic knowledge of their own population structure. We may be observing here a functional evolution principle which demonstrates its own feedback loops. 'Tighter' institutional control requires more organised demographic detail, whilst finer provision allows for tighter policy control ('fine tuning'). The circle is therefore complete. It is perhaps interesting from this standpoint to recognise that this principle may also to a limited degree apply across nations – the governments of the USA, Europe and the USSR having 'finer' demographic data to hand than many Asian and African countries. Perhaps we observe here a form of self-regulating institutional control which is to our benefit; when knowledge is weak, the means of control are crude. This may be advantageous since fine control is not beneficial when on spurious courses – for global issues, the 'correct' course is not yet obvious. If we did have much more finely structured demographic detail at the global level, then problems could be more precisely stated and alternative policies more clearly examined as to their appropriateness. Stated most baldly, with more detailed knowledge comes the opportunity (but not the guarantee – that is an entirely different matter) to move from prejudice – as reflected in arbitrary ideology – to a more rational, coherent and consistent system of government and government policy.

'Precision of government, based upon detailed sociological understanding', which is itself based upon a detailed collation of social statistics and demographic understanding has been emphasised by many writers (see Freeman and Jahoda, 1978; Kahn and Wiener, 1967). But this says nothing of the ethical and moral standing of the government (see Mill, 1910; Pateman, 1970; Shanks, 1962). Policies of encouragement and inducement (say of increased family size) through fiscal encouragement, taxation and state provision of social welfare, maternity grants, day provision, education, etc, offer a surer means of finer ethical and moral considerations (not to speak of individual freedom of choice) than do crude enforcement of sterilisation programmes or mass propaganda campaigns. As to effectiveness . . . ? (It is interesting to note that the scale of government spending on collecting statistics has reached very high proportions. The Department of Industry spent £7·7 million of 1976 in collecting statistics (£5·6 million the previous year); whilst the Department of Transport's cost of collecting statistics has increased from 550 000 in 1974 to £1·95 million in 1976. The Office of Population Censuses and Surveys spent £1·1 million in 1976. (See

'Spending on Statistics – near public scandal', *The Times*, 2 December 1976, p. 4.))

Social shaping thus finds many routes, many outlets and many dependencies on demographic insight; the more detailed the mapping of population distribution and the greater our understanding of social and cultural mechanisms, the greater the potential for policy. Let us examine these problems at three levels of complexity – though these levels are not entirely independent: (1) Global demographic issues; (2) National demographic monitoring (the UK); (3) A more detailed examination of sub-national policy issue in relation to demographic forecasts: Educational Policy.

GLOBAL FORECASTING AND ITS EFFECT ON POLICY

It is not the main purpose of this article to review this area, for which many texts are available (Page, 1973; Glass and Revelle, 1972; Symonds and Gardner, 1973; Myrdal, 1968). However, from the standpoint of 'Uses and Abuses' of forecasting, it is important to make a few remarks. Firstly there are at least three important 'actors' or 'camps' who are concerned with global population forecasts and their implications for social policy: the UN, the pro-Malthusians and the anti-Malthusians. The backcloth for all discussion and argument is the ever increasing (inferred) scale of world population growth, the problems of undernutrition in many parts of the Third World, problems of economic and social development which are underpinned by demographic considerations, and allied problems of employment, education and social wellbeing.

Put very concisely one might summarise that:

(a) the UN is concerned with both immediate and pressing needs relating to present population structures, in particular in the 'underdeveloped nations' of Africa, Asia and Latin America where problems are legion; and also by way of long-term policy with future patterns of population growth. 'Policy' may take many forms: birth control campaigns, food distribution and agricultural programmes, and encouragement of a variety of technological and industrial programmes. Superimposed on this is the educational tradition of organisations like UNESCO.

(b) The pro-Malthusians (Meadows et al., 1972) are of the opinion that, without a fundamental and far-reaching population control programme of worldwide proportions, mankind is doomed to failure due to the outstripping of physical resources, food supply and the like. Problems concerned with pollution, with urban development, with transport, with social disruption, are all seen as inevitable consequences of uncontrolled population growth.

(c) On the other hand, the anti-Malthusians (Cole et al, 1973) do not share this gloom concerning the description, consequences and therefore remedies.

Essentially the latter 'camp' reflects the arguments of two interacting subsidiary groups; the socio-economists (see Freeman's Introduction to Cole et al., 1973) and the technologists (Kahn and Wiener, 1967), and both receive a limited amount of support from a group of agriculture analysts (Lappé and Collins, 1977). The socio-economists would argue that fertility rates adapt to increasing economic, educational and social wellbeing – that the 'insurance value' of large families does not apply as the industrial and economic structure becomes more 'sophisticated'; whilst the second group (those who place their faith in technological development) would agree that man's creative, innovatory and applied technological capacity will enable him to offset all difficulties. Arguments range from the 'green revolution' on the food side (Johnson, 1972) to 'conservation programmes' (Schumaker, 1973; Illich, 1974) and renewable energy resources (nuclear, wind, solar, etc) in relation to materials and energy (Foley, 1976) . Each of these groups becomes involved in support of particular forecasts (see Kahn and Wiener, 1967; Kahn et al., 1977; Mesarovic and Pestel, 1974) which have demographic overtones.

The relevance of all this to population forecasting is twofold: various 'camps' may tend to use techniques which support their own particular case, and/or interpretations (and hence policy recommendations and arguments or focus) will accord with the particular outlook of the protagonist.

Now the gathering of a substantial, reliable and accurate demographic base on a worldwide scale is no mean task. Many countries, especially those of Asia, China, Africa and Latin America – i.e. those with high absolute population base and high fertility-rates (?) – do not have satisfactory census figures. Reference to much of the UN Demographic Yearbook information will reveal sparse and ancient sources. As a consequence of the lack of sufficient demographic data: population distribution, growth-rates, fertility- and mortality-rates etc, it becomes exceedingly difficult to devise a satisfactory 'forecast' and gross errors of aggregation can occur, and indeed have occurred (Revelle, 1967). Witness the methodology of the Club of Rome, through the study *The Limits to Growth* and its subsequent repudiation by, amongst others, the Science Policy Research Unit of Sussex University (Cole et al., 1973) – the latter team placing particular emphasis upon the 'failure of aggregation' and the 'paucity of reliable data', over and above the implications for policy – which ultimately impinges on the growth/no growth arguments (see Freeman's comment on the Tweedledum/Tweedledee aspect of Growth/No Growth arguments in his Introduction to Cole et al, 1973).

Pertinent to this debate are a number of other groups who make and/or interpret population forecasts according to their own lights.

The important thing to recognise in the 'debate' is that the population forecasting, despite the high uncertainty of its technique (see Figure 7.2),

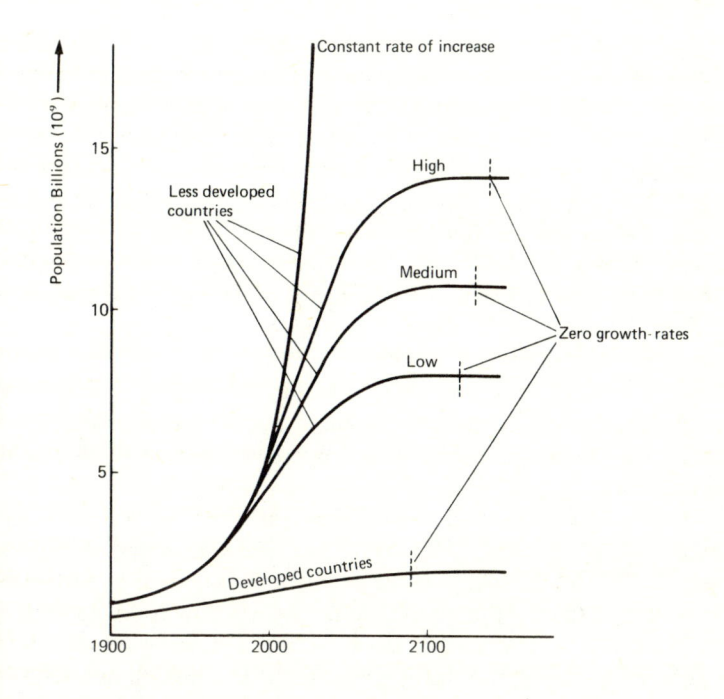

FIGURE 7.2. UN population projections (1974)

Source: U.N. Population Division Projections

serves to engender a climate of opinion in which subsequent policy decisions have an easier or rougher ride.

Some would argue (Lappé and Collins, 1977; Marstrand and Pavitt, 1973) for instance that there is not now, and need not be in the future, a food *production* problem (central to the population issue); that the problem of starvation and under-nutrition relate to supply and to distribution, these issues being underpinned by political and economic considerations. Assuming the validity of the anti-Malthusian arguments and the access to sufficient and reliable empirical data, then the mass starvation observed in various countries (National Academy of Sciences, 1977) and the social engineering characteristics of a nation-wide sterilisation campaign (Visaria, 1976; Banerji, 1976) become major failures of the human race.

In this sense the amelioration of present difficulties, combined with the gathering of reliable demographic information, becomes one of the major prerequisites of twentieth-century man. This is by no means to overstate the case, bearing in mind the scale of human denial.

However, as discussed in 1972 by Stanley Johnson in *A Population Policy of Britain*: 'No one will dispute the proposition that, in the long term, zero population growth is inevitable. This applies as much to the world as a whole, as it applies to Britain. It can be demonstrated that at any positive rate of population growth, if it is sustained long enough, the world will run out of space, energy, food and all other resources necessary to sustain life. But how long is long?' To this we might add whether 'natural brakes', e.g. significant economic development in UDCs, are likely to occur, or whether a more aggressive policy is required? As indicated in the previous paragraphs, there is no clear evidence on this point.

Nevertheless, in response to the question 'How long is long?' the Population Division of the UN produced projections as background material for the World Population Conference, held in Bucharest in August 1974:

In discussing these 'speculative projections' the UK Cabinet Office, in *Future World Trends* (HMSO, 1976) makes several important points. Firstly, 'They did not claim to be predictions but were hypothetical figures, divided from assumptions about the paths that declining fertility might follow in eight major areas of the world, leading ultimately to stable levels of population being approached but by different data in different regions. Bringing about such transitions from high to low fertility in the developing world, and hence reducing the rate of growth in population, implies major changes in their socio-economic structures, as cause and as effect. Even those national governments in the developing world which are already devoting considerable resources to trying to reduce the levels of fertility, focus on the immediate problems of starting on the downward transition rather than on when in the future it might be completed.' Now it should be recognised that although more recent projections have modified somewhat the size of the medium-term population growth, 'nevertheless the earlier long-range projection serves to show the possible order of magnitude at which world population numbers might stabilise'.

In deriving the long-range projections, the UN have made several assumptions – i.e. firstly, that in all cases a smooth transition from present growth-rates to zero growth-rates will occur. Secondly, that the rate of decline in fertility-rate in the developing countries, whilst following the assumption made in the UN's 1970 projections, will not show as rapid a decline as has occurred in the developed world in recent years.

The Cabinet Office document recognises that 'The Sensitivity of these assumptions is demonstrated by taking a 10 years earlier and a 10 years later approach to stability for the developing countries, obtaining so-called "low" and "high" variants respectively, for which the projected stable population of the developing countries become 8 billion and 14 billion. Thus a delay of rather less than one generation in achieving zero population growth could mean an increase of 80% in the eventual population of the developing world.' Thus, how long is long might be seen to be critical! As to policy, it must be recognised that in the absence of worldwide famines or wars, 'rapid population growth in the immediate future is inevitable. Even if fertility-rates were to be reduced to replacement levels now, the existing age structure of the world's population would ensure continuing growth for another two generations. It is this fact which accounts for the long-term sensitivity of total population to stabilisation data.'

The authors of *Future World Trends* state that there has been considerable success in some countries in reducing fertility rates; however, for some of the poorest, e.g. Bangladesh, this is not so. Also certain Latin American and African countries consider that, in order to maximise national resource potential, high population growth-rates should be maintained. We see here empirical demonstrations of the pro- and anti-Malthusian debate.

POPULATION FORECASTS ON A MORE LIMITED SCALE: THE UK PATTERN

We have outlined in the previous section some of the problems which centre upon the interpretation of world population predictions. Is this problem any easier when we move to a smaller unit (say the UK) where there exists a comparatively long history of highly detailed demographic monitoring? Do the more detailed demographic data available allow for a finer, or more sophisticated (in the sense of detailed and informed) discussion of economic and social policy issues? In short, do more sophisticated data provide greater confidence in projections (or forecasts) and thereby lead to a more rational discussion of policy issues? The more informed we are, then the better we can comprehend the implications and consequences of alternative policies (or even recognise that we cannot perceive the consequences, based on past evidences), and the more 'rational' (or less arbitrary) our selection with respect to policy might be.

To this list of questions we might add: exactly what are the major policy/debate areas in the UK which are dependent upon the provision of demographic forecasts?

First as to detail: in the UK, national censuses provide much information, births and deaths are monitored by the OPCS; and on the basis of population distribution, fertility-rates, mortality-rates and net migration figures, projections of population size covering the period up to forty years ahead are made by the Government Actuary's Department on behalf of, and in consultation with the Registrar General of England and Wales, Scotland and Northern Ireland (HMSO, series pp 2 Nos' 7 and 8, 1977).

The underlying assumptions upon which their validity depends, relate to factors affecting births, deaths and net migrations, the most critical assumption being that of future fertility-rates. Figure 7.3 demonstrates the difficulty of making comparatively long-term forecasts, even for a well monitored population.

As can be seen from the chart, the projected population by the year 2000 has varied between 50 million and 72 million. The associated difficulties with respect to any long-term planning which is dependent upon demographic considerations are therefore considerable.

However, as pointed out by the Central Policy Review Staff in *Population and the Social Services* (HMSO, 1977), during the 1970s the methods of projecting the national population have been improved –

POPULATION FORECASTING 155

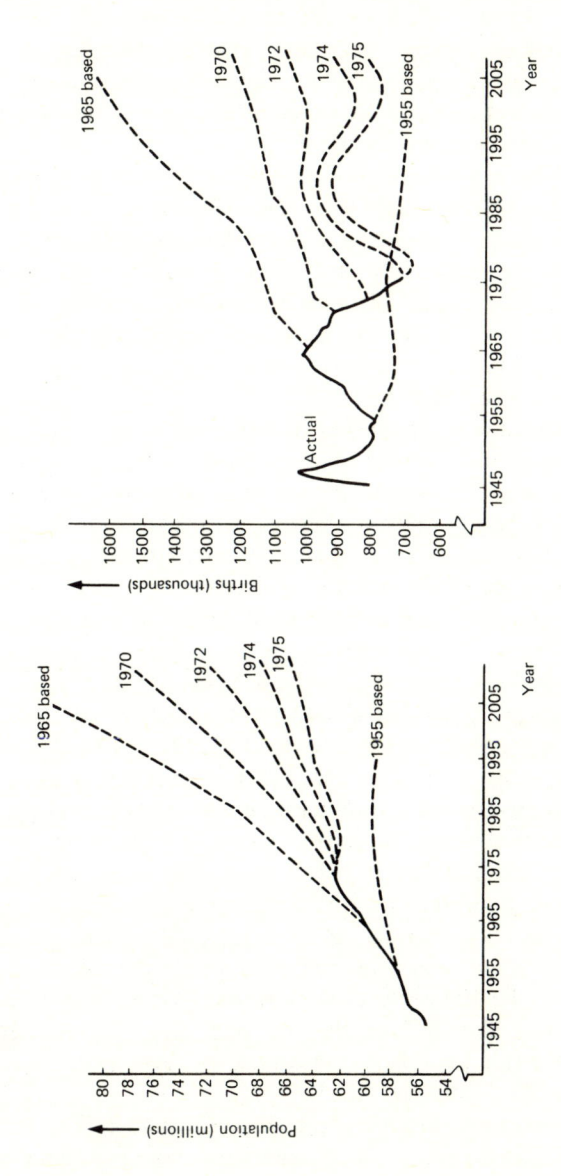

FIGURE 7.3a. Actual and projected population of the United Kingdom*
* SOURCE: *Population Projections 1975–2015*, HMSO (1977), Series PP2 No. 7.

FIGURE 7.3b. Actual and projected live births in the United Kingdom

but even with proved methods the experiences and lessons of past projection errors remain. Secondly, though the projections are not exactly forecasts they are often treated as such (see Appendix 1). Thirdly, for 'social expenditure planning, particularly where programmes are sensitive to demographic changes – it is prudent to consider variant projections and the range of uncertainty implied by them, rather than one central projection'.

Now we asked what are the main policy issues under discussion in the UK which depend upon demographic changes. If we were able to look over our shoulders a mere 5–7 years ago, we should not be far wrong if we decided the major issues and debate centred upon the growth of the British population itself (see for instance, section 4 of Johnson, 1972; *Ecologist*, vol 2, No 1, 1972; Hawthorn, 1973). It is not difficult to see why this was so – the views of the past concerning population growth influenced the 'intellectual climate'.

With respect to 'climate' there was a carry-over effect from the concern with implications of global trends to national levels – even for the developed nations. The World Population Conference in Rome (1954), the second in Belgrade (1968), the setting up of UNFPA (United Nations Fund for Population Activities) in 1967, the World Population Conference in Bucharest (1974), not to mention the UN (6th) Special Session on Raw Materials and Development (in 1974) and another World Food Conference in Rome (1974), had undoubtedly engendered a climate of opinion which filtered down to national governments and various social pressure groups. Added to this was the interest aroused by such publications as 'A blueprint for survival', *World Dynamics* and *The Limits to Growth*. This polemical literature was probably quite influential on various governments' thinking on population development.

One must also admit that the majority of the developed nations were experiencing a significant birth-rate bulge (during the sixties) and this empirical fact would reinforce other thinking (see Figure 7.3b).

The birth-rate increase during the sixties would surely not go unnoticed by governments and would influence policy debate. Indeed, even with respect to the decline which commenced around 1966/67 this would probably not filter sufficiently into public and government cognisance until the trend had been substantial for several years – the 1970 projection was still quite positive!

However, if we just shift our attention by five years and look to 1976 and 1977, we find that the focus of discussion (and indeed the detailed analysis of various government advisory groups) has completely turned about (see Jessel, 1977; Annex 1 to CPRS, 1977), for the central issue at the present time concerns the apparently continuing trend of reduced fertility-rates. (It is of interest to enquire as to whether the publicity which has surrounded the 'population explosion' has in any way influenced the subconscious psyche of Western nations; obviously there are many factors at work.) See for instance, the demographic literature of DES (DES Documents ACSTT (76), Nos 4, 8 and 23) concerning educational policy, the report to the Council of Europe by Jessel, or the Report of the CPRS.

With respect to the latter report, *Population and the Social Services*, which is specifically addressed to 'a possible long-term decline in the birth-rate' and its implications for national social expenditure, the highly detailed report considers a number of variant projections (including a specially prepared very low variant, produced by GAD, OPCS and CSO) which relate to a wide range of age sectors (0–5, school age, 16–65, 65+ etc). This report was the result of cooperative work between the Treasury, DHSS, DES, DEE, the Home Office, the Scottish Office, OPCS, the Government Actuary Department and the Central Statistical Office. It would therefore seem to represent a wide range of thinking and to be potentially of importance with respect to policy formulation in the appropriate sectors. In particular, it underlines the UK Government's concern with obtaining as full information as possible with regard to a reduction in fertility-rates.

The CPRS report will be referred to again in the next section in connection with educational policy. However, since we are particularly interested in the relationship between a more sophisticated demographic data-base and policy-decisions, it is perhaps worth emphasising the CPRS conclusions regarding the relationship between demographic projections, social policy and social planning in the recent past.

They concluded:

(a) That demography is a relevant factor in the planning and policy development of most social programmes, but its influence has been much more direct in some areas, e.g. education (especially teacher training and supply) and regional planning (including new towns), than in other areas, e.g. housing (where growth in the number of households has been more important, and faster, than growth in population).

(b) Where allocation of resources at a regional or sub-regional level is involved (e.g. school or hospital building programmes), changes in population in the country as a whole are often less important than local needs and demands.

(c) Changes in society, social attitudes, social demands and other social policies can often be as important as, or more important than, demographic change (e.g. changes in female activity rates in the labour market).

(d) In some areas, projections of massive population growth, which were subsequently falsified, had a significant effect on policy (especially regional planning, new towns, and teacher supply). There were time lags in adjusting, and subsequently readjusting, to assumed changes in trend. (See next section for more discussion of this aspect in the relation to educational policy.)

The authors then emphasise that given this weak link between demographic changes and social programmes in the past, it is vital to ask:

(a) Are there some social programmes where demographic changes should be taken into account more directly than in the past?
(b) Can planning and policy adjust more smoothly and quickly to changes in trends, e.g. by greater flexibility or closer monitoring?
(c) Can more be done to relate national demographic changes to regional and sub-regional planning and resource allocation?

Answers to these questions depend in part on whether one views governmental procedures as a series of compromises in terms of political bargaining – essentially whether one emphasises power struggles or a rational and equitable role for government. Nevertheless more detailed demographic data – certainly at a disaggregate regional level – assists in answering positively to these questions. Similarly the CPRS report itself is beneficial in establishing a firmer link between demographic considerations and social policy. Even so, if large fluctuations in the birth-rate etc are observed from year to year then this will not help the demographic case; but monitoring and establishment of such fluctuations would at least serve to overcome *demographic rationalisation of political prejudice*. The prediction of the Centre for Policy Studies (OPCS Monitor Ref. pp2 761) that such 'fluctuations in birth-rate are likely to become more dramatic and less conducive to long-term planning on demographic criteria' is of relevance here.

The next section of this chapter focuses on the influence of demographic factors upon current educational policy in the UK. It is perhaps worth keeping the CPRS findings and questions clearly in mind as a means of answering these questions and also in passing judgement on government policy.

THE ROLE OF DEMOGRAPHY IN EDUCATION POLICY: SOME RECENT EVENTS WITH RESPECT TO TEACHER EDUCATION

As pointed out in the CPRS report discussed earlier (*Population and the Social Services*) demographic considerations play a significant role in determining educational policy and financing.

Without some knowledge of incoming pupil and student rates it is impossible to plan effectively for the size and form of the teaching staff. The cost implications are immense, as are the error costs. To a certain degree projections are not involved. For instance the census data on 0–5 year-olds tell us much of the requirements for the primary sector (and the secondary and tertiary, as this age-group proceeds through the educational system). Similarly the age-group statistics for, say, 10–16 years give us fair warning as to the future requirements in the tertiary sector. This is not to say that policy is defined *vis-à-vis* teacher: pupil ratios in the primary and secondary sectors, nor as to the participation rates at university level.

Demographic projections become particularly important, however, with respect to the primary sector because of the lead times required to develop the infrastructure which generates this teaching force.

Similarly, manpower forecasts (at the professional level: medics, engineers, educationalists, etc) play an important and not too successful role in tertiary educational policy. (See also Chapter 6.) This section will primarily concern itself with the role of demographic projections in relation to teacher numbers.

It was indicated above that errors are very costly. If we do not have enough teachers then pupils incur the cost, perhaps irreparably, and ultimately society pays. On the other hand, significant overmanning may place excessive fiscal strain on the public sector, although some would argue that this is an ideal opportunity for society to bestow the benefits of small class sizes upon its young. With respect to the latter argument, one might also introduce a concept of flexible spare-capacity which can be redeployed according to the nature of birth-rate developments; however, the scale of this spare-capacity imposes a not insignificant economic requirement – and the likelihood of this being a strain depends very much on the state of a country's economy (and its values).

If we were to require a very brief summary as to the pattern of UK education policy with respect to the provision of teaching staff, then the pattern over the last quarter of a century would be as follows: the high birth-rate experienced in the late fifties and early sixties placed a heavy load on the primary and secondary sector, and there was an urgent necessity for a crash-programme with respect to the number of places available in teacher training colleges. The Government responded accordingly (though a little late – they had not done their demographic homework). During this period opportunity was taken to initiate the Robbins Report which *laid open the principle of university places for all who might benefit.* The era of educational and academic expansion continued for several years, together with fundamental changes in the secondary sector.

As indicated by a recent policy statement of NATFHE (2266–77), 'The expansion of teacher education in the 1960s was determined by three main factors: the increase in the school population, the decision to increase the length of initial training from two years to three from 1960, and the commitment to reduce overall class size.'

The Robbins Report on Higher Education recommended a very substantial increase in initial training places (130 000 places in 1980 as opposed to then current plans for 82 000 by 1970). As stated in connection with the Robbins Report, 'Robbins also envisaged a degree of diversification taking place in the colleges of education, particularly in the late 1970s when it was expected that the demand for teachers would slacken'. This prediction has proved to be correct.

For now in the late seventies we are observing a dramatic reversal of policy – argued for in the context of a significant drop in the birth rate over a period of years. (See Table 7.1 and Figure 7.4 below.)

Present educational policy is dependent upon the fact of reduced birth-rates over the last few years and also upon the demographic projections for the years immediately following. (See NATFHE 2266–77 and DES Documents ACSTT (76) Nos 4, 8, 20, 23 for a discussion of the influence of these projections on policy.)

Thus 'the reorganisation of the colleges of education during the 1970s is taking place in the context of sharply falling birth-rate projections and school populations. As in the rapid expansion of the early 1960s, *demographic factors have played an important part in policy-making or at least in the rationalisation of political decisions*' (NATFHE, 2266–77, my emphasis). On the surface, the reduction of teacher-training places due to the continuous fall in the birth-rate would appear to be a rational response of government. Why then *'rationalisation of political decisions'*? It is the purpose of what follows to examine the various protagonists in this extremely important social debate as to motives,

TABLE 7.1 Total period fertility-rates (TPFR) and numbers of live births (thousands) in each calendar year 1965–1985, England and Wales

Year	TPFR	Live births	Year	TPFR	Live births
Actual			*Projected*		
1965	2·86	863	1976	1·72	584
1966	2·76	850	1977	1·69	576
1967	2·66	832	1978	1·69	579
1968	2·58	819	1979	1·73	596
1969	2·48	798	1980	1·81	629
1970	2·41	784	1981	1·90	667
1971	2·38	783	1982	1·98	704
1972	2·19	725	1983	2·05	738
1973	2·02	676	1984	2·09	762
1974	1·90	640	1985	2·10	776
1975	1·79	603			

(Source: Table 6, p. 18, *Population Projections 1975–2015*, HMSO Series PP2 No. 7, 1977.)

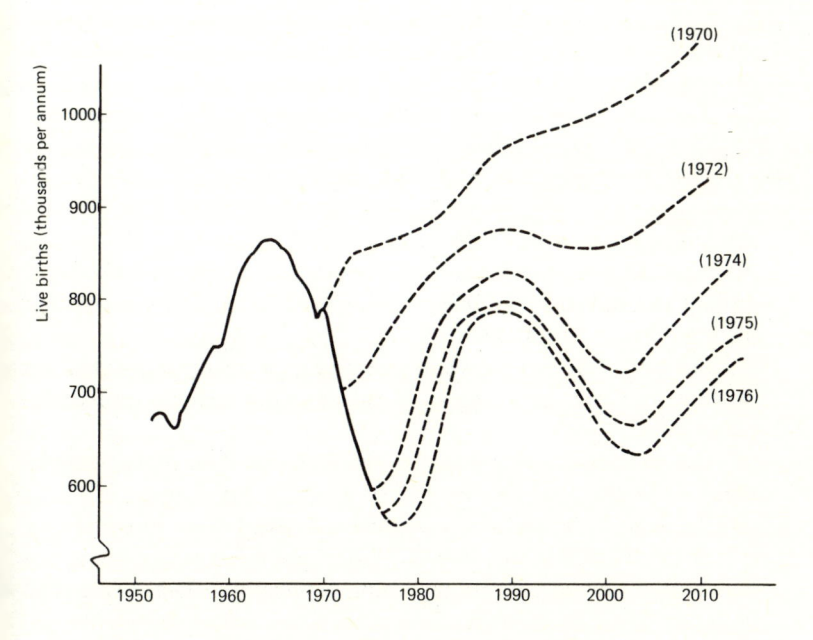

FIGURE 7.4. Actual and projected births: England and Wales. Current (1976-based) projection and four previous projections

arguments and the ways in which demographers' forecasts, etc, are used to support their case – sometimes based on the same demographic 'evidence'!

It is necessary, however, in order to appreciate the motive, to embed the debate in the on-going socio-economic scene in the UK. This might be summarised as follows:

(a) A world recession still hovers.
(b) The UK economy has for many years been one of consistent under-achievement.
(c) Despite the role of North Sea oil, the economy is still not on a sure footing.
(d) IMF loans carried implications for public-sector spending.
(e) Inflation still runs high – if not quite hyperinflation.
(f) The pay restraint of the last two years (the 'Social Contract'), and the erosion effects of inflation on living standards, may result in increasing pressure for wages' and salaries' increase; potential investment funds from North Sea oil, etc, may be redirected from capital investment.
(g) Business confidence for investment in the private sector is low, resulting in pressure for Government funds to be transferred to private industry.
(h) Taxation limits have probably been reached (if not exceeded).

On the social, employment and demographic front:

(a) Unemployment is of the order of 1 500 000.
(b) New entrants into the work-force are of the order of 140 000 per annum and an extra 1 500 000 jobs may be required by 1981 to reduce unemployment to 500 000.
(c) The birth-rate has shown in recent years a steady and significant downward trend, resulting in a substantially reduced pre-school population.
(d) Due to the birth-rate 'bulge' of the sixties (and for other reasons), there is still pressure on the tertiary sector of education.
(e) The education sector received massive fiscal input in the sixties.
(f) There is increasing pressure from several sources for a vocationally oriented education system, especially in later years (and with respect to retraining).

Under such circumstances one might suggest that no expansion in public sector spending can be expected, cuts are politically inevitable, and funds are to be directed into industry as a palliative to unemployment, to generate economic growth through competitiveness, and because certain demographic projections suggesting a reduced load on the educational sector only weakens opposition.

Many of the various protagonists who are concerned with educational policy, and with the ways in which demographic considerations are thought to be relevant, would hold contrary views. Let us therefore consider their use of demographic data and attempt to gain some insight into the role of demographic forecasting in relation to policy-making. The main protagonists and interested parties are shown in Figure 7.5 below. As can be seen from Figure 7.5, there are two main groups of protagonists. On the one hand the Government, who formulates policy

Top-left quadrant:
The UK Government
Dept. of Education and Science (DES)

Top-right quadrant:
Office of Population and Census Studies (OPCS)
Central Policy Review Staff (CPRS)
Centre for Policy Studies (CSSP)

Bottom-left quadrant:
The Robbins Report
The Holland Report
The Russell Report

Bottom-right quadrant:
Association of University Teachers (AUT)
National Association of Teachers in Further and Higher Education (NATFHE)

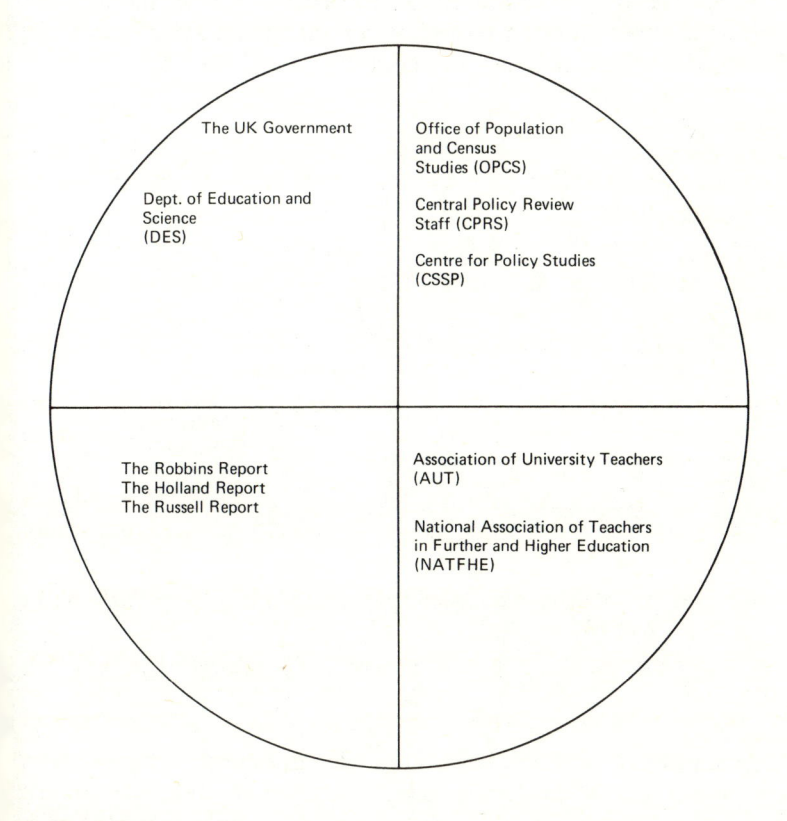

FIGURE 7.5.

and on the other such bodies as the Association of University Teachers (AUT) and the National Association of Teachers in Further and Higher Education (NATFHE), whose motives are varied. The Government is aided by the Department of Education and Science (DES). In this instance various groups provide demographic projection data (forecasts) but by far the most influential source is the Office of Population Censuses and Surveys (OPCS). (Responsibility for the production of the national projections and the assumptions underlying them falls upon the Government Actuary in consultation with the three Registrars General.) Not unnaturally government policy is potentially subject to a wide range of criticism and comment. Nevertheless, by and large all parties are dependent upon the same demographic projections. Interpretation, however, is another matter, as we shall see later.

Now the Government essentially justifies its policies for a contraction in public spending in education (with respect to teacher training and university expenditure) in respect of current demographic trends and future projections, as shown in Figure 7.6 and Table 7.2.

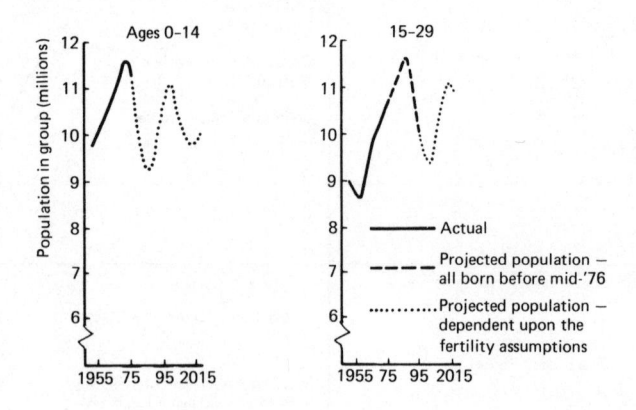

FIGURE 7.6. Actual and projected total population in age-groups England and Wales 1951–2016*

* Source: OPCS Monitor PP2 77/1 – Summary of population projections: mid 1976 based

In describing the projection (and providing detailed yearly estimates up to the year 2016), OPCS state, 'Although the total size of the population is expected to change relatively little over the next 40 years, it

TABLE 7.2 Fertility assumptions – England and Wales*

Year	Current projection TPFR*	Live births (thousands)	1975 based projection TPFR*	Live births (thousands)
1976	1·72†	585†	1·72	584
1977	1·66	564	1·69	576
1978	1·64	559	1·69	579
1979	1·64	562	1·73	596
1980	1·65	570	1·81	629
1981	1·70	593	1·90	667
1982	1·78	628	1·98	704
1983	1·88	671	2·05	738
1984	1·99	720	2·09	762
1985	2·06	755	2·10	776
1986	2·09	775	2·10	785
1987	2·10	786	2·10	792
1991	2·10	791	2·10	799
2001	2·10	654	2·10	677
2011	2·10	711	2·10	744

*Total period fertility-rate.
†Provisional.

is likely that there will be some quite large changes in the age structure ... the number of children under age 15 shows a fall of nearly 2 million between 1976 and 1986, rising again to approach the 1976 level by 1998, but falling steeply again thereafter. ...'

The projected values for individual years being:

TABLE 7.3 Mid-1976 based population projection (England and Wales)

Year	1976 (base)	1977	1978	1979	1981	1991	2001	2011	2016*
000's	11,145	10,901	10,632	10,344	9,810	9,907	10,893	9,745	9,961

Age group 0–14 (1000's)

*These data were not available for use in formulating the White Paper; 1975 based data were used. 1976-based data are provided here since they highlight the continuing downward trend in fertility-rate, which supports in some senses the Government's position.

As can be seen from Figures 7.3a & 7.4, over the majority of the past decade projections of future population size have been modified downwards due to the continued falling birth-rate.

With respect to the short term, the projections used by the Government in determining educational policy are provided in the White Paper *Public Expenditure to 1979–80* (Cmnd 6393, p. 86).

TABLE 7.4 Enrolment projections

				Thousands	
Schools	1975–76	1976–77	1977–78	1978–79	1979–80
Under-fives	418	459	459	459	459
Primary pupils	5363	5274	5141	4974	4785
Secondary pupils to age 16	3746	3813	3849	3846	3814
Over 16	549	581	607	630	654
Non-advanced further education	721	743	765	788	809
Higher education	511	516	523	533	550

(Source: H.M.S.O. Cmnd 6393)

As a result of the Government Actuary projections, the Government's response is to reduce significantly the commitment to teacher training initiated in the sixties, thereby closing or redeploying a high number of teacher training colleges. More detailed discussion of the assumptions is to be found in DES documents such as *Teacher Training in the 1980s; School Staffing Standards; Revised Projections of Pupils in Maintained Nursery, Primary and Secondary Schools; The Teacher Supply Implications of a Training System of 45 000; The Teacher Force in the 1980s*, which both separately and in total serve to consolidate the DES position (and that of the Government) as demographers' projections showed continued reductions in birth-rate trends. On the basis of the demographic data presented to the reader so far, the Government would seem to have a good case.

However, in turning to the forecasts of demand made by NATFHE and the AUT we move into quite different territory.

First let us consider the NATFHE policy statements (the most relevant publications being *Higher Education Draft Policy Statement, The Development of a NATFHE Economic Policy* and *Teacher Education Draft Policy Statement*). (The documents referred to here are draft policy statements not yet issued. Similarly the *Development of NATFHE economic policy* is an internal discussion paper. This writer is grateful to the Association for making the papers available. Similarly, he is also grateful to the Department of Education and Science for making the quoted papers available.) In none of these papers are we provided with either a revised *value* for teacher numbers required (and therefore 'forecast') or a projected value of future student numbers. However, by making fundamentally different demographic and social-economic assumptions to that of the Government, the Association derives a strong case for a significantly higher number than those employed in Government policy.

The NATFHE assumptions and demographic arguments are essentially as follows:

In the first paper cited, (*Higher Education Draft Policy Statement*) they take the Robbins' principle that 'access to higher education for those qualified and wishing to enter it must form a basis for further development and extension of opportunity towards more open access to higher education', and argue that erosion of standards already achieved is unacceptable. Having established their position, they then query the reliability of demographic forecasts and place emphasis upon the CSSP report which predicts fluctuations in future birth-rates and reflects upon its implications for short-sighted long-term planning which make forecasts for student demand 'rigidly or primarily in accordance with demographic predictions'. They argue that

> currently demographic factors are being used as a pretext for relatively short-term economic and political policy and expenditure cuts, just as hitherto they were used as a trigger for political decisions for expansion. Policy-making in higher education in the last 20 years has not been a process of national long-term planning, even when couched in those terms. The CATS, Robbins, Polytechnics and the reorganisation of colleges of education succeeded one another at roughly five-year intervals and have developed as a result of a series of political, social, economic and educational pressures.

The Association argues that demographic projections should be set against a range of social, educational and manpower trends and they predict an increasing demand for higher education.

Factors which are developed to support this increasing demand include Britain's economic performance, increasing demand for skilled manpower, the level of unemployment, the social demand for further and higher education, the effects of raising the school-leaving age, increasing demand from women and girls for training and education, demands for recurrent education and the changing balance between education and vocational and professional training.

Equally they argue that, though ' . . . these factors are tightly intertwined, many of them do not lend themselves to meaningful quantitative prediction over the 10–20 year time-scales of present population trends', but they do speak for an increased demand. They then review growth in each of these areas and suggest that the Government's White Paper projections are of provision, not of demand and conclude that the changes which they (NATFHE) foresee contain enormous potential for growth in student demand in higher education. 'This potential has been largely discounted by the DES, ostensibly on demographic grounds.' Demand in the higher education sector is, of course, also dependent upon adequate provision in the primary and secondary sectors and in their second document, *Teacher Education – Draft Policy Statement*, they address themselves specifically to forecasts concerned with teacher training.

Besides the arguments referred to above – which carry many implications for the primary and secondary sector – they then develop these arguments as a basis for alternative forecasting. Firstly, in reviewing the DES's continually revised predictions for teacher numbers, based on demographic trends (if fluctuations can go down in one year they can go up also . . . ?), they query the value of the forecasts. Secondly, they place emphasis on present and future trends in education at the primary and secondary level, ranging from shortage of particular disciplines (e.g. maths) to the increasing need for in-service training, induction, retraining, curriculum development, etc. Thirdly, they lay emphasis on the appropriateness of a four-year B.Ed. training for teachers compared with the present split in one-year PGCE courses for graduates and three-year courses for non-graduates to college of education courses. The four-year course carries fundamental implications for teacher quality, as does the ratio argument. However, perhaps of greater significance are the implications for non-closure of teacher training colleges, since such a strategy effectively involves a 30 per cent increase in college staff loads and non-closure would allow future options to remain open in regard to the ultimate size of teaching forces, i.e., it would be more flexible to changing demographic and educational needs.

The final document, *The Development of a NATFHE Economic Policy*, takes a more aggressive stand concerning the scale of public expenditure as a means of widening the demographic argument and providing an alternative base for forecasting.

NATFHE consider that their previous statements on educational policy have lacked credibility because in a period of cuts which threaten existing provision, they (NATFHE) have advocated expansionist policies without indicating whether they believe that (1) Resources are to be allocated from other sectors of public expenditure, (2) By increasing the proportion of public expenditure in relation to GNP or (3) Expansionist Policies should be implemented as an increase in GNP permits.

It would seem to this writer that the latter aspect is fraught with difficulties where long-term continuity of planning is required; time-lags in policy implementation may not correspond with economic upswings, and options may be severely restricted if, for instance, extensive college closures occur.

In considering the questions concerning public expenditure, they recognise that whilst public expenditure has a central and crucial regulatory function in controlling economic and social policy, they reject its use in education since it undermines coherent planning. In relation to public expenditure they query whether the UK is out of step with other nations, thus 'public current spending as a proportion of GDP in 1972 in the UK was 20·7; compared with Sweden (25·6); Denmark (23·8); USA (23·2); West Germany (20·4); Italy (16·0); France (14·0); Japan (10·4)'. To this they add a query in relation to 'transfer payments' and distinguish between 'genuine' public expenditure, and on the other hand 'transfer payments' and lending to the private sector, when almost half of the planned public expenditure in the UK is made up of transfer payments (£23 546 million out of £52 035 million planned expenditure for 1976/77).

They then relate cuts in public expenditure to unemployment and also emphasise the structural component to unemployment which carries many future training implications.

These arguments are then integrated under a theme of economic reflation which carries many educational and training implications.

Taking the three documents together they do not (unlike the AUT forecast to be discussed next) provide a quantitative estimate of future educational demand but seek to widen the policy base beyond narrow population projections.

In turning to the Association of University Teachers' forecast entitled *Student Numbers in Universities in Great Britain up to 1987/88*, we encounter a highly detailed forecast, which lists its assumptions, derives a formula for forecasting student numbers in universities which is not reflected in the Government's contraction-policy and finally challenges the Government, by providing a detailed mapping of the AUT's forecasting procedure, and by concluding, 'The DES should state the basis of its planning model so that consultation with the AUT can take place'. The AUT document is addressing itself of course to the forecasting of student numbers in future years, not teacher training places (as for the NATFHE papers); there are certain interdependencies however (see later). (It was stated earlier that teacher education policy and student numbers (demand and provision) are not independent criteria. One might care to consider the effects in significant change in T:P ratios on school performance, early academic attainment, and academic expectations – i.e. aspiration to university entrance.)

The AUT forecasting paper commences by commenting on the DES *'free demand'* forecasting procedure. They state: 'DES planning has (thus) been based on what has been termed "free demand". This is an attractive method of forecasting, it being based simply on the number of 18-year-olds in the population, the proportion of those who have the minimum qualifications for entry to higher education and the number who are willing to enter courses. At any time, the 18-year-old population is known for the next 18 years; this is the only "hard" factor in planning numbers. The other two factors depend, though to differing extents, upon changes in educational, institutional, economic and social factors, past, present and future – *some of which may be determined by government activity or inactivity.*' (This writer's emphasis, i.e., forecasts can be self-fulfilling or manipulatable – the interaction of policy and forecasting being crucial.)

The AUT then comments on the Robbins Report forecast for student numbers in the year 1981/82, i.e., 590 000. It (the AUT) points out that they 'appear to be remarkably close to the 1976 White Paper projection of 600 000 full-time students in Great Britain by this time'. But it goes on to point out

> ... however, the path to these targets has been very different from that anticipated. Only seven years ago, 835 000 students were forecast by DES (Education Planning Paper No. 2, 1970). This was based on assumptions influenced by the very high rates of growth in the mid-1960s. *Education: A Framework for Expansion* (Cmnd 5174 1972) set out a target of 750 000 which has since been reduced to 640 000 and 600 000 in the Public Expenditure White Paper of 1975 and 1976. On 18 January 1977 a revised target was announced of 560 000 full-time and sandwich course students in higher education in Great Britain by the 1981/82 academic year. This reduction was partly justified on the basis of fee increases and the stabilization policy for overseas-student

numbers from 1977/78 onwards.

At the time they were made, it was said that none of the targets was inconsistent with free demand projections. This illustrates the very real difficulty of using 'free demand' for planning.

The AUT indicates that the Government (DES) estimates are now discussed in terms of 'age participation rate' – and as indicated in Cmnd 6393 (the latest Public Expenditure White Paper), the Government, in discussing revised student forecasts, said it would 'allow for a further rise in the proportion of the post-school-age group entering higher education, at present about 14% to 15%'.

As the AUT points out, 'if this age-participation rate becomes a target measure then this can be made the rationale for a *reduction* in student numbers in the 1980s and 1990s', i.e. the Government is shifting the basis of its forecasting technique from 'free demand' to 'participation rate' (and for a demographic decline this would indicate a reduction in absolute numbers). The AUT paper then argues that there are demographic factors moving in different directions and examines:

1. *Demographic trends and historical growth in undergraduates in British Universities*: Where it is argued (a) that the Government's demographic projections are to a certain degree speculative, (b) that a 'ratchet' effect applies in education – relating to raised minimal levels of expectations, involvement etc, once standards are reached, (c) the sharp drop in 18-year-olds in the late sixties did not affect the 'path of growth in full-time students in universities'.

2. *Future growth in undergraduate students aged under 25 years of UK origin in universities*: Where emphasis is placed on (a) the Sex Discrimination Act as potentially influencing higher female intake and (b) teacher training colleges' closure redirecting entry into universities.

3. *Mature students*: Where TUC policy to encourage students is referred to.

4. *Overseas Students*: Government policy is recognised but it is argued that increased tuition fees have not resulted in a significant fall in numbers.

5. *Postgraduate Students*: The AUT feels that this proportion (∼20 per cent) of total university population will remain constant.

6. 'Some additional factors' are then considered:

(a) It argues that school-leaving qualifications will improve and that therefore there will be greater demand.

(b) That there will be an increase in working-class students (TUC policy).

(c) With respect to socio-economic factors and demographic trends (particularly important from the standpoint of this chapter), the AUT refers to an article by Ernest Rudd in the *THES* (19 November 1976) which referred to a 'small sample study carried out by the Office of Population Censuses and Surveys which drew attention to the differential birth-rate by social class. The study showed that between 1970 and 1972 overall births fell by 8 per cent. However, the pattern of births by social class was very uneven: for social classes I and II there was actually an increase in births of 2 per cent; for social class III the fall in births was 9 per cent; whilst in social classes IV and V the number of births fell by 16 per cent. Rudd said that the available evidence suggests that some 60 per cent of undergraduates have fathers in social classes I and II (professional, managerial and intermediate non-manual occupations), about 33 per cent come from class III (clerical workers and skilled manual workers), leaving 7 per cent from classes IV and V (semi-skilled and unskilled manual workers). This shows that there is a distinct inequality in the class share of the total student population. In comparison with this, of the men in the age group that includes the fathers of most students (age 45 to 59), 25 per cent are in classes I and II, 48 per cent in Class III and 27 per cent in classes IV and V. Thus Rudd concludes that the recent fall in the birth-rate may not significantly affect admissions to universities in the late 1980s because the numbers of births in social classes I and II are relatively stable.'

(d) The role of continuing education (see Russell Report, 1973 on Adult Education which emphasises the university contribution).

The AUT forecast is then tabulated thus:

It concludes:

Free demand for entry into universities and higher education at any point in time depends on many factors, some of which are impossible to quantify but could be equally as important: for example, unemployment levels, level of student fees and grants, salary levels and career prospects of non-graduate occupations. Thus 'free' demand is in the hands of the government since it has control over a significant number of these factors. This is implicit in its recent reduction in its forecast of student numbers. When there were few public expenditure

TABLE 7.5 University student population projections (Source: AUT, April 1977)

Source of Numbers and Assumptions for Changes	1974/75	1981/82	1985/86	1987/88
1. Male undergraduates of UK origin under 25 (very slow growth comparable with recent years)	115 000	119 000	121 000	122 000
2. Female undergraduates of UK origin under 25 (growth at the same rate as last ten years)	64 000	93 000	115 000	116 000
3. Change in numbers due to population from 1974/75 level (assuming constant Age Participation Rate (7% in 1974/75), and effective length of undergraduate course, i.e. 3 years)	—	26 000	25 000	19 000
4. Undergraduates (male and female) of UK origin over 25 (continuing growth-rate since 1968/69)	12 000	19 000	25 000	28 000
Sub-total – Undergraduates (1+2+3+4) of UK origin	*191 000*	*257 000*	*286 000*	*285 000*
5. Undergraduates from overseas (male and female) (from 1977/78 stabilised at numbers in 1976/77)	12 000	15 500	15 500	15 500
6. Postgraduates from overseas (male and female) (from 1977/78 stabilised at numbers in 1976/77)	16 000	17 500	17 500	17 500
Sub-total – Overseas students (5+6)	28 000	33 000	33 000	33 000
7. Postgraduates (male and female) of UK origin (assuming postgraduates of UK origin are a constant 15·62% of undergraduates of UK origin – position in 1976/77)	32 000	40 000	45 000	45 000
Sub-total – postgraduates (6+7)	*48 000*	*57 500*	*62 500*	*62 500*
Sub-total – undergraduates (1+2+3+4+5)	*203 000*	*272 500*	*301 500*	*300 500*
TOTAL UNIVERSITY STUDENT POPULATION (1+2+3+4+5+6+7)	251 000	330 000	364 000	363 000

Note: The figures given in the table are for (a) the increase in demographic trends to 1982/83, (b) a higher proportion of female undergraduates under 25, (c) a constant proportion of postgraduates, (d) no increase in the numbers of overseas students after 1976/77, and (e) the numbers of mature students to increase at the same rate as over the last decade.

constraints on higher education, the concept of a 'pure' free demand was a sensible and useful indication for planning but over the course of time the concept has been manipulated to hide both policy decisions and public expenditure constraints.

We can therefore see that the Government's reliance upon 'tight' demographic forecasting is by no means an incontestable operation. To this we might add the demographic 'qualifiers' provided by the recent CPRS Report on 'Demography and the Social Sciences' which emphasises the role of variant projections and the need to retain options due to possibilities of demographic variation away from 'central projections'. Equally, as pointed out in the NATFHE paper, despite the fact that the birth-rate has fallen by over one-third since 1964, the Centre for Policy Studies (Buxton and Craven, 1976) has predicted that 'fluctuations in the birth-rate are likely to become more dramatic and less conducive to long-term planning on demographic criteria. This prediction is based on current trends towards the postponement of families, the reduction in family size and the limitation of family size according to economic circumstances or prospects.'

Finally, an alternative perspective to demographic forecasting based on reduction in fertility is provided by a provocative report on *The Implications of Demographic Change for Social and Migration Policy* presented by the Committee on Population and Refugees to the Parliamentary Assembly of the Council of Europe on 15 September 1977. This report, in considering changes in population structure in European states in the last quarter of a century, and the role of migration with respect to manpower needs, recommended that a climate more favourable to fertility be encouraged by adjustment of fiscal and housing needs to encourage families and to reduce factors which operate against fertility: in particular in relation to women and their role in the working population. Contrary to the concern of most governments with present (and future) large-scale unemployment, the report forecasts that a significant reduction in total work-force will occur due to reduced fertility-rates and that this should not be allowed to develop.

From the standpoint of this study, if such a policy was implementable and effective, one might observe yet another compounding difficulty with respect to demographic forecasting!

We might conclude this section by indicating that the forecasts and policy of governments and associated agencies' forecasts and policy is embedded in a context of economic recession, restrictions on public expenditure, presently decreasing fertility-rates and reduced school population size. The extent to which the forecasts and policy are reliant upon population developments or are seen as rationalisation of policy (NATFHE Doc. 1907a–77) is seriously questioned by forecasts made by other bodies – the scope of demographic forecasting (rather than population projection, see Appendix 1) being more widely interpreted by these latter bodies.

Finally, it is not my purpose here to expound a particular view of the nature of 'society and education', or the responsibility of politicians to the educational arena. However, one might make a few points which are relevant to demographic trends and educational policy. In times of economic deprivation, the economic axe often falls upon the educational sector, and society is the poorer, both in terms of its present and more particularly its future.

Despite detailed work by educational economists, it has not been possible to date to establish any reliable equation which indicates the rate of return to society (in economic, innovatory or social terms) for a particular rate of investment in the educational budget. Proposals have been made (Dahrendorf, 1976) but they are highly contentious. Nevertheless the feedback loop is increasingly recognised and acted upon by governments. This says little of the important non-vocational aspect of education. Of course, from a more simplistic manpower standpoint, a government's prime policy perspective is often in terms of supply and demand of particular disciplines, subjects, professions and trades, over both short- and medium-term periods, which is highly dependent upon manpower forecasting – and has not been short of errors (see Chapter 6).

However, there now emerges on the horizon a possibly different scene for governments to contemplate: continuing and increasing unemployment for a range of reasons (Freeman, 1977). At the same time the 'ratchet effect in education' referred to earlier may help to contribute to a new form of social problem: an unemployed but educated mass of people that may comprise hundreds of thousands, if not millions. It is difficult to see how it will be possible, even under conditions of moderate economic growth, to encourage appropriate labour-intensive industries.

For some analysts the so-called 'service industry' has taken up employment slack from the manufacturing industries; however, more recently others (see Gershuny, April 1977 and December 1977) have fundamentally questioned this role. They see much of the 'service industries' as essentially manufacturing, and therefore subject to similar difficulties (e.g. automation effects) contingent upon the conventional manufacturing sector.

A second possibility with regard to a labour-intensive industry is the 'education industry' itself, employing upwards of a million staff. The industry has an added advantage in relation to educational requirements. At times of teacher reduction, etc this might seem a peculiar or inconsistent claim. However, if we fundamentally re-appraise our notions in regard, for instance, to teacher: pupil ratio and optimum class size, then many possibilities open up. Class ratios of $< 10:1$ would incur labour requirements of $\sim \frac{1}{2}$ million. At the same time the salary cost would be enormous – yet we might consider (a) what ranges of alternative employment exist, (b) the scale of unemployment payments, (c) the nature of future work-force requirements (in terms of skills at both the cognitive and social level (especially if we see long-term continuation of reduced fertility rates), (d) the various benefits to society (and individuals) of a fundamentally restructured educational system.

Such considerations, even in amended form, might seriously modify our forecasting techniques.

Similarly, at a more presently realistic level there has been little or no account or estimate of error-costs associated with the closure of teacher training colleges which might arise in the future in the event of significant fluctuations in birth-rates. Whilst the 'warning time' is less than five years (since it would take around that for any such effect to establish credibility), the lead times associated with the development of educational infrastructures might be considerably longer, with subsequent interim penalties for pupils.

CONCLUDING REMARKS

We have briefly examined here three levels of interaction between demographic projections and social policy, the first at the global level, the second at the level of a single nation (the UK) and finally with respect to a more specialised policy issue within one nation.

It has been indicated that at all levels there is a disquieting lack of reliability of the forecasts, and further that the way in which the demographic data is treated and viewed depends very much on the perceptual focus of the 'interested party'.

Rarely does any party question its own complete range of assumptions, which in turn delimits the nature of the forecast. No doubt this may reflect the inevitable(?) confrontation and polarisation, or position-taking aspects of the political process, which in turn carries many implications for the lack of 'neutrality' of forecasts.

Thus at the global level, irrespective of whether or not one questions the scale of the 'population explosion', there are those who are of a Malthusian turn of mind who would advocate extensive population-control policies and therefore are not particularly against grossly aggregate techniques which unfairly exaggerate the possible scale of future growth. Similarly, they do not emphasise the role of socio-economic development as a moderator of fertility-rates. For the anti-Malthusian, the reverse is true. Intermingled in this debate is the extent to which such analyses of the present and future plight of underfed masses of developing and underdeveloped nations influence on-going policy with respect to agriculture and food provision (or technical aid) — which has an important distributive and developmental dimension.

Ironically, the literature of world collapse due to population developments may have played a more significant (but subconscious?) role in the psyche of the developed nations, who are witnessing a significant decline in fertility-rates when compared with other socio-economic sectors of the world. Such a statement would be extremely difficult to validate however, bearing in mind the wide range of economic, socio-cultural and biological factors which collectively determine fertility-rates.

At the level of a single nation, it can be seen that despite detailed long-term data, it is still difficult to have a high level of confidence in medium- and long-term projections. Whilst this is recognised in some sectors of government — and indeed is reflected firstly in the limited role which demography plays in relation to social planning (see CPRS report) and secondly in the increasing recognition of the need for variant projections which underscore a wide range in future possibilities — *nevertheless a government is not at a loss to use demographic arguments which support current political thinking.*

The aspect being examined here is at the third level, i.e. a more restricted aspect of social policy: educational policy.

It is of interest to enquire here, as mentioned earlier, what would have been the form of educational policy in the UK with respect to teacher education if a period of reduced fertility-rates *had not coincided* with economic recession and internal and external pressure to curb spending in the so-called public sector.

Finally, we may perceive a second cruel irony in the role of demography in social planning and engineering. For as we move from the level of worldwide dimensions to the level of a particular problem in a single nation, then the available demographic data improve (there are many qualifications to this). Yet the far more pressing problems (it might be argued) occur at the wider level — where demographic data are at their weakest. This aspect is particularly important when one considers (and questions) the appropriateness of striving for a *world population policy*. Such a questioning might suggest that limited and 'appropriate' policies in limited areas (nations) based on a sufficient data-bank are a more appropriate goal. But such a philosophy immediately runs into the problem of 'boundaries', whereby the policy of single nations may not be compatible with general global/environmental concerns. The extent to which, and ways in which, one nation's or one culture's thinking can be imposed upon or brought to influence another is central to this issue.

Thus certain sectors of the United States (and the Western world) take up a position *vis-à-vis* rapid population growth in the Third World, but they do not always listen to the Third World's assessment of energy usage by the USA. The population-resource depletion issue is a two-edged sword.

Finally, the influence of demographic thinking (and forecasts) at one level can be an important contributing factor at another level. Thus those policy-makers who for various reasons were concerned to introduce a stabilised, or zero-growth population policy in the UK (see Johnson, 1972; Brown, 1974; Olson and Landsberg, 1975), are not averse to making considerable reliance upon global population predictions as a scene-setter.

The rule would seem to be, if you can find an image (or a mirage) to suit your argument, use it.

APPENDICES

1. Projections versus Forecasts

A fairly comprehensive review of population forecasts for the United States over the period 1790–1960 is provided by Peterson (1961) in his comprehensive text entitled *Population* (see Chapter 11, 'Population Forecasts'). Whilst emphasising the extraordinary success of the earliest simple projections and the inaccuracies of later (and more sophisticated) forecasts (or projections), Peterson also points out that much of what we know about population growth 'has been learned by comparing false predictions with the actual events and trying to understand why the error was made'. However, he also emphasises that the actual act of making the forecast may affect the system which it attempts to describe. Thus, '. . . a population forecast, if it is made a basis for government policy, itself becomes one of the determinants of population change. The very predictions of incipient population decline in the 1930s, for example, may have helped reverse the trend and thus make the forecasts false.' The forecast itself can then oscillate in its role as dependent or independent variable.

With respect to independent variables, when these are given in demographic terms (birth- and death-rates, net migration, etc), then as Peterson points out, 'extrapolation of the past trend is termed a population *projection*. When at least some of the independent variables are given in social or economic terms, or the greater or lesser probability of demographic variables is posited in a social-economic framework, the same extrapolation is termed a population *forecast*. Many extrapolations are not clearly in either one class or the other.' Peterson goes on to state that most population extrapolations are a little of both and that the difference lies only with the temerity of the analyst: 'in the 1930s, when the accuracy of the extrapolations was sometimes uncanny, they were termed "forecasts", while the less successful efforts of the post-war period, though based on precisely the same type of calculations, are called "projections".'

BIBLIOGRAPHY

Association of University Teachers (April 1977), *Student Numbers in Universities in Great Britain up to 1987/88*.
Banerji, D. (1976), 'Will forcible sterilisation be effective?' *Econ. and Political Weekly*, Vol. XI, No. 18, pp. 665–8.
Brown, L. R. (1974), *In the Human Interest: A Strategy to Stabilise World Population*, New York: W. W. Norton.
Buxton, M. and Craven, E. (eds.) (1976), *The Uncertain Future*, (OPCS Monitor Ref. PP2 76/1), Centre for Studies in Social Policy.
Cabinet Office (1976), *Future World Trends*, London: HMSO.
Central Policy Review Staff (April 1977), *Population and the Social Services*, London: HMSO.
Cole, H. S. D. et al. (eds.) (1973), *Thinking About the Future*, London: Chatto and Windus.
Dahrendorf, R. (1976), 'Universities and the Economy', *Times Higher Educational Supplement*, 19 November, p. 5.
Department of Education and Science (1976), DES Documents ACSTT (76) 4: *The Teacher Force in the 1980s*; 8: *School Staffing Standards*; 20: *Revised Projections of Pupils in Maintained Nursery, Primary and Secondary Schools*; 23: *Teacher Training in the 1980s*; 26: *The Teacher*

Supply Implications of a Training System of 45 000
'A blueprint for survival', *Ecologist*, Vol. 2, No. 1, 1972; Penguin Special, 1972.
Foley, G. (1976), *The Energy Question*, Harmondsworth: Pelican.
Forrester, J. (1971), *World Dynamics*, Cambridge, Mass.: Wright-Allen.
Freeman, C. (1977), *Science and Technology in the New Economic Context: Paper on Unemployment and the Direction of Technical Change*, OECD, 3–4 November 1977.
Freeman, C. and Jahoda, M. (1978), *World Futures: The Great Debate*, London: Martin Robertson.
Gershuny, J. (April 1977), 'Post-industrial society – the myth of the service economy', *Futures*, pp. 103–14.
—— (December 1977), 'The self-service economy', *Universities Quarterly*, pp. 50–66.
Glass, D. V. and Revelle, R. (1972), *Population and Social Change*, London: Edward Arnold.
Hawthorn, G. (February 1973), *Population Policy: A Modern Delusion*, Fabian Tract 418 (International Comparisons in Social Policy No. 3).
HMSO, (1977), *Population Projections: Mid-1976 Based: 1976–2016*, Series PP2 No. 8; *Population Projections 1975–2015*, Series PP2 No. 7; *Public Expenditure to 1979–80* (White Paper), Cmnd 6393, February 1976.
Illich, I. D. (1974), *Energy and Equity*, London: Calder and Boyars.
Jessel, T. (rapporteur) (1977), *Report on the Implications of Demographic Change for Social and Migration Policy*, Paper given at Council of Europe, Strasbourg, 15 September 1977, Council of Europe Doc. 4016.
Johnson, S. (1972), *The Green Revolution*, London: Hamish Hamilton.
Johnson, S. (December 1972), *A Population Policy for Britain*, Old Queen Street Paper – Conservative Research Department, No. 18.
Kahn, H. and Wiener, A. J. (1967), *The Year 2000*, New York: Macmillan.
Kahn, H. et al. (1977), *The Next 200 Years: A Scenario for America and the World*, London: Assoc. Business Program.
Lappé, F. M. and Collins, J. (1977), *Food First: Beyond the Myth of Scarcity*, Boston: Houghton Mifflin Co.
Manpower Services Commission (May 1977), *Young People and Work: Report on the Feasibility of a New Programme of Opportunities for Unemployed Young People*.

Marstrand, P. K. and Pavitt, K. L. P. (1973), 'The agricultural subsystem', *Futures* 5 (1).

Meadows, D. H. et al. (1972), *The Limits to Growth: A Report for the Club of Rome's Project on the Predicament of Man*, Cambridge, Mass: MIT Press.

Mesarovic, M. and Pestel, E. (1974), *Mankind at the Turning Point*, E. P. Dutton and Co., Reader's Digest Press.

Mill, J. S. (1910), *Representative Government*, London: Dent.

Myrdal, G. (1968), *Asian Drama*, Vol. 1 (esp. Chapter 10: 'Population and Resources'), Harmondsworth, Penguin.

National Academy of Sciences (1963), *The Growth of World Population: Analysis of the Problems and Recommendations for Research and Training*, Washington DC: National Research Council Publication 1091.

—— (1977), *World Food and Nutrition Study*, Section I: 'Dimensions of the world food and nutrition problem', Washington DC.

National Association of Teachers in Further and Higher Education (NATFHE) (1977), *Higher Education Draft Policy Statement* (Document 1736); *Teacher Education Draft Policy Statement* (Document 1907a); *The Development of a NATFHE Economic Policy: A Discussion Paper* (Document 2266).

Olson, M. and Landsberg, H. H. (eds.) (1975), *The No-Growth Society*, London: Woburn Press.

Page, W. (1973), 'Population Forecasting', *Futures*, 5(2), pp. 179–94.

Pateman, C. (1970), *Participation and Democratic Government*, London: CUP.

Peterson, W. (1961), *Population*, London: Macmillan.

Revelle, R. (October 1967), 'Population', *Science Journal*, pp. 113–18.

Lord Robbins (chairman) (1965), *Higher Education*, Cmnd 2154, London: HMSO.

Rudd, E. (1976), 'What a falling birth-rate will mean to universities in 1982', *Times Higher Educational Supplement*, 19 November.

Russell, Lionel (1973), *Adult Education: A Plan for Development*, Department of Education and Science, London: HMSO.

Schumaker, E. F. (1973), *Small is Beautiful*, London: Blond and Briggs.

Shanks, M. (1962), *The Stagnant Society*, Harmondsworth; Pelican.

Symonds, R. and Gardner, M. (1973), *The United Nations and the Population Question, 1945–1970*, London: Chatto and Windus.

Visaria, P. (August 1976), 'Recent Trends in Indian Population Policy', *Economic and Political Weekly*, Vol. XI, No. 31–3 (Special issue).

8 Shadows on the Seventies: Indicative World Plan, the Protein Gap, and the Green Revolution

PAULINE K. MARSTRAND AND
HOWARD J. RUSH

Use of the term 'forecasting' suggests a well-defined and deliberate exercise. Food forecasting has not always followed that mode and it is difficult to separate attempts at rational planning from actual forecasts. In the 1930s the League of Nations had set up a committee (League of Nations, 1935) to study the causes of food shortages and to make recommendations. After the Second World War the UN carried on this activity, first through WHO, then after the creation of FAO in 1947, by joint action of these agencies. FAO collected information on population and food production, WHO laid down requirements for adequate nutrition, and together they attempted to calculate what would be required. This latter activity can be described as forecasting. We have described elsewhere (Marstrand and Rush, 1978) the difficulties encountered and the reasons for the estimates being too high. These criticisms in no way detract from the good intentions of the agencies in attempting to find out the extent of what was then believed to be a worldwide shortfall in the supply of food and the quantities required to meet it. Without their work the surprising fact of an overall sufficiency of food would never have emerged.

Using figures collected by FAO and by US officials abroad, the US Department of Agriculture has for a long time made its own forecasts of production in various countries on an annual basis, largely in order to advise growers and grain companies in the US of likely trends in prices. Indeed, the on-the-spot predictions of the US man in Delhi, Sydney,

Dakar or Moscow (now done by satellite surveillance!) have a pronounced influence on wheat prices and on production policy.

In 1967 President Johnson's Scientific Advisory Committee prepared a comprehensive report on world resources and demand (USPSAC, 1967) with forecasts of trends based on extrapolation. These strongly suggested that as developing countries industrialised, their rapidly growing populations would exert so great a demand for food that there would be serious world shortages by the mid-1970s. These findings were elaborated by Paddock and Paddock (1967), who predicted world famine in 1975; by Ehrlich, who used them to advocate a policy of zero population growth; by Meadows et al in *The Limits to Growth* and by Mesarovic and Pestel in *Mankind at the Turning Point*. All these authors accepted the stated trends in demand and population growth and their gloomy forecasts were inevitable. In reality, even in the 'disaster' year of 1972 there was enough food to have fed an additional 600 million people to WHO/FAO minimum standards, had it been equitably distributed. By 1977 the grain market is worried about surplus, and American farmers are once again being asked to grow less and the EEC is desperately trying to reduce production of milk and meat.

More recently Buringh et al. (1974), in association with the effort of de Hoogh et al. (1976) to make a more accurate model of the world food system than that of Meadows, have shown that the physical capacity of the world to produce food is in fact much greater than had been assumed by FAO, thus underlining the fundamentally political nature of the problems of famine and hunger in the world.

This chapter will concentrate on the events leading up to and including WHO/FAO effort to meet world food requirements, based on the Indicative World Plan (IWP) for food produced in 1970, as well as the effects of such a plan. This massive attempt to grapple with food problems on a world scale marked a major advance in policy-making. Firstly, it accepted that the welfare of poor people is the responsibility of the whole community of nations and therefore a legitimate field of activity for the UN. Secondly, it endeavoured to make allowance for unequal demand between sections of national communities, and for changes in demand due to economic growth. That the allowance was unrealistically large in the first case and too simply related in the second does not detract from the importance and value of this first world plan, for anything.

The effect of IWP was to stimulate research into methods of increasing production, to reinforce fears about world food shortage, and to create the appearance of a particular shortage of protein. These effects themselves produced good and bad results, some quite unexpected by the UN agencies, by government policy-makers, and by the academic and commercial researchers who became involved. The unwanted results are the shadow on the seventies which has marred the progress of world food distribution.

There are high hopes in the 1960s that a correct analysis of the world food situation and UN guidelines for what should be done would result in increased supply and thus reduce the risk of famine. Because little or no account was taken of the social context in which new technology was to be introduced, the result has been that, while productivity has indeed been enormously increased, famine and hunger have also increased, and the disparity between those who eat and those who do not has been exacerbated.

THE INDICATIVE WORLD PLAN FOR AGRICULTURE

The purpose of the Indicative World Plan for Agriculture was to enable UN agencies to recommend to governments how much food would need to be produced in order to meet expected world demand and to make recommendations on how best to meet this demand. The plan carried out by officials of FAO assisted by member-country governments was an ambitious attempt at looking into the future and influencing it. Set forth in a detailed scenario the plan endorsed specific and general goals which included the introduction of high yield varieties – HYV (encouraging widespread intensive farming as opposed to major increases in cultivated area); the closing of the protein gap (through new HYVs, food enrichment with synthetic amino-acid and formulated protein-rich food products); reducing waste within the agricultural cycle; mobilising human resources (employment to be increased in conjunction with intensification and mechanisation as well as through land tenure reform); and the accumulation of foreign exchange (through expansion of trade and import substitution). The plan was initially criticised on methodological grounds;[1] as pointed out by McLean and Hopkins (1970), the forecast was based mainly on trend extrapolation and assumed that observed shortages arose largely from shortfalls in supply.

Recognising that food intake was 'skewed' by unequal distribution of income, FAO planners calculated a 'safe' quantity which would ensure that 97 per cent of the population would consume sufficient food. This involved adding twice one standard deviation of the distribution of food to the calculated mean requirement. Sukhatme (1972) calculated that this would result in Maharastra requiring almost enough protein to provide four times its actual population with individual average requirements. It was also, we suggest, based on methods which assume that economies can be rationally managed to produce optimal results. As with much of the social planning of the 1950s and 1960s,[2] little account was taken of the unpredictable effects on world markets exerted by the policies of individual governments, especially by industrial countries.

The plan was published in 1970 and shortly after Chacel (1971) criticised it on the grounds that the targets 'might have been set *a posteriori* independently of the IWP'. Whether this is the case or not, or indeed whether it is a fair criticism of any forecasting methodology, seems to us beside the point. The plan is a remarkably complete analysis of the world food situation in the 1960s and the first major attempt at long-term prediction on a world scale. Chacel's criticism does underline the importance of these issues as the dominant ones among agriculturalists and development planners during the late 1960s. By incorporating prevailing beliefs about nutrition and scientific achievement the plan served to legitimate these beliefs, providing an extra boost to the 'Green Revolution' and the 'Protein Gap'.

THE GREEN REVOLUTION

There are two popular views of the 'Green Revolution'. One continues the faith of its founder Borlaug and of the IWP that the high yielding varieties of wheat, maize and rice will continue to spread in the world, more food will be produced and famine will be ended. This view is held by international companies marketing the hybrid seeds, the fertilisers, the machinery and irrigation equipment and by many successful farmers. This is reinforced by the fact that early technical difficulties, like susceptibility to disease, and drowning of short-strawed rice, have been overcome by technical means – mainly by breeding varieties more closely tailored to specific local conditions.

The other view – observing these early failures and the disastrous famines which occurred in districts which had entirely gone over to a new variety and then lost the harvest, the replacement of pulses by cereals in some countries and the problems of amino-acid composition and palatability – believes that the Green Revolution has been an unmitigated disaster; this view is held by many groups desirous of assisting developing countries by encouraging more appropriate agriculture and by other groups which regard all change as deleterious.

We believe that both these views are wrong.

The production of high yield varieties, especially the newer ones developed for specific conditions in conjunction with ICRISAT, IRRI, CYMMIT, are a triumph of applied genetics and do produce much greater yields than local varieties under the conditions for which they are developed. It is no longer true that they are generally less nutritious, less palatable or only able to yield under optimum conditions. They are no more susceptible to disease than other crops grown in monoculture. Wheat has been especially successful in parts of India (Dasgupta, 1977) and the problem of short-straw rice is under investigation.

It is the social aspects of the technology that are problematic.[3] Griffin (1974) reviewed conditions in a number of developing countries and showed that where access to land, credit, machinery and extra labour was unequally distributed, then the increased production achieved by those most able to purchase hybrid seeds and other inputs had a variety of deleterious effects on the poorest, ranging from calling in of land debts, leading to increased landlessness and reduction in day wages, to increased demand for food from middle peasants so that it became even less available to the poorest. Additionally, land formerly under pulses for local consumption might be taken over for the production of cereals for cash sales. Berg, in *The Nutrition Factor* (1973), described the dramatic increases achieved by some countries in the production of food per head 1960–70 and how policies to encourage national food sufficiency, such as supporting prices, acted against the interests of poor farmers and of the urban poor, by raising prices and by reducing the variety of foods available, since pulse production was reduced.

Dasgupta (1977) reviews detailed studies in India of four wheat-producing areas, four rice-producing areas and one production of rice in a wheat area. He shows that after the peak year of 1971 the increases in production were less than expected, partly because of bad weather, but also because of lack of necessary inputs. He concludes that without the new varieties the Indian sub-continent could not have had the remarkable increases in wheat production which brought self-sufficiency within sight in 1971, but that the package of hybrid seed (which must be purchased anew each year), fertilisers, pesticides, controlled irrigation, machinery to gather the increased harvest, together constitute a social system which does not consort well with the societies into which it is being introduced. New agricultural practices require new social practices. Last year's seed is no longer saved – new seed is bought. There must be either an agent or a market; the farmer must save not seed but money. The inputs are expensive, the farmer must grow not only to eat but also to pay off the inputs. This is almost a fundamental ideological change.

In the period of introduction of high yield varieties, little thought had been given to these things. Even when farmers received help with the purchase of inputs they still found it hard to believe that seed saved one year would not give the same good results the next. They did save seed and yields deteriorated. Merchants mixed genuine hybrid seed with local seed. Poorer farmers bought this cheaper mixture. Farmers with capital or credit could exercise control over irrigation water and equipment. It was easier for them to market their surplus.

Increased productivity of food crops must include development of better varieties which respond to improved husbandry, but raised productivity will not follow automatically the introduction of new varieties. Unless governments deliberately counteract the tendency of *any* new technology to increase inequalities between groups in society, by controlling access to credit, prices of produce, accumulation of land and by discriminating in favour of the poorest people, such introductions may increase food production, but will not prevent malnutrition or even famine.

Most developing governments are poor. It is difficult for them to embark on programmes of agricultural development without outside help. Multinational companies with interests in seed production, agricultural chemicals or machinery are a potential source of this help – but can they countenance the different pattern of development which would ensure that the increased production resulted in more food being eaten by the poorest people? Even if this meant reduced or perhaps even negative profit on investment? We think not. Similarly, we find it difficult to believe that governments representing the economically most powerful minorities of their countries will be able to direct development in favour of the poorest – until those wealthier minorities begin to share their wealth and influence, in response to political and social pressures. Not many governments adopted any of the social or institutional adjustments to land tenure and credit availability recommended in Chapters 9–11 of IWP. If they had, the results of the 'Green Revolution' might have been a social as well as a technical success. In the event, adoption of the new high yield varieties could not succeed in feeding the poorest people, and in fact increased the disparities in amounts of food consumed by the rich and the poor. On the basis of the degree of sharing of economic influence it should be possible to predict which countries are likely to decrease malnutrition by increasing food production.

FOUNDATIONS OF A 'PROTEIN GAP'

Concern about nutritional deficiency was given a scientific bent in the nineteenth century, and although subsequently overshadowed by preoccupation with vitamins, proteins had been identified as essential and as associated with nitrogen balance before 1840. Through the early 1900s more separate proteins were being identified and Henderson and others identified the component amino-acids, while Gowland Hopkins recognised that for building human protein only about half the available amino-acids were essential, these being more frequent in the protein of animals, hence first and second class protein. The deprivations of the First World War showed that adults could remain healthy on less than the daily 118 gr of protein thought by Voigt, for example, to be necessary for an active man. In the interwar period interest in protein faded, probably because Europeans and Americans had more than sufficient. In colonial territories, however, concern with malnutrition, especially of children, was increasing, and Williams (1975) reports that when she started work in the Gold Coast (now Ghana) in 1929, kwashiorkor was already recognised as a deficiency disease. She herself treated it with milk or oilseed/cereal mixtures and thought it might involve protein and vitamin deficiency – it was called 'infantile pellagra'. (Pellagra in adults is a disease associated with lack of vitamin.)

Even after the Second World War the immediate goal of the WHO was to identify the extent of food shortage and investigate the potential for alleviating it. In 1949 the first session of the first FAO/WHO Joint Expert Committee on Nutrition did not have protein deficiency on its agenda. The probability that simply increasing the amounts of available staple food might not provide a basis for health among people subsisting on a diet of cassava, yam or the current varieties of maize was raised by Brock (1974) who had been working on kwashiorkor in South Africa. As a result he and Autret were commissioned to study this disease, and reported in 1952 (Brock and Autret). Alerted by this study, UNICEF, FAO and WHO urged the procurement of new protein sources, especially locally. When the Protein Advisory Group of FAO/WHO (PAG) was established in 1955 one of its first tasks was to investigate and comment on protein deficiencies and how they could be alleviated.

The PAG necessarily comprised a group of experts drawn mainly from industrial countries, and the contemporary social context of nutrition research and population forecasting would inevitably have influenced their thinking. Fundamental researching into the formation of protein had spin-off in the production of free amino-acids and thus the possibility of supplementing proteins deficient in, for instance, lysine. Successful application of animal genetics, pasture management and food concentrate formulation resulted in enormous surpluses of milk in the US and Europe. Milk is widely known to be good for babies – why not send surplus milk to starving babies? Human milk is an ideal diet for babies, but it is not a protein-rich food – a fact sometimes overlooked in the subsequent controversy about milk substitutes. In 1956 the US Academy of Sciences National Research Council (NRC) set up a committee to evaluate protein-rich foods for infants. Meanwhile the joint expert committee was attempting to project protein needs and proposed an amount based on the minimum required to maintain nitrogen balance plus a 50 per cent safety factor. PAG made recommendations to the UN, and the General Assembly adopted a comprehensive statement on food strategy, which recognised protein as a key problem. This led to the production of the 1971 strategy statement on action to avert the protein crisis (E71-11-A-17) and the confirmation of the 'Protein Gap'.

Utilisation of bone-meal, fish-meal, leaf proteins and micro-organisms has always been both a local reality and a scientific dream. The blessing of the UN had now been given to development of all kinds of protein to supplement the supposedly protein-deficient diets of the starving millions. Funds became available for research in government, university and industrial laboratories. The protein era had begun.

Probably because concern about *total* food had pre-dated the protein gap, research into high yield varieties of staple cereals, maize, wheat and rice, came to fruition first. With considerable international and commercial support, the 'Green Revolution' was launched, and did succeed in increasing production in many areas. As has been shown by many others: Griffin, George, Lipton, etc, etc, it did not enable the poor to eat, and the early varieties were lower in protein than those they replaced. In addition the profitable growth of HYV replaced the pulses in some regions. Pulses are an important source of protein in a vegetarian diet, supplying amino-acids often deficient in cereals and roots. The incidence of marasmus and kwashiorkor, both now characterised as protein deficiency diseases, increased among the poor, lending validity to the protein-gap concept.

Financial assistance for the development of protein-rich food began with a modest UNICEF grant of 5000 dollars in 1954 for the study of the acceptability of bread enriched with fish flour (Teply, 1966). By 1966 UNICEF and the Rockefeller Foundation had allocated nearly one million dollars for research, development and testing of protein-rich food. Under the guidance of the WHO/FAO/UNICEF Protein Advisory Group, various programmes were undertaken including the provision of pilot plant and laboratory equipment; support for recipe development and acceptability studies; and the adoption of new processing methods for low cost food formulations (Teply, 1966). Worried by a dwindling surplus and the intermittent availability of skim milk, the US AID programme followed the UN's lead with an allocation of 600 000 dollars for a two-year R and D programme in protein-rich formulation food to be carried out by the Agricultural Research Service.

In 1966 and 1968 the UN General Assembly called for the location and development of locally available protein sources and cheap protein supplements. Marketing experts were invited to advise PAG and the World Bank assisted cooperation between companies and developing countries. Several products were developed, using local staple foods, supplemented by local or relatively cheap additional proteins.

While much of the initial research on protein-rich food has been carried out by publicly funded institutions and at universities, the high cost of the elaborate processing equipment required in the production of vegetable protein and the need for marketing and distribution ability, led the major funding organisations to turn towards the food industry as the vehicle with the most readily available know-how to close the 'Protein Gap'. This decision was facilitated by what was considered a successful track record by private enterprise in spreading the 'Green Revolution' (Berg, 1972A). By late 1966 nearly all major transnational food companies had begun the research and testing of protein-rich foods. The variety of low-cost products to come from this R and D effort included baby food cereals, soft drinks and imitation milks (Berg, 1972).

The involvement of many companies was seen by Alan Berg (1972B) as manifesting a desire not to be left behind in possible new market openings. However, Berg also points out that the decision to enter this field was taken reluctantly by many companies because of the obstacle imposed by limited distribution channels, the difficulties in altering food habits and the meagre profit margins available from the poorest segment of the food market. This reluctance was overcome by the usefulness of being seen as cooperating with government, both in the country in which the parent company operates and with those of the less developed countries. The potential use for excess plant capacity also helped stimulate the commitment of private enterprise.

While the eventual failure of nearly every so-called low-cost product demonstrated that the industry's initial fears were well based, it is interesting to note the attitudes, recorded at the time, of two major companies which received grants through US AID's efforts to stimulate commercial involvement.

A vice-president of research for Jackson Inc. stated that 'the AID contract will help us take the technology we have developed into new areas. Admittedly there was some humanism in our motives, but essentially we want a nucleus for future opportunities' (Kropf, 1969). While the size of future investment had not been determined at the time this executive was interviewed, the director and vice-president of the company was quoted as saying, 'Our chairman has said that a 12% return on equity invested is the target.... We want to be successful in this project. We will ship the prototype product down there, and if at any point it doesn't look like it will succeed we'll cut it off' (Kropf, 1969).

An executive of the Pillsbury company (Skulstad, 1969) – the recipient of the first grant from US AID – observed that three basic points determined the company's approach to foreign ventures. These included the growth of nationalism resulting in the closing of export markets, thus the need to maintain a presence by building or purchasing production facilities in foreign markets; the emergence of new markets abroad similar to those in which the company is already successful; and to make more efficient use of a considerable R and D expenditure by spreading it over a broader base.

Multinational food companies are in business to accrue profits, which may not have been compatible with providing a low-cost nutritionally adequate product. However, we do not exclude the possibility that some of the motives were humanitarian ones. Certainly some of the companies involved employed local people, used local products and technology more appropriate to the setting in which they were used. Regardless of the motives, these 'low-cost proteins' were in all but a few instances outright failures. The reasons for this lack of success are numerous. It was perhaps inevitable that with the cost of processing, packaging, transportation and storage, the product would be more expensive than the target population could possibly afford. This was well summed up by Alan Berg's (1972A) implicit recognition of poverty and inequitable income distribution being the causes of hunger – 'Those who require the new foods have no money to buy them and most of those who have the money do not need them.'

The products Pronutro in South Africa, Incaparina in Guatemala and Vitasoy in Hong Kong have been claimed as successful, in spite of a selling price 100–1000 per cent higher than those of the local staple (Orr 1972). Therefore, even when commercially viable, they can only sell to those who can afford to buy. The poorest people everywhere cannot. Orr also reported that they had had little impact on the target populations. Of 46 schemes in 36 countries, 19 had been exploratory only. Twelve were terminated for lack of government support and none had reached the poorest people, unless offered by feeding schemes. The initial reluctance of many companies to enter this market perhaps foreshadowed the eventual discarding of this initiative. However, this is not to say no commercial ventures into the nutrition market have been profitable. It is now common knowledge that large agri-businesses have profitably marketed formula milk foods at comparatively high prices with, for many societies, a resulting detrimental nutritional effect on infant health (Cottingham, 1976, Muller, 1974). The misuse of artificial feeding, caused through misleading advertising and promotion practices, unsuitable hygiene conditions, as well as economic factors, may have exaggerated the increase of malnutrition and mortality in young children in Africa.[4] While the companies making capital from such products were not necessarily involved with the UN or US AID effort, the publicity which those efforts gave to such products, including the seal of approval from some within the medical profession, lent a certain undeserved respectability to the entire range.

Within PAG, awareness was growing that deficiency disease could not always or even usually be eliminated by protein, still less by amino-acids. The work of Gopalan and Sukhatme (1970) showed that marasmus derives from a total deficiency of food, even when the actual diet is not deficient in protein, and Payne etc demonstrated that the physiological requirements of the individual determine whether the symptoms incline more to kwashiorkor than to marasmus. So among the experts there was a growing body of opinion concerned with total nutrition, and aware that lack of food was more important than lack of protein. At the same time the FAO projections 1970–80 showed that average availability of protein exceeded requirements by 70 per cent if evenly distributed and that few countries would have an average *actual* deficiency, although, with allowance for increased demand as incomes rose, the calculated requirements were shown to increase the gap, and by implication, the deprivation of the poor. Having made an early commitment to protein problems, PAG was still apparently reluctant to retract. Although its own estimations of requirements have fallen steadily and despite the current emphasis on protein-calorie malnutrition (PCM) rather than protein alone, the latest estimate is higher and Scrimshaw (1976) has called for an upward revision. This upward revision is to allow sufficient for catch-up growth by children stunted by frequent infection, to meet a desirable rather than observed activity level and to allow for maldistribution. However, even if the estimates are increased, they still do not indicate a protein gap. What does emerge from all field studies is a chronic and increasing income gap.

This history indicates how good intentions, incomplete information and understanding, allied to commercial interests, can lead to misallocation of resources.

The intention to alleviate world hunger led to FAO activity to quantify the scarcity. Prior knowledge of a particular manifestation of deficiency (kwashiorkor) led to the concept of a protein gap. To cope with this PAG was created, and elaborated the concept. The Indicative World Food Plan of 1970, in trying to allow for income growth and population increase as well as adequate nutrition, over-estimated the demand and confirmed the gap. Member governments encouraged research and commercial activity into novel sources of protein. HYV and supplementary food products emerged, creating a need for schemes to use them. Phrases like 'Protein Gap' and 'Green Revolution' caught the imagination of the public in industrial countries, who thus by and large applauded what was happening. But still the hungry multitudes remained.

DISTORTING GOOD INTENTIONS

The criticism within PAG and FAO burst out in 1972–6. Disillusion with the green revolution is widespread. Protein supplementation is discredited and indeed, as Whitehead (1974) pointed out, there is a danger that opinion, and policy, will swing too far the other way.

Some staple foods are deficient in protein, but adequate in calories. In regions which rely on such foods there is a case for adding locally available foods richer in protein to the diets, especially of young children and those recovering from infection. Since these populations would hardly have survived had they not traditionally made such additions, it would be worth finding out what they add and why it is in short supply, and how supply could be increased.

Supplementing meals primarily through schools and health centres are the largest of nutrition intervention undertakings (Berg (1972B) estimated a cost in 1972 at nearly three-quarters of a billion dollars each year, representing 95 per cent of all funds directed to nutrition in developing countries). These programmes are also among the most controversial, for while the feeding programmes reach anywhere from 40 million to 125 million in upward of 105 countries this still covers only a fraction of the number at risk. In reviewing the literature on those supplementary feeding programmes supported through food aid[5] made available by the World Food Programme and the US government's PL480 programme, Simon Maxwell (1977) observes that 'the period of greatest danger and greatest damage occurs between the ages of six months and two years so that by the time a child is old enough to enter school, if he has survived, the damage has probably been done'.

Advocates of supplementary feeding point to the benefits of providing additional food to millions through existing facilities while at the same time increasing school attendance and providing an avenue for more attentive and receptive students (Berg, 1972B). No doubt there are also political and social benefits of such programmes. Critics of the programmes, as well as questioning whether the beneficiaries are in fact those actually at risk also point to the high costs in terms of both material resources and staff resources which might otherwise (Berg, 1972B, Maxwell, 1977) be spent on projects with a greater nutritional impact. Maxwell concludes that 'supplementary feeding has not normally been an efficient intervention tool because of administrative difficulties, high leakage and the problem of dealing with nutrition problems in a poor environment'. He concurs with Ofledal and Levinson (1974) who point once again to the likely failure of nutrition programmes which do not redress family income constraints.

For the therapeutic treatment of children already ill there is a place for supplementary feeding on a temporary basis, but it can never replace measures to increase local food supply and accessibility. Programmes based on exotic foods, e.g. milk, require education and infrastructure (water supply) as well as follow-up care, and are thus not suited to all situations.

Where supplementation is applied, it must be on the basis of free distribution to those actually needing it, otherwise if it finds a way onto the commercial market it will not be available to them. There is thus little chance that producing protein-rich foods for the needy can be a commercially successful operation. A bizarre result of the WHO/FAO/PAG activity and the Indicative World Plan has been to predict a protein shortage, call up research and commercial resources to close it, create a market, and leave the target populations still suffering from kwashiorkor and marasmus.

INDICATIVE WORLD PLAN

The Indicative World Plan was just that. It never claimed to be a forecast. It was, however, a normative plan, which outlined goals for world food supply and made recommendations for industrial and developing countries which could make achievement of the goals feasible. Among these goals were production of sufficient food to meet expected effective demand, to enable developing countries to reduce food imports and to provide more employment. Policy recommendations included reform of land tenure, and improved access to inputs and agricultural credits.

We would not agree entirely with all the goals and recommendations. For instance, increasing supply to meet 'effective' demand necessarily excludes people too poor to exert an economic demand, while land reform to produce units of economically viable size under high yielding crops would not, in all circumstances, benefit poor farmers. Desirable nutritional standards are specifically excluded as goals, although nutritional theories strongly influenced estimated requirements for food in many subsidiary reports of FAO. The assumption was that a sufficiency of food would keep prices down, to the benefit of lower income groups.

It appears that the political pressures exerted on governments led them usually to ignore the politically sensitive policy changes recommended by IWP and to adopt only the technical solutions such as the Green Revolution and new sources of protein. The Plan legitimised the previously held concept of food and land shortages, and thus boosted research into high yield varieties. The 'protein problem' identified by Brock led directly to the protein gap concept and the development of novel proteins to enrich deficient diets. High yield varieties and novel proteins were both already under investigation by commercial laboratories; the plan offered an opportunity for companies to cooperate with governments, and for aid to be channelled into joint enterprises. Jacoby (1977A) notes that there were over one hundred transnational corporations active in the FAO's Industrial Cooperative Programme.[6] Through control of manufacturing, of 'package' inputs, the development of formula foods and involvement in export of cash crops, industry has responded to IWP's recommendation for cooperation in development, but as Jacoby (1977A, B) and George (1976) have well documented, not generally to the advantage of the poor.[7]

Thus the legacy of IWP has been to legitimise certain solutions to the problem of feeding the world population, while selective use or abuse of the Plan by policy-makers has resulted in an increased gap between rich and poor despite an overall increase in world food production per head.

NOTES

1. Chacel, in listing the main methodological objections, includes the following: that the plan represents only partial coverage of FAO member countries; some developing and nearly all developed countries are excluded; the projections use as a data base national account surveys covering only a three-year period; the plan is not explicit enough about the interrelationships with the industrial and tertiary sectors or the relationship between rural and urban activities; and that the plan is inflexible in that no allowances are made for changes in national policy.
2. For example, tariff protection in the EEC discouraged the entry of US grain into Europe, thus adding to the world market surplus of wheat. Low world prices encouraged the use of wheat for animal feed, and a whole new intensive fatstock industry. US grain was donated as food aid, disturbing local markets and prices.
3. These have been extensively reviewed in numerous publications. See Poleman and Freebairn (1973) for a varied and balanced account.
4. While the quality of the product is not in question and the formula-milk companies have claimed that they cannot be held responsible for its misuse, the advertising and promotion of these formula-milks have been clearly shown as leading to this misuse. Such practices as the use of saleswomen dressed as nurses to 'push' the products in maternity hospitals and clinics, as well as providing free samples and feeding bottles to mothers without sterilising facilities or a regular source of safe water, have been seriously criticised. Many mothers who cannot afford the high price of this 'modern' product dilute the formula to make it last, thus unknowingly starving their children.

    Eight milk multinationals have signed a code of advertising agreement, since these practices have been brought to light. Whether they will abide by this non-binding document remains to be seen.
5. It should be kept in mind that although supplementary feeding programmes are the major attempt at directly influencing nutritional status and that nearly two-thirds of its resources come from food aid, it still represents only a minor proportion (11%) of food aid. The remainder is divided between aid which goes to market sale (65%), food for work projects (16%), and emergency feeding (7%).
6. Since the time of writing, ICP is no longer incorporated within the organisation structure of FAO.
7. The one hundred transnationals include firms involved in food production, the food trade, the manufacturing of farm machinery and trucks, large

chemical, forest and paper industries. Jacoby (1977A) contends that the continuing participation of agro-industry, 'with its commercial transfer of technical know-how and its insistence on a favourable investment climate will inevitably lead to ever-growing indebtedness and a never-ending balance of payments crisis in the Third World'.

BIBLIOGRAPHY

As well as books and articles referred to in this chapter, this listing includes those which influenced our thinking but have not been directly used.

Abbott, J. C., 'Marketing of new protein foods', PAG (FAO/WHO/UNICEF), September 1968 Meeting, Rome, Document 22/2, PAG Compendium 9/17 G155.

Adelman, I., Taft-Morris, C. and Robinson, S. (1976), 'Policies for equitable growth', *World Development 4* (7) 561–87.

Berg, Alan (A), 'Industry's struggle with world malnutrition', *Harvard Business Review*, Jan.–Feb. 1972.

Berg, Alan (B), 'Supplemental feeding programs', PAG Compendium, 9 May 1972, 8/13 F675, 19–23 June 1972 – 20th PAG Meeting, Paris, Document 1.17/7.

Berg, Alan (C) (1973), *The nutrition factor*, Washington DC: Brookings Institute.

Brock, J. F. (1974), 'Protein requirement', *The Lancet*, September 21, pp. 712–13.

Brock, J. F. and Autret, A. (1952), *Kwashiorkor in Africa*, WHO Monograph.

Bull, D. (1977), 'Protein and Food Nutrition Policies of UN Agencies', University of Manchester, Thesis for M.Sc.

Buringh, P., van Heemst, H. D. J. and Staring, G. J. (1975), *Computation of the absolute maximum food production of the world*, Agricultural University, Wageningen, Netherlands.

Chacel, Julian M., 'On the indicative world plan', *CERES, FAO Review*, Vol. 4, No. 1, Jan.–Feb. 1971.

Cottingham, Jane (ed.) (March 1974), *Bottle Babies: A Guide to the Baby Foods Issue*, Women's International Information and Communication Service.

Dasgupta, B. (1977), 'India's Green Revolution', *Economic and Political Weekly*, *XII*, 6, 7 and 8, February, 240–59.

Dürrenmatt, K., 'Report on the FAO/UNICEF meeting with Food Industries', Rome, 21–25 October 1963. Nutrition Document R.10/ADD.72, PAG/WHO/FAO/UNICEF, July 1964 meeting, N.Y.

PAG Compendium, 1.3/10, B179.

Ehrlich, P. R. and A. H. (1970), *Population, Resources and Environment: Issues in Human Ecology*, San Francisco, Freeman.

FAO (1971), 'Food and Agricultural Commodity Projections, 1970–80', FAO, Rome.

FAO (1970), 'Provisional Indicative World Plan for Agricultural Development, A Synthesis and analysis of factors relevant to world, regional and national agricultural development', Rome.

George, Susan (1976), *How the Other Half Dies: The Real Reasons for World Hunger*, Middlesex: Penguin.

Gopalan, C. 'Kwashiorkor and Marasmus: evolution and distinguishing features' (1968), in *Calorie Deficiencies and Protein Deficiencies*, McCance, R. A., Widdowson, E. M. (eds.), pp. 49–58, London: Churchill.

Graham, George C., 'Protein Food Mixture Developments in Peru', PAG (FAO/WHO/UNICEF) October 1967 Meeting, N.Y. Document 19/1, PAG Compendium 6.4.3/12, E.799.

Griffin, Keith (1974), *The Political Economy of Agrarian Change: An Essay on the Green Revolution*, Macmillan.

de Hough, J., Keyzer, M. A., Linnemann, H., van Heemst, H. D. J. (1976), 'Food for a growing world population', 'Model of International Relations in Agriculture: MOIRA', Economic and Social Institute, Free University, Amsterdam and North-Holland.

Jacoby, Erich, H. (A), 'Agri-Business and the United Nations System', Paper presented to conference of the International Free Trade Unions, April 1977. Brussels.

Jacoby, Erich H. (B) (1977), 'The problem of transnational corporations within the UN system' in *Economics in Institutional Perspective*, (ed.) Steppaches, R., Zogg-Walz, B. Hatzfelot, H., pp. 169–82, Lexington, Mass.: Lexington Books.

Kropf, James, 'Jackson Inc. in Brazil', FAO/WHO/UNICEF, PAG Compendium, Marketing Meeting, Rome 1969, Document 2.22/12.

Lappé, Frances Moore and Collins, Joseph (1977), *Food First: Beyond the Myth of Scarcity*, Boston: Houghton Mifflin Co.

League for International Food Education (1971), *The Food Industry in Asia: Its Potential for Providing Low Cost Nutritious Foods*, Washington, DC.

League of Nations (1935), *Quarterly Bulletin IV* (2).

Lipton, N. (1977), *Why Poor People Stay Poor*, London: Temple Smith.

Marstrand, P. K. and Rush, H. J. (1978), 'When enough is not enough:

the world food paradox', in *World Futures: The Great Debate*, C. Freeman and M. Jahoda (eds.), London: Martin Robertson.

Maxwell, Simon (1977), 'Food Aid and Supplementary Feeding: Impact and Policy implications', Mimeo.

McLaren, D. S. (1974), 'The Great Protein Fiasco', *Lancet*, 13 July 1974, pp. 93–96 and subsequent correspondence in issues of:

31 August 1974, A. M. Altschul; 7 September A. E. Bender; 21 September J. C. Waterlow; J. F. Brock; J. D. L. Hansen; 19 October J. Rivers, J. Seaman and J. Holt; J. & M. Lawless; D. S. Miller; 26 October J. M. Stewart; D. S. McLaren; 21 December R. Passmore; O. Mellander; 18 January 1975 M. Gebre Mehdin, G. Meeuwisse and E. Kopp; 5 April 1975 C. Williams;

McLean, M. J. and Hopkins, M. (1974), 'Problems of World Food and Agriculture: Projections, Models and Possible Approaches', *Futures* (London), August, p. 309.

Meadows, D. et al. (1972), *The Limits to Growth: First Report to the Club of Rome*, New York: Universe Books/London: Earth Island; London: Pan Books, 1974.

Mesarovic, M. and Pestel, E. (1974), *Mankind at the Turning Point: Second Report to the Club of Rome*, Hutchinson, UK, New York: Dutton/Reader's Digest Press, US.

Miller, D. S. and Payne, P. R. (1974), 'Strategy for a hungry world', *Nature*, 251, 20 September 1974, pp. 176–7.

Muller, Mike (1974), *The Baby Killer*, London: War on Want.

Oftedal, O. T. and Levinson, F. J. (1974), *Equity and Income Effects of Nutrition and Health Care*, Princeton University; quoted in Maxwell, S., 1977.

Orr, Elizabeth (1972), *The Use of Protein-Rich Foods for the Relief of Malnutrition in Developing Countries: An analysis of experience*, Tropical Products Institute, G73, August 1972.

Paddock, W. and P. (1967), *Famine 1975*, Boston.

Poleman, T. T. and Freebairn, D. K. (eds.) (1973), *Food, Population and Employment: The Impact of the Green Revolution*, New York/London: Praeger.

Protein Advisory Group of the UN System (PAG), 'The Global Maldistribution of Protein: A Growing Trend', PAG Statement No. 25, Protein Maldistribution, 21 September 1973, in PAG Compendium F798 13/25.

Scrimshaw. N. S. (1976), 'Strength and weaknesses of the committee approach', *New England Journal of Medicine*, 15 January, 136–42, 22 January, 198–203.

Shaw, R. L., 'Incaparina, the low cost protein-rich food product', PAG (WHO/FAO/UNICEF) R.10/ADD 92, PAG Compendium, G118 9/12.

Skulstad, C., 'The Pillsbury Company', Harvard Business School, PAG FAO/WHO/UNICEF, PAG Compendium, 9/27 G265, Marketing Meeting, Rome, 1969, Document 2.22/11.

Sukhatme, P. V. (1972/3), 'Protein strategy and agricultural development', Presidential address to 31st Annual Conference Indian Soc. of Agricultural Economics, Varanasi (UP) March 31, 1972. Pub. in *Indian Journal of Agricultural Economics*, Vol. XXVII, No. 1, January–March 1972, pp. 3–24.

Teply, L. J., 'Protein-Rich Foods: Research , Development and Testing', Nutrition Document R.10/ADD.105, PAG (WHO/FAO/UNICEF), August 1966 meeting–Geneva, PAG Compendium 6.4.3/10 E775.

UN ACAST (1968), *International Action to Avert the Impending Protein Crisis*, UN, Geneva.

UN E.71-11-A-17 (1971), 'Strategy Statement on Action to Avert the Protein Crisis in Developing Countries', Report of Panel of Experts on the Protein Problem, UN, Geneva.

UN General Assembly (1965 and 1968), Resolution 2416 (XXIII) of 17 December 1968, Declaration on World Food Problem, Proc. UNCTAD, Vol. 1, Add. 1.

UN FAO/WHO/PAG (1970), 'Lives in peril: protein and the child', *World Food Problems*, No. 12, FAO, Rome.

UN WHO/FAO/UNICEF. PROTEIN ADVISORY GROUP (1956–1976), PAG, Documents, Bulletin, Statements, FAO Rome.

US President's Science Advisory Committee (1967), 'The World Food Problem', Report of Panel on World Food Supply, White House.

Waterlow, J. C. and Payne, P. R. (1975), 'The Protein Gap', *Nature* 258 (5531) November 13, pp. 113–17.

Whitehead, R. G. (1973), in *Proteins in Human Nutrition*, pp. 103–117, Porter, J. W. G. and Rolls, B. A. (eds.), AP London and New York.

Whitehead, R. G. (1974), *Lancet*, 3 August, pp. 280–1.

Williams, C. (1975), 'On that fiasco', *Lancet*, April 5, pp. 793–4.

9 The Accuracy of Long-term Forecasts for Non-Ferrous Metals*

WILLIAM PAGE AND HOWARD RUSH

INTRODUCTION

Investment projects in the mining and smelting industries generally have long time horizons, in that five to ten years may pass between initiating an exploration project and having a mine come into production. Thus the industry has a strong interest in looking ahead at future production capacities and technologies and at the market for its products. However, the industry has the problem of desiring good medium- and long-term forecasts while, it seems, being sceptical of the possibility of ever being able to obtain them – a good forecast being, in this context, one which presents a fairly accurate picture of the environment in which the particular company, nation or other group will be operating, so that its own planning can be on a sound footing.

The aim of this study was to see how justified this scepticism might be, and to see if there was any formula employable by forecasters that would increase the likelihood of their being able to present decision-makers with accurate forecasts.

In this chapter, we briefly summarise an analysis of around ninety forecasts made since 1910,[1] and then focus in more detail upon three specific postwar forecasting exercises. Because the former set was located by searching through the major mining journals, they are referred to as the 'journal forecasts', and they include forecasts made by official bodies (including companies and government agencies) as well as by individuals. The focus is upon non-ferrous metals.

THE JOURNAL FORECASTS

Deciding whether the individual forecasts had proved right or wrong was much easier than might be expected; the majority were expressed in relatively black-and-white terms. Low grade copper ores in Chile were indeed 'developed in abundance' (Douglas, 1910), but the expectation that Malaysia's tin deposits 'will become exhausted in a not distant future' has yet to happen sixty years later (*Mining Journal*, 1913). The same applies to most of the few quantitative forecasts; when US per capita steel consumption was expected to be between 0·59 and 0·73 tonnes in 1970 (Pehrson, 1945), and was actually 0·68 tonnes, we can classify the forecast as right. In the few cases where a forecast was too vague for assessment, or right for clearly wrong reasons, or presented other problems, they were ignored; this involved 32 specific forecasts (8 per cent of the total).

This left 372 suitable for analysis and, perhaps surprisingly, 68 per cent were right, and 32 per cent wrong. The sub-group with the worst accuracy level (precious metals) still had more than half its individual forecasts proved right, and the winner (forecasts of price) scored 84 per cent.

Are the sceptics wrong to disbelieve forecasts, as this result suggests? One explanation of the result could be that the forecasts were generally self-fulfilling, but we reject this on the grounds that the real world is too complex to make it plausible that one forecast (even if presented by a company president) could lead to, say, a high long-term world price for a major commodity, or to a major new market developing. (Of course, the forecasts may well reflect general contemporary expectations, and those general expectations may have influenced events, but that is a different matter. Also, forecasts of specific matters at, say, the level of a particular mine may be self-fulfilling, in that they become part of the plans for the mine; but our forecasts are far from that level of incestuous detail.)

It is perhaps more pertinent to suggest that, in general, these forecasters have played it safe by discussing the least controversial of possibilities in the broadest of terms, rather than putting their heads on the block with unorthodox views. For instance, a 1921 forecast argued that, despite the prevailing depressed metal markets, an 'ever-increasing output' had only been checked 'temporarily' (*Mining and Scientific Press*, 1921); but quantities, prices and dates were steered clear of. We can speculate that more detailed forecasts originated within commercial enterprises, but they were not going to be published for the benefit of competitors.

What factors were associated with accuracy? More post-1940 forecasts were correct than were earlier ones (75 per cent versus 56 per cent), and several possible explanations can be examined.

1. Is accuracy increased with more sophisticated forecasting methods? Our results might be partly explained by increased post-1940 sophistication – but our data does not support this, because 'Simple Methods'[2] were used more in the post-1940 period (up to the 1960s) than before (in 65 per cent of post-1940 exercises, as against 50 per cent in the earlier period), and secondly, because the more sophisticated methods do not appear to have a markedly higher success rate:

	Simple	Intermediate	Explicit Models
% of individual forecasts proving correct	73%	67%	75%
total number	162	180	55

2. Postwar forecasters themselves may have been more sophisticated, extracting more lessons from the past, making fewer naive errors, and so on. To the limited extent that this could be gauged, our evidence does not support it. It is hard to find a qualitative difference between the forecasts in the two periods, and the only practical quantitative measure suggested greater prewar sophistication: six of the twenty-seven prewar exercises contained explicit warnings as to the reliability of forecasts, as against only five of the sixty-three postwar forecasts.

3. Do shorter time-horizons lead to greater accuracy? Unfortunately, too many of the forecasts were too vague on their time horizons to permit a useful test of this idea – reflecting our earlier observation on the safe way the forecasts have been presented.

4. Do wider-ranging studies have greater accuracy than narrower studies? On an *a priori* basis, this relationship could be argued either way (and then tested against the pre-/post-1940 difference); operationally, we generally define narrow studies as those that focused upon one metal, and broader studies, upon two or more. By a fairly narrow margin, narrower studies had higher accuracy (73 per cent of their forecasts proving right, as against 65 per cent of the others); this factor does not fully explain the inter-period difference.

5. The postwar world may have been 'easier' to forecast, so that the greater accuracy of its forecasts says more about the real world than

about the forecasts per se. As a measure of 'easier', we took a measure of the year-to-year fluctuations around the trend, for world production and New York price, of four major metals (aluminium, copper, lead, zinc); an index (the standard deviation of the year-to-year fluctuations) was obtained for each metal for each decade from 1910 to 1969, and it strongly supports the view that the postwar world has been more stable and thus, one can argue, with hindsight, easier to foresee. For instance, the 1950s and 1960s saw less fluctuation in production than any of the prewar decades, and the 1960s, less price fluctuation than any prewar decade.

Thus our overall conclusion is that a surprising number of these forecasts were proved correct, but most of them were rather vague and probably of little direct use to decision-makers. No single factor appears to be well correlated with accuracy, and perhaps the major reason for greater accuracy since 1940 has been the relative stability of the period, rather than anything to do with the forecasts themselves.

One last observation concerns what the forecasters left out. Quantitative measures are not appropriate here, but our impression is that most key developments were anticipated, but rarely in any detail (and, of course, some anticipations proved wrong); and one can point to omissions, such as some forecasters not mentioning the increased economy of use of materials, or missing specific developments such as aluminium beverage cans. Most importantly, we find virtually no anticipation of large changes originating outside the industry, but having a great effect upon it – such as the Great Depression and the Second World War or, more recently, environmental control and Third World politics.

We now turn to three major forecasting exercises, all undertaken since the war and all with a much larger quantitative element; these are cases where necks have been stuck out.

THE PALEY COMMISSION

This report, "Resources for Freedom", has as its central task an examination of the adequacy of materials, chiefly industrial materials, to meet the needs of the free world in the years ahead. Even a casual assessment of these years would show many causes for concern. In area after area, the same pattern seems discernible: soaring demand, shrinking resources, the consequent pressure toward rising real costs, the risk of wartime shortages, the ultimate threat of an arrest of decline in the standard of living we cherish and hope to help others to achieve. If such a threat is to be averted, it will not be by inaction.

This Commission, created by President Truman in January 1951 and presenting its report in June 1952, is commonly acclaimed as the most important long-term forecasting exercise in the minerals business. It is a good report from the perspective of the hindsight reviewer: their target date was relatively clear (the mid-1970s), they made their assumptions explicit, and they stuck their necks out on numbers. We start by assessing their quantitative forecasts and look at what went wrong; then we consider their qualitative forecasts.

The report warns that, 'Projections ascribed to the "year 1975" . . . should not be regarded as applying at that literal point in time, but rather considered as a plausible shape of things in the decade 1970–1980' (Vol. 1, p. 2); this is stressed throughout the report. Given that they were writing about events then twenty-five years away, it is reasonable to respect this request. Not so obvious is exactly how to respect it; while the mid-1970s have been a period of world recession, the years 1972–4 saw a major boom build up and end, and the years yet to come before 1980 are an unknown quantity. Thus which year or years are characteristic of the decade?

1972 has been used in this evaluation, as the last year without major boom or recession. While conceding that this is not an entirely satisfactory solution, we can note that the results so obtained reflect such great divergencies from the forecasts that taking a recession year instead only modified the conclusions, rather than negating them.

The quantitative results are shown in Figure 9.1. (This analysis excludes their forecasts for non-metals.) Each forecast of future demand or production has been compared with the statistics for 1972, and the forecast expressed as a percentage of the actual; thus percentages under 100 per cent show under-estimates and those over 100 percent, over-estimates. Following the report's own procedure, a distinction is drawn between the USA and Other Market Economies. (The Communist countries, with their 'barbarian violence' and 'threats . . . of a new Dark Age', are not projected for.)

The figure shows disappointingly little convergence around 100 per cent (i.e. accuracy). For the USA, only eleven (16 per cent) of the seventy checkable forecasts were between 80 per cent and 120 per cent of the actual figures, although ten of the 51 for OMEs (20 per cent) were within the range. The tendency in the US forecasts was to over-estimate future quantities: 48 of the 70 forecasts (69 per cent) were over-estimates. The

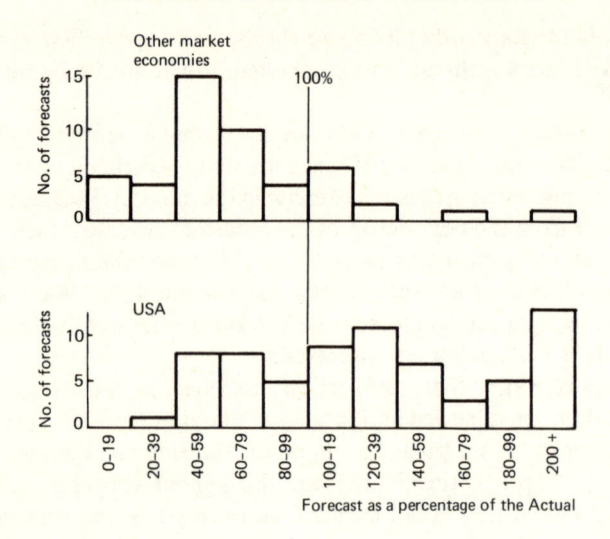

FIGURE 9.1. The Paley Commission: Distribution of outcome
Note: This figure summarises Tables 9.1 to 9.4

position is reversed for OMEs; 39 of the 51 forecasts (76 per cent) were underestimates. Thus the real discrepancy between US and OME levels has proved significantly smaller than anticipated.

The majority of these forecasts were about consumption levels, with a few on production; we take the former first. Table 9.1 summarises the forecasts for total consumption for some metals in the USA and OMEs, and the outcomes. For the USA, these particular results are better than the overall US results; 39 per cent (or 7 out of 18) are within 20 per cent of the actual figures (for 1972), in contrast with only 16 per cent for the overall. However, not one of the OME forecasts is in this range; most of these forecasts have turned out to be between a quarter and a half of the actual, and there was only one over-estimate (antimony).

The Commission presented end-use breakdowns for US consumption for iron and steel, copper, lead, zinc, tin and antimony; 41 such forecasts were given that can be checked against statistics (and were also included in Table 9.2). Seven of these (17 per cent) were within 20 per cent of the actual figures (as against 39 per cent for aggregated demand). This could suggest that greater aggregation leads to greater accuracy, but this conclusion would be based on weak evidence because, if we take as a base for comparison the six relevant aggregate demand forecasts, rather than all of them, we have only one which is within the 20 per cent range.

Table 9.2 gives more information on the outcome of the end-use

TABLE 9.1 Paley Commission: Forecasts of annual demands in the 1970s compared with 1972 actual demands

Units: '000 short tons

	USA Forecast for 1970s	USA Actual 1972	Forecast/Actual %	Other Market Economies Forecast for 1970s	Other Market Economies Actual 1972	Forecast/Actual %
Iron ore	100 000	81 900	122	61 000	404 800	15
Crude steel products	150 000	124 500	138	124 000	280 900	44
Iron castings	22 000	—	—	—	—	—
Bismuth	1·75	1·46	120	·75	?	?
Chromium	1 960	558	351	1 230	3 500	35
Cobalt	20	19·5	103	13·0	39*	33
Manganese	1 242	1 366	91	1 058	?	?
Molybdenum	35	25·8	136	13·5	63	21
Nickel	200	246	81	64	309	21
Tungsten	7·5	7·1	106	27·5	35·3**	78
Aluminium	3 600	4 701	77	2 400	5 600	43
Antimony	28	19·9	141	50	29	170
Cadmium	12·5	6·3	198	6·0	12·4*	48
Copper	1 800	1 951	92	2 050	4 024	51
Lead	1 200	954	126	1 500	2 201	68
Magnesium	500	1 109	45	—	—	—
Mercury	2·4	2·0	118	—	—	—
Tin	94	49	192	122	199	61
Zinc	1 500	1 206	124	1 700	3 289	52

*1974.
**Non-communist world production less US consumption.
(Source: U.S. Bureau of Mines)

TABLE 9.2 Paley Commission: distribution of outcomes of end-use forecasts for the USA.

Forecast/Actual	Total	Iron, steel	Copper	Lead	Zinc	Tin	Antimony
0–79%	12	3	3	3	1	0	2
80–120%	7	2	1	2	1	0	1
over 120%	22	2	1	3	3	6	7
Total	41	7	5	8	5	6	10

forecasts. It shows that nearly twice as many items outside the 80–120 per cent bracket were over-estimates rather than under-estimates (which fits in with the exaggeration of the overall US forecasts). Iron/steel and copper are the only exceptions. (The immediate reasons for error are discussed below.)

Table 9.3 gives more information on the forecasts for total demand in OMEs (for which areas very few end-use breakdowns were offered). As already observed, there was a strong tendency to under-estimate future demands. Of the nineteen under-estimates, fifteen are attributable to under-estimating demand for all five metals in Europe (less the UK) and Japan, and to under-estimating demand for steel and tin in all but one region.

TABLE 9.3 Paley Commission: distribution of outcomes for consumption forecasts in the six regions included in 'Other Market Economies'

Forecast Actual	Total	Canada	Australia New Zealand	UK	'Free Europe'	Japan	Other
0–79%	19	3	2	1	5	5	3
80–120%	8	1	2	4	0	0	1
	3	1	1	0	0	0	1
Total	30	5	5	5	5	5	5

The report also gave future estimates of mine production in the USA and OMEs, and secondary (recycled) production in the USA. Table 9.4 shows the outcome for the six metals that can be checked. No systematic bias emerges for US mine production; while lead and copper production have turned out to be double the expectation, zinc and antimony

TABLE 9.4 Paley Commission: distribution of outcomes for mine and secondary production

Forecast Actual	US Mine	Recycled	OME Mine	Total
0–79%	2	1	3	6
80–120%	2	0	2	4
Over 120%	2	3	1	6
Total	6	4	6	16

Metals: Copper, lead, zinc, tin, antimony, cadmium (for cadmium: smelter production).

Source: U.S. Bureau of Mines

production have been considerably less. In contrast, the levels of recycling in the US have proved considerably less than forecast, except for zinc (where the actual was nearly three times the forecast tonnage).

In keeping with other under-estimates for the OMEs, their production has greatly exceeded expectations. For instance, nearly 4·2 m short tonnes of zinc were mined, not 2·5 m; and 4·55 m tons of copper, as against the expected 3·05 m OME tin production, on the other hand, was put at 216 000 short tons, and was actually 215 200 tons.

Thus, by and large, the Paley quantitative forecasts have been a pretty poor set, tending to over-estimate levels in the USA (but with plenty of under-estimates too), and under-estimate levels in other countries. What reasons can be put forward for this?

A number of basic assumptions underlay the Paley forecasts, concerning population size, gross national product, the output by various economic sectors, and so on. Table 9.5 compares their expectations of total growth from 1950 to the 1970s in several parameters in the USA with the actual growth (to 1972). What is noteworthy is that, in all cases bar two (new railway equipment and shipbuilding), the growth was under-estimated – but, as we saw, metal demand was generally over-estimated. Thus we can speculate that, had they forecast these parameters correctly, then many of their metal forecasts would have been even further off the mark.

In a recent review, Cooper (1975) suggests three possible reasons for this discrepancy. He firstly explores the idea that the trends for metal demand as forecast by Paley were, in one sense, right, but led to increased prices and thus to demand levels that were lower than they otherwise would have been. If correct, one would expect the larger over-estimates to be associated with the greater increases in prices; as he says, the evidence for this is in fact weak. Secondly, that demand for primary metal was over-estimated could be because secondary supplies were greater than expected (thus reducing the need for primary metal); this suggestion is not helped by there having been less recycling than generally expected, not more. Lastly, demand could have been as forecast, the discrepancy being explained by increased net imports of materials in manufactured goods; although Cooper points out that his evidence is not definitive, it does not seem to support this suggestion either.

There are at least two further possibilities. One is that growth in the manufacturing and other materials-using sectors was over-estimated; the evidence of Table 9.5 suggests the opposite to be true. Otherwise, the rate of improvement in the efficiency of use of materials may have been

TABLE 9.5 The Paley Commission: Expected total growth in some economic parameters between 1950 and 1970s, compared with actual growth by 1972

	Units	Forecast for 1970s	Actual 1972
Population	Number	27%	38%
Labour force		27	39
Dwelling units in use		50	60
Phones in use		50–85%	156
Gross national product	Money	100	123
Gross private domestic investment		40	50
Construction		30	52
Residential construction		15	76
Private non-residential construction		50	380
Demand for new producer durable equipment		50	150
New passenger cars		15	39
New motor vehicles		33⅓	60
New railroad equipment		100	33
Demand for new agricultural machinery		0	52
Demand for new consumer durables		40	285*
Shipbuilding	Gross tons	0	−12

*Personal consumer expenditure on durable goods.
Source: US Dept. of Commerce: Statistical Abstract for the United States.

under-estimated — that less material is required to do a given thing than they expected.

To check this second hypothesis, we need to find in the Report forecasts of how much of a metal will be required by a given industry for each unit of output. Unfortunately, we find very few such instances, but the four we have found and can check on do appear to support the hypothesis. In 1972, the US construction industry appears to have used only 48 per cent of the steel that Paley expected, per unit of output; the automobile industry used only 27 per cent, railroads 15 per cent and agricultural machinery, 14 per cent. These latter figures are so low as to be startling, and suggest that the comparison is not with identically defined measures. Substitution of steel by other materials must also help explain these figures. (The *US Dept. of Commerce: Statistical Abstract for the US* was used for this exercise; their figures for 1950 steel consumption were different from Paley's in all four cases and so, for consistency, the Paley 1950–70s growth-rate was applied, not to the Paley 1950 figures, but to the Department's. Thus this problem should have been minimised.)

As regards Other Market Economies, their economic growth was also under-estimated (as was their metal consumption). For continental Western Europe, GNP was expected to grow by around 2·5 per cent p.a.; in fact, the figure has been more like 5·5 per cent, the 2 per cent for the UK has been more like 3 per cent, Canada's 3 per cent has been nearer 5 per cent, as has the 4 per cent for Australia; and Japan hit 10 per cent, not 4·8 per cent. Given the lack of further information on their thinking, it is perhaps impossible to identify what exactly went wrong in this part of the report.

In summary, the Paley Report got most of its forecasts significantly wrong, under-estimating economic growth-rates inside and outside the USA, under-estimating metal demand outside the USA, and tending to over-estimate it inside. We can agree with both Cooper (1975) and Cosman (1974), who point out that the rates of economic growth since the last war have been exceptional in historic terms and higher than anyone could have reasonably foreseen. The rate of technological progress has contributed to this, and appears to be the source of several of Paley's errors in the forecasts for the US.

Despite all the foregoing comments, the final conclusions of the Report have stood the test of time: it is still sensible for the US Government to encourage the investment of risk capital in mining, to continuously monitor the mineral supply position in the US, and to stimulate research and development into the technology of mineral supply and consumption. But perhaps there are some aspects of the minerals business that never change (even if their relative priority and details do change), and these three may be amongst them. Thus hitting them may not be greatly to Paley's credit – but missing them would certainly have been to his discredit.

THE ROBERTSON TIN STUDY

The International Tin Council, under whose auspices this study was undertaken, is a joint producer-consumer intergovernmental body whose responsibilities include monitoring long-term trends in tin supply and demand. In 1961, the ITC decided that, 'in view of the difficulties that have been facing the world tin industry in recent years and which might continue for some time in the future, it was desirable to undertake a detailed inquiry into the long-term position of the industry' (p. 9). The target date of 1970 was taken as near enough to be useful, but sufficiently far away to indicate long-term trends.

Many of the quantitative forecasts, which we look at first, were made dependent upon the price of tin; £700, £900 and £1100 per ton were the price levels used. In general, the higher price was associated with greater production but lower consumption. In fact, the LME annual average price has not been as low as even the high figure for any year since 1964, when this report was published; in three years between then and 1970, it was over £1200, over £1300 in one, over £1400 in two, and was £1530 in 1970 itself. Correcting metal prices for inflation always involves controversy, especially when several countries and currencies are involved. But certainly, the actual price has been closest to the highest of the three prices, if not in excess of it.

Of the 78 forecasts[3] for which no specific price was given or which were based on £1100/ton, ten (13 per cent) were within 5 per cent of the actual 1970 figure, and a further five within 10 per cent. Only one of these forecasts was less than half the actual figure, but seven were double the actual. Figure 9.2 shows this in more detail.

These results combine forecasts of consumption and demand, which may be unfair because under-estimating price may have led to under-estimating production but over-estimating demand. This result is indeed the case; 12 of the 25 production forecasts (based on £1100 or no price) were under-estimates, as against 17 of the 53 (32 per cent) of the consumption forecasts. Thus Robertson's basic model may have been right, but he plugged the wrong prices levels into it.

For this to be the case, one would expect the consumption forecasts to be off the mark by a roughly constant degree, and the production forecasts to be off by another but roughly constant degree. Figure 9.3 shows this not to be the case. Following our forecast/actual measure, the middle one-third of the outcomes for consumption covers a range of nearly 40 percentage points (from 100 per cent to 137 per cent); and for production, a range of over 30 points (from 93 per cent to 125 per cent); the remaining two-thirds lie outside this range. Whatever it is that might constitute a roughly constant degree of error, this would not seem to be it. Thus, without yet having looked at Robertson's model, the problem appears to go deeper than simply having used the wrong price levels.

Reference to 'Robertson's model' is in fact misleading, because the forecasts did not generally originate from him. A series of question-

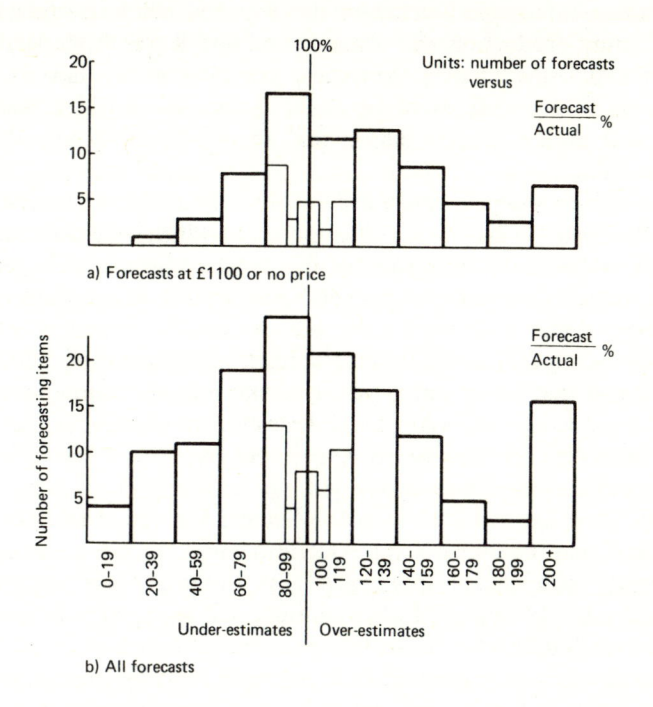

FIGURE 9.2. The Robertson Report: Distribution of outcomes (aggregated)

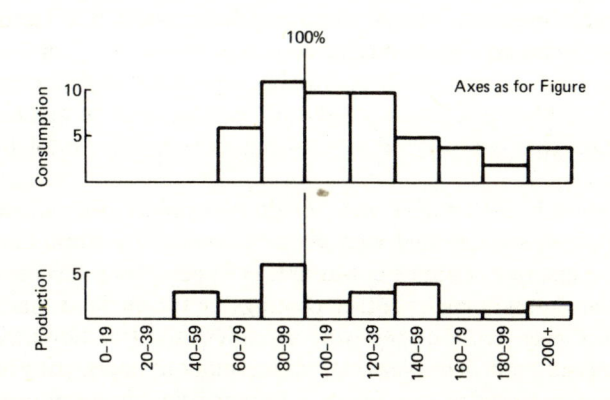

FIGURE 9.3. The Robertson Report: Distribution of outcomes (disaggregated; £1100 or no price)

naires was sent to governments and they supplied their own estimates for their future production and consumption and it was Robertson who wrote it up. Unfortunately, the Report only gives the results and not the basis on which they were obtained (information which was not requested in the questionnaires, and so not generally available to Robertson).

For those especially interested, we can illustrate the success and failures. Forecasts based on £1100 or no price which were markedly too low include primary tin consumption in Western Germany (70 per cent of the actual), Denmark (78 per cent), and smaller Asian countries (79 per cent); Malaysia's production was put at 73 per cent of what it actually was (dredge output being correct, at 103 per cent, but it was anticipated that gravel pump output would roughly double), and two minor producing areas were also under-estimated: the UK (71 per cent) and Latin America (less Bolivia), at 56 per cent.

Instances where consumption was put at over 150 per cent of the actual figure are Austria, Sweden, Greece, Finland, India, Turkey, Thailand, and the similar Latin American countries; UK consumption in tinplate, solder and 'miscellaneous' (148 per cent, 135 per cent and 189 per cent respectively), and Italian consumption in tinplate was expected to be over double what it was (219 per cent). Production by dredge in Thailand was over-estimated (157 per cent), and by hydraulicing in Malaysia (its virtual disappearance not being anticipated); production in Indonesia, Mexico, Canada and 'Other Asia' were all forecast at over 150 per cent of the actual.

Moving to successes, forecasts which were within 5 per cent of the actual figure were total primary consumption in the EEC ('The Six'), in Portugal, Spain and South Africa; consumption of tin in tinplate in the EEC; and mine production by dredge, open-cast and underground methods in Malaysia (but not her total production), total Thai mine production (but not any of its sub-components), and total Bolivian output.

Robertson himself makes many qualitative points, often drawing on acknowledged sources, and virtually all of these have stood the test of time. For instance, tinplate consumption has not been severely hit by aluminium, glass, plastics, other coatings or frozen food, and where there have been battles, they were as anticipated (for beverage cans, motor oil cans, etc). The observations on solder have generally held up: solder is indeed used more economically in wiring, car radiators still use it, glues and resins have not ousted it from many other mechanical joints, and so on. Various changes in bearing metals did indeed roughly cancel out, leading to a fairly constant total demand, but the growth of plastics in this area may have been over-estimated. The estimated world use of tin in bronze and brass did not change much (bearing out Robertson's conclusion); Germany and the USA were wrong in anticipating significant declines for themselves, although Australia was right in doing so.

The production, smelting and trade in tin are roughly as qualitatively expected. While French exports of tinplate did not decline (thus, a wrong forecast), Bolivian mine output did indeed grow to as good as 30 000 tons (although her state-owned industry may not have yet reached as sound an economic footing as hoped for). Again, releases of tin from the US stockpile have played a significant role in the market, as anticipated.

Although the Report is long and contains much information, little of it helps in seeing why some forecasts were better than others. Few clues are given as to the methods used, although we may suppose that any relatively sophisticated method (e.g. econometric and model-building) would have been mentioned if used. As the report says of European tinplate, 'These estimates, it must be stressed, should be treated with caution. As the Italian reply [to the questionnaire] points out, "our estimates for 1965 have been extrapolated to 1970 and therefore their reliability ... is greatly reduced".' (p. 31)

Two further points can be made. Firstly, the qualitative observations on tin consumption (just mentioned) drew heavily on senior staff of the Tin Research Institute, a highly respected organisation. That they were generally correct supports the view that professionals often know what they are talking about; on the other hand, we do not know the standing of the other forecasters contributing to the report and, in particular, of those who got things wrong.

Secondly, there is evidence, albeit limited, of systematic biases in the forecasts originating in some countries. For instance, Italy tended to over-estimate, and Germany to under-estimate, their respective future requirements; why, we cannot say. For instance, the levels of industrial output or the rate of technical change may have been estimated wrongly, or apparently definite plans for new tin-using plants may have turned out differently.

In summary, it is hard to evaluate this Report except in terms of the accuracy of the forecasts it contains; the methods used to derive the forecasts, and the use to which the results were put, are both unknown quantities. However, Robertson suggests that 'it is likely that the Report and the meetings of the Working Party led to more attention being paid to long-term issues. A series of major conferences followed on a wide range of issues affecting the tin-mining industry. The discussion on reserves, however uncertain such figures may be, gave greater confidence to consumers that there was plenty of tin in the ground. Previously there had been serious doubts about reserves and only scattered information.' (Personal communication.)

Lastly, we return to prices and the choice of which to use. As Robertson says, the choice was reasonable at the time, but what upset things were disruptions in several of the major producing countries. 'Non-economic forces had a great effect on the industry in the sixties. The former Belgian Congo was torn by civil war. The Indonesian tin-mining industry was badly hit by the loss of foreign skilled labour and foreign capital which followed the nationalisation of the industry. Its decline was also precipitated by acute management problems which took years to sort out. The Bolivian industry suffered from similar problems.' (Personal communication.)

Thus once again, the forecasts for a metal have been rendered less accurate by events partly outside that specific industry.

'RESOURCES IN AMERICA'S FUTURE'

This study was led by Hans Landsberg, Leonard Fischman and Joseph Fisher for the US research institute, Resources for the Future Inc., and published in 1964. In stating the general purpose of the study, the authors say, 'By the year 2000, the United States probably will have well over 300 million people who will want and expect even higher levels of living than those of today—better diets, better housing, more consumer goods of all kinds. . . .' Defence, overseas aid and the space programme were expected to continue, and this all leads to the question: 'Can the United States over the balance of the twentieth century count on enough natural resource supplies to sustain a rate of economic growth sufficient for their attainment?' (p. 3)

Their approach was to make some central underlying assumptions about the future in general and then to consider economic activity and material resource requirements by major economic sectors. Added together, this generated high, medium and low projections of US consumption of many individual materials; potential supplies were then compared to these requirements. Table 9.6 shows their forecasts for demand for some major metals in the US by 1970.

In assessing these forecasts, we are fortunate in being able to draw on

TABLE 9.6 Outcome of RFF forecasts for USA: primary metal demand*

	Units (short tons) millions	1960 Actual	Forecast for 1970 Low	Forecast for 1970 Medium	Forecast for 1970 High	Actual 1969–70–71 average	Medium 1970 forecast Act. '69–71 av. %
Copper	millions	1·69	1·45	1·97	2·44	1·83	107
Lead		·62	·47	·68	·98	·90	76
Zinc		1·02	1·03	1·34	1·73	1·16	116
Aluminium		2·06	2·44	3·42	5·07	5·36	*64*
Iron ore (iron content)		66·5	67·9	89·9	114·3	81·9	110
Manganese	thousands	64	37	55	90	64·0	111
Tin		118	139	183	230	145	86
Nickel		520	610	770	940	*444*	126
Chromium							*174*
Molybdenum		15·9	22·4	30·7	38·9	24·5	125
Tungsten		4·6	6	8	10	7·1	112
Cobalt		4·5	5·4	7·1	9·0	6·0	118
Vanadium		2·0	2·3	3·1	3·7	7·3	43

* For the non-ferrous metals, these figures include gross exports as part of the primary demand, following the manner in which RFF calculated primary demand; for the ferrous metals (iron ore downwards, less tin), only domestic industrial demand for primary metal is included. The actual figures have been italicised when they lie outside the RFF range.

Sources: RFF forecasts from various appendices; Actual figures from US Bureau of Mines: Minerals in the US Economy, Ten Year Supply-Demand Profiles; US GPO, 1975.

a hindsight review by Landsberg himself. He remarks that 'very few (of the) projections are out of the ball park . . . (and) . . . some projections are strikingly close to reality' (p. 6).

Table 9.7 gives thirteeen projections for primary metal demand in the USA in 1970 and compares them with the average actual figure for 1969–70–71. Seven of the thirteen medium projections (54 per cent) were within 20 per cent of the actual figures, although only two (copper and iron ore – both important commodities) were within 10 per cent. At the other extreme, the medium projections for aluminium and vanadium were 64 per cent and 43 per cent, respectively, of the actual figures; the medium projection for chromium as 74 per cent above the actual. However, only two of the thirteen actual figures lay outside the ball park (aluminium was above the high, chromium below the low).

In total, there were four under-estimates and nine over-estimates, suggesting a marked tendency towards the latter.

Thus our conclusion is slightly less favourable than Landsberg's own, the differences in the results being attributable to our taking a fuller list of metals and to having different actual figures – perhaps reflecting definitional problems in different sources. (Also Landsberg has revised some of the 1970 forecasts slightly, by correcting their Base Year estimates (i.e. 1960) to make them agree with later RFF estimates of the 1960 quantities.) As might be expected, the comparison of projections with outcomes becomes less favourable when one takes relative changes rather than absolute levels. Previously, only two of the thirteen medium projections of absolute levels were more than 40 per cent away from the actual; however, twelve of the thirteen medium projections of changes were this far out (including two with the wrong direction of change – and for which simple percentage errors cannot be calculated on the same basis). In fact, three were more than double the medium change forecast, and three less than half. An error of even 40 per cent or more in estimating how much new capacity would be needed is immense (although we have yet to look at whether the authors had such uses in mind).

Some other forecasts were also given for metals, including end-use breakdowns and gross exports (included in some of the above forecasts) and production of metal from scrap (which, added to the above forecasts, gives a total metal consumption). For the four base metals and aluminium, the secondary production figures (i.e. from scrap) were all over-estimated, the same tendency as in Paley; two were within the range forecast (that for aluminium being only 3 per cent away from the actual); the other three lay outside the range, tin being the extreme case in

TABLE 9.7 Accuracy of the RIAF aggregated forecasts (relative changes)

	Units (long tons)	1960 Actual	Change fcst. for 1970 Low	Medium	High	Actual change	1960–70 Fcst. change (Medium) / 1960–70 Actual change
Copper	million	1·81	−·26	·30	·80	·33	91%
Lead		1·02	−·03	·21	·51	·37	57
Zinc		1·04	·01	·33	·72	·38	87
Aluminium		2·09	·39	1·38	3·05	2·44	57
Iron ore		133	3	47	96	−51	(Wrong direction)
Raw steel		99	9	42	79	18	233
Manganese		1·14	−·06	·27	·60	·41	66
Tin	thousand	62	−26	−9	25	4	(Wrong direction)
Nickel		128	23	70	122	81	86
Chrome		520	90	250	420	−10	(Wrong direction)
Molybdenum		15·9	6·5	14·8	23·0	33·2	224
Tungsten		4·6	1·4	3·4	5·4	10·2	300
Cobalt		4·5	·9	2·6	4·5	11·9	460

Source: as for previous table.

percentage terms (the medium forecast being 250 per cent of the actual).

In the case of lead, the under-estimating of primary demand (the medium was 76 per cent of the actual) was helped by the over-estimating of secondary production, so that the total demand forecast was nearer the mark (the medium now being 91 per cent of the actual). However, for tin an under-estimated primary demand became an almost equally over-estimated total demand (from 86 per cent to 116 per cent), and for copper, an over-estimate of 7 per cent became one of 14 per cent. For zinc and aluminium, the change in outcome is only 1 per cent. Thus errors tended to cancel one another in only one of the five cases.

Gross exports were included for these metals. They were right in anticipating negligible exports of three metals, and copper hit the low forecast. Aluminium exports were the only deviation from expectation: over one million tons, way above the high of 160 000 tons.

The forecasts for each metal were based on end-use breakdowns, giving us a further opportunity to compare individual projections with reality. Unfortunately, definitional problems and changes in the sub-headings used in collecting statistics make this a very limited opportunity. On the one hand, their medium projection for the use of aluminium in building and construction was within 10 per cent of the actual (forecast 1·08m tons, actual 1·20m); the 0·86m expected for transport proved to be 0·94m (suggesting cancelling errors, because an important assumption about aluminium car engines proved unduly optimistic). More aluminium was used in packaging than in even the high projection. The use of copper in transport in 1970 was below their low projection (225 000 tons against 240 000, and a medium of 273 000); copper consumption in building and construction was within the range, but very close to the low (low: 431 000 tons; actual: 450 000; medium: 663 000).

Some other comparisons are so way out as to suggest different definitions being used, although one cannot always be sure. Their range for aluminium in 'Electric Power Construction' was from 60 000 to 240 000 tons; the actual for 'Electrical Construction' was 600 000 tons; this probably reflects both definitional problems as well as under-estimating. To compare copper consumption in 'Electrical Power Construction' with 'Electrical and Electronics' is clearly mistaken, especially when the former list of end-uses also contains 'Consumer Durables' and 'Producer Durables'.

This said, we have identified twenty-five end-use projections for non-ferrous metals that we believe can be evaluated relatively fairly (some mentioned already). Of these, seventeen (68 per cent) of the mediums were over-estimates, thus showing the same general bias as in the aggregate forecasts. Seven (28 per cent) were within 10 per cent, eleven (i.e. four more) within 20 per cent, but nine were over 60 per cent out. Twelve (48 per cent) lay outside their high-low range.

Without any pretence of being able to do any better, one can still express disappointment at such results. This is made more so if we take into account the breadth of the range covered by the high–low projections. Of the two projections of primary demand where the range missed the actual, the high is 54 per cent above the low in one case, and double it in the other. In all other cases, the high was at least 60 per cent above the low. The breadth of the ranges is made yet more apparent by looking at them in terms of the changes expected in comparison to the base year (1960); examples typical of types include copper (a 1960 level of 1·69m tons declining by 0·24m or increasing by 0·75m), zinc (up by 0·01m to 0·71m, from 1·02m) and nickel (an increase of between 21 000 to 112 000 tons, on a base of 118 000).

The existence of such a wide range raises the question of how useful such projections can be. For instance, the nickel or zinc industries would have received little guidance regarding whether to build new smelters or not (and copper, whether to close smelters or not). Here it is fair to raise one of Landsberg's own hindsight remarks: the need 'to tell the consumer in unmistakable terms the purpose of the projection' (p.13); the aim of the RFF study was not to provide direct guidance on investment programmes, but to test the adequacy of reserves against possible demand levels.

Although the Report says much about the adequacy of reserves and supplies, it is not so easy to assess these sections; they are more qualitative and less specific on timing, being mainly concerned with the whole period up to 2000. What one can say – and it is a respectable compliment – is that little, if any, of it permits the present-day reader to feel superior. For instance, there are no indications of panic on discovering projected cumulative demand to outstrip known reserves, but instead a calm argument that this indicates a need for further exploration. On the other hand, the discussion does tend to remain at a broad level; the authors do not, for example, stick their necks out on specific future production costs or reserve levels.

Despite this qualified approbation for their discussion on supply, with hindsight we can see two significant omissions: pollution and Third World politics. The former is mentioned under a section on water, with no inkling of mine or smelter pollution problems; there appears to be no explicit reference to producer government cartel formation, nationalisation and the like. Both these issues have been dominant over the last few years, and we can also suggest that, as with many of the omissions in the journal forecasts, these are also issues with origins outside the narrowly-defined metal-producing and -using industries.

Landsberg describes such omissions as the missing of the 'emergence of new societal perceptions and goals' and as not 'divining changes in public policy, both at home and abroad' (p. 12). A further example of this concerns the steel alloying element, chromium, whose demand was over-estimated by 74 per cent. Part of the problem lay with the Rhodesian situation, that country being a major source of supply; substitute elements were used in its place. Other lessons he draws are also worth mentioning.

There is 'the difficulty in forecasting direction and speed of technological change'. One instance he quotes is that of the aluminium engine block for cars; this 'seemed to be a reasonable idea, given the lighter weight, resulting fuel savings, etc' (pp. 7–8), and secondly, at the time of projecting, eight US car models had adopted such an engine. The seven who then reverted to cast iron blocks did not do so until the book was in print. Lead and tin revealed two further instances of technological change occurring more slowly than anticipated; the life of car batteries did not increase so much, and the thickness of tin on tinplate did not decrease so much. It seems worth highlighting the point that, in these instances, it was not unexpected technological developments that upset the picture, but rather a lack of development that had been expected. These instances run contrary to the conclusions from the analysis of the Paley Commission.

Then there were the 'changes in major parameters, e.g. rate of population growth'. The medium projected population size for the US in 1970 was 210 million; the actual was 205 million, only 2·5 per cent less. In many cases, the changes were more significant that the absolute levels; for instance, the demand for many consumer durables was partly related to the number of new households being created. On the medium basis, they expected a growth of 30 million between 1960 and 1970; the 25 million actually achieved as 17 per cent less. On the other hand, the actual 1970 size of the labour-force was 25 per cent above the 1960 level, not 18 per cent. Gross national product was almost exactly as anticipated: $740b in 1960 dollars) against the projected $730b; an actual increase of $240b against the expected $230b. This is within the error limits of the GNP measurement, and was a remarkable achievement.

Landsberg adds, 'Facile reliance on past relationships between sets of time series that exhibit sturdy constancy in the past but may hide internal divergences liable to break loose during the projection period. . . . ' For instance, the proportion of GNP to be allocated to residential construction was over-estimated with the resultant over-estimates of the various elements in such construction – including the demand for timber and related materials. Another general principle was the implicit assumption of stable relative prices of material; demand was first assessed, without, considering price changes; then the adequacy of reserves was tested; and, as Landsberg says, the implications of, and for, price were not brought out.

SUMMARY AND CONCLUSIONS

Our first conclusion is as might be expected: that the forecasts in the three major studies (Paley, the Robertson tin report and the study by RFF) have generally turned out to be off the mark and, in some cases, very seriously so. In contrast, the conclusion from the analysis of the journal forecasts may be surprising: that nearly 70 per cent of their forecasts can be classified as right. How do we explain his apparent contradiction?

Fairly easily, by pointing out that the three major studies went in for much quantification, while the journal articles generally steered clear of quantification. The way we analysed the qualitative forecasts meant that, had RFF or Paley said, for instance, that the demand for lead was 'likely to grow significantly over the next ten (or twenty-five) years', then we would have said these items proved correct; as it is, their forecasts were 126 per cent and 76 per cent respectively, of the actual US figures, and so we have implied that they were in error. Equally, had we been present when some of the 'correct' qualitative forecasts were made, and bullied the authors into inserting numbers, perhaps our evaluation would now be different. Thus the two sets of forecasts can only be compared with caution, as the same criteria for accuracy cannot be applied to both (a brief qualitative item cannot be satisfactorily described as 80 per cent correct, say, and a quantitative forecast that is 80 per cent of the actual value cannot be satisfactorily described as 'right' or 'wrong').

This takes us back to a key comment made in the journal section: to what extent are the qualitative forecasts actually saying very much? We suggest that their apparent accuracy may be partly the result of the broad and ill-defined meaning of many of the individual forecasts, screens that the three major studies did not generally hide behind.

Whether the vaguer nature of the journal forecasts is important to the user or not depends upon the use; we shall return to this.

The analysis of journal forecasts considered a number of hypotheses on what factors were associated with accuracy. We can now put the results of the analyses of the other three studies into the pool, and attempt to draw some final conclusions. We should not expect to find accuracy 'determined' by just one factor; we should almost certainly be looking for some contribution from many. Unfortunately, it does not seem possible to obtain all the information that would be necessary to discover the true importance of each of the possible individual factors; given the potential complexity of the various interactions between them, such a task might be virtually impossible for conceptual reasons, let alone pragmatic ones.

Firstly, we look at the influence of the one factor which is not under the control of the forecaster (or the commissioning agent), so as to get it out of the way: the historical period in which the study was done. We saw from the journal articles that there is no strong evidence that forecasters were improving their skills, up to at least the mid-1960s. Although more of the postwar journal forecasts have proved correct than of the prewar, it is equally arguable that the postwar forecasters had an easier task, because in some respects, the postwar world (up to the early 1970s) has been more stable. We could also add that RFF, publishing in 1964, perhaps did better at forecasting US demand in the 1970s than did Paley twelve years earlier (e.g. 7 of the 13 such RFF medium forecasts were within 20 per cent of the actual levels, as against 7 of the 18 for Paley); but many other factors could explain this (including, of course, the shorter time horizon for RFF).

Now we turn to factors which are more under the control of the forecaster (or his commissioning agent) and which, our evidence suggests, may have a bearing on accuracy.

How broad a study? Those journal forecasts which limited themselves primarily to one metal produced slightly more accurate forecasts than the broader ones which looked at two or more (73 per cent of forecasting items in the former category have proved correct, as against 65 per cent of the latter. This principle is not supported by the results of the three major studies. As just mentioned, 7 of Paley's forecasts for total US demand of 18 metals, and 7 of the 13 of RFF, were within 20 per cent of the actual value; this is 39 per cent and 54 per cent respectively. One would thus hope that more than 54 per cent of the Robertson demand forecasts have proved equally good, as they were all for tin. But no — only 40 per cent (for tin at £1100/ton or no specific price). While noting this, we may still care to give more weight to the conclusion based on ninety exercises (the journal forecasts) than on three — although the conclusion based on the ninety was not a strong one.

How large a team to use? Although there are several possible explanations for the apparent difference in accuracy between the two sets of forecasts, it could be that the form of publication itself — journals versus books — is relevant, in so far as this indicates the scale of the original forecasting exercise. It is possible that the lone author, perhaps using a few unacknowledged sounding-boards, could be a more accurate forecaster than a team or a committee, where there may be inhibitions against the less conventional view. (The so-called delphi technique is based on this premise, and social psychologists can offer some evidence for it.) The results of our analysis are consistent with this view, but that is not proof of a causal relationship; and even if it was, one would still want to know what was the underlying mechanism.

How expert should the forecaster be? Clearly, all the forecasters covered in this review had some knowledge of the areas in which they were forecasting (or else their work would not have been published in this form). The analysis of the journal forecasts asked whether 'top people' (company presidents, etc) had a better track record than the others; the minimal evidence available did not back this up very much. The three major studies involved eminent people, and they certainly did not score top marks. Thus this study does not indicate that eminence goes with accuracy.

What type of method to use? This study could not examine the track record of the most recent forecasting methods (cross-impact matrices, simulation models, delphi, etc), simply because they are recent innovations. However, the analysis did show marginally different accuracies to be associated with different methods; the most accurate forecasts were associated with the use of what we called Explicit models, followed by Simple methods, and with Intermediate methods being least accurate. While the differences were marginal (and, were tests available, would probably not be statistically significant), we may wonder whether the conclusion is supported by the analysis of the three major exercises. The tin study must be omitted because we do not know what method or methods were used, but we do know that the other two used Explicit models. But again, we cannot compare the accuracy of their quantitative forecasts with that of the more qualitative journal forecasts, and so we cannot draw definite conclusions about the effects of method.

What precision should be aimed at in the forecasts? This study appears to confirm the idea that, the more precise and detailed the forecast, the less likely it is to finally prove correct. It is a great pity that the fall-off in accuracy with increasing precision and quantification is as great as the comparison of the two sets of forecasts appears to suggest. Although it is pleasing to know that the track record of broad forecasts is not too bad, it would be much more useful to know that some faith could be placed in exact forecasts of, say, demand by metal and by market. This study does not provide such reassurance.

Are forecasters generally prone to any particular biases? 132 of the wrong forecasts in the journal set could be labelled as over- or under-estimates of future changes; the majority (63 per cent) were under-estimates. The converse is true for the three major studies (68 per cent of the tin study forecasts for total demand were *over*-estimates, 69 per cent of the RFF total demand forecasts, and 82 per cent of the equivalent Paley forecasts for the US – but only 7 per cent of the non-US Paley demand forecasts).

It is disconcerting to find this difference, and there is no obvious explanation for it; there is not, for instance, any special concentration of over- or under-estimates in any particular area, such as base metals or rates of technical change. The only exception (which cannot explain the difference) concerns the larger, wilder ideas, such as nuclear blasting, the rise of the less-used metals (such as indium in general, or titanium in the transport sector), or non-bauxite sources of aluminium; these forecasts were often highly optimistic.

We could not help noticing that the forecasts generally said little about future developments outside the narrowly-defined metal-producing and -consuming industries, except for the odd comment on future levels of economic activity or population size, for instance (and for those forecasts made in the early 1940s, on the return to peace; and in the years following, on the Cold War). It also seemed that the forecasts were rendered less accurate by such developments in the real world. For instance, Paley's forecasts for Other Market Economies assumed what turned out to be very pessimistic expectations of economic growth outside the USA; the tin study used price levels which were based on little future political disruption to tin production; and the RFF forecasts for the rest of the century, if not so far, will be messed up by the effects of pollution control, international politics, and other post-1960 developments. The same principle applies to many of the journal articles.

What this study cannot show (because of lack of instances) is that more accurate forecasts result from looking at broader social and political issues. It could be that forecasts of such matters would generally prove wrong, and so bring down the metal forecasts based on them. And, of course, assumptions about such matters are made in the reviewed forecasts; it is just that the usual assumption is implicit and is that of no significant change.

There is one last conclusion, which concerns the value of this kind of study. As was mentioned at the outset, very little information was available on each of the forecasts so that, for instance, we could say little about the real usefulness of the various forecasts. Although it was not made explicit, the present authors are very aware that accuracy is not the only parameter of interest; indeed, some of the least accurate forecasts (including Paley) may still have been some of the most useful, and the fact that they were used could, in some cases, have been responsible for their negation. The authors also acknowledge that some of the more influential forecasts may have been kept in-house, and so could not have been encountered in this survey. Finally, we believe that any future researchers of this area should first note the conceptual and pragmatic problems of untangling the various factors influencing forecasts and their outcomes, problems which have hindered us in the search for clear-cut conclusions.

NOTES

* An abridged version of this chapter was published in *Futures*. See H. Rush and W. Page, 'Long-term Metals Forecasting: the Track Record, 1910–1964', *Futures* 11, August 1979, (4) pp. 321–337.
1. The full analysis can be found in W. Page and H. Rush: *Long-term Forecasts for Metals: The Track Record, 1910–1960*, Occasional Paper No. 6, Science Policy Research Unit, April 1978.
2. Forecasting methods were divided into three categories: Simple Methods, employing no formal means of handling data or theory; Explicit Models, employing some simple but formal model relating trends and/or factors; and Intermediate Methods, using trend extrapolations or similar techniques. This classification is not entirely satisfactory, as it is based only upon information contained in the published documents, and has subjective elements; but practical solutions to these two drawbacks were not apparent.
3. The following analysis excludes these forecasts: (i) those for 1965 (the year after publication); (ii) those which are only a different way of presenting others (e.g. when forecasts of total tin consumption and of tin use in tinplate are given, a derived forecast of the latter as a percentage of the former is excluded); (iii) those for which 1970 data does not appear to be available (including reserves; the reserve estimates available for 1970 and given by others are in fact taken straight from this report). The 78 forecasts analysed in the paragraphs immediately following are only those that Robertson presented in tables; others are discussed later. Statistics for 1970 itself, have been used (rather than, say, the average for 1969–70–71) because, by and large, 1970 was not atypical of the period (in the way that, when analysing Paley, 1975 may be suggested as atypical of the 1970s).

REFERENCES

Anon. (1913), 'Future Scarcity of Tin', *Mining Journal*, 11 October p. 979 (cited as unspecified forecast in a publication called *Der Eisenhändler*).

Anon. (1921), *The Future of Mining*, Mining and Scientific Press 2 April 1921, pp. 444–6.

R. M. Cooper (1975), *Resource needs Revisited*, Brookings Papers on Economic Activity, 1: 1975, pp. 238–45.

C. H. Cosman (1974), *Some thoughts on Long-Term Supply/Demand Forecasting for Materials Twenty-five Years after Paley*. Paper to First World Symposium on Energy and Raw Materials, Paris.

James Douglas (1910), *The Future of Copper*, Mining and Scientific Press, 8 January, pp. 86–7.

H. H. Landsberg, *Projections in Retrospect*, paper presented at 104th AIME Annual Meeting, council of Economics, New York, February 1975. (We would like to thank Mr Landsberg for making some very useful comments on an earlier version of this analysis.)

The President's Materials Policy Commission: Resources for Freedom (5 vols); US GPO, June 1952; generally referred to by the name of its Chairman, William S. Paley.

Elmer W. Pehrson, 'The Mineral Position of the United States and the Outlook for the Future', *Mining and Metallurgy*, April 1945 p. 204.

W. Robertson (1965), *Report on the World Tin Position with Projections for 1965 and 1970*; London: International Tin Council. (We would like to thank Mr Robertson for very helpful comments on an earlier draft of this section.)

(Sources for 'Actual' figures include Metallgesellschaft AG: Metal Statistics, 1965–75, Frankfurt-am-Main, and various publications of the US Bureau of Mines)

10 Forecasting the Forces of Nature

JOHN GRIBBIN

Most of the forecasts discussed in this book concern events which are, to a greater or lesser degree, influenced by human activities. In such a situation, it is inevitable that the dynamic interaction of the forecasts themselves with those human activities will change the situation, possibly so that the original forecast is no longer relevant; certainly there is danger in too ready acceptance of a sociological forecast of a unique 'future' either in general or in some specific regard, and all such forecasts must be regarded as inputs to the social system, with feedback from the social system continually modifying the nature and applicability of the forecast as conditions in society change. Forecasts of natural events, on the other hand, might be expected to offer more rigid views of 'the future', at least in detail, and to be much more clearly testable in terms of success or failure – if the weather forecast predicts blue skies and sunshine, but we actually experience heavy rainfall, we all have a clear assessment of the value of the forecast.

So there is a sense in which forecasting the future pattern of events produced by the changing forces of nature – drought or flood, earthquake, tsunami and so on – might be regarded as simpler than sociological forecasting. We have removed one element, the feedback from society into the forecast, from the system. This in itself suggests the value of looking at such forecasts of natural events, and the reaction of society to both the forecasts and the forces of nature, as a 'control' against which reactions to sociological forecasts might be calibrated, at least qualitatively. It turns out, however, that even where natural forces are dominant, the influence of mankind's activities may be beginning to be felt, and here some of the simple feedbacks inherent in forecasting – or rather, inherent in making forecasts public – can be studied in isolation. While this leads to some interesting tentative conclusions about the nature and value of forecasts in general, and the apparent psychological need for forecasts in the human community, the difficulty of the whole area of study also provides food for thought for anyone venturing into what would seem to be the much more complex area of forecasting in situations where the human feedback may dominate.

WEATHER AND CLIMATE

The obvious starting-point for any review of forecasting techniques applied to natural systems is the much maligned weather forecast. The time-scale of the conventional forecast, running from 24 hours to a week or so ahead, is rather small compared with most time-scales discussed in this book, but does highlight one problem inherent in all forecasting: the interpretation of statements of probability. This communication difficulty is one aspect of the broader problem of presenting forecasts intelligibly, with the minimum of jargon, if they are to be understood and used effectively by a wide audience; at least some meteorologists are well aware of this problem, as Figure 10.1 indicates.

In some parts of the world, official weather forecasts are issued as statements of probability, and although these provide scope for jokes that a forecast of a 50 per cent chance of rain means that you should carry half an umbrella, the 'man in the street' is, in fact, well versed in the mysteries of probability from such pastimes as gambling on horse-races, and is well able to interpret such information effectively. This kind of forecast has another advantage for the forecaster – it is never obviously 'wrong' since it never says that the weather 'will be' of a certain kind!

More importantly, however, this aspect of the forecast can be turned around and considered from the point of view of the user – the man in the street, the farmer, or whoever. Now, because the probabilistic nature of the forecast is not concealed behind an aura of infallibility, the user can see much more clearly that the value judgements based on the forecast must be his own. The man who gambles by leaving his umbrella at home and gets rained on can only blame himself; the farmer who plants seed in the hope of rain is doing so in the light of his own judgement of the risk involved, considering the best available evidence. Unfortunately, in spite of the educational effects of gambling on horses, many people, including people in positions of responsibility who use all kinds of forecasts and should know better, still need educating to interpret such statements of probability.

The difficulties involved in educating recipients to interpret pro-

FIGURE 10.1. Weather forecasts: visual presentation
The 'Clo' system of weather forecasting, based on clothing units, developed by A. Auliciems, of Queensland University. This system represents an attempt to present forecasting in terms easily understood by the layman, rather than in technical jargon. (Reproduced with permission from F. K. Hare and A. Auliciems, *Weather* (1973), 28, 478.)

babilistic forecasts become more apparent when we consider a situation in which the forecast is that the weather will be dry, probability 90 per cent, yet it does in fact rain. Few people will have carried umbrellas in such a situation, and many will feel aggrieved at their soaking, even though it is 'their own fault'. A crucial issue here is the overall success rate of the forecasts in the past. As long as '90 per cent' forecasts really do come true nine times out of ten, the user will probably shrug off the odd occasion when things go wrong even if he does not fully appreciate that a probabilistic forecast is never 'wrong' in the naive sense. The onus is on the forecaster to get the *probabilities* right – which is as it should be.

The value of an educated understanding of such forecasts is shown very clearly by consideration of the potential benefits of properly used climatic forecasts of an actuarial kind, on a variety of time-scales. Popular discussion – and too much of the scientific debate – about climatic change has focused on the nature of overall trends, including whatever trend we may now be living through. But for all planning on the time-scales envisaged by agriculture, industry and government any long-term trend in, say, temperature of about $0.2°C$ per decade, either up or down, is of much less significance than information about the likelihood of severe extremes of weather occurring each year as a result of climatic shifts.

This is not the place to discuss the physical basis of present understanding of climatic change and forecasts of future shifts in the global climatic regime (see Lamb, 1972 and 1977; Gribbin, 1978a,b), but it does now seem that with a relatively modest research effort it would soon be possible to provide forecasts of likely extremes to be encountered within a given period of a few years or a decade or two, which could provide a basis for an actuarial approach to relevant planning.

At the shortest time-scale which can reasonably be said to involve climatic forecasting, rather than weather forecasts pure and simple, we might look at the value to be derived from an ability to predict at a reasonable level of confidence the kind of seasons we might expect a year or so ahead. Such forecasts, based on extrapolating the meteorological approach to meet up with the overall picture produced by an understanding of climate, are already feasible and can be made with rather more confidence, and a greater degree of success, than the one-month 'long range' forecasts which are now provided by, for example, the UK Meteorological Office. Why, then, does no one provide such forecasts? The chief reason seems to be precisely because it is felt that the potential beneficiaries from such seasonal forecasts – those involved in agricultural production – could not make effective use of them until the success rate becomes substantially improved.

The problem is highlighted by considering an extreme case. Suppose that interpretation of the developing meteorological patterns, comparison with similar patterns known to have occurred in the past, and computer modelling extrapolating from the present situation, all point to the likelihood of a 'backward' Spring with little rainfall and late frosts, and suppose that this forecast is available in the preceding Autumn. If such a forecast could be made with 100 per cent confidence the value to agriculture would be enormous, with appropriate precautions taken to ensure that crops did not develop in the fields until after the frost risk was past. If, however, the forecast was that the predicted pattern of events had about a one in ten chance of occurring, all farmers would ignore it and carry on with traditional patterns of planting and so on. So, where, between these extremes, does the probability of a correct forecast become great enough to cause concern?

I would argue that even a 10 per cent probability of getting at least the extremes correct is sufficient to justify issuing appropriate forecasts, *provided that the recipients understand their nature.* All farmers are gamblers, and individuals (or individual agri-businesses) are much better placed to decide, in terms of their own strengths and weaknesses overall, including financially, whether a particular risk can be accepted at a particular time. The farmer who gambled on the forecast's being wrong, and lost his crop, would be as much responsible for his own actions as the farmer who gambled on the forecast's being right, delayed planting and then saw a fine mild Spring in which his neighbour's crops raced ahead. The fact that more information on which to base such judgements had been supplied, complete with uncertainty estimates, from an outside source – almost certainly, a government source – would in no way shift the responsibility for the gamble in the field onto the shoulders of the outside source of the information.

Perhaps the situation becomes clearer when we look at a slightly longer time-scale and at the prospects of experiencing a certain number of severe seasons within, say, five or ten years. This is precisely the area in which climatic research now stands poised to achieve a breakthrough, given appropriate support. In the middle part of this century, we experienced several decades of particularly bland, even-tempered weather, compared with the conditions that seem to have been 'normal' over the past thousand years or so. Various events, such as the European drought in 1976 and the severe Winter in the eastern US in 1977, suggest that this pattern may be changing, returning us to a pattern more like that of the nineteenth century, with more hot Summers but also more cold Winters, more frequent droughts but also more frequent floods. To those who argue this case, it is no coincidence that the Winter of 1977 was the worst in the eastern US for a hundred years, and rather than indicating a gap of a further century before such a Winter will come again, the evidence is that a shift in climate has brought a return to conditions in which such Winters can recur. The task which should now be tackled by the climatic forecasters is to determine, from all of the available evidence, how often such conditions might recur in the next few years. The kind of planning required to cope with such extremes on a once-in-a-century basis is quite different from that appropriate if the chance of recurrence suggests three such Winters in the next ten years – and that is exactly the kind of information which is becoming available.

This has clear policy implications, and suggests that the main thrust of present 'official' research on climatic change is misdirected. Too much emphasis has been placed on the longer-term, slow changes in mean parameters (rainfall and temperature especially) and too little on the prospect of increased variability about the mean. A decline in temperature of a few tenths of a degree over a decade or more is not something to worry the agricultural industry unduly; changes far greater than this are already coped with on a year-to-year basis, and by emphasising the existence of the longer-term changes in mean parameters climatologists mislead agriculturalists, and others, into thinking that the changes are far too small to worry about.

It is difficult to put the cost of increased variability in cash terms (but see Table 10.1); an example from southern England in the mid-1970s

TABLE 10.1 Effects of climatic change in wheat yields in six states of the USA.*

Climatic change	North Dakota	South Dakota	Kansas	Oklahoma	Illinois	Indiana
			Changes in wheat yields (bushel/acre)			
			No change in temperature			
Change in precipitation (%)						
−30	−3·70	−1·85	−2·84	−2·81	+3·08	+3·24
−20	−2·49	−1·58	−1·80	−1·56	+2·25	+2·18
−10	−1·07	−0·67	−0·85	−0·62	+1·22	+1·10
+10	+1·21	+0·42	−0·76	+0·31	−1·41	−1·13
+20	+2·39	+0·60	+1·41	+0·30	−3·02	−2·28
+30	+3·62	+1·42	+1·99	−0·02	−4·84	−3·45
			No change in precipitation			
Change in temperature (°C)						
−2°	+1·18	+0·47	+1·44	−2·00	+2·36	+1·69
−1°	+0·68	+0·87	+0·74	−0·28	+1·16	+0·88
−0·5°	−0·36	+0·47	+0·37	+0·04	+0·62	+0·44
+0·5°	−0·41	−0·55	−0·38	−0·40	−0·64	−0·46
+1°	−0·86	−1·17	−0·77	−1·16	−1·24	−0·94
+2°	−1·90	−1·64	−1·57	−3·76	−2·69	−1·93

*Average yields under 'standard' climatic conditions are: North Dakota, 25; South Dakota, 21·1; Kansas, 25·9; Oklahoma, 25·2; Illinois, 36·3; and Indiana, 36·3 bushels per acre. Data from Thompson (1975).
(Source: Thompson (1975) Science vol 188.)

TABLE 10.1 (contd)

| | *Changes in wheat yields (bushel/acre)* | | | | | |
Climatic change	North Dakota	South Dakota	Kansas	Oklahoma	Illinois	Indiana
	A decrease of 2°C in temperature					
Change in precipitation (%)						
−30	−2·52	−2·29	−1·40	−4·80	+5·44	+4·93
−20	−3·32	−1·14	−0·35	−3·56	+4·61	+3·88
−10	−0·06	−0·03	+0·59	−2·62	+3·58	+2·80
+10	+2·38	+0·89	+2·30	−1·69	+0·94	+0·57
+20	+4·41	+1·07	+2·86	−1·70	−0·66	−0·58
+30	+4·80	+0·98	+3·43	−2·01	−2·48	−1·76
	A decrease of 1°C in temperature					
Change in precipitation (%)						
−30	−2·62	−1·88	−2·10	−3·09	+4·24	+4·12
−20	−1·81	−0·71	−1·06	−1·83	+3·41	+3·06
−10	−0·56	+0·29	−0·11	−0·90	+2·38	+1·98
+10	+1·89	+2·33	+1·49	+0·04	−0·25	−0·25
+20	+3·07	+1·47	+2·16	+0·03	−1·86	−1·40
+30	+4·30	+1·39	+2·73	−0·29	−3·68	−2·58
	A decrease of 0·5°C in temperature					
Change in precipitation (%)						
−30	−3·33	−2·29	−2·47	−2·77	+3·70	+3·69
−20	−2·13	−1·11	−1·42	−1·51	+2·87	+2·63
−10	−0·87	−0·20	−0·48	−0·58	+1·84	+1·55
+10	+1·58	+0·80	+1·19	+0·35	−0·79	−0·68
+20	+2·76	+1·07	+1·79	+0·34	−2·39	−1·83
+30	+3·99	+0·98	+2·36	+0·38	−4·22	−3·01
	An increase of 0.5°C in temperature					
Change in precipitation (%)						
−30	−4·11	−3·31	−3·22	−3·21	+2·44	+2·78
−20	−2·90	−2·13	−2·18	−1·96	+1·61	+1·72
−10	−1·48	−1·22	−1·25	−1·02	+0·58	+0·64
+10	+0·63	−0·13	+0·36	−0·09	−2·05	−1·59
+20	+1·98	+0·05	+1·04	−0·10	−3·66	−2·74
+30	+3·21	+0·03	+1·61	−0·42	−5·48	−3·91

TABLE 10.1 (contd)

| Climatic change | Changes in wheat yields (bushel/acre) |||||||
	North Dakota	South Dakota	Kansas	Oklahoma	Illinois	Indiana
An increase of 1°C in temperature						
Change in precipitation (%)						
−30	−4·56	−3·92	−3·61	−3·98	+1·84	+2·31
−20	−3·35	−2·75	−2·75	−2·72	+1·01	+1·25
−10	−1·93	−4·66	−1·62	−1·79	−0·02	+0·17
+10	+0·19	−0·66	−0·01	−0·85	−2·65	−2·06
+20	+1·53	−0·19	+0·65	−0·85	−4·25	−3·21
+30	+2·77	−0·65	+1·22	+1·18	−6·08	−4·39
An increase of 2°C in temperature						
Change in precipitation (%)						
−30	−6·71	−4·39	−4·41	−6·57	+0·39	+1·32
−20	−4·39	−3·22	−3·37	−5·31	−0·44	+0·26
−10	−3·14	−2·39	−2·42	−4·38	−1·47	−0·82
+10	−0·69	−1·13	−0·82	−3·45	−4·10	−3·05
+20	−0·49	−0·67	−0·16	−3·45	−5·71	−4·20
+30	+1·72	−1·12	+0·42	−3·77	−7·53	−5·38

however, serves to indicate the potential value of seasonal forecasts to farmers. In 1976, after late frosts which damaged Winter-sown crops, many farmers planted maize, almost in desperation. The crop did exceedingly well in what proved to be a record-breaking, sunny, hot Summer, and as a result even more farmers planted even more maize in 1977. That Summer turned out to be cool, wet and cloudy, and the crop failed by a long way to live up to expectations. Yet the climatic pattern which brought the cold, wet Summer was already clear in the preceding Winter, and formed the basis of at least one correct seasonal forecast (Gribbin, 1977). If farmers had had access to that forecast, and taken it at face value, they could have avoided the losses from maize by planting other crops.

Rather than developing further the research effort involved in understanding long-term patterns of climatic change, a shift of policy to direct research funds towards the study of climatic variability seems indicated, with as first objective a reliable seasonal forecast. The scale on which such an effort might be made would be appropriate to a group such as the EEC, and the budget required for effective results to be produced would be small by the standards of such a community. Indeed, it would be small compared with the cost of damage caused by one severe season in one country, as the experience of the Winter of 1962–3 in Britain shows (Gribbin, 1975). After a spell of 48 days of intense cold, *The Economist* commented that the period had been 'the most expensive two months since the war' and estimated the cost – in terms of increased fuel bills, repairs to cars damaged in accidents or rotted by salt on the roads, increased food prices, repairs to burst pipes and so on – as £1000 million. Insurance companies alone paid out £15 million on claims directly related to the severe cold of that one 48-day period. Many of these claims, related to burst pipes and the like, could have been avoided by simple and cheap precautions, such as lagging, had anyone suspected the severe weather was coming. In my view, reliable seasonal forecasts could be provided within a year from initiating a suitable research effort, at a cost certainly less than £15 million! And not just the insurance companies would benefit. Taking again an example from Britain, as temperatures drop below freezing, demand for electricity increases by 200 megawatts for every 1°F fall in temperature, with a 25 knot wind on a freezing day boosting demand by a further 700 megawatts. The list is endless.

But it does not even matter, it should be stressed, that we may not be able to say *which* three out of the next ten Winters will be severe (if, indeed that is the forecast), although such an ideal would, of course, be highly desirable. Take the example of the rail system in Britain. In a very severe Winter, like that of 1962–3, the British rail system is adversely affected to a much greater degree than would be caused by the same amount of snow in, say, Canada. This is because in Canada such Winters are common, and the capital investment in snow-ploughs, equipment to keep points operating in severe frost conditions, and so on is not merely justifiable but essential if there is to be an effective rail system at all. In Britain, if such Winters are rare (the worst before 1962–3 was in the mid-1940s) the cost of preparedness may be more than the cost of occasional disruption, and therefore unjustifiable. The whole picture changes if three such Winters are expected in ten years, instead of two in the past 30 years, with clear implications for investment and long-term planning.

This, perhaps, is the optimum time-scale for integrating climatic forecasts into the machinery of society today – a decade or so ahead. The cynics argue that the only time-scales of interest to politicians are those which fit within the four- or five-year pattern of elections (see Schneider, 1976), but the existence of national and supra-national agencies which operate on much longer time-scales in fact keeps climatic forecasts on the decadal time-scale very much within the reaction time of our society to any outside change or influence. The European Economic Community is a clear example of an organisation which both covers an area large enough to require consideration of climatic changes and their effects on agriculture and other activities, and possesses centralised machinery to investigate such influences. The time-scale involved in response to a climatic 'crisis' (if one exists) has been estimated, in this case, as some five years to identify the crisis (this phase is now coming to an end), 3–10 years to develop new strains of crop to meet the changing conditions, and perhaps 7 years to get the resulting crops in widespread use on the farms (Mackenzie, 1977). Even allowing for some contraction of this time-scale, if faced with an extreme situation (which does not seem likely to arise in the immediate future), the ability to forecast the extremes of climate likely to be experienced over the next decade or two seems to fit exactly with the response time of the machinery needed to ensure that the crops in the field are able to withstand the expected extremes. Panic measures are inappropriate; fears of either a new ice age or a dramatic global warming are irrelevant on the time-scale of interest; and what is needed in practical terms is just an indication of the probable limits of weather in the immediate future. This provides a classic example of the value of *relevant* forecasts, on an *appropriate* time-scale and with uncertainty limits defined, to the activities of mankind.

EARTHQUAKES

Having found an example of an almost ideal application of forecasting natural events in terms of value to society, however, it is wise to look at the other side of the coin. The problems posed to society by the growing ability of Earth scientists to predict severe earthquakes show clearly that even an accurate forecast may be a 'bad' one, in human terms, and raise important questions concerning the desirability of providing forecasts in all cases. The moral and ethical problems of this aspect of forecasting the behaviour of the forces of nature are clearly of great relevance to the more general issue of potential abuse of forecasts in other areas.

Once again, the problems are related to the probability of a forecast's being accurate, although in the case of a major earthquake the stakes involved may be so high that a fairly small probability of such a disaster is cause for a great deal of concern. This is where the problems come in. Now, a 10 per cent chance of a major earthquake in a location such as Los Angeles is certainly sufficient to justify some kinds of precaution – but nine times out of ten there will be no large quake following such a 'prediction'. The major difficulty is that certainly when there is no quake, and very probably even when the forecast quake does arrive, 'on schedule', the adverse effects resulting from the issue of a public warning may be worse – possibly far worse – than the effects of the quake alone if no warning had been issued.

These difficulties are exacerbated – not eased, as we might naively expect – by the fact that the promising methods of earthquake prediction now being developed provide a much longer advance warning for large earthquakes than for small. (The situation is further complicated by the likelihood that the uncertainty attached to such a forecast varies over the time from the initial forecast until the earthquake occurs. The 'first warning' is likely to be relatively vague and uncertain, with a confident forecast coming only in the later stages.) Using studies of the change in velocity of shock waves (P and S waves) in the rocks as a guide to the occurrence of earthquakes (see Table 10.2 and Bolt *et al*, 1975) the warnings range from a day for a magnitude 2 earthquake through 3 months for one of magnitude 5 and up to six years for one of magnitude 7. (The magnitude scale is logarithmic; magnitude 2 is about the smallest felt by human beings, magnitude 3 ten times greater and so on; the San Francisco earthquake of 1906 was about magnitude 8·3.) The implications of such advance warning of the possibility of major disaster have been spelled out in a scenario developed by Eugene Haas and Dennis Mileti, and reported in some detail by Aaronson (1977).

TABLE 10.2 Duration of precursory changes in velocities of P and S waves

Earthquake magnitude	Duration
2	1 day
3	1 week
4	1 month
5	3 months
6	1 year
7	6 years

Source: Bolt et al. (1975).

This scenario takes the example of a prediction three years ahead of an earthquake of magnitude 7·3, involving an urban area of California. News of the prediction is first leaked to news media by seismologists in the form of evidence showing a 25 per cent chance that such an earthquake will occur at the designated time; within a year, property values have fallen, new construction has been halted, and the cost of earthquake insurance in the region is becoming prohibitive. Then, the prediction is refined and officially released in the form of a warning that there is now seen to be a 50 per cent of a quake of magnitude 7 or greater occurring in two years' time. The result, according to the scenario developed on the basis of discussions with news media, businesses and government groups in California, is that many families leave the area, businesses close and unemployment rises; just before the expected quake, residents remaining in the area stockpile essential supplies, areas below dams and in other high risk regions are evacuated, and troops are moved in to prevent looting and civil disturbance.

All this, a disruption of normal life over a period of years, produces a high economic and social cost, for a situation in which there is an even chance that there will be no major earthquake in any case. More urgent warnings, on shorter time-scales – even of rather smaller earthquakes – raise obvious problems if they may cause a panic reaction, mass exodus from a city or cities with resultant disruption of communications, and opportunity for the unscrupulous to take advantage of the chaotic situation either through straightforward looting or arson and provocation of mob violence. These are all factors which must, unfortunately, be looked at closely given the nature of our present society when the value of an earthquake forecast is being considered in practical terms.

It is quite clear that we can envisage a scenario in which the damage caused by publicising the forecast is worse than the damage caused by the forces of nature being forecast. If such a situation arises, should the forecast be suppressed? If the forecast could be used only as a secret warning to build up official preparedness for disaster, so that a quick and efficient response would minimise the after-effects, would such action be morally justifiable? And who should make a decision on whether or not to issue a warning in each specific case? Clearly, we return again to the interpretation of probabilities in forecasting, and the poor ability of our society to cope with predictions based on probabilistic forecasts – even the insurance industry, which should be able to make proper use of actuarial risk estimates, would be unable to cope in the Hass-Mileti scenario outlined above. Those who make forecasts must be willing to accept their role in interpreting the implications of their forecasts and educating both administrators and the general public to understand them in concrete terms; it is no longer acceptable to argue, as some have done even in the case of the development of nuclear weapons, that the role of the scientist ends at the door of his research institute. If non-scientists need 'educating' in regard to interpretation of probabilities and scientific language, equally scientists must be 'educated' to appreciate the difficulties of non-scientists in making the best use of their information.

IMPACT OF MAN ON THE ENVIRONMENT

Our concern here is chiefly with the uses and abuses of forecasts, and the potential for abuse of scientific forecasts can be seen clearly by looking at the interactions through which man is now changing his environment. These anthropogenic influences alter the basis of scientific forecasts about future natural environmental changes, while the forecasts themselves may alter the human influences which are changing the environment. Scope for abuse of the forecasts – by scientist or non-scientists, deliberately or inadvertently – abounds in such a situation.

Present debate centres on two critical issues: the possibility of a pronounced global warming brought about by the 'greenhouse effect' of carbon dioxide released into the atmosphere by burning fossil fuels; and the possible threat to the stability of the ozone layer of the stratosphere posed by the use of fluorocarbon propellants in spray cans, and to a lesser extent by high-flying aircraft such as Concorde. While recognising that other human influences on the environment are also causing concern in some quarters, we shall look only at these two examples here as case studies. The implications for the use of forecasts apply equally in other areas.

Concern about CO_2-induced warming is now at an early stage, and no action has yet been taken to change the course of events, which has been developing since the beginning of the Industrial Revolution, rather more than a century ago. It is estimated (Kellogg, in Gribbin 1978a; Singer, 1975) that the rise in carbon dioxide concentration in the atmosphere over this period has been from some 280–290 parts per million by volume (ppmv) to the present 320 + ppmv. Plausible forecasts indicate a continuing rise to 380–390 ppmv by AD 2000 and a doubling of the present level by the middle of the next century. Because carbon dioxide is essentially transparent to incoming solar radiation, but absorbs and reradiates the infra-red radiation from the warm land (or sea) that would otherwise be lost to space, an increase in CO_2 concentration leads to a net warming of the Earth. The figures quoted would imply a warming by $0.51°C$ by AD 2000 and $1.5-3°C$ by the year 2050.

Other effects of mankind's activities probably add to this warming trend, especially in the longer term – beyond 100 years. In Kellogg's words, 'our estimate, based on the best theory and best models of the climate system that we know how to construct, is that this rate of warming will be appreciably larger than any change of mean surface temperature we have seen in the past 1000 years, and could roll back the clock to 4000 to 8000 years ago when the Earth was warmer than now'.

This scientific forecast has interesting significance in a social context, not least since while a slightly warmer Earth might be a 'better' place for mankind in terms of ability to support the greatest population most easily, the redistribution of rainfall and the rise in sea-level produced by such a warming would profoundly affect the distribution of desirable places to live on the Earth's surface. Drier conditions in central North America and Canada, with wetter weather across North Africa, down into East Africa and across the Middle East and India, are just a few of the likely changes which would alter the distribution of global 'breadbasket' regions and the patterns of world trade. For much of the developing world, the pattern of a warmer Earth might seem highly desirable; for much of the industrialised world – ironically, the very nations responsible for the anthropogenic warming – the changes might be such as to cause a decline in importance in the global market-place, quite apart from the hazards of inundation of cities such as London, New York and Amsterdam as the polar caps melt and sea-level rises.

Assuming the forecast is indeed accurate, what action should be taken as a result? The industrialised nations responsible for the change, in which the scientists who make the forecasts live and work, might regard it as an urgent priority to find ways to minimise the release of carbon dioxide, in order to maintain the *status quo* as long as possible. If so, they would by implication be condemning some of the dry, overpopulated regions of the globe to a continued struggle for effective food production, a struggle which could perhaps be greatly eased if the warming trend persisted. There is no clear 'right' or 'wrong' use of the forecast in this – any use made of it (even the choice to ignore it) must be an abuse in some other context. This seems typical of the use of forecasts of all kinds; use and abuse are inextricably linked, and it is difficult to distinguish between good and bad outcomes from actions taken on the basis of forecasts. Some will benefit, others will not, whatever action comes into consideration, the criterion for judging success or failure (use or abuse) must surely be that the least overall harm is done. In that case, the scenario of a warm Earth resulting from work such as that of Kellogg does have a clear relevance to policy-making. If, for example, a deliberate decision is taken to attempt to maintain the *status quo*, then there is a moral obligation on the nations which at present have ample food to ensure its distribution to the have-nots. Equally, if the benefits of a warmer Earth were seen as outweighing the disadvantages, and a certain degree of warming was encouraged by advertent action, there would be a moral responsibility on the beneficiaries – largely have-not nations at present – to help those who would be hard hit by the changes – the present 'haves'.

Even with a clear forecast of a change in the natural balance of the environment, the implications for policy-making are far from clearcut. Where there is uncertainty in the forecast the policy situation becomes even more complex. But as the example of the fluorocarbon/ozone layer scare has shown, the mere existence of a forecast, however insecure its base, can provide the impetus for a major shift in policy with long-term beneficial effects. This raises the puzzle of why these changes cannot be made without the lever of a dramatic doomsday forecast, and suggests that the accuracy of a forecast is by no means the sole criterion on which to judge its success, even when the forecast is concerned with the physical, rather than the social, sciences.

The ozone layer controversy developed in the 1970s, initially through concern about the effect of exhaust gases of high-flying SST aircraft on the chemical balance of the stratosphere. In 1974 a study by Sherry Rowland and Mario Molina was published which suggested that fluorocarbon gases used as propellants in many spray cans posed an even greater threat to the ozone layer, because of their long life in the atmosphere and their ability to catalyse reactions which break down ozone (Rowland and Molina, 1974; Molina and Rowland, 1974; see also GDI, 1977).

Ozone is produced naturally by a series of photochemical reactions, and is concentrated in the stratosphere, reaching a maximum density at altitudes around 25 km. The concern about the supposed 'threat' to this layer centred on the nature of this layer as a filter which screens out the most intense solar ultraviolet radiation, preventing it from reaching the ground. If unscreened, such radiation would cause sunburn and skin cancer in people and animals, as well as damaging crops; links between ozone concentration fluctuations and minor (or even major) climatic changes received little attention alongside such emotive speculations.

The forecasts were, and are, far from precise. If wastage of ozone resulting from introducing fluorocarbons into the atmosphere does occur, and if use of this material continued at 1974 levels, the estimates of the effect on ozone concentrations over a 50-year period range from a 1 per cent decrease to a 20 per cent decrease, with the most likely forecasts seemingly those at the lower end of this range. Even the worst is equivalent to moving from the latitudes of the northern US to those of the southern US, and there is evidence that the *natural* fluctuations in the dynamic equilibrium that maintains the ozone layer produce changes by 20–30 per cent on time-scales ranging from months to decades, while lurid pictures of the fragility of this 'delicate bubble' that protects the Earth ignore the fact that it has been around in much the same form for some 1800 million years. The ozone layer is a very rugged part of the atmospheric system and mankind's disturbances have constituted, and will constitute for the next two or three decades at least, a very minor perturbation (see Gribbin, in GDI, 1977).

In spite of this evidence, the scare produced a very quick reaction from both industry and government policy-makers. Largely, of course, the impetus for this reaction came from the response of the public, which saw a 15 per cent drop in sales of aerosol sprays in the US in 1975 as the story received widespread publicity. First in the State of Oregon, then elsewhere, the use of fluorocarbon propellants was banned, and the product began to be phased out of all except 'essential' (chiefly medical) use. From November 1977, aerosol sprays that still use fluorocarbons in the US have to carry a warning, by edict of the Food and Drug Administration: 'contains a chlorofluorocarbon that may harm public health by reducing ozone in the upper atmosphere'. But this is far from the end of the story.

The backlash against the spray can hit indiscriminately at all such products, including the 50 per cent in 1974 that used other propellants (by late 1977, only 10 per cent of aerosol sprays manufactured in the US used the fluorocarbon propellants) and even now the controversy is expressed in terms of 'ban the can' rather than 'ban the fluorocarbons'. Even in January 1978 a Reuter's report (published in *The Times*, January 24, page 4) used the following words in describing Sweden's decision to ban the can: 'Sweden has become the first country in the world to enact legislation against *most aerosol sprays* on the ground that they may harm the planet's atmosphere' (my italics). This tangling up of the issues enabled 'ecological' pressure groups to use the ozone layer threat (real and imagined) to gain a platform from which to condemn the use of spray cans in general, and to establish a public reaction against all such products (although it remains to be seen how far this reaction will extend).

Arguments against spray cans, in terms of wasteful packaging, wasteful use of energy in manufacture, and so on, can be made, and were being made before the ozone controversy blew up. But the reaction against 'the can' came only from the emotive force of a largely spurious forecast of the dire consequences of the continued use of one type of propellant. There is no doubt that the forecast which led to the controversy and debate was entirely honest and founded in a genuine concern for the environmental impact of the fluorocarbon propellants. But what if, in a similar situation, a pressure group with a genuine concern about the desirability of some technological product were unable to obtain a platform for their views and were encouraged to put forward outrageous (but superficially plausible) 'forecasts' of environmental effects of this kind?

A NEED FOR URGENCY?

In all of the examples of forecasting physical changes in the environment outlined here the urgency, or lack of urgency, has seemed to be an important feature of the forecast — more so than justified in common-sense terms. Change in the way society goes about things can be brought about through the impact of an urgent forecast, whether or not the forecast itself is accurate — to some extent, this applies to the furious debate and widespread reactions following the publication of *The Limits to Growth* (Meadows et al., 1972). Human nature does not seem to be able to respond in a calm, orderly manner to changing situations, but either to do nothing at all or to react urgently to crises, real or imagined.

The role of forecasting, then, might be seen in this context as providing the stimulus for action by creating the impression of a need for urgency when tackling problems which, in fact, lack immediacy. By creating a crisis to react to, the forecaster forces society to debate the issues; a 'bad' forecast is seen, now, as a forecast which stirs little debate, while a 'good' forecast is one which maximises the response to the envisaged crisis. So both *The Limits to Growth* and the Rowland-Molina forecasts can be regarded as highly successful and useful. Any forecast which comes true, on the other hand, is almost certainly 'bad' in that it has not produced any change in the prevailing patterns of events — except for a forecast of continuation of the *status quo* in an already ideal world, which hardly applies here and now.

Equally, the distinction between use and abuse of forecasts becomes blurred on close inspection. The earthquake example cited above shows that the best use of a forecast might indeed be to ignore it, while abuse would be any use of it at all. The morality issues involved in using such forecasts, the questions of blame or responsibility for damage resulting from such use, seem, even in the case of forecasts involving the forces of nature, to be the most important issues which need to be discussed and resolved. If there is a lesson to be drawn from 'simple' forecasts of this kind for the more complex areas of sociological forecasting it can only be the obvious, but often overlooked, message that forecasts are not an end in themselves but a beginning, a catalyst for debate and decision-making which should, almost invariably, result in the original 'forecast' bearing little relation to the actual development of events.

REFERENCES

S. Aaronson (1977), 'The social cost of earthquake predictions', *New Scientist*, IPC Magazines, March 17.

B. A. Bolt, W. L. Horn, E. A. Macdonald and R. F. Scott (1975), *Geological Hazards*, Berlin and New York: Springer-Verlag.

GDI (1977), *A Ban on Aerosols*? Proceedings of Conference held at Gottlieb Duttweiler Institute, Zürich: GDI, Rüschlikon.

J. R. Gribbin (1975), *Our Changing Climate*, Faber & Faber.

J. R. Gribbin (1977), Forecast prepared for Wall's Ice Cream, published in shortened form in the company's *Annual Report*.

J. R. Gribbin (ed.) (1978a). *Climatic Change* London and New York: Cambridge University Press.

J. R. Gribbin (1978b), *The Climatic Threat*, London: Fontana, New York: Scribner's.

H. H. Lamb (1972), *Climate: Present, Past and Future*, Vol. 1 Fundamentals and Climate Now, London: Methuen.

H. H. Lamb (1977), *Climate: Present, Past and Future*, Vol. 2 Climatic History and the Future, London: Methuen, New York: Barnes & Noble.

L. D. M. MacKenzie (1977), 'Interpretation of Climatological Data by Agricultural Policy-Makers in an EEC Context' (Wye College, Centre for European Agricultural Studies, discussion meeting on 'Climate Change and European Agriculture'; proceedings to be published).

D. H. Meadows, D. L. Meadows, J. Randers and W. W. Behrens III

(1972), *The Limits to Growth* New York: Universe Books.

M. J. Molina and F. S. Rowland (1974), *Nature*, 249, 810.

F. S. Rowland and M. J. Molina (1974), *Chlorofluoromethanes in the Environment*, AEC Report No. UCI–1974–1, US Atomic Energy Commission.

S. F. Singer (ed.) (1975), *The Changing Global Environment*, Dordrecht: Reidel.

L. M. Thompson (1975), *Science*, 188, 535.

S. H. Schneider and Lynne Mesirow (1976), *The Genesis Strategy*, London and New York: Plenum.

11 Telecommunications

S. ENCEL

Communications is a prime example of the links between physical technology and social organisation (or social technology). The social technologies of speech, language, and writing are basic to the communication process. Language may, in fact, be described as the essential social technology which makes group existence possible. The development of communication methods could plausibly be used as the basis of a historical sequence superior to the primary-school chronology of Old Stone Age, New Stone Age, Bronze and Iron ages. An alternative, based on communication, might run through rudimentary speech, grammatical speech, written language, mathematical notation, printing and mass literacy, to the age of mechanisation and electrification of communications media. The growth of modern cities, in particular, is bound up with mechanical and electrical means of transport and communication, and coincides closely with the revolution in these two related activities which started around the year 1830.

The appetite for communication services in contemporary society is sometimes expressed through the concept of an 'information industry'. This concept is not new; indeed, it dates back to the founders of classical and neo-classical economics. Adam Smith argued that improved knowledge was a key factor in increased productivity, and attributed the early growth of industry in Scotland to the superiority of the Scottish educational system. A century later, Alfred Marshall described knowledge as man's 'most powerful engine of production', and attempted to calculate the economic value of investment in education. Most of the neo-classical economists who followed Marshall, however, neglected this topic, partly because neo-classical theory tends to take production methods for granted (Lamberton, 1971). In the 1950s, the subject resurfaced, and the 1960s saw it become a central concern of economic analysis. A landmark was the work of Fritz Machlup, which picked up Marshall's concerns and extended them to cover the whole of the 'knowledge industry'. Using a number of heroic assumptions, Machlup estimated that 29 per cent of GNP in the United States could be attributed to the production and distribution of knowledge, and that 9 per cent of GNP was spent on 'communications media' (Machlup, 1962). These results were widely quoted for years despite obvious defects in categorisation (e.g. Machlup's heading of 'information machine' included musical instruments, signalling devices, and typewriters). More recently, Porat has completed a massive re-analysis of American business statistics to produce a more refined version of Machlup's results. He distinguishes a primary sector that sells information goods and services to satisfy both intermediate and final demand, and a secondary sector including information services produced and consumed without any market-place transactions. Porat's estimates are expressed in terms of value added within the US economy, the figures being 27·8 per cent for the primary sector and 20–24 per cent in the secondary sector (Porat, 1976).

In Australia, Lamberton has re-calculated work-force data to demonstrate the level of employment in the information industry. In 1911, the number of persons whose occupation was primarily concerned with the production and distribution of information increased from 8·5 per cent in 1911 to 17 per cent in 1947 and 27·5 per cent in 1971 (Lamberton, 1977). The Australian Telecommunications Commission, established as a separate entity in 1975, employs approximately 1·2 per cent of the total Australian work-force. By comparison, the telecommunications divisions of the British Post Office Corporation employ about 1 per cent of the UK labour force, and a further 0·4 per cent are employed in the manufacture of equipment supplied to the Post Office.

TELECOMMUNICATIONS AND FORECASTING

The picture of an information-based society is a major clue to the nature of forecasting in the telecommunications sector, where it has proved to be a powerful stimulus to the assumption that growth is both necessary and inevitable. This assumption was also stimulated by the actual speed of growth within the sector, and the rapid rate of innovation in the manufacture of telecommunications equipment and the introduction of new systems.

Telephone ownership is the most important single index of growth in telecommunications. Generally speaking, telephone ownership rises in parallel with increases in GDP per head. A French study shows that telephone ownership has grown logarithmically in most countries over the past century, so that the number of phones per 100 people can be expressed as a logarithm of GDP per head. (*Plan et Prospectives*, 1970). In Britain, for instance, telephone ownership grew at roughly the same rate as GDP per head throughout the 1960s. In the period 1969–74 the number of telephones per 100 people rose from 23·3 to 34·1. Traffic increased even faster, so that the number of calls per subscriber per year rose from 174 to 207 during the same period. Telex, a virtually unknown service in 1950, rose to 30 000 installations in 1970 and to 50 000 in 1974, and the Post Office Corporation estimated in 1970 that by 1980 the number would rise to 140 000. Data terminals, which did not exist in 1950, rose to 12 000 in 1970, 30 000 in 1974, and were expected to rise to 300 000 in 1980. Capital investment, which was 420 millions in 1970, was expected to double by 1980 (Little, 1970).

In the United States, where telephone penetration has been more than 90 per cent for a number of years, investment is a better guide to growth than telephone installations. In 1970, capital investment by telephone companies was 10 billion US dollars, and was expected to reach 20 billion by 1980. The installation of cable television was expected to cost 50 billion during the decade. Total investment in telecommunications in the decade 1970–80 was expected to reach a total of 250 billion dollars (*Business Week*, 1974).

On a world scale, these national rates are reflected in a sustained growth of network traffic which requires a doubling of facilities every 7–10 years in most of the developed countries, and growth at even higher rates in developing countries. International traffic on main arteries has been doubling every 3–5 years. Growth-rates of this order not only generate euphoric forecasts and limitless expectations, but also require extremely difficult and expensive decisions about installations, employment, organisation, and tariff policies. As a result, most large telecommunications operators have taken a special interest in forecasting and have commissioned studies from various 'think tanks' or set up their own long-range forecasting units.

In the earlier stages, forecasts about telecommunications were predominantly the work of engineers and manufacturers. Growth was taken for granted, and the only forecasting technique used was simple extrapolation. The language of forecasts was characterised by the use of simple sentences and the indicative mood; qualifying clauses and conditional verbs were largely absent. The Chief scientist of ITT predicted in 1971, for instance, the extensive use of videophones, data terminals, computer-assisted school instruction, personal radio telephones, access to computers through push-button phones, electronic mail, cable TV, digital transmission, broadcasting by satellite, mobile phones, voice-data, the tele-diagnosis. He emphasised, moreover, that these predictions were minimal rather than maximal, and concluded that the growth of transport and telecommunications was 'one of the greatest contributions to understanding among men' (Busignies, 1971).

Optimism about the rapid growth and utilisation of new telecommunication technologies is matched by optimism about the social benefits which would flow from technological change. A study of interactive television credited this medium with the potential to 'reduce the unit cost of education to the point where our society could afford to provide open and equal access to learning opportunities for all members throughout their lives' (Parker and Dunn, 1972). A report by the US National Academy of Engineering, which looked at the role of telecommunications in urban development, concluded that it was a powerful force for the improvement of the quality of urban life. (National Academy of Engineering, 1971). A RAND Corporation report on a similar theme describes the beneficial effects of modern communications on urban ghettos by improving education, increasing community awareness, and disseminating information about social welfare (Dordick et al., 1973). A report prepared for the MITRE Corporation predicts a variety of social improvements to be achieved by interactive television – economic, organisational, occupational, political, administrative, cultural, recreational, and legal (Jones, 1973). The benefits to be derived from the videophone were expounded a few years ago in a report commissioned by Bell Telephone. According to the authors, the videophone will speed the decentralisation of office activities, so that computer key-punching, for instance, need not be done in a central office; hence, it will reduce the demand for transport and so conserve fuel (Dickson and Bowers, 1973).

It is significant that many of these reports have been commissioned by the manufacturers of telecommunications equipment and other electronic devices, or emanate directly from the firms themselves. In this way, they serve as self-fulfilling prophecies which stress the ineluctable pressure of demand for new products on the one hand, and the social benefits to be expected from them on the other. The two factors are clearly reflected in a report prepared by the Institute for the Future, in which much of the information comes from the suppliers of the equipment. The study, which looked at market demand, predicted a rapid growth in community antenna television (CATV), which would bring about improvements in education, the decentralisation of business, access to information, shopping facilities, entertainment, person-to-person communication, recreation, and tourism (Baran, 1970). Elsewhere, Baran has stressed the value of telecommunications as an antidote to urban centralisation, declaring that it would provide a 'healthy and much needed counterpoise to the excessive magnetic attractions and cohesive bind exerted by urban concentrations' (Baran and Greenberger, 1967).

Public authorities which supply the services rather than the hardware are equally capable of promoting optimistic forecasts to confirm their programme for continued expansion. Thus, two experts closely associated with the British Post Office have written:

> Technological advances will not only contribute to the growth and improvement of telephone services, they will also make possible and economic a number of new telecommunications services such as fast data and facsimile transmission (including an electronic mail delivery service), conference television, videophones, and visual display (data access) information services. They could also enhance the range of entertainment sound and television services available in the home, and provide audio-visual services for education and community purposes via broad-band distribution networks (Bray and Reid, 1975).

Such optimistic predictions continue to be made, but since the early 1970s they have increasingly been accompanied by critical and sceptical analysis of the underlying assumptions. These criticisms draw attention to certain common points: (a) the dominance of crude forms of technological determinism; (b) lack of thought for second-order effects in areas such as employment, competition with other public services, availability of resources, and security; (c) the self-serving character of many forecasts sponsored by major suppliers; (d) neglect of the social inequities stimulated by the growth of relatively expensive facilities.

Parker notes the influence of technological determinism on policy choices when he writes that 'policy-makers may be merely trying to maintain their power by keeping in step with historical inevitability or they may be influencing the course of history. In either case, the focus should not be on the technology itself, but on the social policy options and the probable consequences of these policy choices' (Parker, 1975). Again, as Pool remarks, telephone policy involves choices which are not equally cost-effective, and there is no law of nature that societies will always choose the policy which makes the most cost-effective use of the available technology. Technological determinism is only conceivable in circumstances where some Darwinian or rational process rewards the good choices and penalises the bad (Pool, 1977). Conrath and Thompson have drawn attention to the misleading implications of the concept of 'breakthroughs' in communications technique. An analysis of prospective breakthroughs suggests that most of them do not offer much return in the form of social benefit. Their principal value lies, rather, in more efficient logistics and the release of labour for other purposes (Conrath and Thompson, 1973).

Cherry, commenting on the difficulties of forecasting demand for telecommunications services, criticises over-simple assumptions about the relation between demand and supply. The effects of improved communications technology are not simple or unidirectional, but fraught with paradoxes and uncertainties. In the case of telephones, for instance, the considerations affecting demand for business connections are obvious, but the demand for residential telephones is a distinct phenomenon, and the nature of the difference is not well understood (Cherry, 1971). Another kind of concern arises from the difficulties created for the ordinary user by increasing complexity and sophistication, as a RAND study points out. 'It is by no means clear what the consequences are of supplying a greater and greater number of people with tools whose implications they scarcely understand. . . . Perhaps there is an upper limit to the degree of complexity a system can tolerate before breaking down, unless the individuals operating and using it have themselves changed as much as the systems they use.' The problems of privacy, of error, of harassment, of criminal use, and the concentration of power in 'Big Brother' are of growing importance (Goldhamer and Westrum, 1970). Alan Westin, who has paid special attention to privacy, underlines the need to use the few years of lead time available to us before these possibilities grow beyond our power to control (Westin, 1967). A similar concern is expressed in the report of the Canadian 'Telecommission', which identifies a basic social right to communicate, and goes on to examine the dangers generated by the exercise of this right, especially in the invasion of privacy. 'Technology can give society just about anything it wants: but what does it want? . . . How should society exploit the promise of technology while safeguarding against its evident dangers?' (Information Canada, 1971.)

The nature of the forecasting problem is well expanded in a paper by Michael Tyler of the Long Range Studies Division of the British Post Office. The key issue, he suggests, is to distinguish between future 'demands' and future social 'needs'. Long-range planning must take account of changes in the external environment such as economic growth, changes in urban and regional settlement patterns, the supply of energy, and developments in other sectors, notably transport. In addition, the Post Office has social objectives and responsibilities, and the study of its interaction with the broader social environment is a matter of social responsibility as well as commercial necessity (Tyler, 1973). In other words, forecasts can only be made in relation to objectives. The future of telecommunications will not be determined by ineluctable processes but by choice. A decision to make the telephone universally available, for instance, would have quite different consequences from a policy aimed at developing satellite communications. A French report takes this line, arguing that the telephone should be, and will become, 'a consumption good as indispensable as electricity' (DATAR, 1969). A similar view is taken by Dennis Gabor, who believes that the main value of the telephone is to provide a substitute for travel, which has become an increasingly uncongenial activity. Hence, the telephone should become universally available. The logic of this argument leads him to argue that the videophone and facsimile newspapers are of trivial importance; however, wired television should be developed, especially as it can also provide a wide-band channel for computer links (Gabor, 1970). Maddox also contends that the telephone should be treated as a utility like education and transport, and paid for accordingly (Maddox, 1972). Otherwise as Katzman (1974) notes, the effect of new communications technology is to widen the gap between the 'information rich' and the 'information poor'.

A report prepared for the British Post Office Long Range Studies Division by Colin Buchanan and his associates at Imperial College, London, also comes to the conclusion that the most effective policy is to spread the availability of the basic telephone. An analysis of expenditure on telecommunications showed that the largest growth during the 1960s had been in telephone installations. As technology advances, the average real cost of installation falls, and revenue rises faster than might be expected because of the relatively rapid increase in long-distance calls, which cost proportionately more than local calls. These facts were reflected in the rate of residential connections, which rose faster than consumer expenditure on telephone services (Buchanan, 1972).

Buchanan also points out that the share of the telephone in the aggregate demand for telecommunications services would be even greater if it were accessible to the whole population. As it is, the demand for new services is inflated because it largely comes from people who already have telephones. In particular, it came from the business sector, where 27 per cent of spending on telecommunications was on non-telephone services. Buchanan expects a steady rate of growth in this proportion, so that it should rise to about 50 per cent by the end of the century. From 1962 to 1970, business expenditure on the telephone rose by 49·3 per cent; on non-telephone services, by 41·8 per cent. Buchanan's forecast implies that a point of inflexion in the growth curve will be reached as non-telephone expenditure moves closer to equality with telephone expenditure, after which the rate of growth of the former will exceed the latter. However, he does not expect this point to be reached until the latter part of the 1980s, when the ratio should be about one to two.

Domestic customers, on the other hand, are not showing the same demand for non-telephone services, and the continuing annual increase in the number of calls per subscriber (about 3 per cent) suggests that the basic telephone is by far the most potent service as far as the domestic user is concerned.

TELECOMMUNICATIONS, TRANSPORT, AND DECENTRALISATION

A particular motive for forecasting in this area has been the attempt to use telecommunications as a device for reducing the transport problems created by massive urbanisation and the consequent growth of traffic and traffic congestion. As cities grow and become more dispersed, the incentive to cut down travel on the one hand, and the need to improve contact between geographically scattered people on the other, work together to impel the use of communications as a substitute for transportation.

Alex Reid, director of long-range studies for the British Post Office, criticises the naïveté of thinking which assumes, without significant research, that technical advances like conference television will have a radical impact on communication patterns. Some forecasts, he notes, assume a complete break-up of the contemporary city as a result of advances in communications. Individuals would increasingly work at home and communicate electronically, either with one another or with a central office. The available evidence, in fact, demonstrates that telecommunications and personal travel interact in two contradictory ways — reduction in travel through substitution, and increase in travel through stimulation (Reid, 1971). A Canadian study of contact between city pairs (Montreal and Toronto in particular) also found that telecommunications and transport may work as complements rather than substitutes, and that persons doing business frequently by remote communication were likely to make *more* business trips rather than less (Lewis, 1973).

The decentralisation of office activity through remote communication has attracted attention in a number of countries, notably England, France, and Australia. Office activity is, in principle, susceptible to decentralisation through the use of telecommunications. Offices are bound together because they are communication-intensive activities needing a wide variety of rapid interpersonal contacts between workers. Innovations in communications technology may change the need for these activities to be tied to the central business districts. Business tasks such as accounting, bookkeeping and data processing have already shown that they can be moved to the suburbs, leaving the head office in the CBD. With the extended use of conference television, audio-telephone conference links, CCTV and rapid facsimile, more meetings may be held without the need for physical gathering of persons (Thorngren, 1970).

In Britain, there has been a concerted effort for many years to move offices out of London to the provinces and reduce the pressure on office space, housing and transport in the London metropolitan area. Decentralisation of government offices is a major policy of the Civil Service Department; private office decentralisation has been actively promoted by the Location of Offices Bureau, a government-sponsored organisation. The effects of these policies have been examined in detail by the Communications Study Group at University College, London. Among other things, the CSG has examined the possibility of replacing face-to-face meetings with conference television, audio-conference links, and videophones. So far, these studies do not suggest that telecommunications services can radically affect the need for a CBD, thus changing the urban traffic situation, but they do show that organisations with a high level of internal communication would gain from decentralisation. Narrow band services (i.e. audio facilities) are significantly cheaper than the cost of rents, salaries and overheads in the CBD, which are normally high. Broad band services (i.e. visual systems), which are more expensive, are less attractive, although they might be of value within a smaller radius of movement. In this case, however, the value placed on the saving of time would have to be unusually high (Short, 1976).

Another CSG report by Elton notes how transport and telecommunications services should be jointly considered at the planning stage.

For instance, telecommunications, especially of the interactive variety, should assist community participation in the planning process. Transport and telecommunications should be seen as complementary in the areas of health, social services and education. The installation of free or cheap telephones for the elderly and disabled, as done in the city of Hull, illustrates one way in which telecommunication supplies a need for which transport is unsuitable. Unfortunately, he remarks, the Post Office is not receptive to social issues, since there is always more money to be made from business phones. Elton's conclusion is worth quoting:

> There is more at issue than the extent to which telecommunications will substitute for travel. Inasmuch as the two are competing alternatives, the history of other technological innovations suggests that each will concentrate on what it can do best. The use of telecommunications relative to the use of travel will come to depend upon the importance of speed relative to that of social interaction. . . . It is necessary to provide opportunities for transport which strike an appropriate political balance between social costs and benefits to different sectors of the community. There are dangers in ignoring telecommunications, because the marginal value of an improved opportunity (travel) depends on the value of its alternative (telecommunicate) (Elton, 1973).

The Buchanan Report, already referred to, does not encourage facile optimism about the possibilities of substitution. Buchanan argues that the invention of the telephone was the decisive even in the history of telecommunications, and that this has manifestly not led to a more static way of life. 'The notion of the all-telecom society pursued to its bitter end seems to finish up with everyone in bed surrounded by buttons, which does not appear to be the direction in which the restless human seeks to go.' The relationship between transport and communication should be seen in terms not of substitution but of complementation. Thus, they regard the continuing decentralisation of economic activity as a highly probable development for the rest of the century. This could, in its turn, generate a further need for transport between centres, and telecommunications could be exploited to reduce this form of physical movement. One way of achieving this would be to encourage the growth of regional centres with a high level of telecommunications facilities, perhaps in the form of 'neighbourhood communications centres'. Expensive facilities, such as the videophone and conference TV, could be installed at such centres on a public access basis and used to obviate a variety of journeys, e.g. into the CBD. In this way, a relatively short journey would be complemented by remote communication over a much greater distance.

The pessimism shown by Buchanan is manifested even more sharply by Cetron, in a report prepared for the US Department of Housing and Urban Development, which looks at probable changes between 1970 and 1985 (Cetron, 1973). The relevant conclusions are as follows:

(a) Advanced telecommunications technology, while highly beneficial to some segments of society, will prove detrimental to others; in particular, it is likely to benefit the middle-class residential areas and to have a negative impact on the central city areas by accelerating the decentralisation of business and commerce, thus increasing the number of journeys.

(b) Major urban developments in this period are unlikely to be influenced by telecommunications. However, the service sector is particularly sensitive to the use of advanced technology as a replacement for paper transactions.

(c) Shopping from home and working at home will primarily benefit the more affluent sections of the community.

(d) The most important impacts are likely to be in technical training, public services (including transport and security), and health services.

THE NATIONAL TELECOMMUNICATIONS PLAN, AUSTRALIA

A somewhat unusual forecasting exercise was undertaken during the years 1973–6 by the Australian Post Office, which was confronted in the 1960s by massive growth in the system, exceeding previous estimates and causing serious difficulties in coping with demand. A few statistics will indicate the rate of growth. Between 1950 and 1970, telephone services of all kinds rose from 759 000 to 2 704 000 – a threefold proportionate increase. The number of telephone connections, which was 10 per 100 people in 1939, increased to 21 per 100 in 1960, 31 per 100 in 1970, and 35 in 1974. The total number of internal calls rose from 957 million in 1950 to more than 2 860 million in 1970 and 3 422 million in 1973. Telex services rose from 95 in 1955 to 12 857 in 1974, and telex messages from 5 178 to more than 21 million per year in the same period. Revenue from telephone rentals rose from $A11·6 million in 1950 to $A126·6 million in 1970 and $A235·8 million in 1974; internal calls produced $A28·2 million in 1950, $A280·8 million in 1970, and $A517·3 million in 1974.

Revenue from international phone calls rose from $A117 000 in 1950 to $A11 million in 1970 and $A28 million in 1974. The contribution of telecommunications to GNP rose from 0·94 per cent in 1950 to 1·55 per cent in 1970 and 1·7 per cent in 1974; the communications industry as a whole (including postal services, radio and television) contributed 1·78 per cent of GNP in 1950, 2·86 per cent in 1970 and 2·92 per cent in 1974 (Lamberton, 1977).

In Australia, as in many other countries, a national authority has a virtual monopoly of communication services, apart from private operations in the area of broadcasting. From 1901, when the present federal system was established, until 1975, all postal, telegraphic, telephonic and similar services were operated by the Post Office, which was the largest single employer in the country. The monopoly of services is linked with a monopsonistic market situation for equipment. Hence, policies about the development of telecommunications services have a decisive influence on the industries which supply the hardware, as well as profound effects on the employment situation. Again as in other countries, the forecasting of demand and the planning of services are affected by basic commitments to a monopolistic position and the supply of services as a public utility at the lowest possible cost. They are also affected by two major pressures on the system, i.e. the enormous growth in traffic and the rise in labour costs. Both point in the direction of new technologies which can cope with greatly increased traffic and also require fewer people. These objectives are recurrently in conflict with each other. Rapid growth of traffic produces demands for immediate solutions to improve the capacity of the system, which are liable to conflict with longer-term possibilities. Because of the long lead time involved in the development and implementation of radically new technologies, some of them still in the experimental stage, planning is constrained towards incremental improvements using technological advances of an intermediate character, which must remain in operation for a certain number of years to amortise the original investment.

The upsurge of demand for telephones in the 1950s led the Australian Post Office to engage in its first major forecasting exercise, the Community Telephone Plan of 1960. The perspectives on which this plan was based were twofold: an increase in population from 12 million to 33 million within fifty years, and an increase in telephone penetration to approximate the North American figure. The new network would be added to the existing structure by a combination of replacement and expansion, and would provide the physical base for additional forms of telecommunication – telex, mobile phones facsimile data transmission, and videophones—for which demand could not at that stage be anticipated. The plan was based on a mixture of simple extrapolation and technological determinism. Extrapolation depended upon demographic projections coupled with a steady increase in the ratio of phones to population; technological determinism took the form of assuming a continuing demand for telephones, without inquiring into social forces which could affect this demand, such as a rise in individual expectations for telephone service and changes in the structure of the work-force. The principal technological decision was therefore related to telephony, i.e. a move from traditional British switching equipment to the crossbar system developed in Sweden and the USA. Australian telephone engineers maintain that this was a correct decision which allowed for the increase in traffic, by comparison with Britain where the Post Office refused to adopt crossbar switching.

The Community Telephone Plan succeeded in its medium-term objectives, partly because of its own erroneous assumptions. The plan provided for a doubling of telephones in 12 years, from two million in 1960 to four million in 1972. The latter figure was actually reached in 1974. Population growth in the meantime was much less than projected, reaching 14 million instead of 20 million. The demographic error was compensated by two related factors: the increased rate of growth in demand for telephones, which enabled the Post Office to press for budgetary allocations sufficient to achieve the projected rate of installation, and the high rate of economic growth in the 1960s, which made it possible for the increased funds to be raised.

By 1972, it was clear that new forecasts were necessary, especially as the unsatisfied demand for telephones was rising. (In January, 1974, there were 105 000 applications pending, of which 21 000 were deferred applications.) A new federal government was elected in December 1972, and promptly took two decisions. One was to set up a royal commission of inquiry; the other was the establishment of a national telecommunications planning branch within the Post Office. The royal commission report, presented to the Federal Parliament in 1974, recommended that the Post Office should be split into two corporations, dealing with postal services (the Australian Postal Commission) and telecommunications (the Australian Telecommunications Commission). The logic of this decision was based on the familiar complaint that profitable telephone services were being used to subsidise unprofitable postal services, and that the necessary expansion in the telecommunications sector could only be achieved by freeing it from these obligations. With the expansion of the 1960s, the cost of subsidising postal services (other than letters, which *are* profitable) became a drag on the system, caught between the subsidy problem, rapid rises in the cost of labour and materials, the unforeseen growth of demand, and the advent of new and expensive technologies.

The royal commission report (implemented in 1975) removed the first of these four problems, but left the others to be contended with by the new ATC. In the meantime, the National Telecommunications Planning Branch, set up in 1973, was given the task of producing comprehensive policy guidelines for the rest of the century. Its brief was 'to identify future community needs and obtain appropriate managerial and governmental agreement to long-term objectives for the development of telecommunications in Australia'. The director of the project wrote in an introductory memorandum that while planning was concerned with the supply of telephone and telegraph services to meet an established demand for a familiar product, the planner was doing no more than react to a given socio-economic situation. 'The services now in prospect could have a significant effect on the structure of cities, transport, the economy, education, and the nature of information media as well as general life styles. Changing political, sociological and economic needs or constraints will in turn strongly influence the range and structure of telecommunications services provided. The future is clearly not "surprise-free".' (Newstead, 1973) This statement reflected the general realisation that massive technological changes could have massive social consequences, and that perspectives based on linear extrapolation and incremental growth were inadequate.

The NTP team comprised an interdisciplinary group of thirteen members, eight of them engineers and five with social science backgrounds, who met regularly and prepared a large number of papers for circulation and discussion. In addition, ten external studies were commissioned, covering a wide range of topics from mobile services to an analysis of the information industry. From an early stage, the NTP group adopted the principle that 'open planning' and public participation were desirable, and twelve open seminars were held between November 1973 and March 1975, dealing with topics such as broadcasting, manufacturing of telecommunications equipment, urban and regional planning, computers, education and industrial relations. The study programme concentrated on three main directions: (a) technological possibilities which would set the bounds for services that might become available by the year 2000; (b) macro-economic and micro-economic factors which would limit demand and the availability of resources; (c) social factors pointing to future demands and the possible consequences of introducing new services. (Wion, 1978)

The actual conclusions of the *Telecom 2000* report, which was published early in 1976, are not, in themselves, particularly surprising. They envisage the continued extension of the basic telephone service, and the development of new technologies and services to expand the range of services available. The report is cautious and sometimes sceptical about the level of public interest in such things as cable television, videophones, and conference television. It expects investment in the system to continue at a level of something between 3 and 6 per cent of gross fixed capital expenditure. This depends upon an annual growth-rate of 3 per cent in GDP, and an annual population increase of 1·1 per cent. These growth-rates, the report predicts, will lead to an increase in real income per head, and the 'likely income distribution' resulting from this increase will lead, in its turn, to the general availability of services. The reduced unit cost of services, brought about by technological advances, will also contribute to this outcome. Hence, there is a vast potential for new services in private homes. Also, the rate of growth in demand for telephone services will decline in the 1980s as it approaches saturation, although the growth of traffic in proportion to services will continue.

The report thus endorses a continued programme of expansion of the existing network and the addition of new services. It also supports the introduction of a domestic satellite system, the case for which stems from 'the desirability of introducing a video-conferencing facility between capital cities'. This would be extended progressively to other centres, and ultimately it would provide the basis for video-telephone connections to individual subscribers.

The weakness of these arguments is that they are not supported by adequate economic and social evidence. Economic growth and technological change do not lead to increased economic and social equality or equity. Technology reduces costs in some directions and increases them in others. Economic growth is most unlikely to continue at the levels experienced in the 1950s and 1960s, and it is not safe to infer that any surplus generated by a reduced rate of economic growth will be available for capital investment in telecommunications. The introduction of satellite transmission can only be achieved through extra costs, which means a negative impact on resources available for other media. This, in turn, will provoke policies designed to recoup the costs of satellite transmission, which are likely to promote the use of video media, possibly at the expense of other media, with consequent dislocations. There is little evidence of any significant demand for video-conferencing. Since *Telecom 2000* was published, it has become apparent that effective demand for the installation of satellites will come not from ATC but from the private sector. This is indicated, for example, by the pressure exerted by the newspaper proprietor, Mr Kerry Packer, who has invested heavily in promoting television programmes like 'World Series' cricket matches and presumably considers satellite transmission as a way of maximising returns on these investments.

These criticisms of *Telecom 2000* should not, however, obscure the fact that it has broken new ground by introducing more sophisticated economic, political, and sociological perspectives than those customarily associated with forecasting in this sector. This may be seen from the following recommendations of the report:

(a) support for 'open planning' and consultation with users;
(b) field research and comprehensive trials of advanced services, with emphasis on user involvement;
(c) on-going interdisciplinary research;
(d) planning should ensure that future services do not result in a widening of existing social inequalities.

In pursuit of the 'open planning' objective, the report was printed in large numbers and widely distributed, and the public was invited to respond by writing to the ATC. Just over 200 responses were received, 45 from institutions of higher education, 20 from government officials, 13 from private individuals, 11 from within ATC, and 8 from companies supplying equipment. Few of the responses were actively hostile to the report, and those which did express hostility were concerned mainly with criticism of excessive technological optimism. There was only moderate enthusiasm for new services using advanced technology, and a stress on making the telephone universally available. This viewpoint, which echoes the recommendations of some of the consultants to the NTP, has obviously affected the policy of the ATC. The original objective of 90 per cent telephone penetration by the year 2000 has now been advanced 10 years. Many of the responses welcomed the ideas of open planning and the continuous monitoring of social trends, although considerable scepticism was expressed about the feasibility of these objectives.

A particularly interesting consequence of the NTP exercise was the use of the telephone to provide a technological basis for a social welfare programme in the city of Brisbane. Brisbane, with a total population of approximately 900 000 people, is a low-density conurbation poorly served by public transport, and administered by a single municipal authority, the Brisbane City Council. Within this sprawling metropolis there live something like 30 000 persons who are tied to their homes by age, infirmity, or small children. In 1975, the city council looked into the possibility of coping with isolation by providing telephone or radio links, and opened negotiations with the ATC concerning the use of audio-conference facilities (which can be used simultaneously by ten subscribers). While negotiations were proceeding, the *Telecom 2000* report was published. The social worker in charge of the 'Telelink' project invited the NTP team to support the city council in its negotiations with the ATC, and the Minister for Posts and Telecommunications finally approved a concessional arrangement in July 1976. At the end of 1977, about fifteen Telelink groups were in regular operation, and reports on their effectiveness show a high level of satisfaction. The Department of Veterans' Affairs has also set up Telelink groups among its clients. Apart from providing persons isolated through age or infirmity with a 'psychological neighbourhood', Telelink makes it possible to conduct instructional programmes with both adults and school-age children who cannot attend classes.

The success of the Telelink scheme is being monitored through a study of housebound persons in the Brisbane metropolitan area, which will include the participants in Telelink groups and will compare their reactions to physical isolation with those of the control sample.

SUMMARY AND CONCLUSIONS

Because of the monopolistic character of telecommunications, much forecasting is of a self-interested character, done to confirm the rationality or inevitability of existing arrangements and to confirm optimistic expectations about continued growth and technological innovation. Forecasting exercises are liable to confirm what we already know, i.e. that business services are more profitable than domestic services, and that effort should therefore be concentrated on the former rather than the latter. A more open style of forecasting, which invites public contributions, may produce unpalatable conclusions. The case of NTP shows a rather unusual determination by a monopolistic supplier to step outside this situation, and perhaps it will inspire emulation.

REFERENCES

Baran, P. and Greenberger, M. (1967), *Urban Node in the Information Network*, Santa Monica: RAND Corporation.

Baran, P. (1970), *Potential Market Demand for Two-Way Information Services*, Menlo Park: Institute for the Future.

Bray, W. J. and Reid, A. A. L. (1975), 'Telecommunications Developments in the United Kingdom and their Social Implications', *IEEE Transactions*, vol. COM-23, no. 10.

Buchanan, C. and associates (1972), *Transport, the Urban Environment, and Telecommunications 1971–2001*. British Post Office, Long Range Studies Division, Report no. 1002.

Busignies, H. (1971), 'Trends and Future of Telecommunications', *Signal*, November–December.

Business Week (1974), 'The Revolution in the Phone Business', 6 November 1974, pp. 64–74.

Cetron, M. (1973), *Impact of Advanced Telecommunications Technology on the American City*, Washington D.C.: Department of Housing and Urban Development.

Cherry, C. (1971), *World Communications: Threat or Promise?* New York: Wiley-Interscience.

Conrath, D. W. and Thompson, G. B. (1973), 'Communication Technology. A Societal Perspective', *Journal of Communication*, 23, pp. 47–63.

DATAR (1969), *Schéma Directeur des Télécommunications*, Paris: DATAR, p. 46.

Dickson, E. and Bowers, R. (1973), *The Video-Telephone: A New Era in Telecommunications*, New York: Praeger.

Dordick, H. S. et al. (1973), *Telecommunications in Urban Development*, Santa Monica: RAND Corporation.

Elton, M. (1973), 'Developments in Communications: Implications for Planners' Conference paper on Transportation and the Environment, University of Southampton.

Gabor, D. (1970), *Innovations*, London: O.U.P.

Goldhamer, H. and Westrum, R. (1970), *The Social Effects of Communication Technology*, Santa Monica: RAND Corporation.

Information Canada (1971), *Instant World*, Ottawa: Queen's Printer.

Jones, M. V. (1973), 'How cable television may change our lives', *The Futurist*, October, pp. 196–201.

Katzman, N. (1974), 'The impact of communications technology', *Journal of Communication*, 24.

Lamberton, D. M. (ed.) (1971), *The Economics of Information and Knowledge*, Harmondsworth: Penguin.

Lamberton, D. M. (1971), 'Structure and growth of communications services', in Tucker, K. A. (ed.), *The Economics of the Australian Service Sector*, London: Croom Helm.

Lewis, C. B. (1973), Personal communication.

Little, Arthur D. (1970), *World Communications Study*, Boston: Arthur D. Little Inc.

Machlup, F. (1962), *The Production and Distribution of Knowledge in the United States*, Princeton: Princeton U.P.

Maddox, B. (1972), *Beyond Babel*, London: André Deutsch.

National Academy of Engineering (1971), *Communications Technology for Urban Development*, Washington D.C.

Newstead, I. A. (1973), *Report on Proposed National Telecommunications Plan*, Melbourne: Australian Post Office.

Parker, E. B. (1975), 'Social Implications of a Computer/Telecommunications System', conference paper on Computer/Telecommunications Policy, Paris: OECD.

Parker, E. B. and Dunn, D. A. (1972), 'Information technology: Its social potential', *Science*, 176, p. 1392.

Plan et Prospectives (1970), *Postes et Telecommunications*, Paris: Armand Colin.

Pool, I. de S., (ed.) (1977), *The Social Impact of the Telephone*, Boston: M.I.T. Press.

Porat, M. U. (1976), 'Defining the information sector', *Bulletin of the American society for Information Science*, 2, pp. 34–5.

Reid, A. (1971), 'What telecommunication implies', *New Society*, 30 December 1971.

Short, J. et al. (1976), *The Social Psychology of Telecommunications*, London: Wiley.

Telecom 2000 (1976), An Exploration of the Long-Term Development of Telecommunications in Australia, Melbourne: Australian Government Publications Service.

Thorngren, B. (1970), 'How contact systems affect regional development', *Environment and Planning*, 2, pp. 409–27.

Tyler, M. (1973), 'Developing Communications for the Future', Unpublished paper, Long Range Studies Division, British Post Office, London.

Westin, A. F. (1967), *Privacy and Freedom*, New York: Atheneum.

Wion, F. W. (1978), 'Do Engineers Know Everything'. Conference paper, Institution of Engineers, Australia.

12 Long-range Forecasting and Policy-Making — Options and Limits in Choosing a Future

BJORN WITTROCK

POLICY ANALYSIS, FORECASTING AND FUTURES STUDIES

Policy-makers, policy analysis and policy planning
In the 1960s and 1970s policy-makers in Western Europe and North America increasingly emphasised the need to bring systematic knowledge and analysis to bear upon the formulation, planning and implementation of programmes and policies in all fields of policy-making. At an organisational level this was manifested in the creation of bodies for analysis, evaluation and forecasting attached to government offices and agencies. This development was perceptible in most OECD member countries. Thus, in the United States such bodies were established in all major departments and agencies in the 1960s.[1] In Western Germany a special planning department was set up within the Federal Chancellor's Office. In the Netherlands what came to be known as the De Wolff Commission worked out a proposal for the organisation of a scientific basis for a more integrated long-term government policy, eventually in 1972 resulting in the creation of the Scientific Council for Government Policy.[2] In Sweden new bodies for policy analysis, advice and forecasting were gradually introduced in the Government Offices from the mid-1960s, initially in the fields of national physical planning, regional development, defence planning and economic forecasting. In the early and mid-1970s delegations and expert groups came to be attached to most ministries to help achieve a closer connection between

on the one hand current research and policy analysis and on the other actual policy-making in the given fields of responsibility.

This development is related to a redefinition of the role of science policy within the OECD area leading to an increased stress on mechanisms to ensure the utilisation and direction of scientific activities towards the fulfilment of social and, in a wide sense, political objectives.

However, it is also related to the emergence of special, more or less formalised, techniques of analysis and planning. One such important technique was, of course, PPBS (Planning – Programming – Budgeting System), introduced first in the US Department of Defense in the early 1960s and from 1965 and onwards also in other parts of the executive. PPBS shares with other techniques such as cost-benefit analysis, systems analysis and econometric modelling a basic reliance on the validity and applicability of elements of economic theory to the whole range of policy-making.[3]

A systematic analysis of policies is part of the process of preparing and planning policies to be carried out. But what kind of measures policy-makers undertake will vary considerably between different sectors of society even in a given country, e.g. between the planning objects of major weapons systems in defence planning and composition and pricing of products of various branches of industry respectively. Thus, the degree of control exercised over planning objects by policy-makers will vary. But then an increased emphasis on the importance of systematic analysis and preparation of policies will entail a shift away from any narrow general conception of planning and towards a generic concept of planning. Such a generic interpretation of the concept of planning is clearly brought out in a number of official Swedish reports and documents during the 1970s. Planning does not then result in the listing of definite decisions to be made and measures to be carried out at definite points in time. Planning rather involves the systematic preparation of decisions that may have long-term consequences, and the aim of this activity is not the specification of future commitments but to guarantee that policy-makers will in the future have as wide a range of options open as possible.[4] This latter planning conception seems furthermore to be well in line with the delimitations proposed in theoretical literature on planning by authors such as Yehezkel Dror and Erich Jantsch.

It can be noted that both conceptions of planning, i.e. as an activity resulting in a listing of decisions to be taken and implemented in a sequential fashion, and as a systematic preparation of a basis for alternative decisions, will ideally yield an ordering of a finite set A of decisions $\{d_1, \ldots, d_n\}$. However, the ordering will be structurally different in the two cases. In the second option-oriented one the ordering relation R in the set A, $\langle R, A \rangle$, will not be connected in A and there will be a partial ordering of the set of decisions. In the first case, which can be called simple planning, R will be connected and there will be a simple ordering of A.

Of course, cases of what can be termed complex planning are possible, where simple planning obtains for one subset of the set of decisions and option-oriented planning for another one. If the time horizons of the members of these sub-sets are not significantly different, then, *ceteris paribus*, the occurrence of complex planning indicates that policy-makers exercise different degrees of control over the policy fields that would be regulated or affected by the decisions of the different subsets.

Policy-makers, long-range forecasting and futures studies
The late 1960s witnessed the posing of fairly fundamental questions concerning the long-range prospects of highly industrialised and technology dependent societies. An interest of this sort was manifested in the concern about the human environment, in the OECD's reassessment of relationships between science, economic growth and society and the demand for an orientation towards so-called qualitative aspects of growth, and in efforts to undertake systematic studies of sequences of events stretching far into the future.

Against the background of, on the one hand the emergence of techniques of policy analysis and planning – in most countries originally mainly in connection with defence and military planning – and on the other hand a widely felt concern about long-term human prospects, the growing interest in long-range forecasting and futures studies during the late 1960s must be seen as a very natural phenomenon. However, the precise shaping of such forecasting and studies was, indeed, highly open to different interpretations and influences. Despite this fact most kinds of futures studies and cross-sectoral long-range forecasting seem to imply a deviation from other forms of policy planning and policy analysis in at least three respects. Firstly, they are oriented towards a time period of sufficient length to permit decisions about qualitative changes that go beyond what would appear to be feasible within the framework of major present commitments and restrictions. Secondly, in a long-term perspective there will be no one-to-one correspondence between problems identified by forecasters or futurologists and the policy problems handled within different existing administrative units. This will lend long-range studies a more open-ended character than is customary in short-term planning. It will mean that such studies will tend to be of relevance to a number of different groupings of policy-makers and other interested parties. Unless policy-makers exercise a high degree of control over planning objects and can also be expected to do so in the future, it will then, even in a narrow perspective, be difficult to argue that a tight direction of cross-sectoral long-range studies by the policy-makers of some specific organisational unit is reasonable. Thirdly, long-range and cross-sectoral forecasting and futures studies have often encompassed an effort to use or to reconstruct theories or theoretical assumptions other than the basically economic ones underlying much of traditional policy analysis.

VALUE DIMENSIONS OF FUTURES STUDIES

It is not surprising that interest in futures studies has also emerged in Sweden. However, specific features of this interest must be emphasised.

When in June 1971, on the initiative of Olof Palme, the then Prime Minister, a governmental commission was set up to review the field of futures studies, a prominent motive was a perceived need to elaborate a conception of futures studies that was opposed to the one underlying 'most futures studies produced so far . . . sponsored by military establishments and by the world's major multinational corporations' – to quote Alva Myrdal, chairman of the commission and then a member of the Cabinet. It was feared that such 'studies may be based on scales of values that are not democratically acceptable. We must avoid any "colonising of the future" by powerful interest groups, national or international.'

Some main value dimensions that can be discerned in the report of the Myrdal group, *To Choose a Future* (August 1972), are:

– opposition to any form of technological determinism and the focus on degrees of freedom of conscious action and choice in the long run;
– the idea of a need for public participation and involvement in the work of futures studies;
– a sense of international obligation or solidarity; futures studies should not be oriented in such a way that they 'are liable to come into conflict with legitimate aspirations among the majority of people in a developing country'.

It is only fair to say that these value dimensions of futures studies have never been seriously questioned in public Swedish debate or by people directly participating in projects of the official Swedish Secretariat for Futures Studies. However, it is equally fair to state that the precise relationships between these value dimensions and the actual activities of futures studies have not been unambiguous. In fact, even if attention is restricted to the sketching out of a future development with the help of some specific technique, say scenario construction, a number of different interpretations of possible roles of the value dimensions emerge. Thus, they can serve as starting-points for the definition of specific objectives to be reached or conditions to be satisfied in a future set of states of affairs. But they may also figure as phenomena to be given either exact or cursory consideration in the construction of scenarios. Surely, they may also have methodological implications that can be spelled out, or they may just serve as a starting-point for discussions among forecasters or futurologists without necessarily imposing well-defined restrictions upon their actual work. In the studies discussed below, all these interpretations have been relevant, but generally their proper formulation in individual cases has been found to be more problematic than was often initially expected. The different interpretations indicated above can be given the following more precise formulation, where the term scenario refers to a finite sequence of states of affairs of some definite length:

1. every scenario must include an assessment of the state of each member of the set of explicitly stated values and norms;
2. restrict (1) to apply to a sub-set of the scenarios or to a sub-set of the set of explicitly stated values and norms;
3. a satisfaction of certain specified values and norms is put as a requirement upon scenarios to be presented;
4. possible methodological implications of the acceptance of given value premises are spelled out;
5. assumptions of changes in values and norms are made in the construction of scenarios;
6. explicitly stated values and norms serve as a starting-point for discussions within for example a project group on the possible use of value premises or value dimensions according to some interpretation (1)–(5).

EMERGENCE AND ENVIRONMENT OF THE SWEDISH SECRETARIAT FOR FUTURES STUDIES

Emergence and organisation of Swedish futures studies
The appointment of the Alva Myrdal commission in 1971 was not only a reaction to an international development but also in many ways a response to an already manifested interest in futures studies on the part of several bodies within the country.

In the 1960s there had been contacts between the Swedish National Defence Research Institute and the RAND Corporation in the field of futures studies, initiatives for the creation of some formal body had been taken by Liberal Members of Parliament, and a concrete proposal had been worked out by the Academy of Engineering Sciences. There had also in the 1960s and early 1970s been discussions on futures studies in the Government Research Advisory Board, which formed a background for the work of the Alva Myrdal commission. However, in contrast to France or the Netherlands there was no strong domestic tradition in terms of existing policy-planning bodies entrusted with the handling of problems of cross-sectoral long-range forecasting. When, therefore, on the recommendation of the report *To Choose a Future*, a Secretariat for Futures Studies was established early in 1973, the potential and possibilities of this body were open-ended in several respects. The Secretariat was attached to the Cabinet Office. Given the Secretariat's orientation towards comprehensive issues not neatly falling within well-defined ministerial boundaries, this meant that in a sense it was situated at the cross-roads of different organisational units within the central executive.

In June 1974 a parliamentary reference group, composed of members of all parties in Parliament, was set up, establishing a direct relationship between the Secretariat and Parliament. In May 1975 Parliament decided, following proposals from the Conservative, Liberal and Centre parties, that this reference group should be given the status of an Executive Committee and that the Secretariat should be separated from the Cabinet Office, and in October 1975 this change was put into effect and the Secretariat was in administrative and budgetary terms transferred to the Ministry of Education. However, the importance of this change for the actual work of the Secretariat and its project groups should not be exaggerated. The Secretariat has remained a body within the central governmental system, working in a highly open fashion and having constant and close contacts in both ministerial and parliamentary quarters. Recently, a governmental commission, stressing the importance of the Secretariat's having relationships both with the Government Offices and governmental commissions and with Parliament, proposed that the current organisation of official Swedish futures studies should be retained.

Policy-making in the Government Offices
The performance and impact of the Secretariat's futures studies and forecasting activities will, of course, to a large extent be conditioned by characteristics of policy-making in the Swedish governmental system. Three such characteristics can be briefly mentioned.

Firstly, the Ministries, constituting the Government Offices, are fairly small bodies; the total number of Ministries now being 14, each with a staff in the region of 50–200 people, all categories included. This smallness facilitates close contacts and an efficient cooperation in the handling of the large amount of issues and policy matters that have to be dealt with in the Ministries. It also, however, necessitates an orientation towards the processing of the policy matters of mainly short- or medium-term nature upon which action has to be taken.

Secondly, non-routine policy matters that require a more extensive review and investigation than is possible to undertake within the framework of the Government Offices proper are regularly delegated to a governmental commission. Such commissions often include representatives of different governmental and non-governmental parties involved. They can prepare the given issues for an extended period of time and enjoy a fairly independent status. The number of commissions of enquiry has in recent years tended to be some 300, some 70–100 new ones being appointed each year.

Thirdly, the position and authority of a Cabinet Member heading some Ministry is normally, no doubt, a strong one. The administrative apparatus of the Prime Minister – the Cabinet Office – is small in numbers and although its coordinating functions were strengthened during the last years of the Social Democratic Government, it cannot be regarded as a body performing a long-term, cross-ministerial planning function.

Forecasting activities of the Secretariat for Futures Studies
A main task of the Secretariat for Futures Studies has been to initiate, coordinate and support project groups reviewing long-range trends and tendencies in central areas of policy-making and planning and outlining alternative courses of development and action. The Secretariat has, of

course, also an important role to play in work relating to the presentation and utilisation of project results. In addition to this, the Secretariat is a source of knowledge and service to the Government Offices and to governmental commissions in the fields of futures studies and technology assessment. This has taken the form of supply of information, informal contacts, organisation of seminars and participation in policy preparation. The Secretariat, furthermore, maintains an extensive system of contacts outside governmental bodies in an effort to stimulate a general public debate on future-oriented issues, and most reports from the Secretariat are characterised by an ambition to present results that are both reliably documented and intelligible to non-specialists. This has probably contributed to the amount of attention devoted to many of the reports in the press and other mass media.

Four project groups, composed of both academic scholars and administrative professionals, were set up in 1974–5. The themes of the projects – Energy and Society, Resources and Raw Materials, Sweden in the World Society and Working Life in the Future – were selected through a process that involved both discussions with representatives of different ministries and an analysis of the comments from some 130 governmental agencies and non-governmental organisations on the report *To Choose a Future*.

This first generation of project groups – so far having issued some 40 reports – finished their work late in 1977 or early in 1978, and new projects are now under way dealing with the following themes: Care in Society, Sweden in a New World Order, the Vulnerable Society – focusing on the interaction of complex technical systems and problems of social and individual trust – and Forecasts and Political Futures Planning.

A project group consists of 4–6 full-time members but well over 20 persons may contribute to reports in an expert capacity and on a part-time basis. The groups enjoy an independent status from the Government, but each of them has an inter-ministerial reference group, headed by an Under-Secretary of State, continuously following and commenting upon its work. Although both plans and reports can be discussed at the meetings of reference and project groups, it is not the task of the inter-ministerial group to approve project reports for publication. The Secretariat's futures studies activities are financed via the Government budget, the sum for the year 1978/79 being 3·7 million Swedish crowns.

Typology of futures studies
In the report *To Choose a Future* a typology of futures studies was elaborated under two main headings:

(A) Proximity to application of the results of studies, where a distinction was made between the following three categories: (1) studies that may serve directly as planning inputs and as a basis for long-term planning; (2) oriented basic research having at least a potential effect for the amelioration of planning; and (3) so-called autonomous futures studies that should neither directly nor indirectly be guided by the requirements of existing governmental planning bodies.

(B) A hierarchy of the levels of aggregation at which society is being studied, ranging from a global to an individual level, and where the levels can be used in the classification both of bodies utilising results of futures studies and of social phenomena being studied.

Futures studies and forecasting of the Secretariat for Futures Studies are mainly to be assigned to category (A1), and have dealt with phenomena at most of the levels in the hierarchy of aggregation, e.g. climatic changes at a local, regional and global level, relationships between income distribution and energy consumption conservation of individual households, and the operation of multinational corporations in the field of resource policy.

DIMENSIONS OF RELATIONS BETWEEN LONG-RANGE FORECASTING AND POLICY-MAKING

At least six dimensions seem to be relevant in accounting for relationships between policy-making and long-range, cross-sectoral forecasting. These dimensions will be briefly described in the present section and further examples pertaining to them will be given in the following sections. The empirical material cited below comes from observations and interviews at the Swedish Secretariat and its project and reference groups in the years 1974–9

Cooperation with advisory bodies
The time horizon of long-range forecasting is, as already mentioned, long enough to permit forecasters to assume that major current restrictions and commitments do not have to apply. But this entails that the set of policy-makers relevant in an advisory or directing capacity to a certain extent must be indeterminate. Then different *patterns of*

cooperation between forecasters and members of formal advisory bodies will also be open.

In the case of the Swedish Secretariat's futures studies such differences are apparent. Whereas the reference group of one of the projects, Energy and Society, has formally convened only once – this, however, not preventing a close and continuous cooperation between the project group and the chairman of the reference group – another project group, Resources and Raw Materials, has held regular meetings with its reference group every second or third month.

It can be noted that there have been hardly any cases for any of the project groups of efforts on the part of ministerial representatives to directly control the contents of the work of the groups, e.g. by demanding a formal approval of a report before its release to the public. The only incident that has occurred, which by some observers and newspapers was interpreted as a case in point, even led to a parliamentary debate.

The effects of a pattern of regular cooperation with a formal advisory group of civil servants and policy-makers seem to be twofold. First, it tends to create favourable conditions for a gradually increasing appreciation, trust and acceptance of the given forecasting activities. It is clear that, for example, the Swedish group studying resources and raw materials, came to be very generally accepted by the interests represented in the inter-ministerial reference group.

Secondly, the existence of a formal group regularly commenting upon the work of forecasters cannot but indirectly influence the general perspective of forecasters. The number and precise composition of advisory bodies in terms of policy-, time-, and, possibly, research-orientation, for example, will then be a significant matter, not least in the handling of relations between short-, medium-, and long-term forecasting.

Planning conception and impact of forecasting
The general option-oriented conception of planning, outlined above, that is now predominant in Swedish public planning, will affect the requirements and possible impact of forecasting. Within a policy-making setting, criteria of successful forecasting will be formulated in terms of effects on the perceived range of policy options and of mechanisms generating changes in given policy areas. But, surely, these types of criteria do not necessarily mean that a forecast deemed successful will be the most specific account of the most probable line of development, that then actually occurs. Concerning both specification,

probability and success of a forecast in terms of the coming about of a predicted sequence of events, then, there may be good reasons for a deviation from these kinds of ideals, if an option-oriented conception of planning is accepted. Furthermore, in connection with the Swedish Secretariat's futures studies some ministerial observers have emphasised that for them the actual experience of, and participation in, forecasting and futures studies activities have been more important than reading final results and forecasts.

Cross-sectoral forecasting and sectoral competence
Relations between cross-sectoral forecasting and sectoral forecasting competence will inevitably have an effect on the carrying out of long-range cross-sectoral forecasting. At a cognitive level the existence of strong sectoral forecasting will usually mean that the given policy area is well-defined by policy-makers who then have a well-structured view of the field. The long lead times in the introduction of new technical systems makes energy policy a natural area for the evolution of a forecasting tradition, primarily perhaps in connection with electrical energy.

In the Swedish administrative and planning system, energy forecasting has been performed by several public bodies; the Energy Forecasting Commission sketching out alternatives for the periods 1975–85 and 1985–2000, the Delegation for Energy Research up to the year 2000, the State Industry Board and the Central Dispatching Board, coordinating organisation for major electricity producers, private and public. At the ministerial level the main responsibility for the translation of these forecasts into policy planning has been with the Ministry for Industry.

By and large, contacts between energy forecasters and planners were well developed when the futures study on Energy and Society was initiated, originally in the form of a joint venture of the Secretariat and the Energy Policy Delegation, a coordinating body of Under-Secretaries of State that was set up during the oil crisis of 1973–4 and later dissolved.

Distinguishing features of the Energy and Society project were its ambition to trace longer-term consequences of decisions than had earlier been customary, to understand the driving forces behind choices of energy systems even if this meant going beyond the kind of data, often producer oriented, that were amenable to established forecasting techniques. Although the project enjoyed the close collaboration of the chairman of the reference group, an energy policy adviser to the Government and former Director General of the State Power Board, there is no doubt that originally the project was looked upon with some scepticism among parts of what might be termed the Government Offices informal network of people involved in the preparation and planning of energy policy.

The area of resources and raw materials falls within the domain of responsibility of several Swedish ministries, primarily those of Industry, Agriculture, Housing and Physical Planning, Foreign Affairs, Commerce and Defence. Contacts between the futures studies group on Resources and Raw Materials and these Ministries seem generally to have been smooth and in some cases, e.g. that of the unit for national physical planning in the Ministry of Housing and Physical Planning, very close.

The same conclusion is valid concerning relations between the resources project and a number of governmental commissions, in particular perhaps in the case of the minerals policy commission doing forecasting of developments during the coming 10-year period.

For both the Resources and Raw Materials project and for that on Sweden in the World Society, there seem to be grounds for suggesting that cooperation with governmental units to some extent has been facilitated by the relative absence of strong in-house forecasting competence and commitments of a similar broadly conceived orientation.

Needless to say, the existence of such cooperation is of great value in terms of access to professional competence and to factual material not yet published. However, it must certainly always be related to questions about the possible effects of such cooperation on the basic conceptions of forecasters concerning what constitutes the relevant policy problems.

Redefinition, closure and turbulence
It is, as indicated above, a defining characteristic of long-range, cross-sectoral forecasting that forecasters should consider the possibility of major *redefinitions* of given policy areas. Of course, a redefinition of what constitutes the main policy problems and appropriate public measures may be under way among policy-makers even at the time when forecasting activities are being performed. Surely, such a situation may have a profound impact on relationships between forecasters and policy-makers. Furthermore, it is obviously important whether or not a concomitant of such a redefinition is that a considerably larger set, or different set, of people will be involved in reviewing the given field than those normally active in the preparation and implementation of policies.

Thus, the dimension of the relative *closure* of forecasting and policy processes must be considered.

Finally, a review and redefinition of a field of policy, whatever the degree of closure, cannot but be affected by the fact that it is conducted in a stable or a *turbulent* organisational and political environment.

Swedish energy policy in the 1970s provides an excellent example of a movement away from a situation of closure and stability into one of redefinition, of erosion of closure and of turbulence.

Before 1973 energy policy in general and nuclear power policy in particular had, by and large, not been a controversial issue on the political agenda. Up to then all parliamentary decisions on nuclear power had been unanimous and problems were formulated in technical and non-partisan terms. The following years witnessed a change which involved energy policy being a decisive issue for the outcome of the 1976 election and being a main cause of contention within the new three-party Government that emerged in the Autumn of 1976.

In accordance with the functioning of the Swedish political system different aspects of energy policy have been considered by a series of governmental commissions, and in December 1976 a comprehensive reviewing of the field to serve as a basis for a parliamentary decision in the Autumn of 1978 on the fundamental features of energy policy up to 1990 was entrusted to a politically broadly composed Energy Commission.

There are clearly discernible indications that in this situation of flux, the project group on Energy and Society of the Secretariat for Futures Studies has been successful in transferring central elements of its conception of the long-term options and limits in choosing energy systems to the bodies performing a review of the field. Perhaps this should not be surprising considering the fact that the project group, although smaller in terms of manpower and budget than the Energy Commission – to which linkages exist – and sharing with it a comprehensive view of energy policy, had been active for some 2 years when the commission started its work and moreover considers energy alternatives well beyond 1990, i.e. the time horizon of the Energy Commission. The interesting and basically distinguishing feature of the futures study group has, however, been its insistence upon a simple formulation of the problem of a retention of freedom of action in the choice of long-term energy systems and upon the need not primarily of sophisticated techniques of forecasting but of a firm understanding of the driving forces and basic generating mechanisms determining the emergence of systems of energy production, distribution and consumption. This orientation has, as will be indicated subsequently, necessitated a reconstruction and integration of knowledge from traditionally separate fields. Thus, the understanding of a complex policy problem, 'p-problem', has been tightly interwoven with the studying of composite problems of knowledge, 'k-problems'.[5]

FORECASTING AND POLICY-MAKING

It is often argued that forecasting has to rely on the validity of theoretical assumptions.[6] Such assumptions may in some cases constitute an ordering and have the form of an explicit theory. In other cases, however, a set of well-formulated theoretical assumptions relating to the given field of interest may not be available in advance. This does not necessarily entail that forecasting activities within this field will have the character of sheer guess-work. Possibly, assumptions might be formally derived from other assumptions that are well-formulated or they might be partially reconstructed from our knowledge of the given and adjacent fields. In any case, the fact that theoretical assumptions of necessity underlie all forecasting activities will be of importance in at least five different ways to such forecasting as is related to problems of long-range planning and policy-making.

Forecasting, policy-making and choice
Firstly, policy-making will involve reference to actions that may be performed and to the possibility of choosing between alternative courses of action. Now, this poses the problem of choice. There is, of course, a large literature describing the problem of evaluating and choosing from a given set of alternatives to which possible consequences and their probabilities have been assigned. There is also a large literature describing the problem of defining how a social choice is to be reached from a set of individual interests or preferences.[7]

As already mentioned, the element of choice and action has been a prominent one in the conception behind Swedish futures studies, and *To Choose a Future* even states 'that the most fundamental motive for studying and analysing remote futures is to enable us to take genuine decisions at the right time, i.e. to shape the future rather than let it be passively shaped for us'. Given this orientation it is worth noting that it has not implied an emphasis on the problems of defining a social choice function or of proposing formal criteria of rational choice. The focus has not been on the formal process of choosing from a given set of alternatives but instead on the problem of defining these alternatives in distinct and concrete terms. This also includes an effort to identify long-range restrictions on freedom of action.

Such an orientation underlies all the reports of the project group on Energy and Society, where main layers of restrictions have been discerned pertaining to

— the interplay between on the one hand energy policy and on the other political objectives concerning economic growth, full employment, income distribution, solidarity with the developing countries, environmental protection, working environment and climatic and ecological effects;
— technical characteristics of the energy system concerning the nuclear fuel cycle; and
— characteristics of the social and economic regulating system affecting energy policy.

A major conclusion of the project is that the set of feasible options is largely determined by: (1) the amount and quality of energy used; (2) the existence of large, complex technical systems of energy production, e.g. the nuclear fuel cycle; and (3) organisational inertia, the given organisational and administrative apparatus and set of rules being adapted to already operating technologies and having an effect on inter alia the cost structure and competitiveness of different technologies via the rules of the capital market.

In the long run, the group argues, the only possible alternative to an energy system based on nuclear power, including breeder technology, and/or coal, is constituted by a system based on renewable energy sources. However, for this to be a realistic alternative it is necessary for the state actively to create the proper conditions for it, not only by supporting research and development for this purpose but also by political and organisational measures designed to control the amount and quality of energy used – e.g. by affecting private consumption that has become increasingly more energy-intensive – and the form of the energy transmission and distribution system, e.g. by influencing the choice of heating systems based on electricity or water.

The group's comprehensive orientation towards the problems of the retention of freedom of action and of needs to undertake public measures to actually retain that freedom can at present also be discerned in the works of several Swedish commissions and delegations reviewing energy policy.

Forecasting and basic mechanisms
Secondly, forecasting of relevance to long-range planning will have to be related to problems of policy-making and planning. The Swedish Secretariat's futures studies have focused on policy-relevant problems that largely cut across the sectoral boundaries of different ministries and agencies. But such problems tend to have rather an open-ended character, and there is obviously no simple one-to-one correspondence between such problems (p-problems), and problems of knowledge (k-problems), of some given scientific discipline having access to structured sets of data and to well-formulated theories. It may even be the case that the interesting properties of a problem of policy-making cannot be related to any member of any set of well-formulated theories at a given point in time. Forecasting, necessarily relying on some theoretical assumptions, will then have to start out from a reconstruction of some basic generating mechanisms within the given field of interest. Precisely this happened in the work of the Swedish futures studies groups. Thus, a fundamental task of the Energy and Society group was to undertake a delimitation of the comprehensive energy policy problem, including an identification of relevant restrictions and generating mechanisms.

The perspective of freedom of action in the choice of energy systems, outlined above, is tightly interwoven with the conception that energy problems should be seen in terms of the transformation over time of combinations of energy technologies rather than in terms of physical scarcity of energy resources. But, of course, a formulation of this type is open to many analytically different interpretations. The formulation is thus entirely consistent with William D. Nordhaus's view that the driving force behind the transformations over time in the utilisation of energy technologies is the cost of production.[8] It has already been pointed out that the conception of the Swedish energy group is a different one, where costs of production are seen as highly dependent upon interrelated technical and organisational systems, that are open to change through acts of political will. These different interpretations of the problem of transformation also indicate that fairly fundamental ideas of the nature of society and man's place in society — e.g. concerning the possibility of consciously bringing about changes in given states of affairs — are relevant for the theoretical assumptions underlying forecasting activities.

One of the other studies, *Working Life in the Future*, identified three main aspects: firstly, a macro-perspective on working life, including demographic forecasting up to the year 2025, studies of the composition and durability of the labour force, relations between production and concepts of needs; secondly, working life from within, including topics such as organisation of work, experiments of workers' self-government, and technical change; and thirdly, the role of work within the total life situation of human beings, including questions about interrelations between working life, family life and educational life.

Considering the fact that the whole area of working life in Sweden is in process of changing, accompanied by public debate, with new legislation being discussed or in the stage of implementation, and new forms of research being initiated, a successful futures study in this field would undoubtedly meet with great interest in many quarters. However, although a number of reports, that have met with interest, have been or are about to be published, the project group did not succeed in outlining any coherent courses of future development. One major reason for this probably is that it was not found possible to encompass the different fields of the study and the mechanisms assumed to be operating within these fields within a comprehensive theoretical framework sufficiently precise to give structure and sufficiently open-ended to permit knowledge from the wide range of areas to be included. But then, neither could there be a consistent set of assumptions underlying inclusive forecasting in contrast to the successful forecasting in a separate field such as demographic development.

It is interesting to note that the inter-ministerial reference group of the project 'Working Life in the Future' seems to have been quite active in the initial phase of the project, the members of this reference group sharing much of the general public feeling of the importance and, possibly even urgency of discerning the long-term implications of current trends and changes in working life.

Forecasting and uncertainty

A third problem, related to the second one about relations between p-problems and k-problems, concerns the handling of uncertainty.

The relation between an action or a set of actions performed at a given time and possibly ensuing sequences of states of affairs will often be uncertain even if the set of states of affairs considered is a very restricted one.

This should, perhaps, not be surprising considering the following circumstances: Firstly, given a finite set of logically independent states of affairs $\{p_1, \ldots, p_n\}$ that may or may not obtain on, say m, successive points in time, the number of possible sequences, 2^{mn}, will soon become large when m increases.[9] Secondly, knowledge about mechanisms bringing about a change from p_i at time t to $\sim p_i$ at $t+1$ is limited. Thirdly, a restriction of the domain of interest to a particular, definite set of states of affairs presupposes, if it is to be well founded, that no unforeseen factor significantly affects this set during any of the m points in time. Obviously, such an assumption is a far-reaching one that may in given instances not be tenable.

Now, when different alternatives can be assigned numerically comparable probabilities, there are established methods for dealing with uncertainty.[10] However, in cross-sectoral and cross-disciplinary long-range forecasting this condition often does not obtain. One reason for this might be that assumptions underlying one alternative are drastically different in the case of another alternative. A mild form of this might occur in economic forecasting if the technical composition of production is assumed to be significantly different in different alternatives. A more difficult form would be — as has been the case in at least one of the Swedish studies — if a change of the entire basic political and economic organisation for decision-making is a distinguishing feature of the separate alternatives. There are some indications that there might be difficulties in justifying and transferring such perspectives to civil servants and politicians. This is, perhaps, in a sense trivial, but it points to an interesting conclusion: in long-range forecasting qualitative uncertainty will be a recurring and familiar phenomenon, which cannot be looked upon as constituting a primarily technical problem. The handling of such uncertainty by sectorally organised planning and policy-making will unavoidably entail difficulties.

Policy-making, short-, medium- and long-term forecasting

A fourth problem, connected with the last two, concerns the time horizon of forecasting and futures studies. The long term is usually interpreted to mean that major present commitments and restrictions do not necessarily apply so that, as already mentioned, decisions about qualitative changes are seen as possible. But if the results of such studies are to serve as inputs into current planning and policy-making processes they will have to be somehow related to short- and medium-term concerns. It must then be possible to establish non-arbitrary relationships between states of affairs described in a short-, medium- and long-term perspective respectively. Efforts to achieve this objective can follow at least three different lines.

Firstly, forecasting instruments used in short- or medium-term surveys may be adapted so as to cover a more extended period of time. Within the framework of the econometric model system of the Swedish

Ministry of Finance, now of the Ministry for Economic Affairs, a special model has been constructed for the purpose of calculating development paths during the 20-year period following the normal 5-year period of medium-term surveys. This model has also been used by the futures studies group on Resources and Raw Materials. In this case four sets of alternative assumptions about the development of the global market of raw materials were formulated and corresponding to these four different developments of the Swedish economy up to 1990 were described.

The difficulty with this type of approach is, obviously, twofold. A number of relationships between basic variables must be assumed not to be open to drastic changes even in a long-term perspective, which is somehow at odds with the defining characteristics of a long-term perspective. The second difficulty is that most of medium-term forecasting is itself only indirectly related to policy-making. Thus, medium-term economic surveys serve in Sweden as an important informational basis for decision-makers, predominantly in the public sector, but are not really presented in the form of a policy document listing decisions that have to be taken and implemented.

Secondly, a long-range forecast can be explicitly based on the set of basic generating mechanisms that have been identified. The Energy and Society project group have thus outlined two widely different energy systems for Sweden in the year 2015, one system entirely based on renewable energy sources and the other one on nuclear energy. An important characteristic of these alternatives is that their time-scale is, as mentioned above, more extended than that of the alternatives of the Energy Commission, for example, which include forecasts up to 1990. This permits the discerning of alternatives that are really qualitatively different although clearly related to options and decisions of a short-term nature.

The numerical calculations for these alternatives are based on assumptions about what is physically and technically possible and feasible, given the long lead times in the introduction of new, but technically possible, energy sources and given some simple restrictions concerning Sweden in 2015: population (same as today), production of goods and services (increase by 100% from 1975 till 2015), number of dwellings (increase by 40% from 1975, with a slight increase of space per dwelling), specific energy consumption (a decrease from 1975 till 2015 by 20% in industry, 50% in the services- and transports-sector, and by 30% in dwellings). Obviously, this form of calculation is related to the group's emphasis on a conception of freedom of action and to the identification of restrictions in terms of the interplay between technical and organisational systems open to change by acts of political will rather than primarily in terms of the operation of price mechanisms.

Thirdly, regardless of the specific technique chosen in long-range forecasting, an effort can be made to review existing policy-relevant knowledge. The system of inter-ministerial reference groups for the studies of the Swedish Secretariat for Futures Studies was intended to ensure a policy-making focus of this kind. Project groups have also, as has already been described, co-operated with a large number of ministerial units, agencies and governmental commissions. Such contacts may, surely, have a profound impact on both forecasting activities and on the utilisation of forecasts.

Forecasting and alternative developments

It is often stated that long-range forecasters must be sensitive to weak signals indicating possible alternative developments that might be of decisive importance in a long time perspective, although such signals might be currently only partly or vaguely discernible. It is then sometimes suggested that so-called intuitive forecasting techniques are appropriate in the description of these kinds of possible sequences of future events. Examples of such techniques are scenario construction, delphi and brainstorming techniques respectively. Of these, scenario techniques are both more widely used, e.g. in Swedish defence planning, and have a better methodological reputation than the other ones.[11]

Scenario construction is the only one of these so-called intuitive techniques that have been used within futures studies of the Swedish Secretariat. Three of the project groups of the 'first' generation worked with scenarios but for only one of the groups, that focusing on foreign policy issues and dependencies of Sweden in a world society, do scenarios play a major role in the final report.

But if, following the description given earlier, the domain of interest can be represented by a finite set of n logically independent states of affairs, possibly obtaining on m different points in time, then of course the problem remains which of the 2^{mn} possible developments to sketch out. It is, as has already been mentioned, a basic motive behind futures studies that alternatives to be considered should not be restricted to those strictly conforming to currently prevailing notions among policy-makers and what is politically and organisationally feasible in a short-term perspective. Thus, if the set of logically possible developments is denoted by L, the set of short-term feasible ones by F, the empty set by ϕ and the operation of difference on sets by $\setminus$, then the set of possible developments to be considered in cross-sectoral, long-range forecasting, P, must satisfy the following two conditions: (1) $P \subset L$; and (2) $P \setminus F \neq \phi$.

Of course, additional conditions have to be formulated to ensure that L is restricted beyond the delimitations of (1) and (2). But the interesting fact is then that this probably cannot be satisfactorily done if we have not got a definite idea of what constitutes an interesting future regularity, i.e. a regularity that may possibly obtain in a future but does not necessarily do so, at least not in full measure, at present. The specification of such possible regularities is, in turn, not primarily a problem of defining in formal terms a set of necessary and sufficient conditions of adequacy. As far as sufficient conditions are concerned, that would probably be a vain effort.[12] We are not relieved of the need to gain an understanding of what is actually bringing about changes in relevant states of affairs. If a main conclusion of the Swedish studies on Energy and Society and on Resources and Raw Materials is warranted, i.e. that the main problems and obstacles in these fields are not of a technical or physical but of a political and economic nature, then, obviously, what is needed is a well-formulated theory that accounts for the precise operation of such obstacles.

NOTES

1. G. T. Allison, 'Implementation Analysis', Paper delivered at the Uppsala Quincentennial Symposium on Politics as Rational Action, 10–14 October 1977, pp. 2 ff.
2. R. van Gendt (1976), 'The Scientific Council for Government Policy: Indirect Advising on the central level', *Planning and Development in the Netherlands* VIII (1976–I), pp. 34–43.
3. G. T. Allison, *op. cit.*, pp. 3–5.
4. *Forskningspolitik. Betänkande av forskningsrådsutredningen*, SOU 1977:52, Stockholm: Liber Förlag, pp. 123 ff; *Forskningsråd. Betänkande avgivet av forskningsrådsutredningen*, SOU 1975: 26 Stockholm: Liber Förlag, pp. 274 ff; *Om Planering vid Statliga myndigheter*, Statskontoret Stockholm: Liber Förlag, 1977, pp. 12 ff; *Proposal for a Reform of the Swedish Budget System*, Ministry of Finance, Stockholm: Allmänna Förlaget, 1974, pp. 42–5; *Statsförvaltningen planerar: aktörer, rollfördelning, samverkansformer*, Statskontoret Stockholm: Liber Förlag, 1974, p. 7.
5. Cf. B. Wittrock (1977), 'Sweden's Secretariat: programmes and policies', *Futures* 9, August 1977, pp. 352–6.
6. J. Clark and S. Cole (1975), *Global Simulation Models – A Comparative Study*, London: John Wiley Interscience, pp. 59 and 107; M. Edman, 'Det finns ingen naiv prognosmetodik', in *Kunskaps – och begreppsproblem i framtidsstuder*, ed. S. Schwarz, Stockholm: Försvarets Forskningsanstalt, 1975, pp. 1–27.

7. Some recent contributions are: C. d'Aspremont and L. Gevers, 'Equity and the informational basis of collective choice', *Review of Economic Studies* 44, 1977, pp. 199–209; S. Strasnick, 'The problem of social choice: Arrow to Rawls', *Philosophy and Public Affairs* 4, 1976, pp. 241–73.
8. William D. Nordhaus, 'The allocation of energy resources', *Brookings Papers on Economic Activity* 4, 1973:3, pp. 529–76.
9. Cf. G. H. von Wright (1969), *Time, Change and Contradiction* London: Cambridge University Press; G. H. von Wright (1971), *Explanation and Understanding*, London: Routledge and Kegan Paul, pp. 43–82; G. H. von Wright (1974), *Causality and Determinism* New York: Columbia University Press, pp. 13–35; G. H. von Wright, 'On the Logic and Epistemology of the Causal Relation', in: *Logic, Methodology and Philosophy of Science IV*, (eds.) P. Suppes et al., Amsterdam: North Holland Publishing Company, 1973, pp. 293–312.
10. L. Ingelstam (1976), 'Basic Problems of Planning', in: *Trends in planning*, (eds.) C. G. Jennergren et al, Försvarets Forskningsanstalt, Stockholm, pp. 12–14.
11. L. Albertson and T. Cutler, 'Delphi and the image of the Future', *Futures* 8, October 1976, pp. 397–404; B. Cazes, 'The future of work – An outline of a method for scenario construction', *Futures* 8, October 1976, pp. 405–10; P. F. Chapman. 'A method for exploring the future', *Long Range Planning* 9, February 1976, pp. 2–11; S. Hellman, 'Swedish defence planning', *Futures* 9, February 1977, pp. 79–86; W. Kennet (1976), *The Futures of Europe* Cambridge University Press, Cambridge, pp. 27–9; P.-A. Julien, P. Lamonde and D. Latouche, *La Méthode des Scénarios*, Travaux et Recherches de Prospective, Délégation à l'Aménagement du Territoire et à l'Action Régionale (La Documentation Française, Paris, 1975); M. Palmer and G. Schmid, 'Planning with scenarios – The banking world of 1985', *Futures* 8, December 1976, pp. 472–84; B. Schwarz, 'Long-range planning in the public sector', *Futures* 9, April 1977, pp. 115–27.
12. Cf. P. Gärdenfors (1976), 'Relevance and redundancy in deductive explanations', *Philosophy of Science*, 43, pp. 421 ff.

13 The Political Limits to Forecasting

(Extracted from *Margins for Survival – Political Limits in Steering Technology*. Copyright 1976, 1977 by Edward Wenk, Jr.)

EDWARD WENK, JR.

INTRODUCTION

Today, everyone lives in greater jeopardy of servitude or extermination than at any recent time in history. More people are simultaneously exposed to common dangers, and a larger number of different perils are occurring in tandem. Threats are thus manifest to the entire species. Most of these hazards evolve from inadvertent effects of technology; not so much from the presence of scientific knowledge and only somewhat from villainy, but rather from ignorance, human error and lack of imagination as to possible future consequences. Because technology is symbiotically and intricately interwoven with human culture, institutions and social processes, intervention to deal with these predicaments is the responsibility of the salient organisations that synthesise and represent collective social choice – the national governments. Indeed, the major choices involving technology are already made by government as to both ends and means.

These decisions are manifested in public policies that become the steering mechanisms in a pluralistic society. But in the heat of social action to deal with day-to-day issues, sight seems lost of the role of policy to bridge the present and the future.

Since the first responsibility of government is collective security, one would expect heightened attention in the political theatre to continuous, concerted and sensitive attention to the way ahead. One would expect a discipline of careful search for solutions and an appetite for better decision aids.

Yet the slow uninterrupted growth of multiple hazards has occurred as if the policy-making apparatus were deaf to warning signals about the future. We find the criteria employed in decisions largely favour the short term, without sensitive balance with the long. Both information and disposition seem lacking to examine two crucial questions that underpin policy as though future consequences mattered: 'what will happen, if?' in those issues already commanding attention, and 'what may happen, unless?' in those issues currently ignored.

Many social analysts have stated that human evolution has reached such a critical stage that neglect of future consequences could entail a penalty for decision error so economically expensive, so politically strenuous, so environmentally disastrous or so inimical to the human spirit that whatever the immediate cost or inconvenience, certain trade-offs to keep trends from becoming destiny are deemed worthwhile.

Some change in steering behaviour is thus critically required in our political institutions, leaders and selective processes. Although it would appear simple to identify the key leaders who must deal with such overarching dilemmas and to exhort them to do better, the conditions of decision-making in representative governments are such that circumstances may, in effect, be beyond their leaders' control.

The 'system' is increasingly complex and involves many interactions among participants. Processes emanating from the grass-roots cultural set are predisposed toward instant gratification that engenders political expediency. A vice of psychological as well as operational constraints may deter policy leaders from dealing with the future. We may thus be confronted with a form of social paralysis.

Whatever the philosophical, ideological or intellectual attractions of long-range forecasting as an aid to decision-making, it is necessary to consider that such studies may be simply building a library for non-readers.

The decision process may itself be disabled. To probe further entails two things, describing the present situation using the crude diagnostic tools of purely impressionistic evidence available at this stage of social understanding, and unravelling the behaviour of political institutions and of individual policy-makers.

As we consider the situation, it is clear that decision aptitudes are sharply challenged. The range of alternative is greater. The underlying technical facts are more difficult to comprehend because of their sophistication and specialised jargon, and the consequences of error are more lethal and irreversible. Decision-makers are perplexed by new levels of complexity and hyper-interdependence in our society, accompanied by uncertainty, a heightened pace of social change, and discontinuities in utility of past experience.

Distortions in public communication and gaps in understanding arise, inflaming institutional tribalism and new conflicts from enhanced citizen awareness. Resources less and less match ever rising expectations. Finally, policies designed and pushed in each narrow sector do not operate in isolation but produce unwanted, unexpected and capricious cross-impacts, so that in the absence of a broad perspective, there is little net gain.

Since every decision is a choice of one alternative over another, we consciously or intuitively decide by comparing the consequences of each option. That is, we trace the kind and degree of effects which we imagine that one decision would have now and in the future, compared with alternatives. We endeavour to peer ahead.

The individual decision-maker almost always wants to do the right thing. But most also want to stay in office, to be admired by a constituency or to please the boss. Here are the basic seeds of an internal conflict, because these two compelling objectives may not be compatible. Indeed, they may diverge most conspicuously over the time horizon of expected benefits.

The need to exercise trade-offs between pressures of the short run and recognition of perils from neglect of the long generates high levels of stress in the decision process. It may even be perceived as a no-win situation. Under psychological stress, we know from widespread observations of human behaviour that the short run always claims priority. Choices for reasons of expediency become pathological. Indeed, the entire metabolic process in healthy social choice is disabled.

Stress may thus be a significant key to understanding what is going on.

STRESS IN DECISION-MAKING

As we examine the policy-making apparatus, it becomes necessary to focus closely on the individual decision-maker. For only by such an intimate view can we expose essential psycho-sociological factors that motivate and modulate the act of decision-making.

All choices are attended by anxiety. Some apprehension is triggered by a fantasy of adverse consequences of error in relation to the problem being attacked. But some also arise from awareness that the personal reputation and self-esteem of the decision-maker are at stake. Clearly, there are incentives to a thorough search for and assessment of options in terms of manifold consequences just enumerated.

Janis and Mann[1] identify five patterns of decision behaviour under such stress:

- uncritical continuity of existing trajectories;
- uncritical flip-flop to completely new directions;
- defensive avoidance or delay of a decision;
- panic and frantic search for more and better options;
- cool and thoughtful scanning of options and confident choice.

The first four modes are pathological; the fifth, while never a guarantee of rightness, is assumed most productive.

To elaborate: uncritical continuity is the classical case of bureaucratic inertia, where complacency, custom, institutional imperatives and perceptions of short-term rewards for protecting past decisions dominate curiosity, vision and boldness. Such behaviour is also characteristic of systems that have exhausted available resources or lack incentives or a capability to enrich their perspective, including failure to seek and learn from past errors. Future risks of change are deemed greater than penalties of conservatism.

In the second case with a different emotional setting, emergency warnings are so provocative that almost any motion provides immediate relief. These pressures for impulsive action may arise from sudden menace external to and threatening the entire system, or from internal threats to power and position. The knee-jerk mood induces overreaction to group pressure and expediency. With neither case does the decision make sense out of the impending dilemma. Anxiety levels are low or not sustained.

When stress rises, as in their third category, there may be a no-win perception of damned if you do or damned if you don't. Whenever feasible, the decision-maker tries to shift responsibility to minimise personal risk. In a complex organisational setting, such evasions are almost routine because the decision site is masked by the jungle. There may also be a disposition to delay in the secret hope that the problem will go away. The latter tendency to procrastinate is a widely recognised political stratagem that gains reinforcement from absence of any penalty in the short run for ignoring future consequences. It may be said that inaction in the short run is inevitable. But in the long run, it is intolerable.[2] Of course, if the situation is deemed hopeless, there may be no will to respond.

In the fourth case, if a timetable of imminent penalty accompanies perception of threat, or if new crises appear, or if resources begin to drain away, a sense of peril mounts. A search for answers becomes hysterical; simple and hastily contrived solutions become especially attractive; prejudices tend to become more blinding.

The roster of US policy decisions over the last twenty year is replete with examples of all four modes of decision behaviour under stress. Repeated extension of the Federal Highway Trust Fund with neglect of urban mass transit and intercity passenger trains falls into the first category. So did uncritical concentration of federal research funds on development of nuclear power to the exclusion of other energy sources. The second mode is exemplified by hasty enactment of certain environmental laws, requiring for example return of rivers to a zero pollution condition, or the massive, uncritical funding of cancer research. Delays in dealing with energy policy, health care delivery, and world hunger fit the third class of decision paralysis. Over-reaction to generate a massive space programme in 1958 represents the fourth class. Yet, creation of the Comsat Corporation for commercial communication with space satellite relays is a good example of a reasoned analysis and a cool decision matching technological opportunity with social needs.

With these four pathological responses to threat there is high likelihood of error in judgement. The test of error, incidentally, lies in subsequent unfolding of adverse consequences. There is then revealed whether the decision-maker was both disposed toward and skilled in dealing with the future.

By comparison, the fifth mode is appealing. The threat is carefully analysed. Facts are gathered, structured and interpreted. A repertoire of options is examined and different consequences traced. Resources are assayed, and political will exerted to make a decision.

What an immaculate model of rationality, devoutly to be sought and administered. Our sense of reality tells us, however, that there are serious, ubiquitous and subtle impediments to that utopian condition. Indeed, commitment to such rationality is an occupational hazard of policy analysts.

Four types of deficiencies may defeat rationality. The information process may have any or all of the shortcomings outlined earlier. There are limits to human cognition and freedom from bias. Secondly, there are limits to imagination in creating images of the future. All kinds of social, economic, political, bureaucratic and legal pressures or constraints may be present, and rewards may be absent for the long as well as the short run. Thirdly, intellectual and psychic resources to decide may not match the situation, and physical resources to implement a decision may be clearly inadequate to counter threat. Fourthly, time may be too short to think and to act.

THE TICKING CLOCK

The ticking clock may lie behind some of the problems in dealing with the future as an intrinsic part of policy. The decision-maker, as Veblen has so neatly put it, is subject to a parallelogram of forces whereupon he follows the line of the resultant. He is trapped by a series of permutations enforced by circumstances, external and alien. One of these is the perception that an issue is like a time-bomb that must be promptly defused or it will explode. The second problem in perceived time is a temporal limitation on the political actor to find enough personal time to deal adequately with the issue at hand. Many psychologists confirm that animals under such conditions display pathological behaviour of high stress.

Clearly, the time element in the decision process becomes a major object of study for two reasons, the shortage of time versus need for careful study, and the abnormal stress imposed by the time bind that carries with it seeds of decision error.

Virtually all of these decision processes are self-explanatory and familiar. However, the element of time deserves some interpretation here, as a prelude to later discussion of its relevance to healthy decision activities.

Time in Western culture is readily conceived as a clocking mechanism associated with periods of internally coherent activities that occur in discrete sequence. It is a cruelly irreversible parade of events. In this sense, a decision is not the flash of instantaneous action but simply the symbolic culmination of a series of contributing actions which may have been ignited by perception of a threat, somewhere, a long time before.

Social processes in which the decision and its constituents are embedded unroll at an unrelenting rate, and the chronology of key events may itself reveal interactions and possible cause and effect relationships.

To political actors time is a finite resource, allocated in chunks for varied functions. The policy-maker is thus obliged to budget time for each decision, for collection and analysis of data, generating policy alternatives and their consequences, and choosing. As we see later, both the compression of time available for rational choice, and the unrelenting evolution of external forces, leads swiftly to recognition that time is perhaps the scarcest of commodities, and that the shortage imposes stress that can trigger irrationality.

It is interesting that a public mystique has grown up and even been promoted about how unruffled policy-makers are in their daily tasks. Anyone who has spent time in the office of a Congressman or of a senior official in the executive branch is likely to report quite a different atmosphere. It is hectic. These officials take compulsive initiatives to become involved in every possible activity in which they have a stake. With the interconnectedness referred to earlier, the number of issues involving any single actor is increasing. To be effective, they must take the initiative to involve themselves whenever the opportunity arises, on short notice and with timetables over which they have no control. To be sure, numerous legislative manoeuvres are available to delay or slow action to a more congenial pace, or time-filibusters, congressional committee locks, etc. But by and large, the actors dance to tunes played by others.

Finally, none of the political actors can devote his full time to matters of choice. Chief executives have numerous ceremonial functions; parliamentarians must meet constituents and help solve problems for those at home. All must offer courtesies to representatives of powerful interest groups, at least to listen. All must meet the Press and the public as often as possible to stay in the news. Substantively, negotiating solutions to conflicts takes time. And all politicians are understandably assessing their power and prestige at every juncture, sometimes in an excruciating juxtaposition with the public interest.

Staff play a crucial role in assisting. Usually, they are under instructions to compress issue papers to five pages because the decision-maker lacks time to read. Given the time bind, the suspicion arises that staff act as surrogates for their principals, even in cases where responsibility, much less authority, cannot be legally delegated.

The hot kitchen memorialised by US President Harry S. Truman exemplifies the ambient stress in the decision theatre, all the more a source of torment because decision-makers want to do the right thing. Decision behaviour under stress is thus a test not only of intelligence and judgement; it is simultaneously a test of stamina and character.

There is, however, a basic agony of choice. It is common with individuals dealing with micro-decisions. The patterns of paralysis, defensive retreat, aggression, panic or mature engagement of the problem – the five cases previously enumerated – are well known. At the macro-decision level, the same patterns apply.

Most policy decisions are close. If they were black and white, they probably would have already been made at lower levels. With decision-makers on the fence because of obscurity of consequences rather than irresponsibility, small influences can nudge them either way. The last person talking to a policy-maker before a critical decision has disproportionately greater influence on the decider. Yet as close as a choice may seem at the moment of truth, the difference in consequences years later may be enormous.

The point here is that the contemplation either of uncertain but serious perils, or of long- versus short-term trade-offs, adds another weighty burden.

PATHOLOGIES IN NEGLECTING THE FUTURE

The enigma of neglecting the role of forecasting in estimating future consequences has many sources, and their inventory follows.

The reward structure in politics. As a reality judgement rather than bald cynicism, political survival must be assumed a major factor in choice. In the quest for voter esteem, incumbents are bound to consider re-election schedules and probabilities in selection both of issues on which to decide and of positions. Shorter-term issues are generally more rewarding in affording evidence of success. Other than in campaign rhetoric, political courage or leadership seldom focus voter attention on a healthy balance with the longer term. This question of political survival has a corollary in survival tactics – a preoccupation with the politics of an issue rather than its substance. This tendency becomes all the more pernicious as we discover later that technologically-based policies are increasingly political.

The reward structure in industry. In the private sector the pressures are equally high for immediate performance, although here in economic rather than social terms. Executives are monitored by the quarterly statements of profit and loss, and by indicators of corporate performance on the stock exchange. Within an organisation, promotions are based on individual accomplishments subject to evaluation at frequent intervals. As in public life, a seductive premium seems offered in the private sector for the short run. In neither milieu are officials motivated to contemplate the future because they are not in it; any success that accrues too far in the future would likely bring credit only to a successor, who may later become a competitor or superior after the decision-maker had peaked then declined in power and influence.

Pressures for rapid return on investments. Inflation in pushing up interest rates now makes the cost of borrowing an incentive for choosing investments with a quick return. This tendency is unpredictable, however, and must be qualified by what people guess about future changes in interest rates and their relationship to overall economic climate.

Fretting over uncertainty. A fourth element is endemic frustration because futures are always beset with uncertainty, uncertainty as to social ends as well as technical means. As Walter Lippmann stated so poignantly, energies of our society are soaked up in pragmatic acts simply to survive amidst uncertainty. Leadership does not have 'the ambition to participate in history and to shape the future. Modern men are predominantly isolationists. They are preoccupied with the more immediate things which may help or hurt them. They are marked by a vast indifference to big issues and in this indifference there is a feeling that they are incompetent to do much about the big issues.'[3] Sir Geoffrey Vickers interprets this pathological condition as being trapped by a state of mind: the past is no longer a confident guide to the future, and despite the loss in validity of old assumptions, there is great anxiety and little inclination to extend learning beyond what is widely termed linear thinking.[4]

In a way, this loss in confidence is paradoxical, because in a technological society there is a heightened awareness that the natural sciences are built on high expectations of predicting effects from cause. In complex social behaviour, this confidence is diminished.

A related paradox arises from this science–technology–society interaction because, while research is self-consciously sponsored to reduce uncertainty in a narrow field, increased knowledge on a large scale has the capacity to multiply options which in turn increases uncertainty.

Frustration with complexity. Complexity of social structure and of processes adds a fifth element to that feeling of helplessness. Complexity, as earlier defined, results from the large number of organisational components in technological delivery systems, their functional and cultural diversity, their hyper-interconnectedness, and from changes in all three factors.[5] Sensing these complications, individual units quickly recognise that only their short-run behaviour is relatively independent of the maze of constraints in which they are embedded, compared to interdependence in the longer run. In discussing the 'Architecture of Complexity', Simon then contends that long-run behaviour is dependent on the behaviour of other system properties only in an aggregate way.[6] But given the difficulty of mapping the system and of forecasting the long-run situation, decisions are shaped accordingly; the longer-run ones are simply averted. It is easy to understand why.

Relationships of cause and effect have been undermined by fragmentation and by the novelty, transiency and opacity of new networks. Unexpected repercussions may be triggered in remote districts of the technological delivery system. Not only do simple solutions fail, even formulation of more subtle correctives is inhibited. Complexity can only be deciphered by the human mind – making connections, combinations and associations.[7] But there are limitations to the human intellectual capability to solve these riddles, and a threshold of problem-solving exhaustion.[8] No wonder simple ordered regularity has special appeal.[9] Finally, the presence of organisational complexity also masks individual responsibility so as to remove penalties for abdicating the role of decision-making altogether.[10]

Bliss by selected ignorance. Next, from psychological research, Donald N. Michael contends that threatening prospects of the future will be ignored no matter how serious, if no means for reducing that threat are defined along with the emergency warning.[11]

This condition is made worse by the pace of change, the relentless stream of new problems demanding attention before predecessors were adequately disposed of. Indeed, there seems to be a scarcity of time, even to think.

The scarcity of time. There is no scarcity of information. But we may be suffering from excessive quantity and inadequate quality. More to the point is whether there is time to search for and interpret needed data. Telephone and Xerox technologies clog communication channels and distract people from choosing their intellectual priorities to deal with long-term strategies as well as day-to-day tactics. As the complexity of decisions increases, and the margin for error shrinks, there should be spirited incentive to invest more time in relevant information gathering and analysis. On the contrary, however, the tyranny of more numerous decisions and the hectic pace in most decision theatres whittles down time available to contemplate longer-term effects. At the same time, there is precious little multi-disciplinary integration of factual data with value consideration, prepared by independent analysts who have no stake in the outcome.

Impediments to multi-valued goal-setting. While our society boisterously recites a litany of goals, these objectives cannot be put in a master priority list to be ticked off one at a time. The alternatives are not comparable, and a range of potentially impacted parties in organised advocacy are now demanding response; thus tackling all goals simultaneously yields to a squeaking wheel syndrome. And longer-range social goals without energetic advocates are ignored.

Pressures to reduce conflict. The social feedback so devoutly admired in a democracy is often reduced to adversarial contests. With these battlefield conditions, the decision apparatus gets jittery and understandably may relieve discomfort by acting on those short-term issues whose outcome may reduce tension most quickly. Paradoxically, it is primarily citizen militancy that insists on the longer view, an anomaly we examine later.

A key role of the politician is to integrate these differences. At the same time, reconciling legitimate differences for the sake of compromise may obscure the peril. This political practice of seeking compromise has dominated the decision process sufficiently to earn labelling by political scientists as 'partisan mutual adjustment'. In the impetus for such strategies, consideration of longer-run consequences is short-circuited, especially if both protagonists argue only from their short-term perceptions and if immediate relief of conflict, whatever the longer-run penalties, is the prime motivation.

One major exception deserves mention: the case of social intervenors who press for present consideration of future and possibly adverse impact. The resulting project delays tough political bargaining and judicial processes represent a new cost imposed by public participation. Such an increased burden on other institutions in our society that up to now have had no internal disposition to look ahead is forcing a longer-range outlook as a defensive measure. That consideration of the future is forced only by political conflict may itself be symptomatic of a systemic failure.

Governments have tried to deal with this problem of conflict by passing more laws. By such rules, all the players could be expected to know and play the same game. But the law codifies already established social behaviour, generally lacks potential for and has no function of early warning. By itself, the law may only reduce flexibility to deal with the unknown. The predilection of legislators to earn brownie (good measure) points on the basis of laws bearing their name as author may paralyse the system with constraints and conflicts.

Media pressure for the quick fix. Heat on the politicians to discount the future is further increased by technological aids to public accountability. Television exposure demands postures of decisiveness and confidence, more in relation to the thrust of events than to subtle, long-term concepts.

Crises are paraded daily for wide inspection and expectation of simple answers. Whatever predilection the culture has developed for the 'quick fix' is further catered to by promises on the short-run problems. This atmosphere challenges the political will to deal with complex, deep-seated issues with appropriately complex, and perhaps slow-acting remedies. To do so imposes risks that few deciders seem willing to bear.

Concealment of past error. Such a long view of the future may also expose the error of decisions previously made for expediency. As Michael put it, policy-makers are reluctant to admit mistakes, shift gears or stop misguided programmes.[12] The bureaucracy that continues through shifts in political leadership is especially sensitive to such revelations. No small wonder that political prescriptions tend to be 'piecemeal, provisional, parochial, uncoordinated, unsubstantial, and lacking in prophetic moral vision'.[13]

Bureaucratic resistance to change. Ageing bureaucratic institutions are always willing to reinforce that timidity. While all organisations, in and outside of government, are initially created to embody a new idea, such enterprises demonstrate a loss in vitality, a 'half-life' like decay of radioactive compounds. At some point in time, the institutional evolution becomes dependent not on its capacity to sense the pace and significance of change in its function or its performance, but rather on the rate at which the bureaucratic organisation can, or is willing to, change internally. Vested interests dominate either social or intellectual imperatives. When on the defensive, these institutions invest in retaining the loyalty of their adherents and in combating forces inimical to their concealed beliefs.[14] They continue to machine the grooves of original mission, no matter how decayed that function. According to Drucker,[15] the inability to stop doing anything is the central degenerative disease of government. Given their profound dedication to self-perpetuation and aggrandisement, lack of capacity for self-criticism, and well-engraved habits of thought, the notion of change is always threatening; it is thus resisted. As Allison said, the bureaucracy does best tomorrow what it did yesterday.[16] Curiously enough, the more successful an institution has been in the past, the greater is the self-imposed insulation from new ideas. Policy-makers become ambivalent on the cost to them of political energies to move even directly subordinate agencies.

One must have some sympathy, however, for this bureaucratic dilemma. Sincere attempts have been made at long-range planning. In the annual ceremony of budgeting, again the future is heavily discounted. All too often in the budget trimming, proposed new starts are the first elements to be sacrificed. They accumulate in desk drawers for want of resources. Despite the promise of affluence from employment of technology, liquidity of resources to facilitate new starts is non-existent, and entrenched interests cannot be expected to be charitable to a new boy on the block.

A final point needs mention in regard to continuous evaluative feedback on the wisdom of past choices and course correction, as well as to meet new challenges. Change is implicit in self-evaluation, yet this is upsetting to most members of inherently self-protecting agencies. Of the $20 billion spent annually by the US Government for research and development, less than 0·1 per cent is devoted to post facto analysis of effectiveness of the 99·9 per cent.

Risk avoidance, not crisis avoidance. That politics is widely regarded as the art of the possible reflects the presence of irksome constraints on leadership. Given that such leadership is subject to both crisis and pressure, there is a devoutly hoped for bliss of equilibrium. At any level, self-generated change carries the risk of destabilisation. Things can get worse as well as better. When the forecasts of external crisis are too ambiguous and uncertain, and when in the midst of social complexity there is doubt about where the throttles and steering controls lie, latent tendencies to avoid risk that are present in all institutions are conspicuously reinforced. Given the intrinsic difficulties of striking political bargains even in static situations, that requirement is even more demanding in the presence of change. The higher the stress on the deciders, the greater can be their hope for spontaneous correctives and tendencies to head for the safety of the storm cellar.

The failure of long-range planning. In addition, confidence in broad-scale planning has shrunk, partly because projected events often do not happen; the public is fed up with crying wolf over propagandised threats such as that of communism, plans are shaped around a fictional static, homogeneous society, and the public rejects 'top down', master-minded planning as autocratic. Finally, remedial measures often seem counter-productive; continuing to add highway lanes simply does not relieve downtown traffic congestion. Not too long ago, planning was a dirty word associated with socialist political philosophy and dictatorial ambitions. A serious conceptual gap still seems interposed between planners and those being planned for.

No liquid resources. Then there is a scarcity of resources for looking ahead. To consider change and to effect change requires uncommitted intellectual and fiscal capital in the decision theatre itself. Information and analytical capabilities for early warning seem tightly stretched. Contingencies are not treated solicitously in the competitive hurly-burly of resource allocation. Despite the multiplier effect attributed to technology, no reserves have been husbanded anywhere in the system. Without liquidity, incentives to elaborate options diminish because they only become abstract exercises in fantasy.

Barriers in culture. The politicians understand this problem of discounting the future. By and large, they want to embed it in their decision calculus. But they cannot. That is what makes their condition pathological. Given these fifteen manifestations of uncertainty, of complexity, of scarcities, of Babel and of impotence, it may be expecting too much of political leadership to get out in front of the voters, who are themselves buffeted with day-to-day crises, frustrated, demonstrate an appetite for instant gratification, and lack awareness of 'the situation'. The credit card economy so deeply embedded in the Western culture is yet another manifestation of imperatives toward immediate satisfaction.

Thus, we may have to face up to the staggering barrier of public indifference, even hostility, to the long run, stemming from cultural as well as existential attitudes.

The lack of a common and deep appreciation that the future began today is one more source of deafness in the policy apparatus to signals about the future. Citizens' signals as to what they do not want are so weak as to be lost in the buzz of action to alleviate today's discomforts; and the policy-makers are not listening.

These pathologies of the short run are both a source of stress in decision-making and a consequence. To understand the implications, it is necessary to turn to the operational issue of how this psychological setting affects the social performance of technological policy.

CLOCKING AND RANKING POLICY OUTCOMES

Social outcomes of policy can be derived from three sets of criteria, in terms of impacts on the structure of technological delivery systems, on the functioning of the system, and on value preferences of society. While social, economic and ecological effects are included, the political and psycho-cultural impacts have been deliberately emphasised. For purposes of explanation, these impact factors can be transformed into questions about consequences, a type of check-off list for decision-makers.

List A. Political Impacts posed as Questions
  1. How is the decision-maker's political stature altered?
  2. Will conflicts in goals of different interest groups be polarised or reconciled?
  3. Who wins and who loses and how much?
  4. Will existing institutional roles and behaviour be disrupted?
  5. Are new policies consistent with existing policies and laws?
  6. Will new programmes be implemented at appropriate cost and without waste?
  7. Will public confidence be affected in the ability of government to set goals, allocate resources and maintain order?
  8. Will determination be altered of top political leadership to exercise legitimate power in face of obstacles?
  9. Will the role and influence of government be changed relative to private initiative and the play of the market-place?
  10. What future effects are conceivably different from immediate; who will be affected and how?
  11. Will constitutional guarantees and practices affecting individual liberties be modified?
  12. Will maintenance of law, order and safety for citizens, in a sense of community, be altered?
  13. Will there be changes in influence by citizens on policies and their generation?
  14. What will the impacts be on natural environment and on utilisation of non-renewable resources?
  15. Will government be more or less decentralised, with changes in local and state authority?
  16. Will equity be changed in opportunity for individual self-expression and the 'pursuit of happiness'?
  17. Will information capabilities be altered with respect to knowledge generation through research, to analysis and to undistorted dissemination?
  18. Will capabilities be modified for early warning of peril and for contingency planning?
  19. Will government be made more publicly accountable?
  20. Will future opportunities or changes in social goals be inadvertently blocked?
  21. Will the entire system be better able to cope with surprise in its social resilience and liquidity of resources?
  22. What will the effects be on open-mindedness to future change or rate of change?
  23. Will there be a change in the capacity to image the future?
  24. What changes may occur in overall cultural patterns?

These have been put into order according to the swiftness of expected repercussions. These gestation periods of impact may range from weeks to decades. Clearly, the delay in perceiving effects varies enormously from one case to another, so that the rank order is necessarily an abstract average.

These potential impacts are next ranked in the second and third columns of Table 13.1 by the importance accorded each element by a hypothetical policy official and hypothetical citizen. In so doing, we are not here concerned with the intensity of each impact, just how urgent each impacted party considers it is to investigate. The ranking is thus a technique of identifying what for each party are the 'right questions'. As part of their cogitation, if a decision-maker or impacted party can develop corresponding answers as to what could happen, a comparison may then be made with what that person thinks *should* happen. This constitutes a pre-crisis decision assessment.

A major procedural difficulty arises in attempts to order these

TABLE 13.1 Ranking of impacts (Margins for survival)

	Gestation time of impact	Priority for policy-maker	Priority for citizen	Priority for long-term health of society
Continuity in political power of policy-maker	1	1	20	24
Reduction (or increase) in social conflict among interest groups	2	2	6	19
Distribution in direct outcomes of a decision in terms of benefits, risks and costs	3	3	1	20
Continuity of institutional structures, public and private	4	4	13	22
Compatibility with existing laws	5	10	18	14
Economic efficiency (lack of waste) in implementation	6	6	2	13
Continued ability of government to govern	7	7	15	15
Maintenance of political will in leadership	8	5	14	23
Changes in governmental role in relation to private sector	9	9	5	16

TABLE 13.1 (contd)

	Gestation time of impact	Priority for policy-maker	Priority for citizen	Priority for long-term health of society
Indirect and future benefits, reductions of peril (including war) risk and costs	10	12	12	3
Maintenance of democratic traditions, liberty and social justice	11	8	3	2
Maintenance of social cohesion, order and freedom from violence	12	16	4	7
Access of citizens to political process	13	18	7	11
Protection of environment and conservation of natural resources	14	17	9	8
Trends toward state and local authority	15	11	11	17
Changes in quality of life, opportunity for self-expression, equity	16	19	8	12
Strength of information capabilities, scientific research and monitoring	17	13	17	5
Capacity to appreciate the situation; contingency planning for survival	18	15	21	4
Social accountability and public information on government performance	19	20	10	10
Preservation of future options	20	14	16	6
Capability of entire system to cope with surprise (resilience and liquidity)	21	21	24	9
Attitude (hospitality) to future change	22	23	19	21
Capacity to image the future	23	22	23	1
Fundamental changes in cultural framework	24	24	22	18

impacts. Their importance will vary from one decision case to another because the issues are different or because the milieu of the decision is in some transient state of crisis from an adjoining but separate decision. Moreover, there is difficulty in averaging diverse views of either policy-makers or citizens; the average may not be simply a mid-point between extreme positions. But even after admitting these stumbling-blocks, this synthesis reveals a salient pattern of discordance between short- and long-term values when comparing the questions that grip the citizen with those that animate the politician.

In the struggle for power, citizens place high importance on their access to the handles of power, by more intimate participation in the decision process. Politicians, on the other hand, are far more concerned with expanding their personal influence and with maintaining convivial relationships with key institutions in our society on whom they depend for implementation of policy, organisations which display a similar appetite for influence or at least avoidance of boat-rocking. Citizens also may lead their leaders in shifts of social priorities associated with the quality of life.

The fourth column is yet another ranking of impacts, now taking as priority those consequences that influence the long-term health and survival of a democratic society. This might be thought of as a ranking now by a citizen who would not be born until the year 2000. Somewhat contrary to what we might expect, in focusing on the longer term, the order is not merely the inverse of the first column, although a general reversal in pattern appears.

By now comparing the four columns, neither the policy-maker nor the citizen are seen to have given precedence to longer-term, 'iffy' questions. No matter how committed we may be to a humanistic image of the world ahead, it would be naïve folly to expect a universal trade off of the present for the always uncertain future. Therefore the issue is one of balance.

One ranking in the table, that on 'capacity to image the future', particularly the futures we do not want, is so anomalous as to warrant explanation. The importance of this social characteristic has been underscored by C. P. Snow, Kenneth Boulding, Geoffrey Vickers and numerous other social philosophers. Fred Polak puts the case this way: 'The image of the future can act not only as a barometer, but as a regulative mechanism which alternatively opens and shuts the dampers on the mighty blast furnace of culture. It not only indicates alternative choices and possibilities, but actively promotes certain choices and in effect puts them to work in determining the future. A close examination of prevailing images, then, puts us in a position to forecast the probable future.'[17] The validity of this contention is supported by some historical evidence. At one pole were the Dark Ages, seemingly without images. At the other, as Dostoyevsky has suggested in his *Diary of a Writer*, an ethical image of the future has always preceded the birth of a nation. The vision and powerful influence of the Declaration of Independence and the United States Constitution are confirmed by their durability and the social and political forces they evoked worldwide. Given the chaotic situation when they were drafted and the conflicts among the drafters in representing agricultural versus commercial interests, elitist versus populist ideology, slave-holding versus free sub-cultures, the remarkable product could only have emerged from a strong and manifest dedication to a commonly held image of the future.

The absence of images may explain the destruction of Aztec and Inca civilisations at the hands of a few well-armed foreigners; the explosion of the First World War beyond the scope projected by the Prussian General Staff of a limited war game; and on a different scale, the failure of railroad management in the 1940s to perceive the threat to their viability posed by the new highway legislation.

Imaging the future is suggested here as a major element in a survival kit. People who lived through the Depression of the 1930s and the Second World War had some such images of disaster engraved on their experience. But it is difficult for younger people to anticipate what has never been experienced. Indeed, the counter-culture of the 1960s seemed determined to reject all cultural heritages that included some perilous images of the future, and substituted their own emphasis on the here and now.

Imaging the future does not mean prophecy, nor necessarily adoption of a single model. Indeed, that capacity to image may be expressed in the capacity for fantasy, so spontaneously evident in children, perpetuated in myth and folklore, and manifest in the creative activity of adults in play and in the arts. Later the possibility is considered that cultural trends fastening on existential reality abetted by technological artefacts may inadvertently suppress or maim these genetically derived tendencies. Indeed, there is a question as to whether new social trends among the influential elite not to have children may influence their disposition to consider a future that not only excludes themselves but also the progeny of others in their generation.

Needless to say, the ranking by the author is subjective, completely pragmatic, lacking in experimental verification, and, in column four, revealing of his own set of values. Nothing exact is claimed in the table, or needed. Readers might complete their own check-off list and thus be in a better position to consider later arguments. The exact order is not vital to the argument being advanced.

The point is, that under the conditions of stress described earlier and the pathologies of neglecting the future, there seems to be an inverse correlation between the importance accorded these performance criteria by decision-makers and the delay time of impact. That is to say, at the moment of choice, consideration would be given first to the questions having immediate consequences listed, with diminished attention, if not complete indifference, to others with deferred and usually less certain consequences.

It is very dangerous to generalise, by suggesting that all decisions follow the patterns just outlined. Or to conclude that neglect of the long-for short-term considerations is always costly in the long run. Or to suggest that all of the performance criteria deserve equal attention.

In the most cynical interpretation of this list, a choice might be made only on the basis of political expediency by a US president, for example, close to re-election, in trouble with the Congress and the electorate. The bureaucracy and congressional committees are known to push for legislation from ambition to maintain a constituency or to enlarge their influence by committee jurisdiction.

There is another side to expediency that needs mention, because the term is now considered pejorative. Expediency in the sense of a politician's acting on the basis of self-interest to retain popularity with an electorate also reflects behaviour expected in a representative democracy. Voters would rightly object to indifference to their concerns and preferences or arrogant representation. This mechanical responsiveness, however, begs the question of the role of a policy-maker as teacher, to move a constituency from a parochial to a better informed or broader judgement.

And then there is the question of what constitutes expediency. In the increasingly mixed sentiments of a constituency and the general lack of an overriding consensus on any issue, pressures arise from many directions. Each decision is accompanied by complaints of dissenters, often claiming that the representative caved in to pressures. No matter which way a vote is cast, the principal will always appear to step on some group's toes.

Under these baffling conditions, wherein lies any safe route to political survival?

To return to the tabulation of impacts, the second half is of concern not only in terms of slow or hibernating influences. This sub-set of criteria simultaneously defines both the health and the metabolic balance of the entire enterprise. That is, more slowly evolving measures of social performance have to do not only with the substance of a decision but also with the future viability of the decision apparatus itself, the totality of structures and processes in technological delivery.

Thus, the neglect of the future may not only invalidate a particular decision; it may undermine the future capacity to decide. That is, all classes of decision malfunctions outlined earlier are reinforced and likely to debilitate the decision theatre. This is perhaps the most vital conclusion thus far.

At the beginning, we took a position on alarming trends in the nature of the threat horizon. We should also consider trends in decision practice as to balanced consideration of these longer-range omens.

Two contradictory trends seem to be operating. In the first instance, the decisions are getting more political, with implicit incentives for disproportionate attention to the short-run effects. Simultaneously, there are more and more effective voices in our society calling attention to the consequences of neglecting the future. And in that trend, we distinguish shifts in social priorities now given political representation. These trends are not uniform but oscillate in response to pulses of crisis and pressure.

It is thus necessary to examine whether long-term awareness is growing as swiftly as threats on the one hand, and on the other the inclination to act for expediency.

In reconnoitring ways and means to improve decision-making and to locate targets of intervention, it would be folly to examine only the tip of the iceberg. To be sure, policy is emitted from explicit high-level locales. Yet all actors in the technological delivery system share in the decision process, and we need to unravel the kinetics of the technological delivery system previously described to see how it works.

UNDERLYING CAUSES OF SHORTSIGHTEDNESS

Using different sets of diagnostic instruments, we concluded that in regard to long-range threats, there are numerous manifestations of neglect, and that these encourage a preference for achieving outcomes in the short run that critically imperil the health of the decision system. If these initial pathologies that favour the short run are merely symptoms, their relief may prove superficial. Not that we embark on a quest for a single miracle cure. Indeed, we must be prepared to deal with complex problems by complex solutions.

The theatre of the future has often appeared as a special preserve of dreamers, doomsters and science fiction writers.[18] Elise Boulding[19] uses another typology for futurists: technocrats, social evolutionists and revolutionary futurists. Of five groups in the latter category, one is entitled political, non-violent approaches, implicitly suggesting the general lack of political reality in other genres of futurism. Here, we bite that bullet: we consider the future largely in terms of political decision-making about the future.

But while we focus strongly on the Olympus of policy action, the theatre of concern embraces all of the institutions involved in technological enterprise, and all of the forces targeted on the decision-makers that influence choice.

Kenneth Boulding and Harold Lasswell have broken significant ground here, with a proposition that we stand precariously in the midst of great transition, where construction of a livable and enduring society will require a commitment of human energy and enlightenment exceeding that of our precursors.[20] They outline, politically, what we must do:

- understand the predictive behaviour of policy-makers and key institutions;
- forecast what is foreseeable with care and elegance;
- imagine what might be in terms of plausible alternatives;
- determine the strategic availability of more desirable outcomes.

Whatever the temptation to unfurl banners of a selective utopia, and develop the foreseeable, plausible and desirable, we limit this treatise to a less ambitious but perhaps operationally more critical task of dealing with the future in terms of what we do not want. Such boundaries of scholarship, however, do not limit the epistemological arena. The capacity to imagine perils is very much a part of the total appetite of a society for the future, a property C. P. Snow asserts in that 'all healthy societies are ready to sacrifice the existential moment for their children's future and for children after these'.[21]

That frame of mind can be revealed in every aspect of a culture from literature, art, poetry, music, science and philosophy to architecture, consumer goods and entertainment. The stance of policy-makers is inevitably shaped by that social environment, and vice versa. Harmony between citizens and policy-makers does not automatically mean progress. But neither do discord and violence.

With technology imprinting all aspects of our society, and with the winds of conflict blowing more strongly, we must underscore one major new phenomenon, that technological decision-making is getting more political. In institutional terms, technology has tended to concentrate power, wealth and benefit. In uncritical exploitation of natural resources, technology has triggered an unexpected era of scarcity and widened the diversity of the human condition. The question of who wins and who loses becomes more strenuous. Because the selection of ends and means is a matter of political choice, because publicly funded projects have become larger in scale with economically more at stake, and because government regulation limits the freedom of private enterprise, the social management of technology is inevitably more political. The congressional decision to abandon development of SST is a classic example.[22]

Other factors bolster that tendency. Technology generates more options, as with water, coal, gas, nuclear, wind, solar and geothermal sources as energy alternatives. More choices thus have to be made, so that attention becomes more frequently riveted on the decision event. Government tends to play a greater role in all four modes discussed before in stimulation, regulation, using technology directly and investing in social overheads. So in most cases, choice is not left to the decentralised, invisible hand of the market-place; rather, social decisions are driven by circumstances, abetted by television, to high visibility and pinpointed political locale. A ratcheting then occurs in public expectations of crisis abatement, amplified by cultural trends in the abdication of individual responsibility to government. Pressures to satisfy short-term expediency grow more strenuous, and, as we saw, pathological.

We repeat, decisions on technology-intensive public policy are growing more political in the sense that whatever the technical, economic, social or legal implications, more decisions are explicitly boosted to the highest level of policy authority. In growing more political, these decisions are becoming more shortsighted.

Notwithstanding the pejorative inference of 'political' decisions, there is not a pragmatic, much less a theoretical basis for this situation by itself to enhance risk. Political decisions are certainly not, *per se*, bad decisions. For reasons previously advanced, they are not necessarily less rational. There are two major questions, however. Firstly, whether concentration on the short run is at the expense of the longer run in terms of adverse consequences? And secondly, does this growing burden on political apparatus depreciate the quality of decisions in general?

There is a growing view that the factors of complexity, interdependence, political load and atmosphere of conflict may render the system completely ungovernable. That judgement is endorsed by Miles in classical terms of public administration.[23] The critical test is whether government is able to fulfil its most salient responsibility by acting as the public agent for collective security.

To put this point of view even more starkly, there is an obvious trend in capitalist democracies as well as socialist states to provide for 'welfare'. In catering to public demand, the quantity and visibility of these services is second only to military security in importance. In the United States, federal funds in this category now exceed military expenditures.

An alternative view of governmental roles would be to consider collective security against large-scale risks, and not welfare, as the necessary, if not sufficient condition of governmental responsibility. This stance answers to a reversal in the public attitude to 'letting the government do it' as far as reduction in individual risk is concerned, and increased appreciation of, and governmental intervention in, the broader and more lethal threats.

Common sense dictates that no political system can withstand increasing demands indefinitely, although we treat the democratic system as though it were infinitely resilient. Earlier cases alert us to consider whether continued ability to make tough decisions, in time, is vulnerable to thresholds of instability or suddenness of demand, or all the other diseases catalogued earlier.

Thus, the policy apparatus is simultaneously being stressed by more and more difficult choices, by sudden discontinuities engendered by the pace and superposition of technical innovations or eruption of crisis, and by an accretion of political responsibility. Less and less attention is being devoted to adverse effects on viability of the enterprise for each succeeding decision event.

That is to say, the focus of attention on the short run not only neglects future and possibly costly impacts. It increases the possibility of future decision error because the decision machinery increasingly lags in response to threat, and is itself seriously weakened or advanced to a threshold of collapse under the next serious shock. The situation becomes ominous not only because of the potentially irreversible nature of the threats to survival, but also, as was said before, because neglect of the future in current decisions may undermine the long-range capability to decide at all.

THE POLITICAL LIMITS TO FORECASTING

Information is the primary commodity of political choice. If the resilience of the system is exhausted, early warning signals could well be masked by noise. The learning curve of agility to meet novel situations will lag the pulse of crisis and pressure. The increasingly hectic role of policy authorities to harmonise relationships among institutional participants in order to ease conflict could drown out the primary role to deal with the threats themselves.

When the stabilising function of government is lost, the system becomes more sensitive to even minor shocks. The sensation, as Vickers has described it, is of a novice ice-skater, obliged to devote full energies and attention simply to remaining upright, unable to muster the balance and self-confidence to engage in the creative activity of figure-skating or racing.[24] As with human beings, defects in hearing apparatus can cause debilitating instability, a form of institutional vertigo.

We now attempt to unmask the underlying causes of deafness in the policy apparatus to signals about the future. We look first at the systematic malfunctioning of elements in the decision tree that induce too much stress or too little stress for a balanced, healthy consideration of the future, and the maintenance of metabolic balance in the decision system itself. Candidates for such consideration are the policy-level decision-makers, the institutions in our society and the individual citizen.

What is required is a change in behaviour. In our system of minimum coercion, this translates into rewards and penalties for self-imposed change. Many observers of social behaviour contend that individuals change far more readily than do organisations. Institutional viscosity in government and academia, church and industry has always been prevalent, may even be getting more pronounced.

There is a positive side to that inertia. In every society, institutions play a role in pattern maintenance, so that mutual roles and expectations of participants are sufficiently predictable to preserve coherence. By another name this is bald conservatism. Marris has pointed out that conservatism is an impulse to defend the predictability of life, 'as necessary for survival as adaptability'.[25]

Assessing vulnerability to the unknown, however, may not be approached in traditional conservative-liberal terms. Indeed today, these labels are misleading. If, however, certain of our social functions outlined previously have a tendency to be conservative and others versatile and innovative, mismatches and inconsistencies can arise and disable the decision process. For all the processes to be conservative or all to be innovative is also sure to be debilitating in fostering extremes of stagnation or chaos. Perhaps, then, an optimum level of tension between these contrasting currents is essential – to afford internal equilibrium to enhance vigilance as to threat, and alacrity in generating appropriate and timely response.

In what follows, we assume that rather than confront, we accept this ubiquitous property of institutional behaviour with very low expectation as to its reform.

Ultimately what is at stake is meeting political limits in the role of forecasting by changing the behaviour of decision-makers. The problem is not that they *will* not change; they are in a procedural trap such that they cannot. Given the high priority politicians are assumed to place on maintaining their position, power and prestige, and given political energies generally targeted at the shorter run, we cannot expect a change in representative government unless people change.

The root cause of the dilemma and its remedies lie in the cultural setting.

SOCIAL TECHNIQUES FOR COLLECTIVE SECURITY: APPRECIATING THE SITUATION

If there is any single statement of the overarching situation, it is that our most critical task is to restore health to the decision process. So we now engage the self-generated question of 'what should we do?' in new strategies for collective security by including the future in any decision calculus.

Given the sweep of this undertaking and the thicket of technical, economic, legal, political and psychological processes involved, it is difficult to do justice to the fundamental issues. Sorting out 'what's the problem' has been conspicuously brief. Details have been omitted; comprehensive documentation has been short-circuited; interpretation has been simplified; fascination with elegant social science methodology has been suppressed. Yet a composite panorama emerges. As the past becomes less and less a guide for the future, especially where cause-effect processes evaporate as aids to navigation, we become more dependent on the social equivalent of dead reckoning.

Many other explorers of the future have glimpsed this condition and the urgency of new social strategies for collective security. Some have recoiled in gloom. Roberto Vacca believes the technological delivery system is so technically complex as to be beyond human control.[26] Rufus E. Miles concludes that the same system is so politically and socially complex as to transcend the limits of human management.[27] Jay Forrester contends that the major forces at work are almost deterministic and insensitive to policy guidance.[28] Robert Heilbroner argues that the limits to human character predispose the future to a fatalistic, unceasing and irreversible decline.[29]

If choosing is this complicated, one should expect to find inconsistent and conflicting, competing and often *ad hoc* interpretations of the enigmatic social context; a diversity of unanticipated and seemingly irrational behaviour of organisations in response to stimulus of others in the technological delivery system; and a loss in consensus as to coherent action, even loss in agreement as to basic facts on which decisions are to be based (as for example, in dealing with the energy dilemma).[30] It is no small wonder that we just muddle through. Scholars such as Lindblom contend that the only technique of coping is for organisations to make limited moves in a 'strategy of disjointed incrementalism',[31] constantly monitoring and taking stock of the kaleidoscopic environment before taking the next small and presumably surefooted initiative.

Yet, to do nothing, to hope to muddle through, is capitulation to complexity, an admission that we can make no sense from what is happening. 'The consequent triumph of ignorance', predicts Brzezinski, 'extracts its own tribute in the form of unstable and reactive policies.'[32]

While not paralysed by hopelessness, it is very clear that we are at a crossroads. Perhaps our paradigm must be shifted, as Schumaker suggests, to small being beautiful,[33] or as Teilhard de Chardin and Reich propose, to patterns of feeling and of being less aggressive and more cosmic, even mystical.[34] Retooling ourselves is a virtue in its own right, but the track record of sustained voluntary behavioral reform is not convincing. Fear of the devil has generally evaporated. Even the notion of retooling our major institutions does not stir the blood, especially where institutions are so palpably resistant to new ideas that may rock the *status quo* of comfortable accommodation. And few in our society are willing to give organisations even greater precedence over people. Indeed, there is a basic question as to whether society is in a state of readiness to change, and if so, to what?

As Kenneth Boulding sees it, the meaning of the twentieth century is that we live precariously in the midst of a great transition, where a livable and enduring society will require commitment of human energy, resources and enlightenment exceeding that of all precursors.[35] As viewed by John Platt, any such social change must be powered by 'what might be'.[36]

Yet we seem to have exhausted our capacity to imagine that future. To the extent that vision exists, its extreme variations and associated cognitive dissonance reveal what Vickers deems the absence of appreciating the situation, a 'shared system of interpretation to enable humans to influence one another'.[37] This missing foundation is nowhere more dangerous than in the general absence of images of those futures people do *not* want.

The problems are not, as many social critics contend, suffering from the wake of a technological imperative, but rather deficiencies in political and intellectual institutions in foreseeing consequences of no action or the wrong action.[38] Thus, solutions will be found primarily in cultural, institutional and political, not technical, change.

Since the problem is far from simple, we should not expect a strategy for the future to be so either. We are obliged to examine and to consider for remedial action not only the organisational components of the technological delivery system, especially in government, but rather the dynamic processes involved. The cognitive map diagramed earlier pictured this web of social activities and their interactions.

In the first instance, political will would seem to be ignited largely and primarily by what people want. As it relates to improved balance between long- and short-run benefits, will people defer gratification? Will they make the necessary sacrifices? Will chronic anxiety about the unknown increase susceptibility to quick and popular nostrums, or worse, to a yearning for order that is promised by tyrants? The earlier sketch suggested that such dispositions to the short run were engraved in the cultural set so that its fundamental amendment lay in better information and especially a wider appreciation both of threats and of how the system works.

Cultural patterns are the most basic and powerful symbolic templates or blueprints for both the organisation of collective social, and individual psychological, processes.[39] Yet, the cultural setting is the most obtruse and its modification the most unyielding. As real life situations become more complex and unprecedented, the more necessary it is to deal at the highest levels of abstraction. Indeed, basic biological needs and instinctive drives for survival find universal expression in the diverse values and socialisation practices we define as cultures. For millenia, certain of these qualities were transmitted from generation to generation as means for survival, individually and collectively. Given the inventory of dangers now conceived, the past fails as a teacher.

Survival of the species is the goal, but we may need a new survival kit in collective learning and action. Any such actions in a free society will require consensus, underscoring again the criticality of a shared cultural stance based on factual knowledge and understanding, on estimates of threat and on mutuality of expectations. Modern diversity, which is widely admired, carries with it, however, a cultural electicism that seriously debilitates collective decisions. Survival of a humanistic democratic society critically depends on large numbers of people making thoughtful, realistic choices, with the aid of appropriate information.

The problem, as Elliot Richardson sees it,[40] is not just managing complexity and the growing pains of a large social system, but keeping it within the bounds of citizen comprehension. The learning curve for our society seems to be lagging in requirements for citizenship. If learning is possible for an individual, it is also possible for a people. There is even a possibility that people may learn faster than institutions. So that national politics will not continue the charade viewed by some,[41] or the malady of deafness to signals of the future will not continue untreated, the opening wedge of enlightenment is recognition by everyone that steering technology to survive with self-esteem is largely a political act and that citizens rather than politicians write the scripts.

To make explicit rather than implicit the fact that a shared cultural stance is based on shared information reminds us that social systems are communications networks. The commodity of exchange is knowledge and information. Yet, it is a shocking paradox that in the present era, with the exponential growth of technical knowledge, people know so little about what is going on or what perils may lie ahead. Not only is knowledge generated by a new elite of scientists and engineers, it is interpreted and applied by a similar cadre. Here we encounter serious problems in diffusion and common understanding. The problem is clearly not one of deficiency in specialised knowledge. The condition of ignorance arises from the absence of shared data and translation for public understanding.

In raising the question of sensitivity to today's overarching perils, we must admit that each has received a smidgeon of public recognition and symbolic governmental study. But nowhere has there been a study of the subject in all its aspects. We deal with one thing at a time, piecemeal and in response to crisis. Policies are reactive rather than anticipatory. Flaws in technological endeavour are perpetuated.

For one thing, we have entered an era where knowledge is legal property, protected by proprietary fences, patent and copyright. It is tended by its authors and its corporate stewards. Even in academia, tendencies are widely recognised to establish disciplinary boxes, with intellectual turf protected by primitive territorialism and with attempts at inter-disciplinary communication undernourished, undermined or even punished. Paradigms or rigid patterns of thought became artfully ennobled, challenging a few rebels to break through the structure of scientific evolution and to joust with adherents to taxonomy and method.[42] Seldom in the knowledge-generation function is there a sense of broader pattern, a problem rather than discipline orientation to research, or a commitment to foster public understanding of science and technology. The 'citadel of expertise'[43] arrogantly requests support with public funds without a corresponding responsibility for sharing results with the citizen as sponsor. We will shortly deal with this problem in education.

The point here is that a basic deficiency in policy to deal with the future with the aid of anticipatory techniques lies in a flabbiness of citizen interest in the future, as a result of cultural handicaps. The most pressing need is both to widen that perspective so that the individual can gain a better insight into the multidimensional texture of the technological world, and extend it to recognise that bills for today's decision to meet the short-run demand will come due in the future.

Clearly, a better forum is required for the development and exchange of ideas and general perceptions, rather than a staccato of events. The objective is not simply greater effectiveness in problem-solving, but deeper understanding of the problem-setting.[44] The content of such ideas involves a mixture of scientific facts with social judgements. Only such common understanding can permit institutions as well as individuals to cope with the complexity and interdependence highlighted earlier on a day-to-day basis, and to sense the future in terms of consequences of today's decisions or their default.

Earlier, we found examples where people readily deal with the future in terms of what is inevitable – ageing and death, and to a high degree with what were statistically credible and widely appreciated threats – unemployment and war. The class of situations of concern for which there is too low appreciation are those of the adverse consequences of present decisions and of uncertain but catastrophic threats for which similar requirements exist for vigilance, contingency planning and the maintenance of reserve resources. With a more sensitive appreciation of this situation, values could change by integrating self-conscious consideration of the future into the cultural template.

Nevertheless, informed public participation is the point of new appreciation of the future.

Our reasoning is something like this. Policy decisions at the top will systematically include a balanced consideration of the future only if political pressures to do so are sufficiently intense and continuous, and political acts rewarded. Such energy has been evoked locally when threats were personalised; a variety of public interest organisations have issued report cards on incumbent Congressmen and believe that such monitoring and publicity has influenced the outcome of elections. But a general thrust of citizen interest is not now manifested. It is likely only when it springs from a grass-roots creed.

Such a creed could be nurtured by a general education for citizenship that included a greater appreciation for the reality of future impact, of fragmented perceptions and for individual responsibility to foster wise political choice.

At some point, the breadth and depth of public concern for the future becomes a movement. In the US, this has been the rationale of Common Cause. By legitimate intervention in decision-making, it could balance the political forces and bureaucratic inertia that incline to short-term thinking, by making the social cost too high to neglect the future consequences of present decisions. Enhanced grass-roots comprehension and involvement could also reduce the oppressiveness of excessive centralisation, the technical parochialism and social alienation associated with decision-making by the bureaucracy, the elite and the expert.

Now we begin to see a second connection between the roots of culture and the towers of policy-making. With better tools of information, a creed of future concern and heightened involvement, citizens could be intimately involved in long-range planning. Rather than simply assent to policy, the electorate could contribute to it. People would not just be an anonymous mob, catered to or manipulated by the leadership; they could be partners in bottom-up rather than top-down planning and agents for implementation. There could be a 'participatory technology'.[45]

In growing more political, these technological decisions are becoming more short-sighted. Two types of calamities might result. The first is associated with unwanted side effects of contemporary decisions that hibernate only to burst on the scene years later, or in other districts, and for which we find correctives economically intractable, politically unfeasible or ecologically irreversible.

The second type of calamities are those for which we took no action. These are the cases where prevention was not energetically sought and where in the absence of anticipation we find another set of risks. Indeed, it is this threat horizon that may be the most precarious of all: the dangers of nuclear terror, of widespread famine, of global environmental poisoning or of inadvertent climate modification, of urban deterioration, of social chaos from increasing economic disparity among nations, of resource depletion, of system failures, of institutional and policy malfunctioning, from losses in freedom or from pathological shifts in values.

Posting sentries against surprise is at least as old as warfare. Yet we have no civilian counterpart to this military strategy. We do not have systematic process of anticipation on the basis of which pitfalls and crises could be avoided. And yet this is the most fundamental role of government – to provide a collective security against large-scale risks for society as a whole, not simply the reduction of risks to the individual.

People are part of the decision apparatus. Unless they are willing to trade-off instant gratification for some vision of future benefits for humankind generally, and for their own progeny specifically, we will indeed be in difficulty. Unless the public embed the future in their decision calculus, the political leadership will remain in the vice of the short run. The hazard then exists of action or inaction which could debase individual integrity or extinguish humanity altogether. Even before that may happen, the benign neglect of the future may undermine even the future capacity to decide.

NOTES

1. Irving L. Janis and Leon Mann, 'Coping with decisional stress', *American Scientist*, Vol. 64, pp. 657–67.
2. Milton Katz, mentioned in private communication, Harvard University, 18 October 1976.
3. Walter Lippmann, 'Today and tomorrow – Catching up with the times', *Washington Post*, 14 November 1966.
4. Geoffrey Vickers (1970), *Freedom in a Rocking Boat: Changing Values in an Unstable Society*, London: Allen Lane, Penguin, p. 43.
5. Donald N. Michael (1968), *The Unprepared Society: Planning for a Precarious Future*, New York: Basic Books.
6. Herbert A. Simon (1962), 'The architecture of complexity', *Proc. Amer. Philosophical Society*, 106.
7. Todd R. La Porte (ed.) (1975), *Organized Social Complexity – Challenge to Politics and Policy*, Princeton: Princeton Univ. Press, p. 19. Also chapter by Langdar Winner, 'Complexity and the limits of human understanding' and by J. Serge Taylor on 'Organizational complexity in the new industrial state – the role of technology'.
8. John Gerard Rugge, 'Complexity, planning and public order', in Todd R. La Porte, *op. cit.*

9. *Ibid.*; also Garry D. Brewer, 'An analysis of complex systems', in Todd R. La Porte, *op. cit.*
10. Jay D. Starling, 'The use of system constraints in simplifying organized social complexity', in Todd R. La Porte, *op. cit.*
11. Donald N. Michael, *The Unprepared Society*, p. 7.
12. *Ibid.*, p. 86, also Geoffrey Vickers (1965), *The Art of Judgment*, New York: Basic Books, p. 81.
13. Warren Wagar (1971), *Building the City of Man: Outlines of a World Civilization*, New York: Grossman.
14. Z. Brzezinski (1970), *Between Two Ages: America's Role in the Technetronic Era*, New York: Viking, p. 76.
15. Peter Drucker (1969), *The Age of Discontinuity*, New York: Harper and Row, p. 194.
16. Graham Allison (1971), *Essence of Decision: Explaining the Cuban Missile Crisis*, Boston: Little, Brown and Co.
17. Fred Polak (1973), *The Image of the Future*. Translated and abridged by Elise Boulding, San Francisco: Jossey Bass/Elsevier.
18. Franklin Ingwell (ed.) (1973), *Search for Alternatives: Public Policy and the Study of the Future*, Cambridge: Winthrop, p. vi.
19. Elise Boulding (1973), 'Futurology and the Capacity of the West' in *Search for Alternatives: Public Policy and the Study of the Future*, ed. Franklin Tugwell, Cambridge: Winthrop.
20. Harold Lasswell (1951), *The Policy Sciences – Recent Developments in Scope and Methods*, Palo Alto: Stanford Univ. Press; Kenneth E. Boulding (1964), *The Meaning of the Twentieth Century: The Great Transition*, New York: Harper and Row, p. 80.
21. C. P. Snow, 'What is the world's greatest need?' New York *Times Magazine*, 2 April 1961.
22. Edward Wenk, Jr., 'SST – Implications of a political decision', *Astronautics and Aeronautics*, 9 (October 1971), pp. 40–9.
23. Rufus E. Miles (1976), *Awakening from the American Dream*, New York: Universe.
24. Geoffrey Vickers (1968), *Value Systems and Social Process*, London: Tavistock, p. 42.
25. Peter Marris (1974), *Loss and Change*, New York: Pantheon, p. 170.
26. Roberto Vacca (1973), *The Coming Dark Age*, Garden City, New York: Doubleday.
27. Miles, *Awakening from the American Dream*.
28. Jay W. Forrester (1971), *World Dynamics*, Cambridge, Mass: Wright Allen.
29. Robert L. Heilbroner (1974), *An Inquiry into the Human Prospect*, New York: Norton.
30. Jay D. Starling, 'The use of system constraints in simplifying organized social complexity', in Todd R. La Porte, *op. cit.*
31. Charles Lindblom, 'The Science of Muddling Through', *PAR* 19 (1959) pp. 79–88.
32. Brzezinski, *Between Two Ages*, p. xiv.
33. E. E. Schumaker (1973), *Small is Beautiful – Economics as if People Mattered*, New York: Harper and Row.

34. Charles Reich (1970), *The Greening of America*, New York: Random House.
35. Boulding, *The Meaning of the Twentieth Century*.
36. John Platt, 'What we must do', *Science* 166 (28 November 1969), pp. 1115–21.
37. Geoffrey Vickers, *Value Systems and Social Process*, p. vi.
38. Stuart Chase (1968), *The Most Probable World*, New York: Harper and Row, p. 209.
39. George Steiner (1973), *In Bluebeard's Castle: Some Notes Toward the Redefinition of Culture*, New Haven: Yale University Press.
40. Elliot Richardson (1976), *The Creative Balance: A Post-Watergate Look at the American People and Politics*, New York: Holt, Rinehart and Winston.
41. Hazel Henderson, 'Ideologies, paradigms and myths: Changes in our operative social values', *Liberal Education*, (May 1976), Vol. LXII, No. 2, pp. 143–77; *Creating Alternative Futures: The End of Economics*, New York: Berkeley Publishing Co., 1978.
42. Thomas S. Kuehn (1962), *The Structure of the Scientific Revolution*, Chicago: University of Chicago Press.
43. Donald N. Michael, *The Unprepared Society*, p. 78.
44. Geoffrey Vickers, *Value Systems and Social Process*, p. 159.
45. James D. Carroll, 'Participatory Technology', *Science*, Vol. 171, No. 3972, pp. 647–53.

14 Interests, Hopes and Fears – Can We Change the Future?

SAM COLE

INTRODUCTION

This chapter is about the global futures debate and the way in which the very many different visions of the future are presented. The central theme of the paper is the possibility and means of bringing about a more desirable future, as seen through the eyes of some of the principal figures taking part in the debate.

The study here is not a comprehensive review of the futures debate but is rather intended to raise questions, using participants and forecasts as illustrations. Thus we ask which issues are confronted in the debate, what are the 'levers' of change, how these are defined, what are the motives and interest of the participants and how this affects what they say and do. Finally we consider whether anyone does or should take any notice of them. The paper is therefore an attempt to clarify some aspects of the debate by pointing to issues that should not be omitted from our consideration in trying to use the work of forecasters to make our own assessment of possibilities for the future.

WHAT IMAGES ARE PRESENTED?

In a previous study (*World Futures – The Great Debate*) we examined in detail seventeen different forecasts of the world's future that have appeared in the last decade, the assumptions underlying them and their context within the futures debate. Even so these forecasts, which were largely concerned with Malthusian issues (i.e. population and economic growth, resource constraints and environment etc), form a limited part of the whole debate. We again take the same forecasters and personalities as the focus for discussion since this is sufficient for the present analysis.

The best known forecasts, and from the point of view of the Malthusian debate, are *The Limits to Growth*, the 'Doomsday' forecasts of Dennis and Donnella Meadows and Jay Forrester (in *World Dynamics*) and the 'Cornucopian' forecasts of Herman Kahn in *The Year 2000* and *The Next 200 Years*, all Americans. Few people interested in the debate can have failed to see either or both in television spectaculars about the future. More than once they have been set as gladiators in face-to-face confrontation. Simplistically – and there is great danger of over-simplification here – Meadows' view about the global future is that without dramatic corrective action the 'limits to growth' (in terms of resources and environment) will be reached within the next hundred years. The only safe way is to slow down – the world must achieve equilibrium or face 'overshoot and collapse'. Kahn's contrasting view is that 'things are going rather well', 'super industrial society' will emerge in the late twentieth and early twenty-first century. Eventually world economic growth will cease, perhaps 100–200 years from now, but this will be in a 'more or less natural and comfortable way'.

Despite the striking difference in their forecasts, there are also striking similarities. In particular, neither spends much time considering the distribution of growth, high or low. In Kahn's view, 'the closing of the gap will not occur soon'; for the Meadows, 'population growth is the greatest impediment to redistribution'. Other authors, while setting their arguments within a Malthusian framework, concern themselves with other issues: Robert Heilbroner, for example, also an American (in *The Human Prospect*), while predicting 'a grim Malthusian outcome' for developing countries, concentrates our attention on the choice of worldwide totalitarianism or anarchy. His concern with the future is not just a question of economic growth; industrialisation has 'failed to satisfy the human spirit' – a sentiment shared by many writers. For example, René Dumont, a Frenchman, in *Utopia or Else*, also sees the 'threat of revolt' and 'continued confrontation and struggle' between the rich and the poor countries of the world. The late Ernst Schumacher, while objecting to Heilbroner's overly pessimistic view, shared his feeling as to the poverty of our modern spiritual lives. The Fundacion Bariloche in Argentina, led by Amilcar Herrera in *Catastrophe or a New Society?*, for their part refute the Malthusian hypothesis and argue that at the very least 'basic human needs' can be met in a world wide 'ideal society'. Surprisingly (or perhaps not) Soviet views of the future, such as those of Kosolapov (*in Mankinov and the Year 2000*) and Modrzhinskaya (in *The Future of Society*), although less divergent between themselves than Western writers, provide an image of the future advanced industrial society based on 'cybernetics' which is superficially not too different from Kahn's and in some ways even more spectacular — for example, tourist trips to the moon by 2025, life expectancy raised to 100 by the end of the century.

There are many other aspects of the debate — each participant brings something new: Mesarovic and Pestel in their strategy for survival project, *Mankind at the Turning Point*, focus on the complexity and interrelatedness and hence potential for progressive collapse, 'paralysing future orderly development'; Jan Tinbergen (a Dutch Nobel prizewinner), in *The Revised International Economic Order*, also sees the world becoming increasingly complex politically, 'the Cornucopia of growth turning into a Pandora's box — no same person could seriously envisage a world in which the poor live like today's affluent minority'.

Much of this debate springs from the strong environmentalist movement of the 1960s fed by writers such as Paul and Ann Ehrlich in *Population, Resources, Environment*. The debate about possibilities for development has to justify itself against this background. Nobel prizewinner Wassily Leontief's *Future of the World Economy*, arguing that high growth-rates in developing countries should be coupled with reduced rates in the developed countries, is one such example.

We will mention other authors and their contributions later in the discussion but for the moment this is sufficient. It is clear that the debate is wide ranging although underlying the debate is the question of how much growth and for whom, and when should it stop and why. Strong national, ideological and personal interests are vested in the forecasts and the 'solutions to the world's problems' that are offered. To get to grips with these questions we should look more closely at the kinds of changes which are advocated.

Authors support many and varied interests. Rarely do forecasts serve a single interest, and the debate often becomes confused when there is overlap between otherwise diametrically opposed positions. The analytic framework underlying most futurologists' prognoses is often quite unclear, rarely spelled out in any detail, and, even though using the most formal mathematical methods, sometimes self-contradictory.

In this section we attempt to identify some of the interests behind these forecasting exercises. By supporting these interests authors are trying to either change the world in some way or to preserve it from certain changes. The terms 'Malthusian' and 'non-Malthusian' have political connotations, although they are often used almost as synonyms for technological pessimists or optimists. Malthus himself was pessimistic about, and under-estimated, the potential for technological change; but, additionally, his politics were considered by many nineteenth-century writers (especially Marx and his followers) to be exceedingly reactionary – 'a sycophant of the landed gentry'. But on each side of the current Malthusian debate there is a great political diversity. Among the neo-Malthusians, Dumont in *Utopia or Else* and Forrester in *World Dynamic* take opposed positions, yet Dumont (like Heilbroner) uses the quantitative forecasts of *The Limits to Growth* as a starting-point for his radical analysis. A common starting-point appears to give rise in each case to very different policy conclusions. Forrester takes a 'conservative' line on most issues, Dumont a more radical, egalitarian position.

THE NEED FOR VALUE CHANGES

From many of the forecasters considered above, there are calls for changes or reinforcement of values and attitudes. Indeed, often the immediate purpose of the exercise appears to be to influence public values and attitudes. In the 'Malthusian' debate, the central values appear to concern such matters as materialism, attitudes toward the environment and family (family size) and attitudes to others, especially altruism towards poorer nations and toward future generations. Ehrlich, for example, argues that 'the basic solutions involve dramatic and rapid changes in human attitudes, especially those relating to reproductive behaviour, economic growth, technology, the environment and conflict resolution'.

Central to the debate about man's ability to cope with physical threats towards the environment are fundamental differences of opinion as to the proper relation of man to the rest of nature, and these too are reflected in attitudes towards technological change. Despite such divisions of opinion there is consensus among many authors that environmental changes must be accompanied by adjustments to other moral facets of society. Meadows, Ehrlich and Dumont all speak of the wholesale value-changes required in the rich countries. Heilbroner too is adamant that the long-term solution requires 'nothing less than the gradual abandonment of the dangerous mentality of industrial civilisation itself'. Ehrlich and Meadows believe this to be desperately urgent. For Tinbergen preoccupation with economic growth is both 'morally and ethically corrupting'. Bariloche too argues that what happens to the physical environment depends on 'the admitted system of value – the great bulk of values in present society are intrinsically destructive to the environment but one can hardly expect this value to change unless other basic needs are first satisfied'.

It is evident that to some extent the attitudes expressed toward the environment involve semi-religious and fundamental images of the human project. Modrzhinskaya, for example, speaks of 'the planned reconstruction of the surface of our planet'. Ehrlich stresses the 'fascination and profound emotions – the essentially religious feeling aroused by wilderness and wildlife and beautiful scenery'. Modrzhinskaya's image of the 'true conquest of nature' and Ehrlich's or Messarovic and Pestel's view that 'nature will retaliate inexorably and mercilessly against man', might refer to different worlds.

All those authors who believe economic growth is bound to cease in the middle- rather than long-term future, recommend changes in attitudes as especially important. Reformist and radical authors are additionally concerned with redistribution of the world's wealth in order to protect poor countries from possible disaster, arguing that on economic and moral grounds assistance must be forthcoming from rich nations. But again there are differences of view. Dumont, for example, argues strongly for an altruistic spirit which will relieve poor countries of domination, while Mesarovic and Pestel, and the Club of Rome, tend to emphasise self-interested 'world consciousness' through economic interdependence rather than altruism.

Many authors, including the Club of Rome's teams, emphasise the importance of a lengthening of present planning horizons. Mesarovic and Pestel, Heilbroner, and the Meadows team especially, speak of the need to identify with future generations. Mesarovic and Pestel, for example, say 'man must be ready to trade benefits to the next generation for the benefits to himself. If each generation aims at maximum good for itself, homo sapiens is as good as doomed.' Heilbroner, too, considers this a crucial problem for the world of the future to which there is only one possible answer, 'it lies in our capacity to form a collective bond of identity with those future generations'.

FORECASTS AND PROPAGANDA

Suggested changes in value systems are often associated with proposals for or against the reform of political structures. Soviet authors challenge the motives behind Kahn and Wiener's work, arguing that the forecasts of *The Year 2000* were merely made to strengthen an established political system. It is not uncommon for Soviet forecasts to be similarly criticised. For Kahn and Wiener there is little reason to advocate change since, as far as they are concerned, the future is likely to be a more or less 'natural' continuation of the recent past and this is not an unsatisfactory state of affairs. They observe that there is a 'good reason to discount . . . changes by choice'. There are a number of cautions offered. They point to the conflict between desirability and feasibility, 'excessive utopian objectives often prevent even limited gains from being obtained'. In any case Kahn considers that the understanding of future possibilities and long-term consequences of alternative policies 'is ultimately too difficult. . . . Historically such plans tend to miscarry and even when changes occur rapidly the people undergoing evolution or revolution often have the greatest difficulty in predicting the outcome – or even recognising explicitly what is happening – let alone controlling the process.'

On the basis of much of the argument in *The Year 2000* it might appear that Kahn and Wiener dismiss the possibility of directed growth and hence possibilities of achieving explicit normative goals and of long-term planning. The future is apparently largely pre-determined by long-standing 'multifold trends'. But this represents only part of their view. In fact, as with other authors, their argument against possibilities for change appears to be selective. Thus, despite their dismissal of the idea that growth can be normatively directed, Kahn and Wiener suggest that one of the 'causes of the recent speeding up of growth' is the 'contemporary growth cult among nations'. Similarly, their suggestion for 'international legal and arbitration procedures' to resolve international conflict, is not, they say, 'wishful thinking'. This does not 'really require human nature to change: there are reasons in both history and the present for qualified optimism'. When they say that 'there is also a natural inclination not to take seriously the prospect of big changes in the world system' or that 'in any event it is hard to be so confident of the permanence of the current system', this comes as a warning not to rock the boat rather than any positive invitation for change. Essentially, Kahn and Wiener appear to be primarily concerned with the avoidance of deviations from the 'multifold trends', which thus approach the status of natural laws. Deviation is possible but not desirable. Like most other futurologists their arguments are based on the contrast of hope and fear. Unlike others, however, the least desirable future is likely to come from deliberate interference.

The need to adjust one's argument to suit the occasion becomes most clear in comparing Kahn's theories over the decade between his two major publications. The underlying theory of the 'multifold trend' as set out in *The Year 2000* requires that Kahn and Wiener stress the stability of human values and systems. There is only the merest hint of an end to growth. But he has become aware of the possible impact of the environmentalists' protest – much more emphasis is given to keeping the world on course and countering neo-Malthusian (and other) attitudes. 'These views which were surely not generally held ten years ago presumably were created and/or enhanced by the phenomena of *The Limits to Growth*, or neo-Malthusian movement as well as by recent shortages', a perspective which has 'acquired a momentum of its own which if continued will only deepen the malaise it predicts'. Throughout his more recent work, Kahn notes the power of the anti-growth lobby who draw inspiration from the more pessimistic authors. He believes that present lip service that economic growth has to be stopped will have its effect in declining productivity and many other problems within a few years. He is thus accepting that forecasts may have a rather serious impact on people's thinking and activities.

In *The Next 200 Years*, however, Kahn asserts that a bountiful future will be arrived at, in a more or less comfortable way and as the 'marginal utility of wealth and material goods diminishes'. By emphasising the 'topping out' phenomenon Kahn is attempting to neutralise the arguments of his opponents by indicating that their concerns are taken care of in a natural way. Thus although he does not actually believe the work of 'fanatics' should be suppressed, 'this kind of fanaticism, while useful in research and study, can be a disservice if it dominates public discourse'.

In fact Kahn and his colleagues point to what they hope will be the persuasive power of their work and in part justify their forecasts in terms of the need to improve American morale during the Bicentennial Celebration. Their recommendations that 'for the moment, the more growth the better' conveniently support current policies of the government departments and enterprises sponsoring the Hudson Institute. Although they consider that the virtue of their forecast is that 'it may prove accurate', they note that, 'projecting a persuasive image of a desirable and practical future is extremely important to high morale and in general to help the wheels of society to turn smoothly'. To the extent that it can be done we should encourage the evolution of American values in certain directions. Indeed, many of the problems of Western cultures in the late 1960s and 1970s were 'the products of the premature introduction to upper middle-class elites of some of the characteristics of post-industrial culture'. Thus, like more reformist and radical futurists, Kahn and his conservative colleagues recognise a need to manipulate society's goals – although in quite a different direction. As far as possible, however, they continue to promote the stance of historical inevitability. 'People often talk about consciously choosing their future but historically it is clear that only rarely has such a choice been available . . . and usually then under an authoritarian leader'. Yet they must defend their basic optimism about present trends, and ultimately present us still with ambiguities and/or contradictions – 'from now on *if the choice is made* the air, water and landscapes can become cleaner over time – along with continued economic growth'. Kahn and his colleagues are, of course, not alone in their perception of the political role of forecasters. Tinbergen, for example, also stresses the importance of convincing public and political opinion. 'Coordinated and intensified effort should be made, particularly in industrialised countries, to publicise the need to create an international social and economic order which is perceived as more equitable by all peoples. . . . The primary task of many non-government organisations must be to undertake the effort suggested.'

FORECASTING AS A COMMERCIAL AND POLITICAL ENTERPRISE

To some extent all forecasts might be considered merely advertising stunts to promote particular political, or other more personal interests. Although strictly speaking not 'forecasters', the Club of Rome have played a central role in the recent debate, and their apparent early support for the Malthusian position of the Meadows probably reflected more their association with this group than any deep sympathy with the Meadows' analysis. Throughout, they have kept in the limelight by sponsoring and promoting spectacular projects – often immediately preceding major world conferences – but their tactics are to 'switch sell' when these are subsequently discredited. Their position is revealed by the projects they choose to advertise rather than by the projects that they sponsor as a whole. The Mesarovic-Pestel project is typical here: strongly supporting ideas of global management, in which multinational firms would be important but not dominant. Thus *The Limits to Growth* appears as a softening up exercise, selected to provide maximum diffusion of the idea that without some strategy of management the world would face immense peril.

The Club of Rome openly admits that the use of a computer model was primarily an attempt to find a 'vehicle' to attract people's attention. Nevertheless many futurists have a vested interest in their chosen methods. Advocacy of systems-analytic methods has on occasions been as evangelical as the policies prescribed. It can be argued that Forrester used the spectacular and controversial results of *World Dynamics* to highlight his own simulation technique. Forrester, Mesarovic and Pestel and, less forcefully, Leontief, all recommend their own preferred method whilst pointing to the unsatisfactoriness of others. Each, in effect, argues that the world is 'extraordinarily complex', that its main tendencies are beyond the comprehension of the unaided human mind. This, together with the idea that only a holistic (i.e. integrated) analysis is sufficient, is used to support the case for systems models. The attention brought to the methodologies, via the dramatic forecasts, presented has resulted in individual contracts for several million dollars.

In fact, unlike the Meadows, Mesarovic and Pestel's stated concern about 'harmony with nature', resource shortages, and ecological constraints, plays little part in their final analysis. Their direct concern is more with the creation of a 'global consciousness' which will 'identify with future generations' and with 'organic growth'. Ultimately, therefore, their concern appears to be much more with the cure than with the disease. Their model is 'sold' on the basis of its being able to tackle such complex problems – the hallmark of the Mesarovic-Pestel approach is vast diversity within unity'.

Of course, to sell forecasts one has to some extent to gear them to an audience. Thus as indicated earlier Kahn's recommendations concerning more growth supports present policies, whilst the forecasts of Mesarovic and Pestel, too, conveniently place the problems of shortages on supply (and hence technology) rather than on demand (and hence on redistribution), an advantage if one is attempting to sell a model to governments not renowned for egalitarian domestic policies.

Forecasters serving institutions representing many and opposing interests (such as international agencies) have some awkward compromises to consider. The role of the United Nations, for example, is arguably to demonstrate that nations are potentially, at least, united.

Thus an ineffective strategy (which is therefore acceptable because if nothing else it does not damage the *status quo*) may be considered more successful than an effective strategy. This may go some way towards explaining why the strategies from the Leontief study (sponsored by the United Nations) merely reproduce the tried (and failed) strategies of the last twenty years.

Few futurologists therefore, with the exception of the Soviet authors and in a more casual way Wiener and the Bariloche team, care to be explicit about the social theory they are employing to analyse future trends. By avoiding a description of a formal analytical framework most authors present themselves as both ahistorical and apolitical. World modellers, especially, portray their work as a 'general framework for analysis' (Mesarovic and Pestel) which 'can be used for the analysis of different sets of structural and policy assumptions' (Leontief).

THE NEED FOR OVERSTATEMENT

In one way or another each futurologist is aiming to influence public and official opinion. Forecasters operating outside official agencies are prone to overstatement. Although like Khan they may claim to be dubious about the effectiveness of propaganda, or policies, or, as in the case of Mesarovic and Pestel, who argue that 'people will not grasp danger unless personally and seriously affected', forecasters believe that an emphatic warning now is at least worth attempting.

The Limits to Growth was a case in point. As noted earlier, with this forecast the Club of Rome sought a 'vehicle to move men out of their ingrained habits'. Heilbroner, too, speaks of world populations as high as forty billion but afterwards retracts and suggests that with adequate policies a figure of nine billion is possible. In fact the dismissal of propaganda as ineffective is again selective since forecasters are obliged to persuade their audience of the urgent necessity for their own strategies while dissuading them against those proposed by their rivals. This does not apply only to forecasts as opposed as those of Kahn and *The Limits to Growth*. Thus, Heilbroner, in citing the Club of Rome studies, expresses the opinion that 'impassioned polemics against growth are futility' – only disaster will mobilise the 'social will' to slow down the rate of growth. Then, contradicting his condemnation of polemics, he argues that the 'gravity of the situation is shaped by our *appraisal* of our capacity to meet challenges rather than an estimate of the knowable external challenges of the future', and proceeds to polemicise himself.

HARD CHOICES MUST BE MADE...

As with the possibility of changes in attitudes to the environment, there is controversy as to both the obligation for, and ultimate impact of, altruistic actions. For some, altruistic prescriptions are merely misguided; Forrester is quoted by Maxwell as arguing that 'all our problems today are a consequence of 300 years of doing good . . . . The urgent task is to face issues squarely . . . and hard choices must be made'. He observes that 'many humanitarian impulses seem to be making matters worse in the long run'. The 'natural laws' of famine and disease are likely to be more effective, and present suffering may have longer-term benefits. In fact, he argues, 'the developing nations should attempt to emerge no further'.

Spengler has somewhat more faith than Forrester in the ability of the poor to stand on their own, but also questions the merits of altruism, and what he sees as the 'Freudian irresponsibility' of fostering 'sub-marginal' man, which is reminiscent of his concern in the 1930s about racial dilution. In those days he argued for a rapid increase in European rather than a rapid decrease in non-European populations.

In *The Year 2000* Kahn and Wiener express the view that questions of distribution pose 'a grave moral problem'. *The Next 200 Years* is more explicit: 'we do not believe that the persistence of income gaps is necessarily tragic or immoral. It is also equally clear, that we would perform a disservice to all including the poor by raising expectations or defining what is a relatively normal, healthy and near permanent condition as a serious moral problem which has to be resolved.' This does not mean that Kahn and his colleagues advocate or expect the continuation of poverty anywhere in the world. 'What most people want is visible even rapid improvement in their economic status and living standards.' If Americans and others do their duty and learn how to spend their wealth, eventually the gap will close, while 'meanwhile the doubling or tripling of the incomes of the poorest that does take place will be a substantial and welcome development'.

Thus the forecasts of both Kahn and the conservative neo-Malthusian are used to support the idea that developing nations should remain poor relative to the rich.

Forrester and Spengler share Kahn and Wiener's view that social reform is largely wishful thinking, but seeing Malthusian limits, take a less sanguine position. Forrester's book shows, he says, that global equilibrium is conceptually possible; whether it can be achieved is another matter. Forrester remarks that 'social systems are inherently insensitive to policy changes selected to alter behaviour'. He appears to have considerably less faith than, for example, Meadows in our ability to organise such a transition.

More reformist writers, in contrast, tend to reject the idea that the future is more or less predetermined and indeed attempt to argue the reverse. World trends can be redirected if the necessary changes in popular attitudes and institutions can be achieved.

The Ehrlichs see change in the attitudes of individuals as the key to population control and to many other measures necessary for the amelioration of the population–environment crisis. For them much of the blame for the dangerous trends they perceive result from the 'consumist' attitudes of industrialisation. They select the many examples of failed technologies in their book to demonstrate the result of thoughtless 'growth mania', thereby hoping to influence these attitudes and raise levels of environmental awareness. They consider that 'current aid programs are economic and political in orientation rather than humanitarian'. In places the Ehrlichs' analysis and rhetoric is similar to that of more radical authors, but their final prescriptions are erratic and confused.

In the future, the Ehrlichs say, a 'new set of national objectives must be established in relation to the rest of the world'. The mechanisms for change that they see are various, but these are often rooted in citizen protest. Time is too short for institutional reform. The vital change in attitudes is possible but to what extent it will actually occur, or be sufficient is, they say, an open question. In the end their advocacy of large amounts of humanitarian aid, therefore, does not totally discount 'some form of triage'.

Although the thinking of the Meadows in many respects follows closely that of the Ehrlichs, in their final analysis they are less despairing. Although they see possibilities for an equilibrium society they seem far less certain on redistribution. Even 'equilibrium would require the trading of certain human freedoms, such as producing unlimited numbers of children, or consuming uncontrolled amounts of resources, for other freedoms such as relief from pollution and crowding and the threat of collapse of the world system'.

Heilbroner's appraisal of the global situation is a dismal one. Humanitarian aid can only hope to be partially successful. Certainly, unlike Forrester, he does not believe international aid to be counterproductive, but he seems convinced of the presence of Malthusian limits.

'Given the magnitude of the change we have sketched out and the competitive struggle for existence that portends, it is highly unlikely that mankind will enjoy a setting in which the potential for identification with "human nature" can be extended to embrace all men and women of other "peoples".' Along with Mesarovic and Pestel, Heilbroner would see Forrester's prescription of neglect of poor nations as leading to global strife, but he sees the kind of managed changed that they advocate as no longer possible; 'our ability to engineer social change is very small. . . . We have become aware that rationality has its limits for engineering social change and that these limits are much narrower than we had thought.' He cannot, like the more radical authors, welcome the advent of more revolutionary governments, although he sees them as inevitable, perhaps essential; the violence of the transition can, however, be ameliorated by accepting the need to choose between anarchy and authoritarianism.

In some respects Heilbroner appears to have become systematically more despondent. Like Kahn and Spengler, he has adjusted his position. In his earlier works (for example, *The Making of Economic Society*, 1970) he argued that 'if the present trend of technological advance is maintained (and there is every reason to believe it will accelerate) . . . by 1980 – or by the year 2000 – a work week of 30 hours or even 20 hours, is by no means unimaginable'. Elements of his thesis are unaltered – he argued then that 'powerful, even ruthless, government may be needed, not only to begin the development process, but to cope with the strains of a successful development program'. He warns of man becoming 'enslaved' to purposes for which it is 'increasingly difficult to find social and moral justification'. It is not too much to argue that he now feels his earlier fears have become reality. 'The great question will then be whether men will use their triumph over nature to achieve a much more difficult victory over themselves.'

In fact many futurists take the stand that mankind is standing at the hinge of history. Titles such as *Mankind at the Turning Point* indicate this tendency. Thus the Meadows say, 'Deliberately limiting growth would be difficult, but not impossible . . . the necessary steps are well within human capabilities. *Man possesses for a small moment in his history*, the most powerful combination of knowledge, tools and resources the world has ever known . . . all that is necessary to create a totally new form of human society.' They claim therefore to be 'somewhat optimistic' and give 'cause for hope'. Nevertheless they are not totally convinced of this. They say, 'probably more pressure on mankind from the environment will be required before the issues will be addressed with enough concern and seriousness. But by then the time to act will be even shorter.'

Tinbergen, too, sees 'sudden and historically important' changes, in particular the oil crisis (which is cited in many current futures studies) as providing a turning-point. He argues, 'history has frequently shown that people in times of crisis, and once convinced of the necessity for change, are prepared to accept policies which demand changes in their behaviour so as to help secure better lives for themselves and their children'. He argues that in such a crisis government repeatedly and inherently underestimate people's preparedness to change. Thus as with many neo-Malthusian forecasts, an attempt is made to promote a sense of crisis – a tight situation, with a specific and often unpalatable solution.

CONFUSION – INTENTIONAL AND OTHERWISE

Confusion in the debate is deliberately encouraged to some extent by an effort to discredit other forecasts or promote one's own. For example, attempts by anti-Malthusian writers such as Kahn, to equate conservative and radical environmentalists, identifying both as 'middle-class elites whose way of life would be little improved by further growth', or conversely as disruptive radicals, are clearly damaging. Furthermore, because radicals see in the ecological threat the opportunity to swell the ranks of those seen to be opposed to contemporary patterns of industrialisation (especially industrial capitalism), the issue has been further blurred. Ehrlich, for example, was once viewed as a doyen of the radical environmental movement, despite his ambivalence on many issues. In efforts at promotion, arguments may become distinctly tortuous. The Meadows, for example, promote the use of system dynamics as a method linking notions of Eastern philosophy and the ecological unity of humanity and nature to the need to build highly complex 'holistic' computer models. Thus romantic ideals of natural harmony are used to support a high-technology methodology.

Terminology too, brings many misunderstandings. Because terms such as New International Economic Order become the jargon of the futures debate, and of international agencies, researchers are often obliged to take the idea on board, but distorted to fit their own thinking. Thus 'collective self reliance' may mean anything from outright autarchy, to a fairly mild form of import substitution. Similarly 'basic needs' may mean the material and social environment necessary for sustainable development providing full participation for everyone (as considered in the Bariloche study) or merely a kind of welfare or charity sufficient to ameliorate the worst aspects of poverty.

But it certainly cannot be claimed that all confusion is intentional, or the result of futurists attempting to resolve implicit contradictions in their work. It is simply that in many cases their positions are sophisticated. For example, the simple division of forecasters into neo-Malthusians and non-Malthusians, particularly in the sense of the former being essentially technological pessimists, becomes quite insufficient. (For the technological optimists the distinction between, say, Kahn and Modrzhinskaya could easily be attributed to different establishment interests.) There are evidently some environmentalists who would argue against further growth largely on the basis of impending physical limits together with romanticised notions of peasant culture or that the world is not what it used to be. Malthusians committed to more egalitarian objectives argue that because there are limits, redistribution is even more urgent, and that while industrialisation may be dangerous, poverty is in no way a romantic way of life. Major changes are needed to ensure a more egalitarian distribution of resources. But even those authors who might be counted as radicals in the debate, such as Dumont, may argue for a return to the 'peasant ethic'.

Although the Bariloche group take a radical stance advocating fundamental socio-political changes and are opposed to the 'Malthusian' position, they are quite unsympathetic to the Soviet position, which they view as being, like that of the West, opposed to the interests of the developing countries, as aggressively consumist. Despite their non-Malthusian arguments they share many of the concerns of the 'non-establishment' Malthusian writers, such as Dumont and Schumacher.

Just as fundamentally different attitudes to nature play a central role in terms of authors' feelings about the future and in the images of human beings which they portray, so do fundamentally different ideas about social relationships. When Modrzhinskaya speaks of the creation of 'highly moral relationships' she is essentially speaking of the creation of an end to capitalist rather than industrial mentality. Nevertheless, the future physical world, and indeed much of the social world too, described by the Soviet writers bears more than a superficial resemblance to that described by Kahn and Wiener. Each author is working with a different idea of what constitutes the quality of life and the priorities and choices involved.

Although the work of different futurists may be described by words such as 'reformist' and 'radical', distinguishing them beyond the simplistic Malthusian and non-Malthusian dichotomy, it is evident that few can be said to be entirely encapsulated in any one of these categories. Kahn, Spengler and to a lesser extent, Forrester, seem to share a conservative paradigm that the world is as it is because that is how it is meant to be and vice versa; Forrester is actually somewhat more reactionary, with many similarities to the original Malthus. But clearly all these have made use of elements of managerial and Marxist thinking; Kahn, for example, plays down the need for reforms, but often portrays conflict as an essential lubricant to the wheels of change.

There are further nuances in the reaction of forecasters to neo-Malthusian ideas. Kahn is essentially a populist in his cultural attitudes. Spengler and Forrester appear to share with other Malthusians a strong nineteenth-century puritan streak. This seems to be a fairly common facet of the Malthusian position although for many it is more or less strongly influenced by a sympathy for impoverished humanity and the natural world. Among the reformists we meet a wider range of views (in part because these authors predominate in the futures debate). Heilbroner and especially Ehrlich oscillate between despair and recommendations for major reforms. But while Ehrlich sees changed values as a prerequisite for major reforms, Heilbroner (like Modrzhinskaya) tends to see these changes following in the wake of institutional transformation.

INSTITUTIONAL CHANGES

While many authors speak of the need for dramatic institutional reform, in some cases (especially Kahn) a great relaxation of government control of private enterprise is envisaged, whilst others argue for a considerable increase. For Modrzhinskaya and her colleagues the possibility of increased prosperity is determined by social structure; they explicitly call for worldwide socialism. Modrzhinskaya in particular takes a firm and classical Marxist line on world development; largely uncoloured by the contemporary debate, this takes the overthrow of capitalism to be the only real issue and as a historical inevitability. Kosolapov too anticipates the disappearance of this system, but presents a more reformist view – at least for the advanced economies – and in part shares ideas of convergence with Kahn and Wiener. However, whereas Kahn envisages socialist countries moving towards mixed economies, the Soviets are very critical of such 'bourgeois futurology' and insist on the creation of a socialist world order.

Environmental and distributional matters can be adequately dealt with but not under the capitalist system. Kosolapov argues that 'in human society objective laws which are independent of man's will or consciousness manifest themselves through the actions of people who have definite aspirations, objectives and social tasks and who deliberately work toward their realisation'. Thus although Kosolapov propounds a determinist theory of evolution, this is not taken to mean that history is independent of deliberate human choice. 'A deliberate and purposeful human activity transforms the world and humanises it with civilisation.' People make their history neither to follow a precharted path of progress nor because they have to bow to the laws of some abstract evolution. 'They make history in an endeavour to meet their needs', needs which arise as a result of the objective world which people inhabit and which they will themselves change, first in order to meet those ends, and then again as they are met and new needs are generated. 'To make actions conform with the achievement of a social objective it is necessary to have a conscious system of management on the basis of the ideal provision and anticipation of the results of these actions.'

For Kosolapov and other Marxists the system of management is inevitably linked to the underlying system of human needs. This is also true, in a sense, for Kahn but unlike Kosolapov for whom 'changes in institutions and culture follow from the emergence of the super industrial society' rather than precede it, occupying a passive rather than an active role. In fact, quoting Marx, Kosolapov states that until the higher phase of communism arrives, the socialists demand the *strictest* control by society and *by the state* over the regulators of consumption and production.

Both these views contrast with the position taken by futurologists of the 'global management' school. The Club of Rome, Mesarovic and Pestel, and the Meadows believe that a management system can be set up to bring this about, employing the methods and models they offer. The Meadows, for example, point out that although the actions required to achieve equilibrium are not readily acceptable, speeding the process requires a form of organisation which they liken to a successful business enterprise. Each of these authors appears to be arguing for more authoritarian forms of government to manage the global economy although few are specific on institutional matters. None, however, makes the case as strongly as Heilbroner.

Only the Bariloche group, in presenting their 'ideal society', have a dramatically different attitude. They point to the 'fundamental fallacy' in both the Malthusian and Kahn's arguments. There are, they maintain, 'sufficient degrees of freedom so that the future is not an occurrence but the result of human actions'. For them, satisfaction of social and ecological objectives depends more on the type of society than on politics.

WHAT USE IS FORECASTING?

It is clear, and it is reasonable, that different participants in the futures debate are fostering a range of personal, social, organisation, national and international interests. The precise mix, in each case, is a matter for speculation although in some cases particular major interests seem fairly clear.

Kahn and Modrzhinskaya are supporters of what are, in many respects, mutually opposed establishments, yet both vociferously criticise the neo-Malthusians and offer futures similar in many respects. However, unlike Modrzhinskaya, Kahn tends to support industrial interests against interference from government. Throughout the debate Modrzhinskaya and Kahn champion their respective blocks. The Club of Rome too may be counted as establishment figures representing the middle ranks of government, and especially European industry. The Bariloche group take up a Third World and specifically Latin American stance. The Japanese Club of Rome, too, display a strong national interest.

Often, although not always, national interests parallel ideological persuasion. The prescriptions made by different participants to the debate tend to contain three elements: recommendations for economic changes (e.g. taxes and tariffs), institutional changes (e.g. to the need for authoritarian government, or enterprises to be of 'human scale'), or moral changes (e.g. the return to the peasant ethic). The emphasis placed on each of these elements is also closely tied to particular schools of thought – each identifies different 'leverage points' whereby history may be changed. The possibility for man to consciously bring about a chosen future certainly is linked strongly to underlying ideology. The 'conservative' Kahn explains why there is 'reason to discount change by choice', reformists such as Tinbergen suggest that 'in a crisis people will accept changes' and Marxists like Kosolapov attribute to man 'predestination as a creator'.

Most futurologists structure their argument by presenting contrasting images of hope and fear, of utopia and despair; but in their attempts at product differentiation and indirect and outright rebuttal a lot of confusion arises. Furthermore the intention of the forecasters is not always simply to produce forecasts.

Futurologists give many reasons for their work. *The Limits to Growth* was presented as a timely and urgent warning. Kahn in *The Next 200 Years* sees himself as offering a morale-boosting alternative – 'an image of hope, not despair'. Heilbroner claims merely to be 'helping people to make sense of things'. It is clear that however the forecasts are presented they see their work and the work of other forecasters as having an impact. Often forecasts are exaggerated deliberately and aimed at a particular audience to be used by a particular group of policy-makers. In some cases arguments appear to be carefully balanced to match a range of interests. The more recent arguments of Kahn, for example, try to assuage or neutralise environmentalist opinion while still providing optimistic forecasts for a commercially minded audience and sponsors. The forecasts of Leontief are designed to be acceptable to the widest range of United Nations delegations even if this means sacrificing credibility.

There is a recognition that administrations pick and choose forecasts (and elements of them) to suit their own purposes. As with much other research there is an attempt to be objective. The use of mathematical models is clearly a thinly veiled attempt to legitimise arguments and there is a 'hard sell' of modelling techniques which may be confused with attempts to sell the forecasts themselves. Even though it is accepted that such works do not give greater accuracy, they are taken as evidence of systematic analysis.

The fact that the present is so often seen as a turning-point raises the question as to what extent images of the future are merely invoked as a justification for action (or no action in the present). In the context of the times a given amount of exaggeration may be needed to bring sufficient attention to a proposal for it to receive public attention. The exaggerated image of the future is used to support exaggerated policies in the present. Thus the environmental 'crisis', the OPEC 'crisis' and so on, and their implications, are played up or down depending on the significance accorded to them by particular forecasters. In practice it is very difficult to 'spot' the indicators which tell of significant changes. In practice even agreement on what have been the significant changes in the past is difficult to come by since interpretation of the past is almost as dependent upon one's worldview as is one's vision of the future.

Consequently quite different forecasts for the long-term may support similar short-term policies or quite different policies may be deduced from a given forecast.

The goals of the forecaster (such as making arguments for or against a particular world order) seem to be more stable than the forecasts themselves. Forecasters appear loth to discard their view of the world although certainly a great deal of modification goes on.

In fact most forecasts (or at least the basic ingredients of them) are not of recent origin apart from, perhaps, the idea of continued growth. The Malthusian image especially is an old one, but so are ideas contained in 'basic needs' and 'post-industrial society'. In a sense we may assume that the ideas are always there, competing for prominence and that they are reinterpreted to be relevant at each point in history. Even in the short term it is not clear where forecasts come from – whether forecasters as a group play a leading role in directing discussion about the future, or whether the forecasts they produce are merely a response to current events. Forecasters have a habit of choosing topics relevant to forthcoming United Nations conferences. The ecology debate took place at a time when certain environmental damage became apparent. Forecasters pointed to the long-term consequences of such tendencies continuing, thus increasing the intensity of the debate. Thus forecasts may enhance tendencies. There is the old argument of self-fulfilling forecasts. Kahn at least argues this to have some merit in the case of his own scenarios of continued growth and for those of his no-growth adversaries.

In *The Year 2000* Kahn recommends that his forecasts be taken with 'several grains of salt'. This obviously applies to other forecasts as much as to Kahn's. Nevertheless even a forecast to be treated with caution may be better than no forecast at all, if only in the sense that issues are highlighted and 'trade-offs' posed. Forecasts clearly have a strong ideological component although for a variety of reasons this is often disguised in presentation. This is unfortunate because even though one may be rightly sceptical of most economic and demographic forecasts (as other papers in this book amply demonstrate) the forecasters do arguably contribute to discussion of important issues. In the day-to-day world of Realpolitik long-term issues and fundamental questions as to the course and purpose of societies tend to get lost.

BIBLIOGRAPHY

R. Dumont (1974), *Utopia or Else . . .* , London: Deutsch.

A. and P. Ehrlich (1970), *Population, Resources, Environment – Issues in Human Ecology*, San Francisco: Freeman.

J. Forrester (1971), *World Dynamics*, Cambridge, Mass: Wright-Allen Press.

C. Freeman and M. Jahoda (1978), *World Futures: The Great Debate*, London: Martin Robertson.

R. Heilbroner (1970), *The Making of Economic Society*, 3rd ed., London: Prentice-Hall International.

R. Heilbroner (1974), *An Inquiry into the Human Prospect*, New York: Norton.

A. Herrera et al. (1976), *Catastrophe or New Society?* Ottawa: I.D.R.C.

H. Kahn and A. J. Wiener (1967), *The Year 2000*, London: Macmillan.

H. Kahn, W. Brown and L. Martel (1976), *The Next 200 Years*, New York: Morrow.

Y. Kaya et al. (1974), 'Global constraints and a new vision for development', *Technological Forecasting and Social Change*, pp. 277 and 371.

V. Kosolapov (1976), *Mankind and the Year 2000*, Moscow: Progress Publishers.

W. Leontief et al. (1976), *The Future of the World Economy*, Preliminary Report, New York: United Nations.

P. Maxwell (1972), 'The shape of things to come? Interview with J. Forrester and D. Meadows', *Internationalist*, Wallingford, May/June, p. 6.

D. Meadows, et al. (1972), *The Limits to Growth*, New York: Universe Books.

M. Mesarovic and E. Pestel (1974), *Mankind at the Turning Point*, New York: Dutton/Reader's Digest Press.

Y. Modrzhinskaya and C. Stephanyan (1973), *The Future of Society*, Moscow: Progress Publishers.

E. F. Schumacher (1973), *Small is Beautiful – A Study of Economics as if People Mattered*, London: Blond and Briggs.

J. Spengler (1966), 'The economist and the population question', *American Economic Review*, Providence, R. I., March, p. 1.

J. Tinbergen (1976), *Reshaping the International Order – A Report to the Club of Rome*, New York: Dutton.

15 The Uses of Forecasting: Some Concluding Comments

TOM WHISTON

The preceding chapters have illustrated a wide range of forecasting exercises, most of them produced not just out of intellectual curiosity, but with the intention of providing an input to the process of policy-making. That this is a very difficult task indeed hardly needs recapitulation; it raises serious questions, however, about what purposes and interests forecasting serves, about policy decision-making and about the relationship of these two activities to each other. A comprehensive treatment of these issues would extend beyond the scope of this concluding chapter. My aim is rather to spell out some of the general lessons inherent in the main text, and to argue from them for a particular kind of forecasting which can be useful.

What interests should forecasting serve? The answer depends, in part, upon the extent to which a producer or a consumer of forecasts is critical of present policies and would like to see fundamental changes.

Many forecasts implicitly support or feed on-going programmes, rather than questioning policy. In this sense there are those (see Gershuny, Whiston, Turner and Cole, McCormick, Encel in this text) who regard the forecasts which they discuss as too narrow in their terms of reference and ultimately self-fulfilling in their effects.

No doubt the elected politician feels that he has a limited mandate, that he must represent a particular part of the political spectrum; that his time horizon for planning is not a very long one; that his policies should show effect during his period of office; that he or his party must seek re-election (see Wenk's chapter); this may then be reflected in the general focus of a forecast which he chooses to initiate or use. Such forecasts often do not go beyond the extrapolation of current trends; they predict more of the same tomorrow.

Other forecasters, however, query the goals implicit in current policies. They do not believe that more of the same is either inevitable or desirable. Wide rather than narrow terms of reference, including the examination of alternative goals of policy, guide their work. Many authors of the foregoing chapters have adopted, implicitly or explicitly, this point of view. There are, then, two ways in which forecasting relates to policy: one as a service to current policy-makers, the other as a service to the wider debate about policy goals.

Both have their justification. If we nevertheless give priority to the second, this is based not only on personal preference but also on the realisation of the major constraints on all forecasting: it cannot predict *the* future. As we have seen, economic forecasting, intended to serve current policy-makers, is often wide of the mark (Blackaby). While the policy-maker therefore takes rightly all forecasting with a pinch of salt as only one input among the many pressures to which he is exposed, using it, understandably, most willingly when it confirms preconceived policies, but ignoring it when it countervenes his plans and convictions, forecasts that aim at influencing the wider public debate and conducted unconstrained by immediate political pressures may in the long run have a greater influence on policy through their impact on the level of public consciousness. Forecasting at the Science Policy Research Unit deals with the unpredictability of the future by insisting on spelling out the course of alternative paths; it aims at fulfilling two purposes: to provide an independent critical assessment of 'in-house' forecasting and to encourage and feed a wider debate about policy goals.

However one must not state this too baldly. In all fairness there are several examples of work undertaken by Government forecasting teams in the UK for instance, where they have adopted a comparatively 'broad view': one might mention the CPRS studies on the funding of government R and D and other studies in relation to the motor industry or the turbo-alternator industry. Similarly several of the studies of the Programmes Analysis Unit (on educational technology, air pollution, marine oil pollution) might be fairly considered to have a comparatively broad perspective in view.

Such studies are no less valuable than 'independent' forecasting activity. What is important to recognise however is the increasing *need* for independence and alternatives in forecasting, for a wide discussion beyond essentially trend-extrapolative approaches, for pluralism in forecasting – with regard to which forecasting outside government has an important part to play.

Nevertheless so-called 'independent forecasting' must also recognise its own inevitable failings, bias and partisanship; and as suggested below one-sided independent forecasts often need to be 'corrected' or balanced by other independent forecasts. The overall aim should always be to provide a catalytic, competing and pluralistic role in widening public debate.

Similarly whilst there are advantages in independent forecasts which 'are formulated by people or groups who may have no direct political power', there are potential dangers resulting from inaccurate or possibly alarmist statements (which may reflect a certain degree of irresponsibility and/or lack of information). However perhaps this is the necessary price we have to pay in order to outweigh the dangers of potential political complicity. The remedy for this lies in part through public access of information and also through a cognisant and involved society which recognises alarmism when it sees it.

Policy-makers may claim that 'in-house' forecasting under their policy directives may reduce uncertainty in their minds about the future; this may be so, but by the same token it leads to 'fixing the future' (Gershuny), at the expense of examining alternatives. There is no question that the narrower forecasts serve a function: that of an intelligence unit which spells out likely consequences within a range of limited and imposed assumptions. But by definition it cannot meet the purposes of critique and input into a debate which goes beyond currently accepted policies.

Perhaps an example will clarify the different functions fulfilled by the two approaches to forecasting:

One of the major areas not considered in this text is that of energy forecasting and its relation to policy. In one sense this is unfortunate considering the central role which energy policy plays with respect to the economic, industrial, environmental and *social* structure of a nation; in another sense there have been so many analyses of energy forecasting in recent years that a separate chapter here might have been redundant. It remains nonetheless a suitable example because both types of forecasting have been applied to it. There are not only extensive government forecasts and the results of public inquiries available (and policy decisions based on them have been made); the future of energy has also been considered in several independent forecasts differing in their sociopolitical outlooks.

World supplies of energy (and in particular oil) have for several years been recognised to be severely limited with respect to current depletion rates; future demand is highly dependent upon assumptions about future economic growth and the efficiency of use of energy, whilst supply depends predominantly on the advance of science and technology.

The important alternatives to oil are at present considered to be coal and possibly nuclear power, unless massive R and D is undertaken for an alternative energy programme. At present an anticipated 'energy gap' over the next two decades has been used to justify an expanded nuclear programme (including the breeder reactor), in the face of public opposition which in some countries at least, has been strong.

Due to the long lead times for plant commissioning, and the associated infrastructure, the temporal identification of any future energy gap is critical, the more so because of many social doubts about a nuclear programme, and also because of the extent to which we have a 'breathing-space' to attempt to develop from an adequate R and D base an 'alternative energy programme' which may make unnecessary the irreversible commitment to an expanded nuclear programme.

Official energy projections are based on the assumption of continued economic growth. This raises two problems – one methodological and one more of a socio-political nature. Firstly as to methodology: the calculated values for future energy requirements varies considerably (see Chesshire and Surrey, 1978) dependent upon whether one takes a 'top-down' approach which derives essentially from a percentage growth value for overall economic growth *or* a 'bottom-up' approach which derives from the summation of individual sectors of the economy. In taking the latter approach various technological assumptions and conservation factors may be included, as well as sectoral shifts in energy demand, which result in a much lower value for energy requirement estimates. This has important implications with respect to the point in time at which we anticipate energy problems and an associated need for an expansion of the energy supply structure.

However, perhaps more contentiously, one must also examine the extent to which we assume continued future growth and its relationship to future energy demand. Several groups – both within and without 'the establishment' have published alternative scenarios which tend to question either the wisdom or practicality of 'growth'. This wider debate and its eventual resolution carries important implications with respect to energy policy.

It is also important to recognise an alternative viewpoint however: namely that one of the basic justifications for an expanded nuclear programme is that it is the preferred route for the provision of base-load electricity on economic grounds *even in the absence* of an hypothesised 'energy problem'. The question then arises as to the extent to which scenarios and forecasts go beyond economic and technological considerations.

This brief summary of the energy situation clearly indicates how the two types of forecasts must differ from each other: Politicians are for good reasons committed to economic growth; some also regard nuclear power as the solution to the energy gap. Within these political guidelines 'in-house' forecasts predictably emerge with very high demand estimates for energy. Independent forecasts not only point out that such estimates must follow from the imposed assumptions; they also provide estimates for what might happen, if the desirable growth-rate is not achieved. What is equally important, they can more easily go beyond economic and technological considerations because they are not tied down to the inevitably specialised concerns of one administrative department and therefore can consider possible consequences for other areas, such as employment prospects, the quality of life or international relations as they may be influenced by the development of the energy sector. In doing so they widen the considerations that enter into the formulation of policy in one sector and raise questions that cut across sectors and concern superordinated policy goals.

It would be wrong to pretend that all forecasts outside political directives realise this potential, or that it is totally impossible for 'in-house' forecasts to query policy goals. But it is easier for the independent forecast to aim at such integrated views of alternative futures, and thereby influence the public debate about major issues. Such forecasting can play an important catalytic role in forming public opinion and in providing a wider intellectual setting from which to make decisions. In many ways its quantitative representations may be open to severe criticism, however its particular strengths lie not so much at the quantitative level but more at that of indicating qualitative consequences of policy. This difference between specialised and integrated forecasting with regard to the ease of quantification accounts for the fact that forecasts built on the simple extrapolation of a trend which is relatively easily quantified, are often regarded as more scientific and hence as more reliable indicators of the future than integrated forecasts. Of course quantification is desirable where appropriate; but where it is built on debatable tacit assumptions the apparent precision hides rather than discloses the major issues.

The simple extrapolation of trends and its subsequent use in relation to policy can be a very self-fulfilling exercise as Gershuny has elaborated in his chapter concerned with transport policy. He made reference to the transport sector as a prime example of an area where alternative views of the future did not sufficiently influence planning inquiries (though we are now as a result of a range of criticisms witnessing a widening of debate). And again in relation to the transport sector, the Roskill Commission was restricted to looking at a Third London Airport rather than considering the longer term infra-structural implications of national airport policy.

There is another advantage to integrated and independent forecasting. Policy-makers are, by and large, limited in their power to shape the future by their national boundaries. Given the inter-dependence of today's world they certainly cannot and do not ignore what is happening outside these boundaries, but it takes second place to what they perceive to be in the national interest and within their power to influence. Independent forecasts, because they are formulated by people who may have no direct political power, are not so restricted. Indeed, the considerable forecasting literature produced by such people all over the world in the last two decades deals as a rule with global relations. Since there are no policy-makers who have power over all nations, such global forecasting has occasionally been accused of being irrelevant to policy. But this is surely short-sighted. As I have argued before, independent, integrated and global forecasting approaches and the process of policy formation via its impact on public opinion. Now it is a distressing but virtually universal feature of public debate that it concerns itself mostly with national affairs. Global forecasting aims at having an impact on this aspect of the debate; if it succeeds – as the debate about *Limits to Growth* did – it has justified itself. It hardly needs adding that the rather one-sided picture of the world which *Limits to Growth* presented must be corrected by other independent forecasters, as has indeed happened in order to advance debate rather than lay down the law about the future. Thus there is another qualification which needs to be introduced to make integrated, independent, global forecasting truly useful: it must exist on a pluralistic base. Since all forecasts are uncertain, the introduction of a single one may bias the debate; competing scenarios of the future may help to enlighten and enliven it.

The value of competing forecasts will thus in the end depend to a considerable extent on the ability of the originators to find means and opportunities for transmitting them to a wide public. It is one of the decidedly positive aspects of the current social climate that the public appers to have abandoned its former deferential stance and demands to be heard, and that politicians have recognised this. Hence the growing frequency of public inquiries about policy issues before decisions are made which may influence the lives of people for generations to come. While this is a decisive development in the right direction, public inquiries have their own problems, foremost among them the role of the expert, as the analysis of the Marina Inquiry (Cole and Turner) demonstrates, and the power to define the terms of reference, which is in the hands of politicians (as the results of the Windscale Inquiry demonstrated, where many broader issues raised by the participating public did not enter into the final report because they were judged to be outside the terms of reference). Nonetheless, the debate took place and lingers on in public consciousness.

The constructive use of forecasting of the type advocated here is thus not easily achieved. But the problems facing the UK and the wider world in the future are of such dimensions that every effort, however small or difficult, must be made to sharpen our anticipations and to attempt to influence policies as best one can, so that the politician's justified interest in the here-and-now should not lead to decisions which commit the future in dangerous directions. Forecasting by itself will not eliminate the dangers. But it may help to strengthen the conviction that the future is not inexorably determined but depends on the *informed* political will of us all.

(*I am grateful to Marie Jahoda for detailed comments on an earlier draft of this chapter.*)

REFERENCE

Chesshire, J. H. and Surrey, A. J., 'Estimating U.K. Energy Demand for the year 2000: a sectoral approach', SPRU Occasional Paper Series, No. 5, February 1978 Sussex University.

Subject Index

Accuracy of
 economic forecasts, 47–8
 mineral production, 201–27
 population estimates, 143–53
 UK population projections, 154–8
 weather prediction, 229–39
aerosol sprays, see ozone layer
AUT, views on education policy, 169, 170–3

Bariloche world model, 30, 324, 337
Brighton Marina Inquiry, 93–107
Britain 1984, 24
British Post Office Long Range Studies division, 254–5
Buchanan Report, The, 254, 257
bureaucratic resistance to change, 300

Cambridge economic policy group, 51
climate
 climate change and food, 233–6
 climate forecasting, 229–46
 economic implications, 232–3
 greenhouse effect, see ozone layer
 ozone layer, 241–5
 world climatic change, 233
closure and turbulence, 278–80
Coal Question, The, 17
collective security, 314–20
Committee on Manpower Resource for science & technology (CMRST), 114–18
conditional and unconditional forecasts, 64–6
Council for scientific policy, 115

De Wolff Commission, 267
demography and education policy, 159–76

earthquake prediction
 accuracy of, 239
 social consequences, 240
economic forecasting
 accuracy of, 47–8
 general review, 42–53
 influence on policy, 48–50
 Keynesian considerations, 42–3
 medium term and long term macro-economic, 50–2
 short term, growth of, 42–4
 short term, technique, 44–7
 treasury model, 48
education policy (dependence on forecasting), 159–76
employment of first-degree science graduates, 125
energy forecasting, 277–81, 346–8

'Fixing the Future', 64–6, 87–9
food
 FAO and food policy, 182–3, 184, 193
 green revolution, 185–8
 indicative world plan for agriculture, 184–5
 multinational companies, 187, 191
 Protein Advisory Group (PAG), 188, 192, 193
 'Protein Gap' and agriculture policy, 188–93
 WHO and food policy, 182–3, 184, 193
 World Food Programme, 194
Forecasting
 and urban planning, 93–106
 as a commercial and political enterprise, 330–2
 choice in, 280–2

Forecasting (*contd.*)
  climatic change, 241–5
  conditional and unconditional 64–6
  earthquakes, 238–41
  economic, 42–52
  food needs, 182–96
  global forecasting and world issues, 323–42
  long-range forecasts, 267–87
  manpower needs, 108–37
  market, 54–63
  mineral requirements, 201–27
  political constraints, 289–320
  population, 143–79
  short-term economic, 43
  social history of, 5–31
  telecommunication developments, 248–64
  transport needs, 64–89
  uncertainty of, 283–6
Future of the World Economy, 325
Future World Trends, 152, 153

global forecasting, population, 143–51
global issues, 323–43
Green Revolution, The, *see* food
greenhouse effect, *see* ozone layer

historical perspective of forecasting, 5–41
House of Commons Select Committee on Science and Technology, 132

'independent' forecasting, 345, *see also* cross-section forecasting
Indicative World Plan for Agriculture, 184–5, *see also* food
industrialisation, effects on forecasting, 18–22
institutional changes, 338–40, *see also* 'value changes'

Limits to Growth, 183, 245, 324, 329, 331, 332, 341, 349
London Airports, *see* transport
long-range forecasts and policy-making, 267–87

long-range forecasts and world issues, 323–43
long-term demand for scientific manpower, 110–11

Making of Economic Society, The, 335
Mankind at The Turning Point, 183, 335,
manpower forecasting, 108–42
Marina Action Campaign, 94, 97–102
market forecasting, 54–63
media pressure, 299
metals forecasting
  accuracy of, 201–27
  mineral production, 201–27
  Paley commission, 204–11, 223
  Resources for freedom, *see* Paley commission
  Resources in America's future, 216–23
  Robertson Tin Study, 211–16, 223
'mixed economy' and planning, 25
multinational companies, *see* food

NATFHE, views on education policy, 160, 168
National Association for the Promotion of Social Science, 18
National Telecommunication Plan, Australia, 258–64
New Atlantis, 10–11
newspaper circulation: market potential, 54, 58–60
Next 200 Years, The, 324, 329, 333, 341

OECD scenario, 25, 52
OPEC crisis, 52, 341
oceanic travel, *see* transport
'open planning' in telecommunications systems, 263
overstatement in forecasting, need for, 332
ozone layer, 241–5, *see also* climate

PPBS, 268
Paley Commission, The, *see* metals
pathologies in neglecting the future, 296–302

INDEX

Plan Europe 2000, 29
pluralism, in forecasting, 26
political and social priorities: mismatch of, 302–9
political limits to forecasting, 289–320
population forecasting
  and education policy, 159–76
  global issue, 149–51
  UK projections, 154–8
pre-industrial futures, 6–9
probabilistic forecasting (weather), 230–2
Programme Analysis Unit, 345
Project Camelot, 23
propaganda (relationship to forecasting), 328–30
'protein gap', *see* food
public inquiries, 102, 106

RAND, 23, 251
Republic, The, 7
Resources for freedom, *see* metals
Resources in America's Future, *see* metals
risk avoidance, 301
Robbins Report, The, 111–12, 160, 167
Robertson Tin Study, The, *see* metals
Roskill Report, The, 82–4, 349

shopping models, 96
shortsightedness of policy-making, 309–14
short-term economic forecasts, *see* economic
social history of forecasting, 5–31
stress in decision-making, 291–4
Student Numbers in Universities in Great Britain up to 1987/88, 169–71
Swann Working Party, 107–37
Swedish Futures Secretariat, 272–5

TRRL forecasts, *see* transport
Teacher training in the 1980s, 166
teacher: pupil ratio, 176

Technological Trends and National Policy, 21
Telecommunications
  and decentralisation, 255–8
  and transport, 255–8
  forecasting, 249–64
  further developments, 249–55
  Telecom 2000, 258–64
theatre attendance: market forecasting, 55–8
'Think-Tank', 23
time considerations (and decision making), 294–6
transport
  'fixing the future', 64–6, 87–9
  London airports: forecasts of demand and capacity 81–7
  oceanic travel, 61–2
  TRRL forecasts, 67–81
  telecommunications and transport, 255–8
  transport forecasting, 64–91
Triennial surveys, 132

UGC and manpower planning, 120–1, 130–1
uncertainty
  conditional and unconditional forecasting, 64–6
  forecasting and choice, 280–2
  uncertainty in decision-making, 297
  unforseeable future, 27–31
Utopia, 8
Utopian thinking, 6–9, 10–14

value changes, 326–7, *see also*, 'institutional' changes
value dimensions of future studies, 270–1

WHO, *see* food
weather prediction, *see* climate
Working Life in the Future, 282
World Futures – The Great Debate, 323

Year 2000, The, 324, 326, 328, 333, 342

Name Index

Aaronson, S., 239
Abrams, M., 54
Abrams, P., 18, 19
Adams, J., 91
Aldiss, B., 19
Allison, G., 300
Amin, S., 34
Armytage, W. H. G., 13
Ash, J. C. K., 52
Ashby, M., 22
Atkinson, P., 34
Auliciems, A., 231
Autret, A., 188

Bacon, Sir F., 10, 11, 32, 33
Bahro, R., 34
Balibar, E., 34
Ball, J. G., 115, 116
Banerji, D., 152
Baran, P., 252
Bell, D., 14
Berneri, 10
Bernouilli, 13, 33
Bernstein, B., 22
Berg, A., 186, 190, 191, 194
Berger, G., 33
Blackaby, F., 2, 345
Blackburn, 32
Blake, William, 14, 32
Blaug, M., 109, 110
Bolt, B. A., 239
Borlaug, 185
Bosworth, G. S., 115
Boucher, W. I., 29, 33
Boulding, E., 310
Boulding, K., 306, 310
Bowden, Lord, 115
Bowers, R., 251
Boyle, C., 34

Bray, W. J., 252
Brech, R., 24
Brock, J., 185
Bromhead, P., 92
Brown, L., 178
Brzezinski, Z., 315
BSSRS, 34
Buck, P., 13
Buchanan, C., 254
Buringh, P., 183
Busignies, H., 174

Cabet, 16
Callenbach, E., 34
Cetron, M., 258
Chacel, J. M., 185
Cherry, C., 253
Chesshire, J., 347
Chomsky, N., 33
Christ, C. F., 52
Clarke, I. F., 36
Cohn, N., 8
Cole, H., 100, 101
Cole, H. S. D., 3, 93, 107, 145, 150, 344, 350
Collins, J., 150, 152
Conrath, D. W., 253
Cook, O., 92
Cooper, R. M., 209
Cornish, E., 28
Cosman, C. H., 211
Cottingham, J., 192
Cox, G. V., 21
Craven, E., 174
Cripps, F., 52
Cullen, M. G., 14

Dahl, R. A., 89
Dahrendorf, R., 175

INDEX

Dainton, Sir F., 114, 115
Dasgupta, B., 186
Davies, R. L., 116, 117
de Montfort, 13
Dickson, E., 251
Dombey, N., 106
Dordick, H. S., 251
Douglas, J., 202
Dror, Y., 268
Drucker, P., 300
Dumont, R., 324, 326, 337
Duncan, O. D., 33
Dunn, D., 251

Easlea, B., 10, 32
Ehrlich, A., 325, 334
Ehrlich, P., 325, 334, 336, 338
Elliot, M., 31
Elsner, H., 22
Elton, M., 256, 257
Encel, S., 3, 344
Engels, F., 15
Enzensberger, H. M., 34
Evans, J., 32

Fels, R., 21
Fetherston, M., 52
Finley, M. I., 10
Finn, R., 33
Fischmann, L., 216
Fisher, J., 216
Foley, G., 150
Forrester, J., 321, 324, 331, 333
Foucault, M., 10
Frank, A., 34
Freebairn, D. K., 196
Freeman, C., 29, 145, 148, 150, 175

Gabor, D., 254
Galbraith, J. K., 24
Gamble, A., 26
Gannicot, K., 109, 110
Gardner, M., 149
George, S., 196
Gershuny, J. I., 3, 107, 175, 344, 346, 348
Gilfillan, S. C., 33
Glass, D., 149
Godley, W., 53

Goldhamer, H., 253
Golub, B., 34
Gopalan, C., 192
Gough, I., 25
Graunt, J., 13
Greenberger, M., 252
Gribbin, J. R., 3, 232, 236, 237, 241, 244
Griffin, K., 186
Griffiths, D., 34

Haas, E., 239
Hailsham, Lord, 115
Haldane, J. B. S., 21, 34
Hall, R. L., 52
Hall, Sir R., 42
Halley, 13
Hanson, A. H., 21
Harper, P., 34
Heath, Edward, 133
Heilbronner, R. L., 321, 324, 327, 332, 335
Herrera, A., 30, 324
Higgins, J. C., 33
Hill, C., 12
Hinshaw, C. E., 21
Hoggins, 13
Hough, 183
Hoos, I. R., 28
Hopkins, G., 184, 188
Horowitz, D., 23
Horowitz, I. L., 23, 24
Howe, E., 32
Hutchings, D., 128
Huxley, A., 34

Iambulus, 8
Illich, I., 150
Irvine, J., 28, 30, 32, 33, 34

Jacoby, E., 195, 196
Jackson, Sir W., 114, 116
Jahoda, M., 29, 145, 148
Janis, I. L., 320
Jantsch, E., 268
Jarret, D., 13
Jessel, 156
Jevons, W. S., 17, 18
Johnson, President, 183

Johnson, S., 152, 156, 178
Jones, F. E., 114, 115
Jones, M. V., 251

Kahn, H., 23, 33, 148, 150, 324, 328, 329, 332, 338, 341
Katz, J. E., 24
Katzman, N., 254
Kellogg, 241
Kelsall, R. K., 124, 128
Kennedy, M. C., 52
Keynes, J. M., 18
Klein, G., 34
Kleinberg, B. S., 26, 29
Kosolapov, V., 325, 339
Kropf, J., 191
Kusch, 34

Lamb, 232
Lamberton, D. M., 248, 249, 259
Landsberg, H. H., 178, 216, 218, 222
Lappé, F., 150, 152
Lasswell, H., 310
Laury, 52
Le Guin, U., 34
Leontief, W., 325, 331, 341
Levinson, 194
Lewin, L. C., 33
Lewis, C. B., 256
Lindblom, C. E., 89, 315
Little, A. D., 250
Livingstone, D., 34

Machlup, F., 248, 249
Mackenzie, L. D. E., 238
Macmillan, Harold, 49, 52
Maddox, B., 254
Malthus, T., 17, 34, 323, 326
Mandel, E., 24, 26, 34
Mann, L., 320
Markovic, M., 34
Marien, M., 29
Marris, P., 321
Marstrand, P., 3, 152, 182
Marx, Karl, 15, 16, 30, 326
Maxwell, P., 333
Maxwell, S., 194
McCarthy, 122, 123
McCormick, K., 3, 344

McCracken, P., 26
McKie D., 92
McLean, M., 32, 184
McMahon, C. W., 25
McNees, S. K., 52
Meadows, D., 145, 149, 183, 245, 324
Mendelson, E., 32
Mesarovic, M., 150, 183, 325, 327, 335
Michael, D. N., 298
Miles, I., 2, 14, 26, 28, 32, 33, 34
Miles, R. E., 321
Mileti, D., 239
Mill, J. S., 18, 148
Modrzhinskaya, Y., 325, 327, 337
Molina, M. J., 243
More, Sir Thomas, 8
Morris, W., 17
Morton, A. L., 10, 11, 16
Moser, 117
Muller, M., 192
Myrdal, G., 149, 270, 272

Nairn, T., 19
Nelkin, D., 107
Newstead, I., 261
Nordhaus, W., 282

O'Connor, J., 25
O'Dea, D. J., 52
Ofledal, 194
Ogburn, W. F., 21, 33
Oliver, W. H., 39
Ollman, B., 15
Olson, M., 178
Openshaw, S., 107
Orr, E., 192
Orwell, G., 34
Osborn, D. R., 52

Packer, K., 263
Paddock, W., 183
Page, W. R., 3, 149, 227
Parker, E. B., 251, 252
Paley, W. S., 24, 207, 208, 209, 210, 223
Palme, Ol., 270
Pateman, C., 148
Pateman, T., 34
Pavitt, K., 152

INDEX

Pehrson, E. W., 202
Pestel, E., 150, 183, 325, 327
Peterson, W., 178, 179
Petty, 12, 13
Pipard, 116, 117, 131
Plato, 7
Platt, J., 322
Polak, F., 321
Poleman, T. T., 196
Pool, I., 253
Porat, M. U., 249
Posner, M., 52
Proxmire, J. H., 21

Rand, 23
Rank, J. A., 55
Reich, C., 315
Reid, A., 252, 255
Revelle, R., 149, 151
Richardson, E., 317
Rippon, G., 94
Robbins, Lord, 110, 160
Robertson, W. H., 211, 212, 214
Rodgers, B., 63
Rose, H., 32
Rose, S., 32
Rosenhead, J., 24, 32
Roskill, 83, 86
Rowland, F. S., 243
Rudd, E., 124, 172
Rush, H. J., 3, 182, 227
Rusell, E., 32
Russell, B., 21

Sandberg, A., 40
Sargent, L. T., 10, 16
Schneider, S. H., 238
Schumacher, E., 150, 315, 337
Scrimshaw, N. S., 199
Shanks, M., 148
Shelley, Mary, 14, 32
Short, J., 256
Simon, H. A., 298
Simon, H. E., 89
Singer, S. F., 241
Skulstad, C., 191
Smith, Adam, 14, 248
Smyth, D. J., 52
Snow, C. P., 306, 310

Sohn-Rethal, A., 10
Spence, 14
Spengler, J. J., 18, 333, 338
Stratford, A., 86
Strauss, E., 12
Sukhatme, P. V., 185, 192
Surrey, J., 347
Suvin, D., 34
Swann, Sir M., 109, 114, 115, 118, 127
Swift, Jonathan, 32
Symonds, R., 149

Tanner, J. C., 89, 90, 91
Teilhard de Chardin, 315
Telpy, L., 190
Thompson, L. M., 234
Thompson, G. B., 253
Thorngren, B., 256
Thunhurst, C., 24, 32
Tinbergen, J., 325, 327, 336
Todd, Lord, 115
Townsend, J., 34
Truman, President, 205, 295
Tulpule, A. H., 89
Turner, C., 106
Turner, R., 3, 93, 107, 344, 350
Tyler, M., 253, 254

Vacca, R., 321
Vickers, Sir G., 297, 306, 313
Visaria, P., 152

Wallace, R., 13
Walton, P., 26
Ward, B., 20
Warren, B., 20, 25
Weingart, P., 32
Wells, H. G., 19, 20, 33
Wenk, E., 3, 4, 321, 344
Westin, A., 253
Westrum, R., 253
Whiston, T. G., 3, 344
Whitehead, R., 193
Whitley, R., 32
Wiener, A. J., 33, 148, 150, 328, 329, 332
Williams, C., 188
Willson, K., 29
Winstanley, G., 30, 32

Winston, D., 8
Wion, F. W., 262
Wittrock, B., 3

Yates, F. A., 12

Yehezkel Dror, 268
Young, R., 10, 32

Zucker, S., 27
Zuckerman, Sir, S., 114